# Records
*of*
# Walker County, Alabama

**including Inscriptions from Cullman, Fayette, Marion, Winston, Talladega and Tuscaloosa Counties..**

**Collected by:**
**Florence Knight Guttery**

**Compiled By:**
**Inez Bozwell Biggerstaff**

**Southern Historical Press, Inc.**
**Greenville, South Carolina**

This volume was reproduced from
an 1959 edition located in the
Publisher's private library
Greenville, South Carolina

This direct ALL correspondence and book oreders to:
**Southern Historical Press, Inc.**
**PO Box 1267**
**375 West Broad Street**
**Greenville, S.C. 29602-1267**

Originally printed & ©: Oklahoma City, OK. 1959
Reprinted by: Southern Historical Press, Inc.
Greenville, S.C. 2005
ISBN #0-89308-812-9
*Printed in the United States of America*

"It is wise for us to recur the history of our ancestors. Those who are regardless of their ancestors . . . . do not perform their duty to the world." . . . . . Daniel Webster.

Dedicated
to
William and Hannah Guttery
Pioneer Settlers of Walker County
and
To All Those Whose Names Appear Here

## Acknowledgement

We wish to acknowledge with special thanks, all those who have been so gracious in helping us make this a complete work by lending us their bible and family records. We feel that these records will add a great deal of interest and information on these particular families.

We would also like to thank Mrs. Lucille Swann of Jasper, Alabama, for getting together the pension applications of the War of 1812 and helping to translate some of the more difficult parts of them. If any mistakes occur it will be because the copies we had were very dim in places so as to make it almost impossible to distinguish some of the names of witnesses and those who acknowledged them. Mrs. Swann made this task a little easier and we are most grateful to her. We also are indebted to her for the 1840 Tax List which is included. This is a very real contribution because the records of Walker County prior to 1871 were destroyed and these records had been preserved by the son or grandson of a former County Clerk.

We would like to thank Mrs. Herman Poe of Corona, Alabama and Mrs. W. L. Lucas for their contributions of some of the cemetery records of Fayette County.

And of course we would like to thank Mr. John McQueen Guttery, Sr. who accompanied his wife, Florence Knight Guttery on the many excursions to the various cemeteries in search of these old records. He not only went along on these trips but copied many of the records himself and we owe him a debt of gratitude for his patience and understanding of this project.

To Mrs. Florence Knight Guttery goes the credit for collecting the records. Her interest was only equalled by her perseverance. It was quite a task to hunt out and go to these old cemeteries, many of them hidden deep in the woods and as is usual in most old inactive cemeteries, buried in bramble. It is not only a laborious task but a hazardous one. Many of these old cemeteries and those who lie there would never have been recorded for posterity, had she not been so keenly interested in the families among whom she has lived all her life. She had a personal interest due to the fact she has known many of these old families and their children since her childhood. She not only collected the records of Walker County but went into surrounding counties and secured records of those counties. I am sure there are many cemeteries yet to be explored, it would be a colossal task to get them all, but we feel that she has, in the 161 cemeteries she visited, gotten a representative list of the early citizens of the county.

It has been a pleasure for me to be associated with this project. It has been hard work, of course, to compile these records and get them published but it has been a rewarding one. It has brought me into contact with some of the most wonderful people I have had the good fortune to know. I have enjoyed every minute of it.

Inez Boswell Biggerstaff

## ERRATA

We wish to correct the following typographical errors, for which we apologize, but in a work as extensive as this, it can be expected that some errors will creep in. Miss Mary Lou Glasgow, to whom I am personally indebted for her patience with me and her understanding, and of course the tremendous effort on her part to meet my deadline, has a full time position and had to do this work at night after office hours. The mistakes are due mostly to the electric typewriter she was using and which she was not accustomed to, as well as fatigue.

Page 1 -10th line from bottom of p. descndants, should read -descendants
" 1 -8th line from bottom of p. origional, should read -original
" 10 -1st column, 9th line, McDkff, should read McDuff
" 21 -Agwd, 8th line, should read aged
" 21 - 10th line, Decsmber, should read December
" 21 -6th line from bottom of p. delcares, should read declares
" 26 -19th line, Statues, should read Statutes
" 26 -23rd line, here to for, should read heretofore
" 27 -11th line, receivwd, should read received
" 28 -15th line, from bottom of p. Novembsr, should read November
" 29 -15th line, Bsng should read Being
" 33 -25th line, dischargsd, should read discharged
" 57 -24th line, Lomg should read Long
" 79 -17th line, from bottom of p. Huchem should read Hyche
" 95 -4th line, Cronnover should read Crownover
" 100 -29th line, name is Hamrick, did not print clearly
" 100 -7th line, name is Camak, did not print clearly
" 101 -15th line, name is Jones, did not print clearly
" 101 -29th line, name is Lockhart, did not print clearly
" 102 - 24th line, date of death of Louisa Davis is 1898
" 103 -3rd line, date is Nov. 13,1879, did not print clearly
" 105 -William R. Jones, birth date should read 1856- 19th line
" 108 -14th line from bottom of p. Bsnett should read Bennett
" 116 -20th line, name of Jagood should read Hagood
" 118 -17th line, Crcwnovsr, should read Crownover
" 128 -28th line, name of Prescost, should read Prescoat
" 128 -29th line, same spelling of Prescoat
" 133 -12th line, Girganus should read Gurganus
" 137 -20th line, Cheatsm,should read Cheatam
" 138 -10th line from bottom of p. Daniles, should read Daniels
" 53 -27th line from bottom of p. Wile, should read will
" 151 -11th line, Willinghsm, should read Willingham
" 154 -12th line from bottom of p. Ne-man, should read Newman the "W" did not print
" 161 -12th line, Strangs, should read Strange
" 162 -23rd line, Bsnton, should read Benton
" 174 -14th line, Siheinick, should read Sihelnick
" 179 -23rd line, Wahefiwld, should read Wakefield
" 159 -26th line, should read Lewis Wade Kilgo, did not print clearly
" 3 -4th line, name is John Boshell, did not print clearly

The first white man to set foot upon the soil of what is now Alabama was probably Desoto in the year 1539. English traders were navigating the Alabama River as early as 1687. Mobile was founded in 1711 but under another name. Due to the many controversies regarding the boundaries and the cessions of land, Alabama became part of one region after another. It did not come under the complete jurisdiction of the United States until 1813. In the year 1817 it became the Territory of Alabama and later in 1819 it was admitted to the Union.

Walker County was erected in 1823 from the counties of Tuscaloosa and Marion. It has an area of 798 square miles within it's boundaries and received it's name from John W. Walker who was president of the Constitutional Convention which formed the first constitution of Alabama. He was from Madison County. He also became the first Senator from the State of Alabama.

Walker County lies in the Northwestern part of the State and it has for it's boundaries, the counties of Winston and Cullman, on the North, on the East, by Cullman, Blount and Jefferson. It is bounded on the South and West by Tuscaloosa, Fayette, Jefferson and Marion Counties. It has an elevation of 500-700 feet above sea level and slopes to the South. There are possibly thirteen different soils in the county which affords a diversified farming. Much of it is covered with a sandy loam which is excellent for fruit growing. However it is not strictly a farming area. There are rich deposits of coal and iron.

The county is drained by the Black Warrior, Mulberry, and Sipsey Rivers and has fine timber forests of Post Oak, Red Oak, Spanish Oak, Beech, Poplar, Gum and Long Leaf Pine.

Many of the families who came to Walker County remained there and raised their families there and have left descsndants who have spread out over many states. Many of them can trace their heritage back to the oldest families of the origional thirteen Colonies. Many of it's young men saw service under the Confederate Flag and lie buried throughout the county. Certainly it can be said, when the roll of the immortal are called, the men of Walker County will be among the first to answer.

The motto of the State is "Here We Rest" and what more suitable phrase could we offer for those whose names are inscribed in this book.

Judges of Walker County and the dates they took office.

Commissioned:
Dec 27, 1823 . . David Murphy, Sr. Judge of the County Court
Nov 27, 1826 . . Samuel D. Reed " " " " "
Jan 31, 1830 . . David Murphy " " " " "
Dec 13, 1833 . . Edward G. Musgrove " " " " "
Jan. 9, 1840 . . John E. Clancey " " " " "
Aug 24, 1843 . . W. B. Taylor " " " " "
Jan 7, 1844 . . Ward B. Taylor (J. E. Clancey resigned)
Apr 30, 1846 . . William Hewlett, (Taylor resigned)
June 19,1847 . . William M. Jones (William Hewlett resigned)
Mar 7, 1848 . . William N. Jones elected Prob.Judge of Walker Co.
Jan 30, 1850 . . William N. Jones appointment to expire 1st Monday in May
May 25, 1850 . . John Erwin elected by the peeple Prob. Judge
May 16, 1853 . . Thomas M. Gabbart elected Probate Judge
May 27, 1859 . . F. A. Gamble elected Judge (Resigned)
May 5, 1862 . . Thomas M. Gabbart appointed by Gov.as Prob Judge
Aug 22, 1865 . . Moses Camak elected Mar. 6, 1865
May 28, 1866 . . Moses Camak
Aug. 15, 1868. . John Brown
Nov. 21, 1874. . J. R. Shepherd
May 9, 1877 . . F. A. Gamble
Sep 14, 1880 . . F. A. Gamble (elected Aug. 2, 1880)
Aug 19, 1886 . . John B. Shields
Nov 1, 1892 . . James W. Shepherd
Nov 3, 1898 . . " " "
Nov 19, 1904 . . " " "
Nov 9, 1910 . . " " "
Dec 29, 1913 . . Chas M Sartain elected, no date of election
Nov 28, 1916 . . Edgar W. Long
Nov. 23,1922 . . Edgar W. Long electsd Nov. 7, 1922
Dec 6, 1928 . . Edgar W. Long
Dec 5, 1934 . . L. C. Garrison
....... 1940 . . L. C. Garrison
....... 1946 . . Lecil D. Gray
....... 1952 . . Lecil D. Gray

Present County Officers- April, 1959 are:
Circuit Court . . . . . . . . Judge Roy Mayhall
Judge Alton Blanton
Probate Court . . . . . . . Judge Nelson Allen
County Court . . . . . . . Judge Gerald Colvin
Circuit Court Clerk . . . Pat Fleming
Tax Collector . . . . . . . T. L. Johnson, Jr.
Tax Assessor . . . . . . . Miss Gladys Gunter
Chairman of Board of Finance . . T. Jeff Land

# 1840 TAX RECORD
## Walker County, Alabama
## William Robins, Collector

Beat 1 - Walker County, Alabama

A. R. Baker
Elias Cunningham
Benjamin Stewart
John Boshell
Peter Baker
Augustine Williams
Robert Boshell
W. S. Knight
Edmon Knight
John Manasco
Nicholas Boshell
John Hardcastle
D. W. Townley
David Leonard
W. Easley
P. S. Johnson
William Leonard
Reuben Keaton
Jacob Stover
David Leonard, Jr.
Richmond Townley
John Romine
David Miller
A. J. Boshell
H. R. Sides
M. R. Miller - 1 slave
Jonathan Sides

Beat 2

Hugh McClelland
Patrick White
G. W. Crawford
Charles Cagle
Nancy Lovett
Valentine Cagle
John Gesire
Wright McClung
J. F. Cagle
William McNutt
A. B. McClain
Jonathan Sides
....B. Cunningham
....M. Easley
Joseph Easley
William P. Pike
Mc. M. Boshell
J. A. Hendon
J. M. McClain
Simeon Smith
D. Blackwell
Johnson Thomas
John Snow
N. C. Sides
P. E. Easley
William R. King
T. J. King
Lucy King
G. W. King
Robert Guttery
William Townley
Vingard Lawson
Giles Burton
John Guttery, Jr.
John Guttery, Agt.
F. C. Irwin
James Loyd
L. W. Baker
John D. Taylor
L. C. Miller - 3 slaves
L. C. Miller - Adm.
Total Tax $61.50
J. Y. Hill
James Cagle
John Taylor
J. A. Simmons
William Stokes
Allen Stokes
Levi Sides
....H. Cagle
William Young
Marvel Scoggins
R. M. White

Johnson King
John King
James Jeffers
Joseph Roe
....R. White
William Jeffers
John Moore
A. J. McNutt
Jesse McNutt
Evan McNutt
Josiah Crameen
G. D. Cleere - 8 slaves
J. W. Blackwell
William C. Blackwell
Henry Cagle
Richman Pace
Alford Stokes
Daniel McKinley - 3 slaves
George Hooker
John Allen
Bradford Raden
James Prewett
T. W. Harvey

Total Tax $24.86

Beat 3

Samuel Tubb
Daniel Tubb
Jeptha Billingly
Elisha Randolph
Thomas Childers
James Pool
T. Pool
Kinney Pool
James Brown
J. H. Alexander - 1 slave
E. S. Pyler
William S. Davis
John M. Davis
William Lollar
William Lollar, Agt.
James Hulsey
W. H. Bradley
William Brown
William Tubb
C. A. Montgomery
R;bert Ford
W. H. Harris
Joseph Richardson
William Dill
William Robertson
Andrew Clements
J. D. Randolph
John Richardson
Alexander Irwin
Micajah Little
Robert Rains, Agt.
John Burton
Samuel Sparks
J. D. Sides
L. W. Bradley
Joel Burnum (guar)
R. P. Harrison
H. W. Hamilton
John K. Heard
Jesse Jackson
William A. Dill
Abner Dill
James Daniel - 2 slaves
Carter Scott
E. D. Baker - 3 slaves
John Irwin
John Irwin, Agt.
N. G. Bagley
James O'Rear
William Riggs
James Dutton
John Kitchens
David Brown
William Tubb
James Glaze
Moses Winters
Lewis Sides
William B. Allen
Absalom Barton
John M. Dupey
John Allen
William Robins
Samuel Lawrimore
P. E. Headrick
Josiah Richardson
James Kitchens
James Kitchens, Agt.
E. D. Baker, Agt.

Samuel Jackson
G. M. Mason
G. W. McDonald
William Thompson
G. Lamkin
John E. Clancey
John Newton
J. H. Baley
Levi Conley
E. G. Musgrove
P. B. Phillips
Jacob Hamilton
T. V. M. Camak
Wiley Wells

Total Tax $61.50

Beat 4

A. G. Lane
F. B. Moore
Eldridge Mallard - 8 slaves
J. D. Lane
John W. Lankford
J. R. Lane
A. McDonald
Ashley Aldredge
John Purdy
Benjamin Davis - 7 slaves
John Davis
William Aldridge
Isaac Brown, Agt.
John McNutt
Lewis Smith
W. G. Hendon
W. G. Hendon, Agt.
James McDade
Y. W. Brazeal
J. M. Lane
David Walden
Charles Tucker
Peter Ingle
James McDonald
Isaac Brown
John Box
William H. Pate - 7 slaves
Willis Manasco
S. W. Moore
N. B. Miller
J. M. Kilgore
Joseph Allen
Dennis Davis
William Hendon
C. M. Wilson
W. D. Chentham
Nathan Bellah
Morgan Brazeal
William McGuire

Beat 5

Hiram Richardson - 1 slave
William H. Snow
William H. Snow, Agt.
John Gurganus
Warren Adcock
Lewis Short
Tob. Richardson
J. H. McElroy
James T. Turner
William H. Wallis
Thomas Thompson - 11 slaves
James Thompson
William R. Medlin
Andrew Reed
James Short, Jr.
Mitchell Short
Thomas Short
Jarret Brown
James Brown
Washington Copelan
John Heard
John Heard, guardian
Richard Beasley
Katherine Earnest
Hamilton Hutto
E. S. Minor

William Rhea
John Smith
William Brown - 1 slave
E. W. Payne
John Reed
James Short, Sr.
Elisha Bachelor (Bacholor)
William Odum
Joel Gray
William Reed
R. W. Minor
Alexander Copelan
Robert Turner
Robert Turner, Agt.
Obediah Copelan
Robert Cain
Jeremiah Thompson
L. T. M. Franklin

Beat 6

Daniel Speegle
E. Speegle
Martin Milligan
C. M. Green
Thomas Manly
F. W. Hamilton
John W. Vest
William F. Lawrence
George Corley
John Orr
Robert Calvert
David Speegle
Thomas Calvert
David Speegle
James Calvert, Adm.
R. H. Davis
Jesse James
William Bradford
D. H. Young
William W. Sheats
H. Milligan
Sanford Weston
Pleasant James
John Shavers
Asher Harris
William Davis
Calvin Guttery
Morgan Guttery
Jesse Trussel
Jacob Beasley
Jonathan Sandlin
Jephniah Woodall
Jonathan Orr
Ishom Parker

Beat 7

C. Conway
John Calvert
W. B. Day
James Blevin
John Blevin
Daniel Martin
Samuel King
A. Stephenson
Russel Brown
Hannah Brown
Henry Inman
H. Stephenson
Joseph Branch
Joseph Branch, Agt.
S. C. Jones
Isaac James
Labon James
D. M. Deskin
Samuel Harbison
J. W. C. Jones
James Livingston
Samuel Livingston
Henry Livingston
T. A. Bell
Jacob Webb
Jacob Webb, Agt.
Samuel Wiley
John Marks
P. C. Clark
John Penn
John Williams
John King
M. Sapp
John Key
Jeremiah O'Rear
J. Y. Key
Hugh Brown, Agt.
L. A. Lay
R. Chaeak

Beat 8

Ned McCarn
Ned McCarn, Adm.
William Reid - 1 slave
William Reid, Adm
James Rice
John Sullivan
Elijah Cannon
J. D. Case
Nancy Reid
John G. Butt
Manly Steward
Silas Williams
James L. Boyd
James P. Rice
Beverly Reid
Jacob Rhodes
W. B. Taylor
John Gravlee
S. C. Chance
Abslom Butt
Elizabeth Keneday
Ashley Reid
Jarrett Myers
James S. Sullivan
James Sullivan
E. H. Burns
Martha McCarn
Martin Ward
Abslom Reid
James Cannon - 4 slaves
Newton Cannon
Joseph Price - 2 slaves
Washington Myers
Champion Sitton
Mary Sitton
Richard Bellamy - 4 slaves
Alexander Burns, Sr.
Alexander Burns, Jr.
John G. Burns
Charles Burns
John Ward
Daniel Burns
John Kemp
David B. Johnson
John G. Godfrey
Joseph Hester
Phillip Sitton, Sr.
R. R. Burns
Rolen Robins
T. C. Rutherford
Phillip Sitton, Jr.
James McFerin
Caleb Reid - 4 slaves
Walter B. Drennen
William Johnson
J. N. Dunn

Beat 9

William Davis
John Peak - 1 slave
James T. Davis
W. H. Gibson
William P. Stovall
William Rogers
E. Jetton - 1 slave
H. P. Butcher
Daniel Davis
James Davis
Robert Bryson
Hiram Barton, Jr.
William A. Hewlett - 3 slaves
Levi Robins
Robert Mills
M. H. Gibson
Jeremiah Shepherd - 6 slaves
James Hancock (Wancock)
John P. Ballenger
B. L. Mills
E. Spaulding
John W, Clayton
Cyrus W. Butcher
John Brake 1
J. Y. Usselton
Jacob Gibson
Silvester Steel
J. A. Gibson
S. C. Doyle
John B. Robins
Isiah Barton
Elizabeth Gibson

Calvin Kemp
Presley Kemp
John Bess
Jacob Myers
Moses Barton, Jr.
Adam Morrow
Mary Morrow
John Morrow
Samuel Morrow
Anderson Russel
Hiram Gibson
George Russel
Anderson Russel, Agt.
Ezekiel Alexander - 1 slave
B. F. Burden
A. Black
James Sutherlan
William Hicks
J. T. McAdams
T. B. McAdams
A. H. Gibson
John Black
Elias Davis
George Gibson
Hugh Black
Hiram Barton, Sr.
Allen Rains
T. B. Franklin
Levi Bates
Y. W. Smith
Moses Barton, Sr. - 6 slaves
F. Drummon
N. M. Burns
James Sanders - 1 slave
John B. McFerin
Hampton Fields
Abraham Nations
L. T. Robins
Avery Barton
W. B. Rains
James A. Barton
John M. Barton

Beat 10

W. N. Dickenson
Y. H. Conway
George Conway
J. H. Croft
A. M. Roberts - 4 slaves
Sarah Jones - 2 slaves
Robert P. Burton - 2 slaves
Samuel Black - 3 slaves
Jacob Sutton
J. T. Cambell
H. Teague
G. W. Phillips
Washington Wilson
Robert Y. Tuttle
Thomas Wilson
Burgess Myers
David P. Rice
William Aaron
James M. Steward
John Claghorn
John C. Myers
Charles Phillips
Stephen Phillips
Brewton Phillips
Jacob Myers
James J. Fuller
William Butt
Jeremiah Alexander
T. J. Callahan
Joshua Callahan
Richard Chilton - 12 slaves
T. R. Conway
Byrd Cole
John Myers
Sarah Myers
John Steward - 12 slaves
Jefferson Phillips
Henry Myers
William Lindsey
James Aaron
John McClendon
Silas Sitton
Elijah Roberts
Thornton Myers
Robert Phillips
Andrew Patton
H. P. Gaines - 8 slaves
H. P. Gaines - Agt.

William Gravlee, Agt.
Eli Henson
John Henson
Martin Magby
David Magby
William Henson, Agt.
Jefferson Phillips, Sr.
Henry Clark
Henry S. Jones
Cornelius Renow
Michael Robins
Jesse Robins, Jr.
Jesse Robins, Sr.
Miles Croney
P. W. Lumpkin
William Conway
William Leonard
Solomon Evans
A. Y. Whitson
James W. Snow
John Lowrimore
James Earnest
Ezekiel Wilhite
A. H. Embry
Abner Alvis
S. Blankenship
A. Y. Johnson
Allen Brown
J. T. Richards
G. K. Robertson
Jesse Files
William Enis, Agt.
Obed Baker
Edward Frost
Samuel Jones
Jesse Hyra - 1 slave
John Birdwell, Agt.
John B. Cole - 1 slave
Abram Clemmons
David Knight
James Holland
Johnson Guttery
Green Inman
Daniel O'Rear
William N. Smith
J. V. Tyra
Thomas Martin
D. W. Harville
Armsted Blevins
Richard Sappington
E. T. Gaines
Est. of J. M. Brown, dec'd.
William Pike
Isom Guttery
Thomas Whitson, Agt.
John H. and Phillip Ellison
John Wadkins
Jeremiah Files - 2 slaves
John Howel
Samuel Comer
James Cochran, Adm.
Samuel Thacker
Jesse Wood
John Carroway
Abner Crawford
F. D. Enis
Berry Ross
Washington Hamner
Greenberry Jones

Beat 11

Abel J. Lovett
William Williams
George Ellis
William Brown
Samuel James
James W. Payne
Richard Prewett
Martin Castleberry
Christopher Borden
Michael Bennett
Nathan Montgomery
Nathan Montgomery, Agt.
Joseph Elkins
S. M. Garrison
Robert M. Clark, Adm.
Preston Payne
Thomas Flowers
Elijah Tollever
J. M. Rains
S. M. Deskin

Beat 13

James A. Jones
James W. Jones
Jesse Lawson
Wiley Rabun
Simeon Covin
Timothy Williams
Tinson Shepherd
James H. Patton
John McDkff
William Davis
John M. Key
T. K. C. Gibson
C. L. King
T. W. Swindle
John B. Raben - 4 slaves
Didama Thacker
William Wiggins
William Courington
Nathaniel Upton
Jacob Clements
Thomas Crawford
Hiram Banks
John C. Holly
John Blackburn - 1 slave
Winton Dunn
Washington Smallwood
James Garrett
John H. Morris
J. T. Gilbert
George Hanley
John Brown
Stephen Busby
Robert Davis, Agt.
P. S. Banks
William Weathington
Jack Taylor
James Cain, Agt.
A. J. Jones, Agt.
John A. Lollar
William Swindle
E. T. Wood
C. R. Key
Isaac Blanton, Jr.
William Cobb
Thomas Williamson
William Hanley
S. E. Cooner
Isaac McDuff
Edmon Rutledge
John W. Knight
William Rutledge
Bolen Courington
Robert Morris
James Blanton
James Odum
C. H. Knight
William C. Guinn
John M. Cranford
John Langyard
William Edgil
George Kilgore
James Harbison
Benjamin Blanton
William G. Cain
James Courginton
Thomas Kilgore
Newton Patton
John Swindle
Robert Davis
Clement Corley - 1 slave
Reece Courington
Edmon Gilchrist - 6 slaves
James Cain - 4 slaves
T. L. Reed

Beat 14

A. C. Sides
S. Y. Ferguson
David J. Sides
Hezekiah Edwards
John Roberts
Elijah Sides
Adam Edwards
William Dowdy
H. C. C. Teagle
James Hughes
P. P. Pike
Hezekiah Edwards, Agt.
Henry Sides
Alford Sides
J. H. Faught
David Sides

Henry Ferguson - 13 slaves
John Sides
William Taylor
Edmond King
G. R. Brock

K. H. Edwards
Henry King
S. P. Taylor
Jesse Livingston
Nathaniel Jackson

Beat 15

A. Stewart
William L. Hicks
J. S. Johnston - 2 slaves
A. J. Ingle
George Tucker
Abner Cromeens
Patterson Dodd
Isom Prince
Aaron Murphew
John Wedgeworth
B. W. Roden
William Dodd
Jacob Stewart
Richard Breazeal
James Sample
Charles Pate
William Hicks
John Cromeens
David Manasco

Peter Ingle
G. W. Day
William West, Sr.
Michael Dodd
William West, Jr.
James Tittle
William W. Clements
C. B. Cagle
John Murphew
Reuben Norris
Berry Dodd
Pleasant Dodd
Martha Stewart
John Boatright
Burrel Cannon
W. B. Manasco
S. R. Pate
Spencer Cromeens
T. M. Peters

Beat 16

A. R. Self
Elias Cathy
Alford Sandlin
Nathaniel Self
Charles Loggi ns
Saniel Sandlin
Jacob Brett
Sherrod Culwell
J. B. Howard
Peter Moony
James C. Hollaway
Peter Baker
......Livingston
......Livingston
......Thomas
......Benns
Calvert, Jr.
Ashley
William Calvert, Sr.
Joseph Dean - 1 slave
Asa Allen

Jesse Sandlin
John C. Loggins
Samuel Fretwell
Major Loggins
Luke Williams
P. M. Alford
Charles Parker
William Cathy
A. M. Finley
P. W. Rhodes
Nicholas Sandlin
........Livingston
........Livingston
........Felton
S. Thomas, deceased
Kinney
Baker
John Elliott
Jonathan Calvert
Samuel Steward
Ezekiel Childres

Number of Beat not shown for the following

| | |
|---|---|
| J. M. Files | Elizabeth South |
| W. R. Leeth, Agt.- 2 slaves | John L. Davis |
| Asa Crosswhite | J. Easley |
| Absolom Little | James Vest - 2 slaves |
| Baker T. Camak | Owner unknown by R. Chilton |
| David Morrison | William Goodwin |
| Hezekiah Key | John Childres |
| Isaac Jett | Elias Fraser |
| J. M. Blackwell | C. B. Hill - 1 slave |

Marriages Recorded in Book "A" - 1879-1888-Walker County

I. D. HIGGINBOTHAM and MARY TOWNLEY, Feb. 1, 1877, at residsnce of Mr. Townley, by Simeon Covin, O.M.G.
GEORGE KILGORE and ELIZABETH WILCUTT, Feb. 15, 1877, at James Silcutt's residence, by Simeon Covin, O.M.G.
SAMUEL J. BUSBY and MARY L. C. BURLISON, Jul. 19, 1877, at residence of John Busby, C. C. Collins, O.M.G.
D. B. LOCKEY (or LACKEY) and EDY WILLIAMS, Jul. 19, 1877, at Widow William's res. W. D. Session, L.M.G.
DOCTOR LOVING and NICY ATWOOD, Jul. 19, 1877, at Richard Atwood's res. H. Barton, M.G.
ROBERT F. HOCUTT and MARTHA A. E. WILLIS, Jul. 26, 1877, at her res. S. A. Smith, M.G.
L. C. KIKER and SOPHRONIA HENRIX, at res. of W. W. Beard W. W. Beard, O.M.G. (No date on this license)
E. L. KIMBRELL and MARY E. TAYLOR, Jul. 30, 1877, at res. of the bride. D. Manasco, O.M.G.
JOHN H. CRANFORD and WILLIE A. PHIFER, Aug. 7, 1877, at house of J. B. Sumner, J. W. Shepherd, J.P. officiating.
ROBERT J. MUGFORD and LUCY BLACK, Aug. 9, 1877, at res. of A. Black. Hiram Barton, M.G.
JESSE KITCHENS and SALLIE SUMNER, Aug. 4, 1877, Wm. Randolph L.M.G.
JAMES DILL and REBECCA RICHARDSON, Aug. 9, 1877, at res. of the bride. F. A. Gamble, O.M.G.
ERVIN KILGORE and SARAH HUTTO, Aug. 14, 1877, at res. of Ann Hutto, Simeon Covin, M.G.
JAMES HENRY HARDEN and GEORGIA AN HESTER, Aug. 13, 1877, at res. of Solomon Hester, Hiram Barton, O.M.G.
JOHN A. GLOVER and CALADONIA FARRIS, at res. of W. W. Beard, O.M.G.
W. R. JONES and AMANDA ROBINSON, Sep. 6, 1877, at res. of bride's father, William Randolph, J.P.
LEWIS GUTTERY and MARGARET ALVIS, Sep. 5, 1877, at res. of the bride, Alexander N. Smith, J.P. officiating.
JOHN M. BLACK and MILLEY T. MITCHAEL, at res. of Charley Beard, Sep. 10, 1877, A. White, M.G.

P. C. WOOD and MAUDY HAYWOOD, Sep. 8,1877, at res. of William Townley, J. W. SHEPHERD, J.P. officiating.
L. D.BAILEY and SAMANTHA J. JACKSON, Sep. 13,1877, at res. of Samuel Jackson, LeRoy Williams, M.G.
JAMES W. SHEPHERD and E. E. PALMER, Sep. 18, 1877, at res. of Mrs. E. A. Palmer, James E. Andrews, O.M.G.
DAVID A. INGLE and MARY S. ADKINS, Sep. 22, 1877, at res. of William Adkins, W. P. Smith, M.G.
LOGAN DAVIS and LANEY DAVIS, Sep. 29, 1877, at Dave Blanton's res. Henry Jackson, O.M.G.
JOHN TURNER and BIRTHY MUSGROVE, Oct. 3, 1877, at res. of Lucy Blackston's, S. Covin, O.M.G.
YORK WALKER and JENNY BOX, Oct. 7, 1877, at res. of Mrs. Milley Box, Squire Cockran, M.G.
E. G. BRYANT and MARTHA L. GILBERT, Oct. 14, 1877, at res. of Thomas McGough, Thomas McGough, O.M.G.
G. W. JONES and GEORGIA ANN BANKS, Sep. 27, 1877, at res. of S. Banks, J. R. Jones, J.P. officiating
JOHN B. LONG and M. C. MUSGROVE, Oct. 11, 1877, at res. of S. T. Shields by F. A. Gamble, Judge of Probate.
WILLIAM T. QUINN and SARAH McPEARSEN, Oct. 21, 1877, at res. of Michael Robins, W. W. Macon, J.P.
DAVID BARRETT and C. A. GRAY, Oct. 29, 1877, at res. of G. W. Barrett, Wilson Shepherd, J.P. officiating
JOHN P. BLACK and MARY A. M. KING, Nov. 5, 1877, at res. of R. W. Miner, J. J. Hamilton, J.P. officiating
J. W. McDUFF and MARY E. FREEMAN, Nov. 15, 1877 at res. of Wm. Copeland. Jas. E. Cox, O.M.G.
D. F. PRICE and SARAH C. SMITH, Nov. 18, 1877, at res. of bride's parents, Wm. Randolph, J. P. Officiating
WM. W. KEY and LAURA S. UNDERWOOD, Nov. 25, 1877, at res. of William Underwood, by A. White, M.G.
SETH RICE and NANCY CONWAY, Dec. 2, 1877, at res. of Mrs. Rebecca Conway, by A. W. Mason, J.P.
MOSES HUNTER and CELIA A. WILLIAM, Dec. 9, 1877, at the res. of the bride, by J. W. Gurganus, J.P.
J. M. LANTRIP and NANCY E. PETERSON, Dec. 9, 1877, at res. of W. J. Peterson, by Daniel Jenkins, M.G.
RUSSELL ALLEN GANT, and MAUDY B. THOMPSON, Dec. 9, 1877, at res. of William Thompson, by J. W. Gurganus, J. P.
D. L. TUBES and J. A. PHIFER, Dec. 8, 1877, at res. of the bride, by Wm. Randolph, J.P.
T. H. GANT and NANCY E. CORLEY, Dec. 17, 1877, by F. A. Gamble, Probate Judge
WM. A. CLEMENTS and MARTHA E. FERGUSON, Jan. 2, 1878, at res. of Henry Ferguson, by J. E. Andrews, M.G.
BENJAMIN OWEN and SARAH C. ROBINS, Dec. 16, 1877, at res. of Michael Robins, by A. W. Mason, J.P.

COLUMBUS DAVIS and SARAH SHEPHERD, Dec. 27, 1877, at res. of Luke Shepherd, M.B.
JOSEPH SMITH and NANCY BLACK, Dec. 28, 1878, at res. of Mrs. McCracken, by J. J. Hamilton, M.G.
V. R.GUESS and F. B. BAGWELL, Jan. 4, 1878, at res. of John T. Bagwell by C. C. Kelly, J.P.
J. M. CLARK and MARY C. KING, Jan. 5,1878, at res. of N. J. King, by A. A. Sides, J.P.
I. P. BOSHELL and FRANCES FILES, Jan. 2, 1878, at res. of R. Files, by David Manasco, O.M.G.
JOHN STUBBLEFIELD and V. E. GUESS, Jan. 3, 1878, at res. of Elizabeth Guess, by C. C. Kelly, J.P.
I. S. KITCHENS and A. E. CARMICHAEL, Jan. 3, 1878, at res. of D. D. L. Carmichael, by John R. Sartain, O.M.G.
J. W. COONER and M. G. THOMPSON, Jan. 2, 1878, at res. of J. B. Thompson, by L. J. Wright, J.P.
GEORGE W. ELLIS and CATHERINE M. WILSON, Jan. 5, 1878, at res. of W. W. Wilson, by W. L. Smith, O.M.G.
JOHN N. ROBERTS and ARRENIA BARTON, Jan. 6, 1878, at res. of Hiram Barton, by Leroy Williams, M.G.
JOHN R. COURINGTON and SARAH M. WAID, Jan. 9, 1878, at res. of James H. Waid, by R. F. Sumner, J.P.
N. A. HUMPHRIES and LULA ALEXANDER, Jan. 10, 1878, at res. of D. Alexander, by R.L. Knight, J.P.
I. S. COX and R. H. FELTMAN, no date, at res. of W. Hudson by F. A. Gamble, M.G.
W. P. McCLESKEY and FANNY E. BURTON, Jan. 10, 1878, at res. of P. S. Burton, by G. A. Smith, O.M.G.
C. H. HOUSEWORTH and JULIA A. DANIEL, Jan. 9, 1878, at res. of Dr. Rosamond by F. A. Gamble, O.M.G.
J. W. RHEA and G. A. THOMPSON, Jan. 13, 1878, at res. of William Rhea, by A. J. Rowe, J.P.
M. L. RUTLEDGE and M. E. KEY, Jan. 17, 1878, at res. of Thomas Key, by R. W. Johnson, J.P.
F. M. WELLS and NANCY E. WILSON, Jan. 17, 1878, at res. of Geo. W. Wilson, by C. C. Collins, O.M.G.
WILLIAM WILSON and CHARLOTTE GAINES, Jan. 31, 1878, at res. of Jack Gaines, by Calvin Holly, L.M.G.
G. W. KEMP and CATHERINE VANDEVER, Jan. 31, 1878, at res. of Mr. Hand, by Jas. W. Davis
HARDY HANCOCK and PICKENS L. VANDIVER, Feb. 7, 1878, at res. of Miss Margaret Vandever, by Jacob A. Jones, J.P.
JOHN W. SANFORD and LOUANNA BUSBY, Feb. 4, 1878, at res. of J. L. Busbee, by H. A. Kelly, O.M.G.
DAVID MILLER and CLEARISSY FEARS, Feb. 6, 1878, by F. A. Gamble, Probate Judge
J. F. MULLENS and MARY A.GADDY, Feb. 6, 1878, at res. of H. S. Gaddy, by Wilson Shepherd, J.P.

G. L. STOVALL and M. S. CUNNINGHAM, Feb. 13, 1878, at house of John Cunningham, by Alvin A. Smith, M.G.
R. W. BRAZEAL and KEZIAH ALDRIDGE, Feb. 12, 1878, by Thomas McGough, O.M.G.
A. J. CONNER and NANCY KEY, Mar. 1, 1878, at res. of J. Key, by R. F. Sumner, J.P.
F. A. THOMPSON and MARY J. GAINES, Mar. 17, 1878, at home of G. S. Gaines, by J. E. Andrews, O.M.G.
W. P. ODOM and NANCY KILGORE, Mar. 10, 1878, at res. of James Kilgore, by Thomas N. Rose, L.M.G.
J. M. BUSBY and E. C. COLE, Mar. 13, 1878, at res. of David Rice, by J. D. Gravlee, M.G.
G. E. COVIN and SARAH I. HUBBARD, Mar. 17, 1878, at res. of John H. Morris, by J. R. Partain, O.M.G.
J. W. COX and SARAH E. CLEMMONS, Mar. 26, 1878, at res. of Thomas Ballard, by J. R. Johnston, M.G.
JOSEPH C. REED and MARY E. RANDOLPH, Mar. 21, 1878, at res. of the bride's father by Wm. Randolph, J.P.
S. E. SPARKS and A. D. LEITH, Feb. 21, 1878, at res. of M. P. Leith, by F. A. Gamble, Probate Judge.
B. F. TURNER and M. E. BRAKEFIELD, Feb. 14, 1878, at res. of R. Breakfield, by W. J. Wilson, M.G.
R. L. JOHNSON and M. E. THURMAN, Feb. 17, 1878, in the public road near my residence, Charles P. Key, J.P.
JAS. M. GLOVER and M. J. BLACK, Feb. 18, 1878, at res. of James Boyd, by James W. Davis, J.P.
JOHN MALONE and EMILY S. J. SEETON, Feb. 22, 1878, at res. of John Seeton, by J. W. Savage, J.P.
JAMES I. McCRORY and MARY SUSAN HAMILTON, Feb. 24, 1878, at res. of Y. L. Gabbert, by Leroy Williams, M.G.
W. H. MORGAN and NANCY DRUMMOND, May 29, 1878, at the res. of Thomas Drummond, by Leroy Williams, M.G.
LOUIS MITCHELL and JULIA A. E. SUMNER, Apr. 5, 1878, at res. of James Sumner by W. P. Smith, O.M.G
JOHN M. PHILLIPS and NINENEY ROBINS, Mar. 31, 1878, at the res. of Gabriel Phillips, by N. Creel, M.G.
DAVID MORRIS and MARGARET VANDEVER, Mar. 31, 1878, at the res. of Thaney Vandever, by Jas. W. Davis, J.P.
W. M. LOCKHART and C. E. GUTTERY, Apr. 9, 1878, at the res. of John Guttery, by David Manasco, M.G.
HENRY PRESCOTT and MARGARET VANDEVER, Apr. 9, 1878, at res. of W. H. Hancock, by Jacob A. Jones, J.P.
WILLIAM NESMITH and ELIZA WHITLEY, Apr. 24, 1878 at res. of G. Whitley by S. J. Wright, J.P.
JAS. S. GANNERT and CEBELLE McDANIEL, May 9, 1878, at res. of W. B. W. Dent, by Leroy Williams, J.P.
JOHN DISON and ELIZABETH DISON, May 16, 1878, married in the public road near my premises, by W. M. Buzbee, J.P.
MERIT KING WELCH and LUCINDA RUSSELL, June 4, 1878, at office of the Probate Judge by F. M. Gamble, O.M.G.

JOHN NORRIS and MALINDA PHELPMAN, June 16, 1878, at res. of Jerry Files, by G. W. Whitley, J.P.
JOHN AARON, Jr. and MARTHA J. KING, June 23, 1878, at res. of R. W. Minor, by James Hamilton, M.G.
COLUMBUS WILLIAMS and MARY BEST, June 30, 1878, at res. of James J. Smith, by John N. Sparks, J.P.
JOSEPH EDWARD and SARAH J. GRAY, June 25, 1878, at res. of C. P. Owens, by S. A. Smith, O.M.G.
R. J. ISBELL and E. ANDREWS, June 26, 1878, at the res. of J. E. Andrews by Evan Nickolson, M.G.
J. P. ROMINE and L. A. TAYLOR, Aug. 8, 1878, at the res. of Davidson Blackwell, By S. A. Smith, O.M.G.
L. W. WILLIAMS and MARY E. DAY, Jul. 16, 1878, at the res. of W. B. Day, by B. E. Mullens, O.M.G.
EDMUND BURK and SARAH O'REAR, Jul. 25, 1878, at the res. of John O'Rear, D. B. Ford, O.M.G.
R. W. KEETON and ELIZA J. RICHARDSON, Aug. 8, 1878, at the res. of Jno. W. Richardson, by C. C. Collins, O.M.G.
GEO. THOMPSON and PHEBA A. HOLLIS, Aug. 8, 1878, at the court house, by F. A. Gamble, O.M.G.
HENRY BUTLER and MARTHA E. CLARK, Aug. 8, 1878, at the res. of R. M. Morgan by Jas. W. Davis, J.P.
R. J. GUTTERY and C. L. BOSHELL, Aug. 18, 1879, by W. H. Burkett, J.P.
V. L. LAWSON and JOSEPHINE LESTER, Aug. 28, 1878, at res. of J. R. Lester, by P. P. Jones, J.P.
JAMES TUNE and E. A. PARKER, Aug. 1878, at res. of S. J. Childers, by R. E. Harris, O.M.G.
HENRY TURNER and DICY BLACKSTONE, Sep. 3, 1878, at res. of "Bud's" Mother, by A. J. Rowe, J.P.
ROBERT BLACKWOOD, JR. and S. J. HARRIS, Sept. 5, 1878, at the home of the bride by L. A. Morris, M.G.
J. W. SHAW and E. A. STUDDARD, Sep. 11, 1878, at res. of Wm. Hendon by W. R. Boshell, J.P.
L. R. HENSON and SARAH M. SWINDLE (no date) at res. of Maderson Busby by A. J. Rowe, J.P.
R. A. WILLIAMS and MARY A. GABBERT, Sept. 18, 1878, at res. of bride's father by Wm. Randolph, J.P.
THOMAS SIMPSON and MARGARET GILMORE, Sept. 22, 1878, at the res. of W. W. Simpson by A. J. Rowe, J.P.
A. H. BLACKWELL and MARGARET SANFORD, Aug. 8, 1878, at home of the bride's father by Wilson Shepherd, J.P.
GEORGE B. McGOWEN and SARAH M. JOHNSON, Sep. 26, 1878, at res. of M. L. Johnson by Thomas McGough, O.M.G.
A. B. SANFORD and MARY HANCOCK, Sep. 29, 1878, at the res. of James R. Hancock, by Jacob A. Jones, J.P.
NEWTON DAVIS and MARY J. MORGAN, Sep. 26, 1878 at res. of Liza Morgan by Jas. W. Davis, J.P.

J. H. WILSON and M. L. RAMEY, Sep. 26, 1878, at res. of M. E. Raney by C. C. Collins, O.M.G.
G. W. HERRON and JANE HERRON, Sep. 26, 1878, at res. of Thos. Herron by Thomas McGough, O.M.G.
G. W. MANUEL and MARY J. DILL, Sep. 29, 1878, by P. P. Jones, J.P
JOHN D. CAMPBELL and MAUDY LOGIN, Oct. 1, 1878, at res. of Bud Sandlin by E. A. Blevins, J.P.
NATHANIEL SELF and MELOMA UPTON, Sep. 30, 1878, at res. of J. R. Martin by W. A. Vest, J.P.
JOHN B. JACKSON and MARY E. HAMILTON, Oct. 3, 1878, at res. of C. C. Hamilton by Wm. Randolph, J.P.
J. B. COBB and SARAH DUNKIN, Oct. 7, 1878, F. A. Gamble, Probate Judge
WILLIAM A. JUSTICE and BETTY A. SHORT, Oct. 8, 1878, at res. of R. Short by Nelson Skelton, L.M.
J. M. FILES and V. C. McCOLLUM, Oct. 10, 1878, at home of Jerry Files by W. H. Burkett, J.P.
W. D. GUTTERY and M. E. ELLIS, Nov. 2, 1878 at res. of James Ellis by A. A. Sides, J.P.
GEORGE ODOM and MANDY COPELAND, Oct. 17, 1878 at res. of L. E. Copeland by H. A. Key, O.M.G.
W. M. THOMAS and R. P. CANNON, Oct. 15, 1878, at res. of Russell Guttery by S. J. Wright, J.P.
J. H. ALDREDGE and MARY E. MATON, Oct. 17, 1878, at my own home by Eld. W. A. Bryan
JAMES E.BURTON and M. F. ELMORE, Oct. 20, 1878, at res. of W. A. Elmore by Leroy Williams, M.G.
RUSSELL M. WILLIAMS and NICEY A. SCOTT, Oct. 22, 1878, at res. of Carter Scott, by R. E. Harris, O.M.G.
GEORGE F. LOCKHART and PERMELIA LOCKHART, Oct. 24, 1878, at res. of ELIza Daniels, by Wm. Randolph, O.M.G.
JAMES M. CAMAK and CARRIE E. LONG, Oct. 24, 1878, at res. of B. M. Long by David Manasco, O.M.G.
D. K. CARTER and NELLIE E. KING, Nov. 1, 1878, at Monteith by J. E. Andrews
S. A. SMITH and LUTICIA MILLER, Oct. 27, 1878, at home of Mrs. Miller by Wm. Randolph, O.M.G.
P. M. BOSHELL and C. D. LATHAM, Oct. 1878, at home of R. T. Latham, by R. E. Harris.
JOHN T. MORRIS and FATIMY STANLEY, Oct. 31, 1878, at res. of J. T. Stanley by J. J. Hamilton, O.M.G.
W. J. PHILLIPS and LIDY A. NATIONS, at res. of M. Phillips, Nov. 7, 1878 by Eld. Sanders, M.G.
A. M. STEPHENS and MARY E. F. PETERSON, Nov. 18, 1878, at home of Wm. Peterson, by Daniel Jenkins.
S. V. BELL and M. A. SMITH, Nov. 21, 1878, at res. of S. A. Smith by James E. Cox, M.G.
W. R. FERGUSON and LEONI DAVIS, Nov. 27, 1878, at res. of V. A. Davis by W. P. Smith, O.M.G.

A. A. WALDROP and M. M. JACKSON, Dec. 12, 1878, at res. of A. H. Johnson by A. J. Rowe, J.P.
R. J. PAYNE and HANEY VANDEVER, Dec. 18, 1878, at res. of the bride, by David Jenkins.
P. E. McALLESTER and SARAH I. FOSTER, Dec. 4, 1878, at res. of E. B. Foster by Wilson Shepherd, J.P.
SAMUEL E. WALTON and M. J. BEASLEY, Dec. 8, 1878, at res. of P. A. Harris, by R. F. Sumner, J.P.
G. W. THOMPSON and PHOEBE L. I. SHERER, Dec. 5, 1878, at res. of Jackson Sherer, Hiram Barton, M.G.
JOSEPH S. SMITH and CHARITY H. WHITFIELD, Dec. 17, 1878, at res. of R. M. Whitfield by W. P. Smith, O.M.G.
R. B. CASTLEBERRY and MARY MOORE, Dec. 11, 1878, at res. of J. P. Moore, by A. A. Smith, M.G.
H. A. THOMPSON and ELIZABETH THOMPSON, Dec. 12, 1878, at res. of Edmon Thompson, by John W. Sparks, J.P.
ISHAM PATE, JR. and ELEMENTINE UNDERWOOD, Dec. 19, 1878, at res. of Wm. Underwood by Jacob Jones, J.P.
JOHN ROLLINS and FRANCES DAVIS, Dec. 25, 1878 at home of Jacob Davis by George Shepherd, L.M.
J. W. HUNTER and MARY A. BLACK, Dec. 26, 1878, at the res. of John Black by J. J. Hamilton, O.M.G.
A. H. YOUNG and ANNIE HUTTO, Dec. 31, 1878, at res. of Miss Hutto by J. W. Gurganus, J.P.
JAMES NELSON and M. A. MYERS, Jan. 1, 1879, by Leroy Williams,MG
H. J. CRANFORD and DOSHA HOLLIS, Jan. 1, 1879, at res. of S. Black by N. Sanders, M.G.
ISHAM GUTTERY and SARAH A. BROWN, Jan. 3, 1879, at res. of James M. Richardson, J. E. Cox, O.M.G.
R. O. KIMBRELL and M. F. BOSHELL, Jan. 10,1882, at res. of J. B. Boshell, by J. S. Steedman, J.P.
C. D. FIKE and M. J. THOMPSON, Jan. 1, 1882, at res. of the bride's father by J. B. Romine, J.P.
R. P. GRIFFIN and JOSEI BAKER, Jan. 15,1888, at res. of Mrs. Mary Sparks by F. A. Gamble, O.M.G.
M. M. AMERSON and MARTHA J. NELSON, Jul. 23, 1882, at res. of J. G. Files by J. G. Files, J.P.
A. S. SPARKS and M. S. STEADMAN (no date) at res. of Mrs. Steadman.
JOHN E. WALTY and JANE CARADINE, Apr. 17, 1882, at res. of the bride, by J. W. Rhea, J.P.
S. L. KEY and M. B. NELSON, Jul. 28, 1882, at res. of Amos Nelson, by M. D. King, N.P.
W. C. TOWNLEY and N. B. GUTTERY, Oct. 3, 1882, by J. S. Steadman, J.P.
JAS. R. HUNTER and MOLLIE O'REAR, Dec. 15, 1884, at res. of E. O'Rear by Ira Robbins, N.P. and J.P.

J. B. GRACE and MARTHA J. BANKS, Dec. 29, 1884, at res. of Mrs. Mary Grace by W. F. Sides, N.P.and J.P.
A. J. KNIGHT and MISS LOU NELSON, Dec. 25, 1886, at res. of S. Nelson by E. H. Harris, M.G.
JOHN MANASCO and CORDELIA WOODS, Mar. 26, 1888, at res. of C. H. Woods by M. D. King, J.P.
BYRON LEETH and M. GUTTERY, Apr. 4, 1888, at res. of John W. Sparks by John W. Sparks, M.G.
JOHN M. KING and MARY ANN BOSHELL, Dec. 3, 1888, at res. of Nick Boshell by W. F. Wright.
W. H. BEASLEY and M. E. GUTTERY, Apr. 11, 1888, at home by L. R. Craig, M. G.
G. J. GUTTERY and E. R. BOSHELL, Mar.6, 1884, at home of John Guttery by David Manasco, O.M.G.
J. F. HUDSON and L. C. TOWNLEY, Mar. 12, 1884, at home of Robert Townley by Isham Guttery, M.G.
LEWIS GUTTERY and MARGARET ALVIS married at the res. of the bride, Sep. 5, 1877 by Alexander Nesmith, J.P.
WILLIAM C. BURTON and ELIZABETH GUTTERY, Oct.10, 1879 by David Manasco, M.G.
JOSEPH T. SHERER and LOU N. GUTTERY, Mar. 28, 1881 by N. L. Hewitt
W. D. GUTTERY and M. E. ELLIS, at res. of James Ellis, Oct. 16, 1878 by A. A. Sides, J.P.
W. C. LOCKHART and C. E. GUTTERY, at the home of John Guttery, Apr. 9, 1878 by David Manasco, M.G.
R. J. GUTTERY and C. S. BOSHELL, Aug.18, 1878 by W. H. Burkett, J.P.
ROBERT W. CARMICHAEL and ELIZABETH BURTON, Aug. 27, 1889, at res. of John Burton by W. D. Boshell, J.P.
B. P. HASSELL and LAVONIA BURTON, no date, at res. of Wiley Davis by J. M. Williams, M.G.
EDWARD LANKFORD and MARY A. KING, Nov. 15, 1888, near Holly Grove by John H. Pool, O.M.G.

Miscellaneous Marriages

MILES CHAPPEL and PRISCILLA PARKER, Jul. 12, 1812, in Bedford Co., Tenn. by John Eppes,J.P.(from Miles Chappel's 1812 War record)
JOHN MANASCO and LOVISA ODOM, Nov. 4, 1797 in Franklin Co., Ga. by Henry Sparks, J.P. (taken from 1812 War record of John Manasco)
JOHN MANASCO, JR. and LUCINDA LUSTER, Feb. 3, 1829, in Morgan Co., Ala.
DAVID MANASCO and JANE KIRKLAND, Sep. 16, 1823 by John Bird, J.P. in Morgan Co., Ala. (Bk.A.p.146, Morgan Co. Marriage Bonds)

JOEL MANASCO and KITTY WILLIAMS, Nov. 30, 1824 by David McClung. (Bk.A.p.66, Morgan Co. Ala. marriage bonds)

Walker County Marriages taken from the Bible

SEABORN J. WRIGHT and ANNIS ELIZABETH BOSHELL, Apr. 18, 1858
ELIZABETH GUTTERY and WILLIAM BURTON, Oct. 8, 1878, at the home of her father, Isham Guttery.

Jefferson County Marriages

ABNER C. DEWEESE and FRANCES COKER, Feb. 3, 1823, by John Brown, J.P.

Family Record

DAVID MANASCO and ELIZABETH R. DEWEESE, 1855

TUscaloosa County Marriages

JAMES CHAPPEL and LUCY FREEMAN, Jan. 18, 1838
RICHARD FILES and MARTHA STANLEY, Oct. 26, 1858, at res. of David Stanley
AUGUSTUS APPLING and MARTHA E. STANLEY, Dec. 17, 1846
WILLIAM HOPPER and BETSY THOMAS, Apr. 29, 1824 by James Rains, M.G.
JOHN STANLEY and ELIZA H. JONES, Dec. 24,1846
JESSE M. STANLEY and MARTHA J. CHAPPEL, Dec. 17, 1850
LEWIS T. STANLEY and SUSAN APPLING, Oct. 25, 1837
DAVID STANLEY and FATIMA THOMAS, Feb. 19, 1827
DANIEL BOON and NANCY E. STANLEY, Dec. 26, 1856, at res. of Benj. Stanley
JOHN M. CUMMINGS and ELIZABETH STANLEY, Dec. 27, 1859, at res. of Lewis Stanley.

The following is taken from a book printed by the Government entitled:

The Executive Documents
Printed by Order of the
SENATE OF THE UNITED STATES
For The
Second Session of the Forty-Seventh Congress,
1882-'83
In Five Volumes

Volume V - Part 5

WASHINGTON:
Government Printing Office
1883

List
of
Pensioners on the Roll
January 1, 1883:
Giving
The name of each pensioner, the cause for which pensioned, the post-office address, the rate of pension per month, and the date of original allowance,
as called for by
Senate Resolution of Decsmber 8, 1882
************

Volume V

**************

Washington:
Government Printing Office
1883
ALABAMA

| No. of Certificate | Name of Pensioner | Post Office Address | Cause for which pensioned | Date of Original Allowance |
|---|---|---|---|---|
| 18,313 | Madison, Susan | Beach Grove | Widow 1812 | Feb.1879 |
| 13,296 | Bevill, Rutla | Do | Do | Dec.1878 |
| 23,434 | Swindle, Eliz. | Do | Do | May 1879 |
| 32,481 | Mathews, Eliz. | Holly Grove | Widow 1812 | Jun.1882 |
| 5,686 | Romine, Nancy | Do | Do | Oct.1873 |
| 11,513 | Kidd, Ailsey | Jasper | Do | Nov.1878 |
| 11,623 | Morris, Sarah | Do | Do. | Nov.1878 |
| 19,933 | Trice, Joseph | Jasper | Surv. 1812 | Dec.1872 |
| 8,853 | Gamble, Jane | Do | Widow 1812 | Sep.1878 |
| 9,236 | Martin, Barton | South Lowell | Surv. 1812 | Dec.1871 |

1812 War Pension Applications of Walker Co. Residents

State of Alabama
County of Walker

On the 26 day of April, A.D. one thousand eight hundred and seventy-one, personally appeared before me John Brown, judge, of the Probate Court, a court of record within and for the county and State aforesaid, JAMES MATTHEWS, agwd, seventy-eight years, a resident of . . . . ., County of Walker, State of Alabama, who being duly sworn according to law, delcares that he is married, that his wife's name was Betsy Jones, to whom he was married in Walker County, Ala. on the . . . day of Nov. 1767, that he served the full period of sixty days on the Military Service of the U.S. in the War of 1812; that he is the identical JAMES MATTHEWS who enlisted in

Captain Jas. Marawheather (Meriwether) Company, Harris' Regiment. . . . . at Wadkinsville, Georgia, on the .... day of August 1812, and was honorably discharged at Milledgeville, Ga. on the . . . . day of January 1813; that he has lost his discharge. That he has drawn a land warrant for 160 acres, that he, at no time during the late rebellion against the authority of the U.S. adhered to the cause of enemies of the Govt., etc............
Signed...........His - James Matthews - Mark

State of Alabama
County of Tallapoosa

On this 12th day of November, A.D. 185 , personally appeared before me a Justice of the Peace, within and for the county and State aforesaid, JAMES MATTHEWS, aged 58 years, a resident of Tallapoosa County, in the State of Alabama, who being duly sworn according to law, declares that he is the identical JAMES MATTHEWS, who was a private in the company commanded by Captain Isam Hendon in the first Regiment of Georgia Militia, commanded by Col. Jeb Thomas in the War with Great Britain declared by the U.S. on the 19th day of June 1812. That he was drafted at Watkinsville, Ga. on or about the tenth day of September A.D. 1814 for the term of six months and was continued in actual service in the War for the term of five months and was honorably discharged at Sparta, Georgia on the 12th day of March A.D. 1815, as will appear by the Muster Roll of his company and that no written certificate of discharge was given him. He makes this declaration for the purpose of obtaining the Bounty Land which he may be entitled to under the Act granting Bounty Land to certain officers and soldiers who have been engaged in the military service of the U.S. passed 28th Sep. 1850.
JAMES MATTHEWS
Sworn to and subscribed before me on the day and year above written and I hereby certify that I believe the said JAMES MATTHEWS to be the identical man who served as aforesaid and that he is of the age above stated.....Signed - William Allen, J.P. (LS)
Cert. 45918 - January 9, 1851
James Matthews
Capt. Merriwether
1st Reg. Georgia Vols.
War 1812
July 1813
March 1814
Sec. service Capt. Hendon
Sep. 1814
March 1815
Ordered 160 acres Sep. 15,1851

James Matthews served from 23 Aug. 1813 to March 1814 under Capt. Merriwether.
2nd Service under Capt. Hedon from 10th Oct. 1814 to March 1815.
Signed Jas. T. Gallaher - Warrant No. 8445 issued and sent 1st Oct. 1851 - Simeon Gookey, Dadeville, Ala.

War of 1812 - Declaration for Original Pension of a Widow - Child or Children under Sixteen years of age surviving.

State of Alabama - County of Walker ............

On this 5th day of December .. A.D. one thousand eight hundred and eighty-one ... personally appeared before me, F. A. GAMBLE, Judge of the Probate Court .. the same being a court of record and for the county and State aforesaid, ELIZABETH MATTHEWS, age 27 ....years, who being duly sworn according to law, makes the following statement in order to obtain the pension provided by Acts of Congress granting pensions to widows: That she is the widow of JAMES MATTHEWS who enlisted under the name of JAMES MATTHEWS...... at ...... on the ........day of ......A.D. 18.. in Capt. Merriwether's Co. Ga. Militia, in the war of 1812 who ....... died......... on the 30th day of April .... A.D. 1857, who bore at the time of his death the rank of .............., that she was married under the name of ELIZABETH JONES, to said JAMES MATTHEWS, on the 30th day of September A.D. 1869 by JOHN GUTTERY Justice of the Peace at James Matthews' house, there being no legal barrier to such marriage; that neither she had been previously married; that JAMES MATTHEWS had been previously and his first wife Maria Matthews died January 15th 1866, that she had to the present date remained his widow; that the following are the names and dates of birth of all his legitimate children yet surviving who were under sixteen years of age at the father's death, to wit:

William Matthews, born Sep. 25, 1870
Rhoda S. Matthews, born Jan. 15, 1872
Aramintta A. Matthews born Feb. 14, 1878
Pinta M. Matthews, born Oct. 14, 1870
(His by herself)

His by a former marriage:
Martha A. Stacks, born Nov. 25, 1821
John Matthews born Aug. 9, 1823
Sarah A. Griffin born Jul. 15, 1827
Elviry(Elmiry) Matthews, born Mar. 12, 1839
George W. Matthews, born Jan. 10, 1841

That she has not abandoned the support of any of his children but they are still under her care or maintenance except Martha A. Stacks, John Matthews, Sarah A. Griffin, Elmiry Matthews and George W. Matthews who have homes and families of their own; that she has not in any manner been engaged in, or aided .... or abetted, the rebellion in the United States; that prior application has been filed by James Matthews and obtained pension certificate No. 10,032
Dated Dec. 23, 1871
That she hereby appoints ............. that her residence is ..... Walker County, State of Alabama and that her post office address is .......... Holly Grove, Ala.
her X mark - Elizabeth Matthews
Att: Wm. Randolph

****************

Benjamin Stanley's 1812 War record

BLWT 33495 - a20 -- 55
Application 11-1-1850 and 4-7-1855
The State of Alabama
County of Tuscaloosa

On this first day of November A.D. one thousand eight hundred and fifty personally appeared before me a Justice of the Peace within and for the County and State aforesaid, Benjamin Stanley aged 59 years, a resident of Tuscaloosa County in the State of Alabama who being duly sworn according to law, declares that he is the identical Benjamin Stanley who was a private in the Company commanded by Captain Willson in the Regiment of Militia commanded by Col. Ezekiel Wimberly in the war with Great Britain declared he was drafted on the 18th day of June 1812 to service on or about the .... day of November A.D. 1814 for the term of six months and continued in actual service in said war for the term of four months and was honorably discharged at Darien, Georgia on the .... day of March A.D. 1815 as will appear by the Muster Roll of said company. He not having his original certificate of discharge. He makes this declaration for the purpose of obtaining the Bounty Land to which he may be entitled under under the Act of granting Bounty Land to certain officers and soldiers who have been engaged in the Military service of the U. S. passed Sept. 28, 1850. Signed Benjamin Stanley. Sworn to and subscribed before me the day and year written. And I hereby certify that I believe the said Benjamin Stanley to be the identical man who served as aforesaid and that he is the age above stated.

Thomas J. Burke (Seal)
Justice of the Peace

Act 28 Sep. 1850
No. 3586 of Benjamin Stanley
Wilson's Comp.
Wimberley's Regiment
War of 1812
11-14-1850
Clements

State of Alabama
County of Tuscaloosa

On this 4th day of December, A.D. one thousand eight hundred and seventy, personally appeared before me WM. MILLER, Judge of the Probate Court, a court of record within and for the County and State aforesaid, JESSE SWINDLE, aged seventy-seven a resident of .........County of Tuscaloosa, State of Alabama who being duly sworn according to law, declares that he is married and that his wife's name was ELIZABETH WASHINGTON, to whom he was married at Tuscaloosa Co., Ala. on the 4th day of March 1824; that he served the full period of sixty days in the military service of the U.S. in the War of 1812; that he is the identical JESSE SWINDLE, who was drafted in Captain John Holshouser's company Col. Copeland's Regiment, Johnston's Brigade ....... division, at Fayetteville, Tenn. on the .... day of January or February 1814 and was honorably discharged at Fayetteville, Tenn. on the .... day of May, 1814; that he was in the Creek Nation on Coosa River most of the time of service, was not in any engagement, that he at no time during the late rebellion against the authority of the U.S. served the cause of the enemies of the Government, etc. that he makes this declaration for the purpose of being placed on the pension roll of the U.S. under the provision of the act approved Feb. 14, 1871, and he hereby constitutes and appoints, with full power of substitution and revocation N. H. Brown, lawful attorney to prosecute his claim and obtain the pension certificate that may be issued, that his office is at Oregonia, County of Tuscaloosa, State of Alabama and that his domicile or place of abode is Tuscaloosa Co. Ala. ........Signed His Jesse Swindle Mark

J. J. ----------?
Lewis Christian

--------------------Applicant

<u>Claim of Widow for Service Pension</u>
State of Alabama
County of Walker

On this 23rd day of October, A.D. One Thousand Eight Hundred and Seventy-Eight, personally appeared before me, Judge of the Probate Court, the same being a court of record within and for the County and State aforesaid (1) Elizabeth Swindle, aged 57 years, a resident of Beach Grove, in the State of Alabama, who being duly sworn according to law, declares that she is the widow of (2) Jesse Swindle who served under the name of (4) Jesse Swindle as a (5) Private in the company commanded by Captain .........in the ........regiment of....... commanded by .........in the War of 1812-15; that her said

husband, etc., etc......................(left blank).
She further states that she was married to the said Jesse Swindle at the city near the town of Jasper, in the County of Walker, State of Alabama, on the 4th day of February A.D. 1869 by one (11) Thomas Key who was a (12) Justice of the Peace and that her name before her said marriage was Elizabeth Wade and that she has not remarried since the death of the said Jesse Swindle; and she further states that the said Jesse Swindle had been previously married to Elizabeth Washington who died 1st August 1868, Tuscaloosa County, Claimant has not been married before, and that her said husband (14) Jesse Swindle died at Tuscaloosa Co. in the State of Alabama on the 7th day of Sept. A.D. 1876 and she further declares that the following have been the places of residence of herself and her said husband since the date of his discharge from the Army, viz; (15) Tuscaloosa County, Walker County, Alabama. ............She makes this declaration for the purpose of obtaining the Pension to which she may be entitled under Section 4736 to 4740 inclusive, Revised Statues and the Act of March 9, 1878 and hereby appoints with full powers of substitution and revocation, THOS C. FULLERTON, of Washington, D.C. her true and lawful attorney, to prosecute her claim. And she further declares that she has heretofor made no application for (16) pension,but her husband Jesse drew bounty land and also applied for pension Act of Congress 3rd of March 1871 and drew pension until his death, and that her said residence is Beach Grove, County of Walker, State of Alabama and that her post office address is Beach Grove, Alabama............Her Mark - Elizabeth Swindle

A. H. McClung
Jno. A. Gravlee
Also appearsd Joseph Atkins aged 62 years residing at Beach Grove in Walker County, Ala. and Sarah Atkins aged 47 years, residing at Beach Grove
No. 26304
Treasury Department,
Third Auditors Office
October 3, 1872
Respectfully returned to the Commissioner of Pensions with the information that the rolls of Captain John Holshouser's Company of Tennessee Militia show that Jesse Swindle, Private served from January 25th 1814, to May 10th 1814. The Captain's name as borne on the rolls is "John Holshouser" and so signed on the roll. ........Auditor

The State of Alabama
Tuscaloosa County

On this 31st day of March A.D. 1855, personally appeared before me a Justice of the Peace within and for the County and

State aforesaid duly commissioned and sworn, Jesse Swindle, aged sixty-one years, of the County of Tuscaloosa and State of Alabama who being duly sworn according to law, declares that he is the identical Jesse Swindle who was a private in Captain Holshouser's Company Colonel Copeland's Regiment of Tennessee Militia in the War with the Creek Indians for the term of three months from the 20th of February to the 27th May 1814 and continued in actual service in said war for near three months. That he has heretofore made application for Bounty Land under the Act of September 28th 1850, and receivwd a Land Warrant, No. 2832 for forty acres which he has since legally disposed of and cannot return now. He makes this declaration for the purpose of obtaining the additional Bounty Land to which he may be entitled under the Act approved March 3rd 1855. Also he declares that he has never applied for or received, under this or another Act of Congress, any Bounty Land Warrant except the one above designated. And he hereby appoints John G. Barr, of the City of Tuscaloosa, Ala. to prosecute his claim and receive his Warrant when issued.........Jesse Swindle (LS)
Witnesses - H. P. King and J.L. Cobb (LS)
J. S. Skinner, Justice of the Peace.

The State of Alabama
County of Tuscaloosa

On this 30th day of October A.D. One Thousand Eight Hundred and Fifty, personally appeared before me a Justice of the Peace, within and for the County and State aforesaid, Jesse Swindle, aged 56 years, a resident of Tuscaloosa County in the State of Alabama, who being duly sworn according to law, declares that he is the identical Jesse Swindle who was a privats in the company commanded by Captain Holshouser in the Regiment of Militia commanded by Col. Copeland in the War with the hostile Creek Indians, and that he was drafted and was mustered into the service of the U.S. at Fayetteville Tenn. on or about the 20th day of February, A.D. 1814 for the term of three months and was honorably discharged at Fayetteville Tenn. about the 27th day of May, A.D. 1814, on account of expiration of term of service, as will appear - he having lost his discharge, on the roll of said company. He makes this declaration for the purpose of obtaining the Bounty Land to which he may be entitled under the Act granting Bounty Land to certain officers and soldiers who have been engaged in the military service of the U.S. passed Sept. 28th, 1850..............Jesse Swindle (LS)
Sworn to and subscribed before me the day and year above written. And I hereby certify that I believe the said Jesse Swindle to be the identical man who served as aforesaid and that he is of the age above stated...J. Skinner, Justice of the Peace.

****************

Declaration For A Pension
Under Act of Feb. 14, 1871
War of 1812
State of Alabama
County of Walker

On this 19th day of April A.D. One Thousand Eight Hundred and Seventy-One, personally appeared before me JNO BROWN, Judge of the Probate Court, a court of record within and for the County and State aforesaid, RARDON BEVILL, aged seventy-nine years, a resident of the County of Walker, State of Alabama, who being duly sworn according to law, declares that he is married, that his wife's name was Rutitia East, to whom he was married in Shelby County, Ala. on the 22d day of March 1847, that he served the full period of sixty days in the Infantry service of the U.S. in the War of 1812; that he is the identical Rardon Bevill who enlisted in Captain Butler's Company 18.... regiment....Brigade..... division at Union Dist. S.C. on the 4th day of July 1812 and was honorably discharged at Fort Johnson on the 13th day of January 1814; that he was Corporal, has drawn a land warrant for 160 acres. That he, at no time during the late rebellion against the authority of the U.S. adhered to the cause of the enemies of the Government, etc.....etc. That his post office is at Holly Grove, County of Walker, State of Alabama, that his domicile or place of abode is ...............
Rardon Bevill (LS) Applicant
Attest: H. R. Guttery - John M. Nelson

State of Alabama
County of Shelby

On the 9th day of November, A.D. one thousand eight hundred and fifty personally appeared before me, a Justice of the Peace, within and for the County and State aforesaid Rardon Bevill aged fifty-six, years, a resident of Shelby County, Alabama in the State of Alabama who being duly sworn according to law, declares that he is the identical Rardon Bevill who was a private, and subsequently a corporal, in the company commanded by Captain George Butter(Butler) in the 18th regiment of infantry commanded by Col. William Drayton im the war with Great Britain declared by the U.S. on the 18th of June,1812 that he enlisted at Union Court House South Carolina on or about the 14th day of July A.D. 1812 for the term of eighteen months and was honorably discharged at Fort Johnson South Carolina on the 13th day of January A.D. 1814, as will appear by his original certificate of discharge herewith presented. He makes this declaration for the purpose of obtaining the Bounty Land to which he may be entitled under the Act granting Bounty Land to certain officers and soldiers of the U.S. passed Sept. 28th 1850. Rardon Bevill(LS) Sworn to and subscribed before me on the day and year above written and I hereby certify that I believe the said Rardon Bevill to be the identical man who served as aforesaid and that he was the age above stated..... H. V. Nabours (LS) Justice of the Peace.

Claim of Widow for Service Pension
State of Alabama
County of Walker

On the 29th day of April A.D. One Thousand Eight Hundred and Seventy-Eight, personally appeared before me Judge of the Probate Court, the same bsing a court of record within and for the County and State aforesaid, (1) Rutla Revill, aged 51 years, a resident of Walker County in the State of Alabama, who being duly sworn according to law, declares that she is the widow of (2) Rardon Bevill deceased, who was the identical (3) Rardon Bevill as a private, in the company commanded by Col. Drayton.... in the War of 1812; that her husband volunteered at Fort Moultrie on or about the 18th of July A.D. 1813 for the term of 18 months and continued in actual service in said war for the term of 18 months, and whose services terminated by reason of honorable discharge at Fort Johnson on or about January 13th A.D. 1814. She further states that the following is a full description of her said husband at the time of his enlistment, Viz: Blue eyes, fair complexion, dark hair, five feet 8 inches high, occupation farmer. She further states that she was married to the said Rardon Bevill, at the city or town ......... in the County of Shelby and in the State of Alabama on the 22d of March, A.D. 1849 by one Rev. James H............(?) who was a Minister of the Gospel and that her name before her marriage was Rutla East and she further states that her husband's first wife's name was Mary Lang. She died in Shelby County, Ala. 3rd of October 1846 and that her said husband Rardon Bevill died at his residence in the State of Ala. on the 12th day of March A.D. 1877 and she further states that the following have been places of residence of herself and her said husband since the date of his discharge from the Army, viz: we remained simetime in S.C. from there he came to Ala. thence to suit me then came to Shelby County, Ala. and thence we moved to Walker County, Ala. She makes this declaration for the purpose of obtaining the Pension to which she may be entitled under Sections 4736 to 4740, incl. Revised Statutes and the Act of March 11, 1878, and hereby appoints Thos. C.

Fullerton, of Washington, D.C. her true and lawful attorney, to present her claim. She further states that she had heretofore made no application for pension but her husband Rardon Bevill drew a pension certificate No. 9083 dated 5th day of Dec. 1871......and that her post office address is Beach Grove, Walker County, Ala......Ruttla Bevill - (her mark).
Witnesses:
Elijah O'Rear
W. F. Sides

Also appeared Elijah O'Rear aged 50 years residing in Jasper, Ala. and W.F. Sides aged 46 years residing at Jasper, Ala.

Treasury Departmet
Third Auditor's Office
November 20, 1871
Respectfully returned to the Commissioner of Pensions with the information that the rolls of Captain George Butler's Company 18th U.S. Infantry show that Rardon Bevill served from the 12th July 1812 to 13 January 1814 when discharged.
Allan Rutherford, Auditor.

************

War of 1812 - Declaration For Pension Under
Act of February 14, 1871
State of Alabama
County of Walker

On the 16th day of October, A.D. One Thousand Eight Hundred and Seventy-One, personally appeared before me Jno. Brown, Judge of the Probate Court, a court of record within and for the said County and State, JAMES ROMINE, aged eighty years, a resident of Holly Grove, Walker County, State of Alabama, who being duly sworn according to law, declares that he is married, that his wife's name was NANCY BIRDWELL, to whom he was married at Madison Co., Ala. on the 14 day of May, 1812, that he served the full period of sixty days in the military service of the U.S. in the War of 1812 and that he is the identical JAMES ROMINE, who enlisted in Capt. James Reid's Company, Col. Steed's Regiment, on the 28 day of January 1814, and that he was engaged in guarding the frontier and scouting for Indians. He has drawn a land warrant for 100 acres...... Signed by: James Romine (his mark).
Witnessed by:
E. W. Miller
L. M. Leith

War of 1812 - Declaration of a Widow For Pension
State of Alabama
County of Walker

On the 19th day of July, A.D. One Thousand Eight Hundred and Seventy-Three, personally appeared before me, D. S. Stovall, Clerk of the Circuit Court .... for and within the said county and State, NANCY ROMINE, aged 78 yrs., a resident of near Jasper, County of Walker, who being duly sworn according to law, declares that she is the widow of James Romine, who served the full period of sixty days in the Militia Service of the United States in the War of 1812, who was the identical James Romine, who enlisted in Captain James Reid's Company, Tenn. Militia,.....etc, at Huntsville, Ala....... Her said husband was inscribed on the Pension Roll at Washington, D.C. on the 3rd day of Nov. 1871, Certificate No. 8635. That she was married under the name of Nancy Birdwell, to the said James Romine, on the ninth day of May, A.D. 1812, by John Cantaberry, Minister of the Gospel, at Huntsville, Ala. there being no legal barrier to the marriage, that her husband died at Near Jasper, on the 28th day of March, 1873, and that she has not remarried since his death, etc..........
Signed: Nancy Romine (her mark).

Treasury Department
Third Auditor's Office
November 29, 1871
Respectfully returned to the Commissioner of Pensions with the information that the Rolls of Captain James Reid's company of Tennessee militia show that James Romine served from the 8th January 1814 to 28th April, 1814.............
Signed by: (name not legible, Acting Auditor.

*****************

State of Alabama
County of Walker

On this 20 day of October A.D. 1855, personally appeared before me a Judge of the Court of Probate within and for the County and State aforesaid, ROBERT MORRIS, aged 73 yrs. a resident of Walker County in the State of Alabama who being duly sworn according to law declares that he is the identical Robert Morris who was a private in the company commanded by Captain Isham Hendon in the Regiment of drafted me commanded by Gen. Floia in this war with Great Britain declared by the U.S. on the 18th day of June 1812 for the term of six months and continued in actual service in said war for the term of fourteen days that he has heretofore made application for Bounty Land under the Act of September 28, 1850, and received

a land warrant no...... for 80 acres which he has since legally disposed of and cannot now return. He makes this declaration for the purpose of obtaining the additional bounty land to which he may be entitled under the act approved the 3rd day of March 1855. He also declares that he has never applied for nor received under this or any other act any bounty land warrant except the one mentioned above.....
Robert Morris...(his mark)
Acknowledged by:
D. L. Stovall
John N. Barton

War of 1812 - Claim of Widow for Service Pension
State of Alabama
County of Walker

On the 27th day of March, A.D. One thousand eight hundred and seventy-eight personally appeared before me Judge of the Probate court, same being a court within and for the County and State aforesaid, Sarah Morris, age 60 yrs., a resident of Jasper, in the State of Alabama, who being duly sworn according to law, declares that Robert Morris, deceased, who is the identical Robert Morris who served in the company commanded by Captain Henden in the......regiment..... of Ga. Militia, in the War of 1812......etc. she further states that the following is a full description of her said husband at the time of his enlistment, viz: 5 ft. 8 inches high, weight 160 lbs, complexion rather fair, hair rather dark. She further states that she was married to the said Robert Morris at the City or the Town of Jasper, in the County of Walker, State of Ala. by one John Holly, on the 26th day of April, 1850 and that her name before her marriage was SARAH EDGIL and she further states that she had not been married before but her husband Robert Morris had been married to NANCY JENT, who died in the early part of the year 1850, and that her said husband Robert Morris died at Near Jasper in the State of Alabama, the 27th day of May, 1865, etc....... She makes this declaration for the purpose of obtaining the pension to which she may be entitled under Sections 4736 to 4740, inclusive, revised statutes and the Act. of Mar.11, 1878 and hereby appoints Tho. C. Fullerton, of Washington, D.C. her true and lawful attorney to prosecute her claim. And she further states that she has heretofore made no application for pension as widow but her husband drew a land warrant No. 20719 and that her residence is near Jasper, County of Walker, State of Alabama and her post office is Jasper, Walker Co., Ala...... Signed: Sarah Morris (her mark).

Acknowledged by:
E. W. Wright
J. C. Thompson
Also personally appeared Elias Wright, age 55 yrs, and Robert Jent, 52 yrs., made affidavit to the above statement.

Robert Morris, Pvt. in Captain Hendon, Col. Thomas Ga. Militia, 1812 ... Filed 3/5/.... date illiegible
Oct. 30, 1858, Robert Morris served under Captain Hendon from the 12th of October 1814 till the 17th March 1815, Signed: R. F. Gallaher - Claimant - Jasper, Ala.

****************

War of 1812 - Declaration of Soldier for Pension
State of Alabama
County of Walker

On the 7th of April, One Thousand Eight Hundred and Seventy-One, personally appeared before me, John Brown, Judge of Probate, BARTON MARTIN, age seventy-six years a resident of Walker County, State of Alabama, who being duly sworn according to the law, declares that his wife's name was MARY ROBESON, to whom he was married the 17th day of January, 1820, in Jasper Co. Ga. and that he served the full period of sixty days in the military service of the U.S. in the War of 1812 and that he is the identical Barton Martin who was drafted in Captain Leonard Worthy's Company, at Monticello, Jasper Co., Ga. on or about the 7th day of August, 1812, and was honorably dischargsd at Fort.........(illegible) on or about the 6th day of February, 1815 and that his capacity and manner of service was guarding comissarys at Fort Bainbridge and Fort Mi.....(??) and that he has received one land warrant calling for one hundred and sixty acres, the number fo which he has forgotten,........etc......... and that his post office is Pleas. Creek Falls(?) of Winston Co., State of Alabama and that his domain or place of abode is in Walker Co., Alabama......Signed: Barton Martin (his mark).
Acknowledged by:
G. H. Guttery
A. J. Guttery

The State of Alabama
Tallapoosa County

On the 9th day of December, A.D. Eighteen Hundred and Fifty, personally appeared before me, Wm. H. Thornton, Acting Justice of the Peace of and for the County and State aforesaid, BARTON MARTIN, aged fifty four years, a resident of Tallapoosa Co.

in the State of Ala. who being duly sworn according to law, declares that he is the identical BARTIN MARTIN who was a Private in the company commanded by Capt. Thomas Worth in the regiment commanded by General Blackshear (given name not known) in the War with Great Britain declared by the U.S. on the 18th day of June, 1812. That he was drafted near Jasper Co. Ga. and continued in actual service in the war for the term of six months and seven days and was honorably discharged at Fort Hawkins, Georgia, on or about the 22nd February 1815, but did not receive a written discharge. He also states upon oath that he is the identical Bartin Martin who was a private in the company commanded by Capt. John Strong in the regiment commanded by Gen. Andrew Jackson.... etc. That he substituted in place of a draftee private who was drafted in Oglethorpe Co., Ga. on or about the 12 Feb. A.D. 1819, for the term of three months but did not receive a written certificate of discharge. He makes this declaration for the purpose of obtaining the bounty land to which he may be entitled under the act of granting bounty land to certain officers and soldiers who have been engaged in the military service of the U.S. Passed September 28, 1850. Signed: Bartin Martin (his mark).

Acknowledged before
Wm. H. Thornton, J.P.(seal)
who states he took the acknowledgement above and believes Bartin Martin to be the identical man who served as aforesaid and that he is of the age stated.

War of 1812 - Claim of Widow for Service Pension
State of Alabama
County of Walker

On this 21st day of September, A.D. One thousand eight hundred and eighty-two, personally appeared before me J. B. Hughes, Clerk of the Circuit Court, same being a court of record in and for the County and State aforesaid, SARAH ANNE MARTIN, aged 55 yrs., a resident of near South Lowell in the State of Alabama, who being duly sworn......etc.......states she is the widow of Bartin Martin, deceased, who was the identical Bartin Martin who served under the name of Bartin Martin as a Private in the Company commanded by Captain Worth in the regiment of Infantry, War of 1812, and that her husband volunteered at Monticello, Georgia, on or about ......day of October, 1812, for the term of ......and continued in actual service for four months and whose services terminated by reason of peace........February, 1812. She further states that the following is a full description of her said husband

at the time of his enlistment, Viz: Was 18 yrs. of age, a farmer, born in Oglethorpe, Co., Ga. 5 feet, 8 inches high, black hair, blue eyes, fair complexion, and she further states that she was married to the said Bartin Martin in the county of Tallapoosa in the State of Alabama, on the 4th day of September, A.D. 1845 by one, John White, who was a Justice of the Peace and that her name before her marriage was SARAH ANN ALLRED. And that she has not remarried since the death of her husband Bartin Martin and she further states that Bartin Martin was married to POLLY ROBERTSON before and that her husband Bartin Martin died at near South Lowell in the State of Alabama on the 26th day of June, 1882. And she further declares that the following have been the places of residence of herself and her husband since the date of his discharge from the Army: First lived in Tallapoosa County, Ala. for 6 years, then in Walker Co., Ala. near Holly Grove about 9 years, then near South Lowell, Ala. in Dec. 1861 and have lived there ever since. She further states she has not heretofore, made application for Pension for Bounty Land Warrant. And that her residence is near the town of South Lowell, County of Walker, State of Ala. and that her post office is South Lowell, Walker County, etc....
Signed: Sarah Ann Martin (her mark).
Witnesses:
Elijah O'Rear
William K. Tetson (Letson??)
Also personally appeared Elijah O'Rear age 51 years residing near Jasper, in Walker County, Ala. and William H. Letson, aged 35 yrs. residing near South Lowell.
Certificate #11825 or 11827, issued Dec. 28, 1871, and signed by Allan Rutherford, Auditor.

********************

State of Alabama
Walker County

That on the fourth day of December, in the year of our Lord One Thousand Eight Hundred and Fifty, there personally appeared before me E. G. Musgrove, an acting Justice of the Peace in and for the said County and State, ANDREW KIDD, aged sixty years, being duly sworn.......etc.........declares he is the identical ANDREW KIDD, who was a substitute in the company commanded by Captain Jonathan Beatty in the regiment commanded by Colonel Hugh Means, in the War with Great Britain and was a substitute and entered service in York Dist, S.C. on the 28th day of Sep. One thousand eight hundred and fourteen for the term of six months and continued in service until the end of the war and was honorably discharged at Haddrills Point in S.C. on the .....day of March, 1815, and was mustered out

of service. I never got a discharge from my Captain the muster rolls will show my service. I make this declaration for the purpose of obtaining the bounty land to which I am entitled to under the act granting bounty to certian soldiers who was engaged in the military service of the U.S. passed Sep. 28, 1850.... Signed: Andrew Kidd (seal).
On the 25th day of April, 1855 Andrew Kidd made application in Tuscaloosa County, setting forth the same claims as stated in the above document, but that he had now received a land warrant #16976 or could be 16776 (lettering blurred) for eighty acres and which he has now legally disposed of. The document was witnessed by: E.(?) C. Clements and Ransom Cory, and acknowledged by Andrew P. Walker, Justice of the Peace.

War of 1812 - Declaration of a Widow For Pension
State of Alabama
County of Walker

On the 4th day of February, 1874 personally appeared before me .........Clerk of the Circuit Court, in and for the said County and State, AILSEY KIDD, aged seventy-six years, a resident of near Jasper, Ala. who states she is the widow of Andrew Kidd, who enlisted in the service of the U. S. in the War of 1812, and that he is the identical Andrew Kidd who enlisted in Capt. Beatty's Company, S.C. Militia, etc.......etc...... Said Andrew Kidd has drawn two bounty warrants of eighty acres each, No. 16976, issued Aug. 4th, 1852, and No. 28768, issued Mar. 31, 1856 that she married under the name of AILSEY BARTIN to the said Andrew Kidd on or about the 15th day of December 1814, by Levi Sides, at Jasper, Ala. and that said husband died at Fayette Co. Ala. the 20th day of March, 1859 and that she has not re-married since his death, etc. she further states her post office is Jasper, Ala. and that her domicile or place of abode is near Jasper, Alabama.....Signed: Ailsey Kidd (her mark)
Attest:
L. B. Freeman
Wm. L. Stanley
Certificate issued No. 12433, March 22, 1878

***************

State of Alabama
County of Tuscaloosa

On the 22nd day of January, 1851 there personally appeared before me a Justice of the Peace for and within the County and State aforesaid, JOHN MADISON, aged 52 years, a resident of Tuscaloosa Co. in the State of Alabama, who being duly sworn.........etc......declares that he is the identical JOHN MADISON who was a non-commissioned officer in the company commanded by Capt. Benjamin Reynolds, in the 39th Regiment of Militia of the U.S. commanded by Col. Williams, in the war hostile Creek Indians. That he enlisted on or about the ....day of October, 1813, for the term of twelve months, and continued in actual service in said war, for the term of ten months and was honorably discharged at Mount Vernon, Ala. on the ....day of August 1814, as will appear by the muster roll of the company and his original certificate of discharge which he has sent on to Washington City. He makes this declaration for the purpose of obtaining the Bounty Land to which he may be entitled under the act granting Bounty Land to certain officers and soldiers who have been engaged in the military service of the U.S.....Signed..John Madison(seal)

Sworn to and subscribed before me on the day and year above written....Thos. Burke, Justice of the Peace
Moses McGuire, Judge of Probate

War of 1812 - Claim of Widow for Pension
State of Alabama
County of Walker

On the 14th day of October, A.D. 1878, personally appeared before me, F. A. Gamble, Judge of the Probate Court, the same being a court of law in and for the said County and State, SUSAN MADISON, who being duly sworn .......etc...... declares that she is the widow of JOHN MADISON, deceased, who was the identical JOHN MADISON who was a private in the company commanded by........regiment of.......commanded by ...........in the War of 1812, that her said husband volunteered in Green Co. Ala. on or about .......day of..........,etc. She further states that the following is a full description of her said husband at the time of his enlistment: Viz: was 5 feet 11 inches high, blue eyes, dark hair, fair complexion, She further states that she married the said John Madison at the city or town of Bedford in the County of Bedford and State of Tenn. on or about the 1st day of August, 1817, by one William Williams, who was a Justice of the Peace and that her name before her marriage was SUSAN TEARCE, and that she has not remarried since the death of her husband, that he died at his residence in the State of Alabama, on the 25th day of May, 1866, that he was never married before. That her husband drew a Bounty Land Warrant, that she lives at Beech Grove, Walker Co., Ala...Signed: Susan Madison (her mark).

## Copy of Discharge of John Madison

By Thomas Pinkney, Major General
Commanding the Sixth Military District of
United States.

To All Who Shall See These Presents, Greeting:
Be it known, that JOHN H. READ, Surgeon of the 39th Regiment of Infantry has issued the requisite certificates by which it appears that JOHN MADISON, a Corporal in the company of Captain Reynolds, of the 39th Regiment of Infantry has been wounded or injured while in the service of the United States, in such manner as to disable him from performing military duty; the said John Madison, is therefore honorably discharged from the PUBLIC SERVICE.
Personal description of the aforesaid John Madison:
Twenty-one years of age, dark hair, grey eyes, fair complexion, 5 feet 9 inches high and by profession when enlisted was a Hatter. In testimony, whereof I have hereunto affixed my signature at Headquarters at Charleston, S.C. this 18th day of July in the year 1814... Thomas Pinkney, Major General, U.S.A.
By the General
Wm. R. Booth
Some of this is very faded and it has been copied as nearly correct as possible regarding the signature of the General Booth.

****************

State of Alabama
County of Fayette

On this 10th day of January, A.D. 1851, personally appeared before me a Justice of the Peace within and for the County and State aforesaid, MILES CHAPPELL, aged sixty years and a resident of Fayette County and the State of Alabama, who being duly sworn according to law, declares that he is the identical MILES CHAPPELL who was a private in the company commanded by Capt. John Jackson in the regiment of drafted militia commanded by Col. Metcalf, in the war with Great Britain declared by the United States A.D. 1812. That he was drafted in Bedford Co., Tenn. on or about the first day of Nov. 1814 for the term of six months and continued in actual service until peace was made and the treaty with Great Britain was ratified. And was honorably discharged by Gen. Carroll on or about the 10th day of April 1815 as will appear by the muster rolls of said company, his certificate of discharge being misplaced. He makes this declaration for

the purpose of obtaining the bounty land to which he may be entitled under the Act granting bounty land to certain officers and soldiers who have been engaged in the military service of the United States, passed Sep. 28, 1850................
Signed: Miles Chappell.
Certificate No. 2249 was issued by the Treasury Department March 11, 1872.
Respectfully returned to the commissioners of pensions with the information that the rolls of Capt. John Jackson's company of Tenn. Militia show that MILES CHAPPELL served from Nov. 13, 1814 to May, 1815.....
Signed by: Allen Rutherford, Auditor.

****************

DANIEL TUBB born Feb. 17, 1794 in S.C. died Mar. 25, 1882 buried in Good Hope Cemetery 6 mi. this side of Cullman in Cullman County, on Highway #69 (above information from Bruce Myers a descendant of Daniel Tubb)

Declaration for a Pension under Act of Feb. 14, 1871 - War of 1812
State of Alabama
County of Walker

On this 23rd day of May, A.D. One thousand eight hundred and seventy-one, personally appeared before me John Brown, Judge of the Probate Court, a court of record within and for the County and State aforesaid, DANIEL TUBBS, aged seventy-six years, a resident of ......,County of Walker, State of Alabama who being duly sworn according to law, declares that he is married, that his wife's name was ELIZABETH RUTLEDGE, to whom he was married on the 16th day of February, 1840; that he served the full period of sixty days in the military service of the United States in the war of 1812; that he is the identical DANIEL TUBBS who enlisted in Captain Thomas Porter's company, Williamson's regiment Coffee's Brigade, Jefferson Division, at Vernon, Tenn. on the ....day of October 1814 and was honorably discharged at Nashville, Tenn. on the ... day of April 1815; that he has drawn two 80 acres land warrants, was in battle at New Orleans....that he, at no time during the late rebellion against the authority of the United States, adhered to the cause of the enemies of the Government, giving them aid or comfort; or exercised the functions of any office whatever under any authority, or pretended authority, in hostility to the United States; and that he will support the Constitution of the United States; that he is not in receipt of a pension under any previous act; that he makes

this declaration for the purpose of being placed on the pension roll of the United States, under the provision of the act approved February 14, 1871, and he hereby constitutes and appoints, with full power of substitution and revocation, B. D. Hyam, of Washington, D.C., his true and lawful attorney to prosecute his claim and obtain the pension certificate that may be issued; that his post office is at Jasper, County of Walker, State of Alabama, that his domicile or place of abode is..........Daniel Tubbs (his mark)
Attest: W. L. Stanley.....A. J. Guttery.

War of 1812 - Claim of Widow for Service Pension
State of Alabama
County of Cullman

On this 21st day of June, A.D. One thousand eight hundred and eighty-two, personally appeared before me, Judge of the Probate Court, the same being a court of record within and for the County and State aforesaid, (1) ELIZABETH J. TUBBS aged 63 years, a resident of Cullman County, in the State of Alabama who being duly sworn according to law, declares that she is the widow of (2) Daniel Tubbs, deceased, who was the identical (3) Daniel Tubbs, who served under the name of (4) Daniel Tubbs as a (5) private in the company commanded by Captain......in the Tenn. regiment of Mil, commanded by.... in the War of (6) 1812; that her said husband (7) volunteered at .....on or about the .....day of.....A.D. for the term of .....and continued in actual service in said war for the term of (8)...and whose services terminated by reason of (8) Honorable Discharge...at....on the ....day of ......A.D. She further states that the following is a full description of her said husband at the time of his enlistment, viz: (10) age about 20 or 21 years- farmer born in the State of South Carolina, Height about 5 ft. 7 or 8 in. Dark hair, blue eyes, fair complexion. She further states that she was married to the said Daniel Tubbs, at Loss Creek, in the County of Walker, and in the State of Alabama on the 16th day of February A.D. 1841 by one (11) William Sides; who was a (12) Justice of the Peace; and that her name before her said marriage was ELIZABETH J. RUTLEDGE, and that she has not remarried since the death of said Daniel Tubbs; and she further states that (13) said Daniel Tubbs was formerly married to one Matilda Sanders who died on Loss Creek, Walker County, Ala. in the year 1840 and that her said husband Daniel Tubbs, died at near Cullman, in the State of Alabama, on the 25th day of March A.D. 1882; and she further declares that the following have been the places of residence of herself and her said husband since the date of his discharge from the

Army, viz: (15) 1st Loss Creek, Walker County, Ala. until about 9 years ago, then on Crooked Creek, Winston County, Alabama, until about 4 years ago, and in the Cullman Co. near the town of Cullman, Alabama for past four years. She makes this declaration for the purpose of obtaining the Pension to which she may be entitled under Sections 4736 to 4740, inclusive, Revised Statutes, and the Act of March 9, 1878.....and hereby appoints, with full powers of substitution and revocation, J. Vance Lewis, of Washington, D.C. her true and lawful attorney to prosecute her claim... and that her residence is near the town of Cullman County of Cullman, State of Alabama, and that her post office address is Cullman, Alabama.....Elizabeth J. Tubbs (her mark)
(Two witnesses who can write their names)
Thaddeus W. McMinn
Hiram Adkins

## BIBLE AND FAMILY RECORDS

FAMILY RECORD

Children of MILES and PRISCILLA PARKER CHAPPELL:

Lucy, born in Bedford Co. Tenn. June 26, 1813, married G. W. JOHNSTON, died Aug. 27, 1838
SARAH, b. Bedford Co. Tenn. Apr. 15, 1815, md. ROBERT BERRY
PERMELIA, b. Bedford Co. Tenn. Feb. 6, 1817, md. J. H. KIRKLAND, died Oct. 26, 1903.
JAMES, b. Bedford Co. Tenn. Feb. 27, 1819, md. LUCY FREEMAN, died Jan. 23, 1896.
SUSANNAH, b. in Ala. Mar.22, 1822, died young.
MARY, b. Ala. Mar. 21, 1824, Md. MR. BERRY.
CATHERINE, b. Ala., Aug. 26, 1826, md. SAMUEL WHITSON.
PALATINE, b. Ala. Jan. 29, 1829, md. JOHN FREEMAN.
MARTHA J., b. Ala. May 29, 1831, md. JESSE M. STANLEY.
LUTITIA, b. Ala. May 4, 1833, md. WM. LUCIOUS STANLEY, died June 25, 1910.
CAROLINE, b. Ala. Aug. 4, 1835, md. NATHANIEL DAVIS.
ELIZABETH, b. Ala. Sep. 22, 1837, md. MR. WYNNE, died Sep. 6, 1910.
JOHN A., b. Ala. Nov. 29, 1840, md........d. in Texas.
ALPHA ANN, b. Ala. May 13, 1846, md. JOHN THOMAS d. in Texas.

Children of James Chappell and Lucy Freeman Chappell:

CORNELIA, b. Feb. 22, 1840 - md. HIRAM HYDE.
EMILY, b. Oct. 19, 1838, died young.
SUSANNAH FRANCES, b. May 14, 1842, md. LEWIS T. STANLEY.
WM. W., b. Nov. 2, 1847, md.............d...............

Chappell Family, cont'd.

CHRISTOPHER COLBERT, b. Jul. 30, 1849, md. and died in Texas
JAMES MARSHALL, b. May 10, 1851
LUCY PALATINE, b. May 10, 1851
MARY TEMPERANCE, b. Jan. 22, 1855
LUTITIA ELIZABETH, b. Jan. 17, 1857, md. THOMAS STANLEY
JESSE M., b. Aug. 27, 1862, md. LELA HAMNER
CHARLES L., b. Jul. 27, 1863

Children of Christopher Colbert Chappell, b. Jul. 30, 1849, married Jan. 12, 1871 - Cornelia Josephine Stanley, b. Jan. 13, 1854, lived and died in Texas.

JOHN HENRY CHAPPELL, b. Jan. 1, 1872, md. CORNELIA GARNER
THOMAS MARSHALL CHAPPELL, b. May 28, 1874, md. MAGGIE BOYLES and secondly, VALORA HAMILTON
RUFUS BENJAMIN CHAPPEL, b. Nov. 10, 1875, md. ADDIE CHAPPELL
ALFRED JEFFERSON CHAPPELL, b. Mar. 14, 1878, md. MAUD HOLCOMBE
ELIZA HESTER CHAPPELL, b. Apr. 5, 1880, md. EDD HOLCOMBE
LUCY BELLE CHAPPELL, b. Jul. 16, 1882, md. LONNIE BRADDEY
JESSIE M. CHAPPELL, b. Oct. 12, 1884, died in infancy
JAMES M.CHAPPELL, b. Jan. 5, 1887, md. JUDY TAYLOR
CHARLES WHEELER CHAPPELL, b. Apr. 16, 1889, md. BESSIE PERSON
SARAH MISSOURI CHAPPELL, b. May. 26, 1891, md. JOHN BLANKS, Nov. 25, 1911
DANNIE LUTICIA CHAPPELL, b. Dec. 16, 1893, md. DAVID McMAHAN
SQUIRE COLBERT CHAPPELL, b. Mar. 29, 1897, md. ETHYCE WALLS
JOHN STANLEY CHAPPELL, of Elgin Texas married PHEBE LEE.

Robert Guttery Bible: Pub. - by Andrew & Judd -1832
Now in possession of Dr. John McQueen Guttery, Jr., Dyersburg, Tennessee.

Births:

ROBERT GUTTERY............................Feb. 26, 1801
SARAH ANN WILLIAMS........................May, 8, 1804
JOHN GUTTERY..............................Aug. 30, 1822
CATHERINE GUTTERY.........................Mar. 22, 1824
WILLIAM GUTTERY...........................Dec. 12, 1825
ISHAM GUTTERY.............................Sep. 30, 1827
B. F. GUTTERY.............................Dec. 8, 1829
ELIZABETH GUTTERY.........................Dec. 17, 1831
J. RUSSELL GUTTERY........................Dec. 12, 1833
MARTHA ANN GUTTERY........................Dec. 24, 1834
A. J. GUTTERY.............................May 11, 1837
L. J. GUTTERY.............................Mar. 27, 1839
ROBERT W. GUTTERY, Jr.....................Mar. 27, 1842
NEWTON W. GUTTERY.........................Mar. 16, 1843

Robert Guttery Bible, cont'd.

Births, cont'd.

SARAH GUTTERY..............................Apr. 6, 1846
HOUSTON GUTTERY............................Sep. 15, 1847
JOHNSON GUTTERY............................Jul. 15, 1850

Marriages:

ROBERT GUTTERY and SARAH ANN WILLIAMS married Nov. 11, 1821 (marriage bond in Hall Co. Ga.)
ISHAM GUTTERY and NANCY ROMINE, Oct. 29, 1848
GEORGE HOUSTON GUTTERY and ALICE CLEMENTINE STANLEY, Jul. 4, 1876
A. J. GUTTERY and A. A. MILLER, Oct. 10, 1867

Deaths:

WILLIAM GUTTERY....... Jul. 7, 1825 (father of ROBERT)
B. F. GUTTERY......... Jan. 22, 1831
SARAH GUTTERY......... June 14, 1846
HANNAH GUTTERY........ Dec. 1, 1854 (wife of WILLIAM GUTTERY, age about 75 years)
L. J. GUTTERY......... May 13, 1862
ROBERT GUTTERY, SR.... Apr. 6, 1877
SARAH ANN GUTTERY..... Feb. 8, 1881
JOHN GUTTERY.......... Jan. 30, 1883
JOHNSON GUTTERY....... Oct. 10, 1881
WILLIAM GUTTERY....... Apr 6, 1890 in Texas
A. J. GUTTERY......... Aug. 11, 1889
GEORGE HOUSTON GUTTERY.Dec. 5, 1911
ISHAM GUTTERY..........June 4, 1922, in Girard, Texas
ELIZABETH GUTTERY......Dec. 6, 1910, m. JAMES BAKER, d. Texas
MARTHA ANN GUTTERY.(CORRY)Apr. 18, 1872
CATHERINE GUTTERY (BOSHELL) 1873, church record.

Marriages not in Bible, taken from Family Records:

JOHN GUTTERY married MARY JOHNSON
CATHERINE GUTTERY married ANDREW JACKSON BOSHELL
WILLIAM GUTTERY, married 1st. ELIZABETH ?..2nd. LUCRETIA SHIRLEY
ELIZABETH GUTTERY married JAMES BAKER
J. RUSSELL GUTTERY married BARBARA SANDERS
MARTHA ANN GUTTERY married 1st. ROBERT CARMICHAEL.. 2nd. JAMES MONROE CORRY
ROBERT GUTTERY, JR. married LUCINDA KING
NEWTON GUTTERY married SARAH JANE........
L. J. GUTTERY married MATILDA KITCHENS
JOHNSON GUTTERY married MARY DISSPAIN

Stanley Bible; Pub. by Edw. W, Miller, 1849
Owned by John McQueen Guttery, Sr., Jasper, Ala.

WILLIAM L. STANLEY, b. Dec. 20, 1816
REBECCA F. STANLEY, Jan. 15, 1831
FATIMA F. STANLEY, b. Dec. 2, 1850, dau. of REBECCA F. and WILLIAM E. STANLEY.
LUTICIA CHAPPELL, wife of W. L. STANLEY, b. May 12, 1833
MARY P. STANLEY, dau. of W. L. & LUTICIA STANLEY, b. May 13, 1855
ALICE C. STANLEY, dau. of W. L. & LUTICIA STANLEY, b. Aug. 17, 1858
VIRGINIA STANLEY, day. of W. L. & LUTICIA STANLEY, b. Jan. 19, 1862
RISSA ETTA STANLEY, dau. of W. L. & LUTICIA STANLEY, b. June 10, 1864.
WILLIAM C. STANLEY, son of W. L. & LUTICIA STANLEY, b. Sep. 22, 1870
JAMES G. STANLEY, son of W. L. & LUTICIA STANLEY, b. Jan. 7, 1873.
JOHN B.STANLEY, son of W. L. & LUTICIA STANLEY, b. Mar. 17, 1876

Marriages:

WILLIAM L. STANLEY and REBECCA F. GAINES were married 3rd Jan. 1850
WILLIAM L. STANLEY and LUTICIA CHAPPELL married 31st May 1854
ALICE CLEMENTINE STANLEY and GEORGE HOUSTON GUTTERY married at home, Jul. 4, 1876.
RISSA ETTA STANLEY and ROBERT WALKER GORDON were married May 14, 1890.

Deaths:

REBECCA F. STANLEY, died Sep. 30, 1851, wife of W. L. STANLEY.
WILLIAM L. STANLEY, died June 20, 1883
LUTICIA STANLEY, d. June 25, 1910 (wife of W.L. STANLEY)
VIRGINIA STANLEY, dau. of WM. L. and LUTITIA STANLEY, d. Jul 14, 1864.
MARY P. STANLEY, dau. of WM. L. & LUTITIA STANLEY, d. Jul. 31, 1879.
JOHN BENJAMIN STANLEY, son of WM. L. & LUTITIA STANLEY, d. Mar. 24, 1881
RISSA ETTA GORDON, dau. of WM. L. & LUTITIA STANLEY, d. Nov. 16, 1946.
WILLIAM CHAPPELL STANLEY. son of WM. L. & LUTITIA STANLEY, d. June 8, 1950.
ALICE C. GUTTERY, dau. of WM. L. & LUTITIA STANLEY, d. Sep. 29, 1956.

Bible of Seaborn J. Wright: This Bible has been lost but the records are in possession of Mrs. John M. Guttery, (Florence Knight) who descends from this Wright family.

SEABORN J. WRIGHT was born......................Sep. 7, 1838
ANNIS E. WRIGHT was born........................Jan. 19, 1839
ALFRED WRIGHT was born.........................Jan. 30, 1859
JOHN O. WRIGHT was born.........................Jul. 20, 1860
MARY J. WRIGHT was born.........................May 25, 1862
ROXANNAH WRIGHT was born.......................Dec. 27, 1864
SARAH E. WRIGHT was born........................Mar. 11, 1867
MARTHA L. WRIGHT was born......................Feb. 6, 1869
MINTY A. WRIGHT was born........................Apr. 1, 1872
LUCIUS B.F. WRIGHT was born....................Aug. 17, 1874
MARGARET WRIGHT was born........................ 1877

JOHN FRANCIS BAKER was born....................Sep. 1, 1859
JOHN FRANCIS BAKER and SARAH ELIZABETH WRIGHT were married at home of her father, Dec. 29, 1889, JOHN L. GUTTERY, officiating.
Their Children:
BEAUREGARD, LUCY, DOLLY, IDA, VIRGINIA, HOPE, JEANNETTE.

Deaths:

SARAH ELIZABETH BAKER, d. Feb. 19, 1945
JOHN FRANCIS BAKER, d. Feb. 19, 1946
IDA BAKER, date of death not shown

Gaines Bible:

JOHN STROTHER GAINES, b. Jan. 9, 1841
BASSHEBA JANE (JENNY) SWINDLE, b. Sep. 15, 1846
JOHN STROTHER GAINES and BASSHEBA JANE SWINDALL married Feb. 24, 1868---Children: MARGARET ANN, SUSAN FRANCES, EUGENE PENDLETON, ELIZABETH, LULA MAE

Deaths:

JOHN STROTHER GAINES, d. Dec. 8, 1887
BASSHEBA JANE (JENNY) GAINES, d. June 6, 1928
EUGENE PENDLETON GAINES, d. Feb. 11, 1930

Bible of Mr. and Mrs. Samuel Sanders, presently in possession of Mrs. Wm. Kitchens

Marriages:

SAMUEL SANDERS and NANCY CAIN were married Sep. 10, 1848.
VENILA LUCRETIA SANDERS and GEORGE D. O'REAR were married Jan. 18th, 1880.
MABEL ISABELLE SANDERS and WILLIAM F. KITCHENS were married Dec. 28th, 1890 at Aberdeen, Miss.
LUCY ESTELLE SANDERS and JOHN H. CATCHINGS were married Nov. 2nd, 1892.
NEVADA HALE SANDERS and CHARLES L. ROSSER were married April 28th, 1895.
LAVONIA CATHERINE SANDERS and SAMUEL B. SMITH were married Oct. 16th, 1895.
SAMUEL MONROE SANDERS and TINIE STURGIS were married Dec. 26th, 1900.

Births:

SAMUEL SANDERS was born September the 23rd, 1826.
NANCY SANDERS was born the 28th of July, 1830.
JAMES REUBEN SANDERS was born August 12th, 1849.
ADKIN CAIN SANDERS was born February 1st, 1851.
TRAVIS HOUSTON SANDERS was born November 1st, 1852.
LUVENIA BERINIECE SANDERS was born April 21st, 1855.
VENILA LUCRETIA SANDERS was born January 24th, 1858.
MABEL ISABELLE SANDERS was born 8th of June, 1861.
SAMUEL MONROE SANDERS was born February 9th, 1864.
LUCY ESTELLE SANDERS was born July 9th, 1866.
LAVONIA CATHARINE SANDERS was born December 11th, 1868.
NeVADA HALE SANDERS was born June 13th, 1871.

Deaths:

LUCENIA BERINIECE SANDERS departed this life, July 31st, 1857.
TRAVIS HOUSTON SANDERS departed this life, August 7th, 1871.
JAMES REUBEN SANDERS departed this life, April 8th, 1871.
SAMUEL SANDERS died September 10, 1902.
NANCY CAIN SANDERS died November 22, 1915.
VENILA LUCRETIA SANDERS O'REAR died March 16, 1934.
SAMUEL MONROE SANDERS died June 7, 1938.
LUCY SANDERS CATCHINGS died September 8, 1945, Ft. Worth, Texas
LAVONIA SANDERS SMITH died October 1, 1953.

Bible of Peter S. Burton - Owned by Mrs. Molly McCleskey Sparks.

Marriages:

PETER S. BURTON and MARY E. TOWNLEY were married June 10, 1855.

Bible of Peter S. Burton, cont'd.

BIRTHS:

PETER S. BURTON was born July 24, 1833.
MARY E. BURTON was born May 12, 1835.
FRANCES E. BURTON was born June 1, 1856.
SARAH JANE BURTON was born May 25, 1858.
GEORGIA ANN BURTON was born Oct. 16, 1859.
JOHN HENRY BURTON was born Oct. 25, 1861.
MARY DICY BURTON was born Oct. 30, 1864.
PINKNEY BURTON was born Mar. 18, 1867.
CHRISTINE LUCINDA BURTON was born May 13, 1868.
DAVID LUCIUS BURTON was born Nov. 25, 1872.
WILLIE DIRE BURTON was born Nov. 16, 1874.

Deaths:

PINKNEY BURTON died Mar. 23, 1867.
DAVID LUCIUS BURTON died Dec. 22, 1873.
WILLIE DIRE BURTON died Nov. 20, 1874.
PETER S. BURTON died Jan. 11, 1900.
MARY E. BURTON died June 5, 1904.

Williams Bible -
Owned by Roxie Williams Hubbard

Marriages:

A. WILLIAMS and MARTHA B. WILLIAMS Jan. 12, 1832 (1st wife)
A. WILLIAMS and SALINA WILLIAMS Nov. 23, 1852 (2nd wife)
MALINDA WILLIAMS and J. F. STURGIS Jul. 25, 1867
J. M. and E. ALABAMA WILLIAMS May 10, 1877
RUSSELL WILLIAMS and NISA ANN Oct. 22, 1878 (2nd wife-EDNA SMOOT)

irths:

A. WILLIAMS was born Jan. 12,1812
MARTHA B. WILLIAMS was born May 14, 1803
SALINA WILLIAMS was born Mar. 10, 1826
JOHN M. WILLIAMS was born Apr. 16, 1836
MALINDA ANNA WILLIAMS was born Jul. 25, 1853.
JAMES M. WILLIAMS was born May 20, 1856
RUSSELL M. WILLIAMS was born Jul. 31, 1858

Deaths:

MARTHA B. WILLIAMS died Aug. 6, 1852
ROBERT M. WILLIAMS died Mar. 15, 1855
JOHN M. WILLIAMS died Apr. 1, 1862
AUGUSTUS WILLIAMS died Feb. 6, 1863
SALINA WILLIAMS died June 13, 1891

Williams Bible Cont'd.

Children of J.M. & Alabama Williams:

VICTOR HUGO
DENA
LULA
GURLEY
FLOYDA
CHARLEY
FRANK
JOHN L.M.
ROXANNA MALINDA
PEARL
MINTA ANN
SANFORD

Bible of M.D. Garner -
Near Sardis Church - Cordova Ala.
Pub. 1868 by American Bible Soc.
Sold by William L. Stanley, 1871-Jasper, Ala.

Births:

MOSES BARTON was born May 9, 1827
MARTHA McADAMS was born Sep. 25, 1829
JOSHUA T. BARTON was born May 13, 1849
TALITHA FRANCES BARTON was born Jan. 30, 1852
MARTHA CAROLINE BARTON was born Sep. 28, 1857
SARAH ANN BARTON was born Sep. 25, 1849
SIDNEY BARTON was born Apr. 4, 1870
MARTHA E. BARTON was born Oct. 31,1872
JOSEPH E. BARTON was born Oct. 22, 1875
MOSES BARTON was born Apr. 20, 1880
JOHN W. GARNER was born June 14, 1856
PERNECIE CORDELIA GARNER was born Mar. 23, 1876
ROBERT A. GARNER was born Nov. 29, 1878
THOMAS B. GARNER was born Oct. 14, 1881
MOSES DALTON GARNER was born Jan. 23, 1884
SIMEY BARTON was born May 8, 1883
CLINTON BARTON was born Feb. 13, 1887
MATTIE WILLIAMS was born Jan. 31, 1893
ERVIL WILLIAMS was born Dec. 11, 1896

Marriages:

MOSES BARTON and SARAH McADAMS married June 8, 1848
JOSHUA T. BARTON and SARAH ANN JOHNSON married Dec. 17, 1868
J. W. GARNER and MARTHA CAROLINE BARTON married Jul. 2, 1874
M. D. GARNER and ETHEL MORROW married Apr. 7, 1904
FLONNIA M. GARNER and DEL C. SHERER married May 16, 1931
THOMAS BENT GARNER and AMANDA JANE BUTTS married Dec. 1899

Deaths:

TALITHA FRANCES BARTON died Sep. 22, 1856
MODY BARTON died Oct. 10, 1880
MARTHA E. BARTON died Dec. 18, 1884
MOSES BARTON died Sep. 11, 1902
MARTHA McADAMS died Dec. 18, 1882
SARAH ANN BARTON died Dec. 21, 1902

Garner Bible Cont'd.
Deaths cont'd.

MARTHA HASE BARTON died Dec. 5, 1915
J. T. BARTON died Dec. 29, 1915
SIMEY BARTON died Sep. 16, 1897
JOSEPH BARTON died June 30, 1942
SIDNEY BARTON died Jan. 4, 1939
J. W. GARNER died Nov. 13, 1939
W. B. MORROW died Oct. 27, 1939
GELLIA E. MORROW, wife of W.B. MORROW died Feb. 18, 1947
J. A. WILLIAMS died June 5, 1935
ERVIL MILLER died Aug. 5, 1942

Bible of John Irvin Lollar
Residence near Jasper

Marriages:

JAMES A. LOLLAR of Walker Co. and MARTHA J. IRVIN were married on the 13th day of July 1865 at the residence of her mother by Rev. W. W. Wilhite
MARY SUSAN LOLLAR was married to J. H. BURTON, March 8,1885
LAVONIA AUGUSTA LOLLAR was married to W. G. CORY, Oct. 1,1893
WILLIAM CLINTON LOLLAR was married to ILLA ROBERTS, Sunday, Dec. 22, 1895
FLORENCE MABEL LOLLAR married Sunday June 21, 1903 to G. W. CHANDLER
TEXANNA ELIZABETH LOLLAR married Sunday 16, 1909 to DR. THOMAS P. DEWEESE
EARL VANDORN LOLLAR married Sunday, May 1, 1910 to MARY LEONA JACKSON
JOHN IRVIN LOLLAR was married Sunday, Dec. 4, 1910 to MARY S. MILLER
WILLIE MORREL (HUDSON) LOLLAR married Sunday, Sep. 3, 1916 to S. E. SPARKS
WILLIAM IRWIN and SUSAN ANN were married Dec. 6, 1842

Deaths:

HENRYETTA CAROLINE LOLLAR died Sep. 30, 1889
MARTHA J. IRVIN LOLLAR died Jul. 12, 1904, age 57 yrs 4mos.12das
JAMES PRICE LOLLAR died Oct. 30, 1914
MARTHA ADELINE LOLLAR died Oct. 15, 1917, age 45 yrs 6mos 24das
HENRYETTA (SHUCK) IRWIN died Oct. 27, 1846
ELIZABETH ANN IRWIN died Nov. 23, 1849
ROBERT HOWELL IRWIN died Nov. 23, 1849
MARY CAROLINE IRWIN died Nov. 26, 1849
REV. WILLIAM IRWIN died Nov. 19, 1849, age 33 yrs 14 das.

Bible of John Irvin Lollar cont'd.

Births:

JAMES MORTIMER CORY, grandson of J. A. and M. J. IRWIN LOLLAR was born Sep. 16, 1894

Meek --- Robinson Family Bible
In possession of Mrs. Charles H. Harpool
1609 Randel Road, Oklahoma City, Oklahoma

Births:

ANDREW E. ROBINSON was born February 22, 1817
NANCY MEEK was born Nov. 28, 1813 (wife of ANDREW E. ROBINSON)
FRANCES DRUCILLA ROBINSON was born Feb. 25, 1842
JAMES MEEK ROBINSON was born Feb. 25, 1842
MARGARET JANE ROBINSON was born Mar. 4, 1843
JOSEPH AMZI ROBINSON was born Jun. 2, 1844
NANCY SUSAN ROBINSON was born Oct. 9, 1845
LEANDER EGGER ROBINSON was born Mar. 7, 1848
WILLIAM ANDREW ROBINSON was born Dec. 23, 1846
JOHN HOPE ROBINSON was born Oct. 28, 1849
JACOB MARIAN ROBINSON was born Mar. 8,1851
JAMES MONROE MEEK ROBINSON was born Jun. 3, 1855
SARAH ELIZABETH GUTTERY was born Aug. 2, 1862 (wife of J. M. M. ROBINSON)
JAMES L. ROBINSON was born Jan. 3, 1883
WILLIAM ANDREW ROBINSON was born May 3, 1888
MAUD ROBINSON was born Sep. 1, 1889
JAMES MEEK was born Mar. 28, 1782
AGNES BLACK was born Jan. 10, 1786 (wife of JAMES MEEK)
MARY B. MEEK was born Oct. 22, 1812
ISAAC J. MEEK was born Mar. 14, 1815
JOHN H. MEEK was born Nov. 29, 1817
JACOB B. MEEK was born Aug. 18, 1819
MARY JANE MEEK was born Apr. 3, 1821
ELIZABETH P. MEEK was born May 3, 1823
MARGARET MEEK was born Oct. 26, 1825
JINCY L. MEEK was born Mar. 15, 1828
LORENZO L. ROBINSON was born May 29, 1908
WILLIE ALLENE ROBINSON was born Mar. 10, 1911

Marriages:

ANDREW E. ROBINSON and NANCY MEEK were married Apr. 21, 1840
ROBERT J. LOVE and NANCY S. ROBINSON were married Jan. 10, 1867
WILLIAM A. BURNS and MARGARET J. ROBINSON was married Sep. 5, 1867

Meek--Robinson Family Bible cont'd.
Marriages cont'd:

JAMES M. M. ROBINSON and SARAH E. GUTTERY were married Jan. 12, 1882
W. A. ROBINSON and BESSIE P. BARKER were married Aug. 14, 1907
JAMES LAVERTIOUS ROBINSON and MAGGIE CAIN were married Jul. 2, 1908
MAUD ROBINSON and GEORGE A. JEFFCOAT were married Nov. 2, 1911

Deaths:

JAMES M. ROBINSON died Jan. 14, 1847, age 4yrs 10mos 20das.
JAMES MEEK died Apr. 25,1854, aged 72 yrs and 28 das.
JOSEPH ROBINSON died Apr. 8, 1856, (father of ANDREW E. ROBINSON)
AGNES MEEK died June 9, 1859, aged 73 yrs. 5 mos.
MARY B. MEEK died Jul. 1, 1815, aged 2 yrs 8 mos 9 das.
MARY JANE MEEK died Sep. 7, 1826, aged 5 yrs 4 mos 4 das.
ISAAC J. MEEK died Sep. 9, 1826, aged 11 yrs 5 26 das.
MARGARET MEEK died Oct. 9 (or 1st), 1836, aged 10yrs 11mos 23das
JOSEPH AMZI ROBINSON died June 30, 1864, aged 20 yrs 28 das
WILLIAM ANDREW ROBINSON died Jan. 24, 1865, aged 18 yrs 1mo 1da
LEANDER EGGER ROBINSON died Mar. 20, 1870, aged 22 yrs 13 das
SARAH ELIZABETH ROBINSON died Jan. 14, 1892, aged 29 yrs. 5 mos 12 das.

While the early members of the Meek and Robinson Family did not come to Walker County, their descendants did come to the county and are buried there. These families came from York County, S.C. to Alabama and both the Meek and Robinson Revolutionary ancestors, as well as Jacob Black, father of Agnes Black who married James Meek, were of York County, S.C. Another of James Meek's daughters, Parmelia Meek married into the Kirkpatrick Family of York Co. and came into Walker County about the same time as did the Robinson and Meek Families.

Robert Guttery, son of William Guttery and Hannah, his wife, descends from Robert Guttery who died in Elbert County, Georgia, 1799, and his wife Elizabeth......surname unknown. Elizabeth died in Hall County, Ga. in 1825 and her estate was settled there by her son Leroy Guttery. Dombhart, in his History of Walker County states that the family of Robert Guttery came from an old Charleston, S.C. family. There were two Guttery or Guthery families in S.C. apparently and both had sons Robert. We have not been able to establish former residence of Robert Guttery of Elbert County and would welcome any data on him. A son John, living in Hall County, Ga., at the time of his mother's death, stated in the 1850 census that he was born in N.C. 1776. We would like to know if Robert of Elbert Co., Ga. 1799, was descended from John or Robert Guttery who were living in Old Lunenburg Co. Va. in 1749-50 in that section of the county which later became Bedford Co. Va. Lunenburg was divided into eleven counties and it is possible that somewhere in that area lies the link that we need, or was he of the N.C. or S.C. group? Anyone having any data please do contact the compiler of these records. Robert Guttery who came to Walker Co. with his parents, William and Hannah Guttery, married Sarah Ann Williams, dau. of Robert Williams, in Hall County, Ga. and represented his father's estate when Elizabeth, mother of William died. Mother and son died the same year, 1825. Elizabeth may have had the name of Johnson before her marriage as the name of Johnson has come down in the family as a given name for a son since that union. Any information, regardless of how small it may be, will be most welcome.

Alice C. Stanley, mother of John McQueen Guttery, Sr. of Jasper, Alabama, was the dau. of William L. Stanley and Lutitia Chappell, dau. of Miles Chappell and Priscilla Parker. Alice C. Stanley married George Houston Guttery who was born in Walker Co. Ala. in 1847 He was a son of Robert and Sarah (Williams) Guttery and was reared on a farm. He was educated at Jasper and Holly Grove Ala. and farmed until the outbreak of the War Between The States, when he joined the forces of the Confederacy and fought with Co. A 56th Ala. Regiment, under the command of his brother, Capt. A. J. Guttery. He served in the command of Gen. Forrest in Mississippi and with Gen. Johnson's Army from Dalton to Atlanta. He was in all of the battles which the forces were engaged, including Peachtree Creek.

In 1866 he came to Jasper and entered into the mercantile business and continued until 1874 when he was elected sheriff of the county of Walker. He served in this post until 1877. In 1878 he again went into the mercantile business and continued until Sep. 20, 1888. The City of Jasper was incorporated Dec. 22, 1887 and he was elected the first Mayor of the City.

In 1876 he was married to Miss Alice C. Stanley, dau. of William L. Stanley, one of the pioneers of Walker Co. and the City of Jasper, and the Treasurer of Walker Co. before and during the War Between the States. There were three children born to this union: Claude, Pearl and John McQueen Guttery, now a resident of Jasper.

Mr. Guttery's father, Robert Guttery was a pioneer preacher of the Primitive Baptist Church and was among the first settlers of Walker County. He immigrated to Walker Co from Tennessee with his father, William Guttery, probably before 1820. William Guttery died in 1825 and is bured near Providence Baptist Church, between Parrish and Oakman, Ala. supposedly on the Phiffer farm, although the exact location of the cemetery is not known. After his death his widow, Hannah, married Daniel Townley and died in 1854, aged about 75 yrs.

Benjamin Stanley, father of William L. Stanley, married Nancy Thomas, (dau. of Joshua Thomas and his wife Rebecca Wheeler) and was a soldier of the War of 1812, serving with the State of Georgia. In 1816 he was living in Clarke Co. Ala. when the Territorial Census was taken and later settled in Tuscaloosa Co. It has been said that his father was Lewis Stanley of S.C. and while we have found a record of one Lewis Stanley in Anderson, S.C. there is nothing there to prove this relationship. It is possible that he went to Pickens Co. or had settled in that county and it is possible that he was from Culpepper Co. Va., though that has not been established. We will be glad to exchange data on the Stanley Family with anyone interested. Tradition has it that the family came originally from Virginia and we would like to establish this fact.

Joshua Thomas, father of Nancy Thomas, who married Benjamin Stanley, left a will in Tuscaloosa Co. dated April 7, 1825. He is mentioned as being deceased Jan. 26, 1833 and may have died much earlier as he is not listed in the 1830 census. His wife ~~Hannah~~ Rebecca died after Aug. 16, 1834. It is not known where or when Joshua Thomas married Rebecca Wheeler or from which state he came to Alabama, but probably Ga. or S.C. He was in Clarke Co., Ala. when his son Jeremiah Thomas married Ann Creighton Dec. 12, 1818. Nancy Thomas, wife of Benjamin Stanley was born in Georgia in 1792 according to the census of 1850. She apparently married soon after Benjamin Stanley received his discharge from the service of the War of 1812. He was discharged at Darien, McIntosh Co. Ga. and it is possible that the family lived somewhere in that vicinity. Benjamin Stanley was born 1791 in S.C.

Ila Thomas, a son of Joshua Thomas, b. 1790, was living in Clarke Co. Ala. in 1830. In 1833 he bought land in Tuscaloosa Co. His wife was Mary, surname unknown. Elizabeth Thomas, another dau. of Joshua Thomas, married William Hooper, Apr. 29, 1824 in Tuscaloosa County. Martha Thomas, dau. of Joshua, was born 1802 in S.C. and married John Weathington. He was deceased in 1843. She was living with her sister Fatima Stanley, in 1850. Mary, another dau. of Joshua Thomas, was born in S.C. in 1803, married Hiram Creighton, Jan. 20, 1820 in Clarke County, Ala. Fatima Thomas, born 1806, married David Stanley, who was born in S.C. in 1794. He was a brother of Benjamin Stanley. John L. Thomas, a son of Joshua, was born 1811 in Georgia, married Margaret, surname unknown. We would welcome any exchange of data on these families, especially the Thomas Family.

Miles Chappell, a soldier of the War of 1812 (see his pension record elsewhere in this book) descends from an old Virginia Family which settled in Surry and Sussex Counties, Va. at a very early date in this country's history. Later some of the family migrated to Amelia Co. Va. and there it was Abner Chappell was born. He was the father of Miles Chappell and was a soldier of the American Revolution from Amelia Co. Va. He later moved, after the war, to Bedford Co. Tenn. and it was in that county where he married for the second time. About 1822, he moved to Howard Co. Missouri where he died. His estate settlement is of record in that county.

Abner Chappell, stated in his application for Revolutionary pension while living in Howard Co. Mo. that he was born April 13, 1763, in Amelia Co. Va. where he lived until 1807, when he removed to Bedford Co. Tenn. He was issued a certificate in May 1833 and placed on the pension roll under the Act of June 1832. His heirs named in his estate settlement were: Robert Chappell, William Chappell, Miles Chappell, Wiley Chappell, and Mrs. Sarah Clay, who was most likely his sister. Miles Chappell came to Fayette Co. Ala. about 1821 and died in Tuscaloosa Co. Mar. 24, 1887. His wife Priscilla Parker Chappell died Aug. 27, 1889 and both are buried in the Sterling Cemetery in Tuscaloosa Co. Their children are listed elsewhere in this book under Bible and Family Records.

The father of Abner Chappell was James Chappell, son of Robert and Sarah.. ..Chappell. James Chappell married first Sarah Hudson and ten children by her. She died and he married secondly Phoebe Archer, dau. of William and Ann Archer who was born in Prince George Co. Va. Sep. 3, 1733. (Bristol Parish Register) By this last wife, James Chappell had two children, both girls, Dorothy and Caty Chappell. By his first wife Sarah Hudson, he had the following children: James, John Abner, Miles, Robert, William, Miles Chappell married Sarah Mann Apr. 24, 1782 and died soon after their marriage.

Abner Chappell of Revolutionary War service, married Susannah Moore, Sep. 4, 1785 in Amelia Co. Va. They had four sons, William, Wiley, Robert and Miles who went to Tenn. with their father.

The first of the name of Chappell to come to this country was Captain John Chappell who arrived on the ship "Speedwell" which weighed anchor at Southampton, England, May 28, 1635, Captain John Chappell was master of the little ship and it is without doubt that he is the first of the name to enter this country when he landed at the Jamestown settlement. However Thomas Chappell, age 21 years, also came that same year and unlike Captain John who returned to England, Thomas remained and it is probably through him that all the Chappells descend. A History of the Chappell Family has been published and is available in some of the larger libraries in their genealogical section.

There were many South Carolina families who came to the new state of Alabama, among them were the Burtons and Boshells also spelled Bouchelle. The Boshell family of Walker County descend from Nicholas Boshell or Bouchelle of Abbeville, S.C. or Old 96th District, as it was known at that time. Nicholas evidently left a widow by the name of Katherine Boshell but nothing is shown in the records that will identify his children. But it would be fairly safe to assume that Nicholas Boshell of Walker Co. Ala. may be a son of Nicholas of Old 96th District, S.C. We would be glad to have any data concerning this family before it left S.C. It would appear from the evidence that it is of Huguenot ancestry.

The Burton Family also came from Abbeville, S.C. and many of their descendants have made Walker County their home. Samuel Black married into this family and also came to Walker County. He and his wife died without leaving any heirs to survive them. The Gant Family was of S.C. also and came from Old 96th District.

The Wright and Knight families probably came from Tenn. to Walker County. The Manasco Family came from N.C. originally, we learn from family connections. The ancestor of this family was probably Jeremiah Manasco, altho we have not been able to document this at present. The Deweese Family may have come from N.C. or Virginia. And they could have been in Kentucky for a time.

Anyone interested in these families please get in touch with the compiler of these records.

New Prospect Baptist Church Cemetery - 2 Miles North of Jasper, Ala.

In memory of ISHAM GUTTERY, born in the State of Georgia, Jan. 6, 1813, died August 17, 1882, age 69 yrs, 7 mos. 11 das. He was a devoted husband affectionate father and an approved Mason. Died in the Faith, he rests in hope of a glorious immortality.
SARAH ANN GUTTERY, born in S.C. Apr. 27, 1832, died Oct.1,1896
NANCY ANN (CONN) KILGORE, wife of J. T. KILGORE, b. Mar. 3, 1859, d. Nov. 4, 1905
JOHN THOMAS KILGORE, Aug. 1,1858, d. Dec. 5,1911
MAHULAH CONN, Jan. 4, 1820 - Apr. 10, 1892
JAMES CONN, Oct. 4, 1807 - Sep. 5, 1893
W. H. LOLLAR, Feb. 14, 1849 - June 4, 1928
MRS. W. H. LOLLAR, Mar. 6, 1860 - Jan. 2, 1931
In memory of AMANDA A. LOLLAR, wife of W. H. LOLLAR, b. Jan. 18, 1855 - d. July 30, 1893
ELIZABETH J. KIKER, wife of L. P. KIKER, Dec. 11, 1831 - July 16, 1882
L. P. KIKER, Mar. 5, 1843 - Dec. 7, 1900
JAMES A. F. KIRKPATRICK, Dec. 29, 1813 - Apr. 12, 1895
ROCINDA A., wife of L. P. KIKER, Jan. 26, 1846 - Jan. 31, 1893
MARY A. KIRKPATRICK, b. Sep. 15, 1815, died Sep. 26, 1891
In memory of M. E. KIRKPATRICK, b. in the State of S.C. Dec. 28, 1836, died Feb. 14, 1853
ELIZA BREAKFIELD, July 18, 1830 - Nov. 15, 1907
WILLIAM O'REAR, Oct. 9, 1826 - May 15, 1904
MARGARET E., wife of J. W. O'REAR, Dec. 3, 1842 - Dec. 15, 192?
In memory of DR. SMITH, b. Feb. 27, 1861 - d. July 23, 1880
RHODA S. SAXON, b. in Fulton Co. Ga. Apr. 20, 1836, d. Feb. 12, 1891
RODA LUCY SAXON, b. in Bowdon Ga. Feb. 10, 1872 - d. Sep. 13, 1890
ARTHUR CROCKER, Co. E 28 Ala. Inf. C.S.A. b.1830- d. Apr. 11, 1902
MARY E. wife of D. A. BREAKFIELD, Feb. 7,1825 - Sep. 15, 1907
D. A. BREAKFIELD, Sep. 3, 1834 - d. Oct. 1, 1899
J. P. MOONEY, Dec. 2, 1833 - Jan. 6, 1915
ANNIE C. wife of J. P. MOONEY, Feb. 8, 1833 - Mar. 13, 1906
NANCY G. KILGORE, wife of W. E. KILGORE, Sep.11, 1831, d. Nov. 21, 1911
J. N. SHERER, May 13, 1828 - Mar. 12, 1896
HARRIETT, wife of J. N. SHERER, Sep. 4, 1829 - Mar. 28, 1909
JOHN B. HULSEY, Co. C. 13th Bn. Ala. Partisan Rangers, C.S.A.
In memory of W. M. SHERER, Jan. 22, 1826 - Oct. 2, 1903
SARAH E., wife of W. M. SHERER, Dec. 3, 1831 - Jan. 18, 1897

## New Prospect Baptist Church Cemetery Cont'd.

ELIZABETH SHERER, dau. of J. & E. KIRKPATRICK, b. in S. C. Nov. 5, 1821, married E. A. SHERER, Dec. 16, 1844, d. Jan. 12, 1902
LT. E. A. SHERER, b. S.C. Jan. 25,1821, d. Feb. 13, 1907
O. C. STOVER, May 1827, d. Oct. 1899
NANCY, wife of O. C. STOVER, d. Feb. 1908
MADISON L. LOONEY, May 23, 1835, d. Aug. 20, 1915
ANNIE ELIZA LOONEY, Oct. 5, 1848 - Mar. 22, 1930

## Oak Hill Cemetery - Jasper, Alabama

ROBERT H. PALMER, Feb. 25, 1856 - Dec. 16, 1937
JOANNA GERTRUDE JACKSON PALMER, Jun. 7, 1871 - Mar. 8, 1955
WILLIAM JOE RICHARDSON - 1881 - 1936
CARRIE G., wife of WM. JOE RICHARDSON, 1884 - 1954
JOHN M. GRAY, 1875 - 1956
FRANCES E. TARRANT, Wife of JOHN M. GRAY, 1877 - 1937
SAMUEL H. DUNSTON - 1878 - 1930
ANNIE C. HAUGHTON - 1852 - 1943
MALCOLM A. OATES, 1875 - 1939
CLAUDE GUTTERY, 1877 - 1936
MAE HAUGHTON, wife of MALCOLM A. OATES, 1881 - 1954
WILLIAM P. KNIGHT, 1859 - 1930
ROMA MANASCO KNIGHT, wife of WM. P. KNIGHT, 1866 - 1932
DAVID H. CHILTON, Dec. 14, 1876 - Jun. 2,1935
EUGENE PENDLETON GAINES, Mar. 11, 1877 - Feb. 11,1930
EDGAR WILLIAM LONG, Jul. 30, 1876 - Jul. 8, 1948
JAMES FREDERICK ALEXANDER, M.D., 1871 - 1926
CLELIA GUTHRIE LEITH, 1868 - 1952
MARTIN LUTHER LEITH, 1868 - 1923
IDA COLE, wife of JOHN W. PHILLIPS, Apr. 15, 1885 - Nov. 13,1932
BEN M. HAY, 1862 - 1939
HARRIS WELBORN, Nov.11, 1850 - Mar. 21, 1929
MARY ANN WELBORN, Mar. 10, 1850 - Oct. 19, 1924
MONROE A. ARGO, 1866 - 1935
MATTIE C. ARGO, 1867 - 1950
AMANDA CAIN BOYLE, Apr. 14, 1839 - Sep. 15, 1907
ROBERT WALKER GORDON, 1858 - 1899
ETTA STANLEY GORDON, 1864 - 1946
LUTITIA CHAPPELL STANLEY - 1833 - 1910
JAMES GUILD STANLEY, 1873 - 1901
WILLIAM CHAPPELL STANLEY, 1870 - 1950
GEORGE HOUSTON GUTTERY, 1847 - 1911
ALICE STANLEY GUTTERY, 1858 - 1956
CHARLES W. STUBBLEFIELD, Apr. 30, 1865 - Apr. 26, 1948
IDA BLANTON STUBBLEFIELD, Dec. 27, 1870 - Nov. 22, 1945
JUDGE JAMES W. SHEPHERD, Dec. 24, 1850 - Nov. 7, 1925
EUSTATIA PALMER, wife of JAMES W. SHEPHERD, Jan. 2, 1859 - Feb. 5, 1929

Oak Hill Cemetery - Cont'd.

R. H. SHEPHERD, M.D., Aug. 25, 1886 - Sep. 9, 1956
INEZ LANTRIP, wife of DOCTOR R. H. SHEPHERD, Dec. 8, 1897 - Apr. 2, 1954
LOUVINNIA MILLER, 1848 - 1908
ROBERT LEE LITTLE, 1871 - 1905
A. T. PALMER, 1853 - 1892
SALLIE B. PALMER, 1855 - 1939
CLAUDE PALMER, 1881 - 1898
ROBERT PALMER, 1889 - 1889
CRAIG PALMER, 1882 - 1924
CRAIG PALMER, JR., 1919 - 1930
CHARLES MANLEY SARTAIN, 1870 - 1940
JACK CURTIS, 1918 - 1919
EDWIN C. DILWORTH, Apr. 2, 1878, Nov. 8, 1933
HARROLD CALDWELL DILWORTH, M.D., Jun. 11, 1902 - Jul. 16, 1933
CORNELIA DILWORTH, Jun. 19, 1842 - Mar. 27, 1929
STEPHEN PRICE DILWORTH, Jan. 23, 1846 - Oct. 25, 1917
T. BOLTON DILWORTH. Jul. 28. 1870 - Apr. 29, 1929
C. C. SMITH, 1952 - 1932
MOLLIE, wife of C. A. SMITH, 1867 - 1945
JAMES J. LONG, Jul. 25, 1854 - Jul. 20, 1932
ROBERT Y. LONG, Nov. 3, 1861 - Jun. 15, 1947
CHARLES D. LONG, Feb. 21, 1857 - Oct. 26, 1930
CHARLES D. LONG, JR., Jul.12, 1894 - Jan. 9, 1929
GEORGE H. GUTTERY, JR., Mar. 3, 1899, Mar. 4, 1941
EZRA WILSON COLEMAN, Aug. 10, 1861 - Oct. 13, 1904
NANCY PRISCILLA SHIELDS, wife of EZRA W. COLEMAN, Jun. 21, 1869 - Nov. 18, 1953
ROBERT WOOTEN LONG, Mar. 19, 1864 - Oct. 1, 1910
GAYE LONG LACEY, Apr. 6, 1880 - Jun. 19, 1923
FRANCIS MUSGROVE LONG, May 1882 - Nov. 1932
JOHN B. LONG, 1857 - 1907
LYCURGUS BRECKENRIDGE MUSGROVE, 1856 - 1931
J. C. MUSGROVE, Apr. 11, 1860 - Jul. 30, 1904
ELIZABETH CAIN, Aug. 18, 1835 - Jun. 18, 1917, married June 6, 1853 FRANCIS ASBURY MUSGROVE
JAMES LAWRENCE SOWELL, M.D., Mar. 19, 1868 - Nov. 26, 1952
JOSIE PLEASANT SOWELL, b. Jan. 7, 1869, d. Sep. 11, 1954
WALTER GODFREY GRAVLEE, b. Mar. 31, 1838, d. Aug.29, 1915
WALTER FORREST GRAVLEE, Apr. 16, 1864 - Oct. 9, 1950
THOMAS PETER LAMKIN, 1844 - 1928
NANCY MATILDA LAMKIN, 1854 - 1936
WILLIAM BROCKMAN BANKHEAD, 1874 - 1940
FLORENCE McGUIRE BANKHEAD, Jul. 9, 1889 - Jul. 1, 1952
JOHN HOLLIS BANKHEAD, Sep. 15, 1842 - Mar. 1, 1920
TALULLAH BROCKMAN, wife of JOHN HOLLIS BANKHEAD, Dec. 12, 1844 - May 11, 1922
JOHN HOLLIS BANKHEAD, II, Jul. 8, 1872 - Jun. 12, 1946

Oak Hill Cemetery, Cont'd.

Sep. 3, 1867 - Feb. 19, 1921 - Here Lies LOUISE BANKHEAD PERRY LUND, Who by good deeds laid up a fortune which she has gone to enjoy.
WILLIAM HAYNE BANKHEAD PERRY, only son of COLONEL WILLIAM HAYNE PERRY and his wife LOUISE BANKHEAD, born at San Souci, S. C. Mar. 16, 1897 died Nov. 3, 1915, Jasper, Ala.
Sacred to the memory of my precious mother MARY ELIZABETH McAULEY, b. Nov. 9, 1822 - died Mar. 26, 1915
CHARLES B. CROW, Ala. 2nd. Lt. Co. M. 342, World War I, b. Mar. 17, 1897 - died Jul. 8, 1955.
LULA EMMA DODD, wife of CAINE O'REAR, Mar. 11, 1888 - Sep. 6, 1936
SAMUEL J. CHILDERS, Dec. 8, 1847 - Aug. 22, 1926
FRANCIS L. CHILDERS, Oct. 11, 1838 - Apr. 21, 1913
THOMAS M. CHILDERS, Sep. 11, 1876 - Jul. 29, 1930
IDA SMITH CHILDERS, Jul. 11, 1878 - Apr. 4, 1952
MARVIN M. CHILDERS, Jun. 21, 1904 - May 12, 1930
ELVIRA, wife of W. R. WINDERS, Apr. 7, 1839 - Dec. 21, 1910
J. H. CRANFORD, Mar. 12, 1855 - Jul. 31, 1934
ANNIS E. CRANFORD, Nov. 25, 1870 - Jul. 3, 1936
BETTYE MORRIS LYON, Nov. 25, 1847 - Jul. 5, 1935
ASA CRANFORD, Dec. 25, 1878 - Sep. 10, 1953
STEPHEN CRANFORD, Dec. 25, 1878 - died 1930
WILLIAM H. DUFFEE, Dec. 9, 1832 - Aug. 1908
ELIZABETH GRAVLEE DUFFEE, Nov. 2, 1848 - Apr. 2, 1929
ELLA DUFFEE, May 18,1874 - Mar. 25, 1949
J. R. GUNTER, Jun. 1, 1861 - Aug. 25, 1914
MARY E. (MOLLIE) GUNTER, Dec. 22, 1866 - Feb. 12, 1956
PAUL GUNTER, Sep. 6, 1890 - Jan. 29, 1952
D. L. STOVALL, 1830 - 1905
M. JANE STOVALL, 1840 - 1900
A. B. STOVALL, 1864 - 1917
EULA L. STOVALL, 1870 - 1937
MURRAY P. STOVALL, 1902 - 1955
RICHARD H. SMITH, Feb. 17, 1846 - Apr. 3, 1917
REBECCA J. SMITH, Aug. 1, 1850 - Sep. 25, 1915
EDWARD W. SMITH, Sep. 28, 1886 - Dec. 4,1911
THOMAS JACKSON AMISS, Jan. 22, 1864 - Nov. 20, 1928
FANNIE CROCKER AMISS, May 9, 1872 - Nov. 17, 1954
WILLIAM AVERY BATES, 1869 - 1927
AMANDA CURTIS BATES, 1880 - 1949
WILLIAM GRADY BATES, 1897 - 1945
ANDREW M. STOVALL, M.D., 1857 - 1928
NANCY E. STOVALL, 1868 - 1926
F. H. McANNALLY, Feb. 18, 1859 - Mar. 22, 1927
A. C. McANNALLY, Apr. 28, 1857 - Jan. 3, 1925
MARTHA SPROUL CRANFORD, 1876 - 1951

Oak Hill Cemetery Cont'd.

CLARENCE H. CRANFORD, Jul. 1, 1896 - Oct. 11, 1918
EDITH CRANFORD MARTIN, 1911 - 1945
JESSE L. KING, 1864 - 1918
LUCINDA KING, 1869 - 1938
S. HAMILTON, Dec. 6, 1870 - Aug. 11, 1943
MRS. S. HAMILTON, Dec. 19, 1873 - Nov. 23, 1942
CRAIG, son of MR. and MRS. S. HAMILTON, Nov. 13, 1913 - Oct. 9, 1922
JOHN BRABSON SHIELDS, Aug. 25, 1840 - May 13, 1930
CAROLINE ELIZA LONG, wife of JOHN BRABSON SHIELDS, June 29, 1845 - Mar. 27, 1933
JOHN BRABSON SHIELDS, dau. of JOHN and C. E. SHIELDS, May 15, 1880 - Oct. 11, 1948
J. R. KILGORE, 1855 - 1928
MARY E. KILGORE, 1857 - 1940
AMY KILGORE CAMPBELL, 1889 - 1955
JAMES ANDREW HUGGINS, Apr.30, 1861 - May 6, 1931
MARY JANE HUGGINS, Feb. 10, 1859 - Mar. 17, 1931
JOHN E. LACEY, 1857 - 1941
MOLLIE L. LACEY, 1867 - 1943
MILDRED VIRGINIA LACEY, 1891 - 1918
JOHN HENRY HAYES, Oct. 13, 1843 - Nov. 21, 1908
MILDRED FILES HAYES, Apr. 27,1846 - Sep. 18, 1895
JACK, eldest son of EDGAR and ANNA L. Q. HAYES, Nov. 16, 1903 - Apr. 22, 1915
JOHN HENRY, son of OSCAR and MARY HAYES, Jun. 24, 1908 - Sep. 28, 1909
THOMAS L. LONG, 1860 - 1931
AUGUSTA SPRATT LONG, 1869 - 1947
HENRY SPRATT LONG, Ala. Capt. 117 F.A. 31 Div. World War I, Aug. 24, 1890 - died Sep. 19, 1850
BENJAMIN BROCKWAY, son of T. L. LONG and M. A. LONG, Jul. 17, 1895 - Oct. 4, 1896
SAMUEL SANDERS, Sep. 23, 1826 - Sep. 10, 1902
NANCY SANDERS, wife of SAMUEL SANDERS, Jul. 28, 1830 - Nov. 22, 1915
JOHN SHORT, Nov. 31, 1909, age 90 years, a good soldier.
JOHN MORGAN ROQUEMORE, SR., Apr. 13, 1862 - Jun. 26, 1952
WILLIAM S. PAYNE and wife MOLLIE N. PAYNE, (no dates)
A. R. BURCHFIELD, Jul. 27,1864 - Oct. 18, 1902
LUCINDA WOODS, 1822 - Nov. 22, 1909
REV. R. M. GUY, Apr. 29, 1858 - Sep. 1, 1912
LAURA E. GUY, May 6, 1860 - Sep. 25, 1914
C. L. ROSSER, May 10, 1862 - Aug. 20, 1911
CHARLES THOMAS ROSSER, Sep. 12, 1903 - Feb. 26, 1955
W. L. KITCHEN, Aug. 30, 1866 - Oct. 9, 1938
JAMES P. SHAW, 1873 - 1944
PERRY SHAW, 1902 - 1943

Oak Hill Cemetery Cont'd.

GADSIE ROBINS WILLIAMS, 1868 - 1955
DAN M. ROBINS, 1874 - 1952
JOHN H. ROBINS, 1881 - 1943
CUSTUS L. ROBINS, 1878 - 1951
ALICE F. ROBINS, 1866 - 1944
MAUDE R. COBB, Nov. 14, 1885 - Aug. 22, 1956
O. F. COBB, Nov. 14, 1888 - Aug. 3, 1935
FRANK L. SMITH, Aug. 26, 1910 - Jan. 13, 1926
W. NEIL SHERER, 1916 - 1953
JOHN M. SHERER, Jul. 25, 1886 - Dec. 5, 1947
EUGENIA A. POWELL, LAMERT, Sep. 22, 1846
BONNY JEAN LAMERT, Oct. 30, 1867 - Feb. 5, 1911
GRACE CECILIA GORDON, 1898 - 1937
WILLIAM L. SWINDLE, May 10,1909 - Feb. 26, 1934
ALBERT SIDNEY PRESTON, Apr. 23, 1865 - Oct. 1, 1952
RUHAMA ANDERSON SHERER, 1879 - 1939
LECIL DEAN GRAY, 1881 - 1937
GERTRUDE MILLER GRAY, 1887 - 1949
CHARLES Y. HUGGINS, 1881 - 1928
MARGARET S. HUGGINS, 1882 - 1942
REV. C. C. BUTLER, May 1, 1880 - Mar. 7, 1935
GEORGE KUDER, b. GROVELAND, Livingston Co. N.Y. Aug. 25, 1829 - d. Feb. 12, 1896
AMELIA KUDER, 1835 - 1918
DON A. McGREGOR, Feb. 19, 1866 - Nov. 4, 1942
DON A. McGREGOR, JR., Oct. 28, 1901 - Dec. 26, 1942
SHERIFF LACEY, May 7, 1853 - Jul. 27, 1953
ELLA McCOLLOUGH, wife of SHERIFF LACEY, Apr. 1858 - Jul 7, 1927
EARNEST LACEY, Oct. 11, 1877 - Nov. 29, 1942
INEZ EDWARDS, wife of ERNEST LACEY, Aug. 31, 1898 - Aug. 4,1955
LORENE LACEY WOODS, wife of GEORGE W. WOODS, Dec. 1893 - May 19, 1940
DOROTHY LACEY WOODS, May 1916 - Nov. 1919
CECIL LACEY, 1860 - 1942
DOUGLAS ROWE, wife of CECIL LACEY, Mar. 1881 - Jan. 1953
CHARLES E. TWEEDY, May 21, 1880 - Aug. 13, 1955
WILLIAM J. KNIGHT, Jun. 12, 1919 - May 27, 1956
WALTER L. GUTTERY, May 1, 1878 - Oct. 11, 1945
JESSE O. LONG, 1874 - 1934
SAMUEL M. SANDERS, 1864 - 1938
ALBERTINE STURGIS SANDERS, 1876 - 1946
LAWRENCE B. SANDERS, 1907 - 1938
M. O'REAR, Nov. 13, 1907 - Jul. 27, 1931
GUY O'REAR, Feb. 21, 1882 - May 11, 1927
VESTA BRIGGS, wife of GUY O'REAR, Feb. 28, 1881 - Jul.20, 1918
CALVIN SUMNER MIGHT, Feb. 3,1859 - Feb. 21, 1921
BELLE C. MIGHT, D. Sep. 15, 1956, age 99 years, 7mos. 8 das.

Oak Hill Cemetery, Cont'd.

JOHN B. RICHARDSON, Jul. 20, 1854 - Jan. 12, 1911
BERT S. RICHARDSON, Aug. 19, 1883 - Mar. 23, 1941
MARY ALICE WILSON, Jul. 29, 1878 - Feb. 3, 1955
HARVEY WILSON, Feb. 24, 1900 - Oct. 12, 1951
JOHN B. LOLLAR, Nov. 30, 1835 - Aug. 29, 1914
HARRIETT ELIZABETH, wife of JOHN B. LOLLAR, Feb. 11, 1835 Mar. 10, 1915
J. A. O'REAR, 1865 - 1917
QUEEN LOLLAR O'REAR, 1869 - 1897
JUDGE J. B. APPLING, Feb. 18, 1841 - Oct. 21, 1901
WALLER R. APPLING, Aug. 26, 1872 - May 16, 1899
MATTIE J. APPLING, Feb. 4, 1877 - Feb. 17, 1902
THOMAS P. DEWEESE, M.D., Apr. 6, 1860 - Feb. 2, 1932
CLARA V., wife of THOMAS P. DEWEESE, Nov. 19, 1869 - Oct.5, 1908
ANNA ELIZABETH DEWEESE, Nov. 30, 1867, Feb. 1, 1953
NANCY SANDERS, wife of SAMUEL SANDERS, Jul. 28, 1830 - Nov. 22, 1915
SAMUEL SANDERS, Sep. 23, 1826 - Sep. 10, 1902
EMILY WINSLETT, wife of JOHN WHIT LONG, Aug. 1908 - Aug. 1954
KATE WALLACE WINSLETT, Oct. 1885 - Jun. 1954
GEORGE O'REAR, Nov. 13, 1854 - Jan. 20, 1939
VENILA L. O'REAR, wife of G. D. O'REAR, Jan. 24, 1858 - Mar. 16, 1934
HARRY HAZELTON, 1877 - 1915
VARILLA GAINES HAZELTON, wife of HARRY HAZELTON, 1874 - 1954
.............., wife of T. H. HAZELTON, Jun. 3, 1843-Dec.24,1904
MAJOR THOMAS HAZELTON, 1840 - 1912
JAMES FRANKLIN HALEY, Feb. 28, 1832 - Jul. 10, 1911
PRISCILLA JOANNA SHIELDS, wife of JAMES FRANKLIN HALEY, Oct. 8, 1845 - Jan. 28, 1934
A. B. LEGG, 1859 - 1946
LIZZIE LEGG, 1860 - 1945
MARY EARL LYNN, no date
STACIA M. LYNN, Jun. 22, 1876 - Dec. 8, 1899
S. EARL LYNN, 1876 - 1942
H. P. GAINES, Apr. 25, 1850 - Nov. 6, 1923
CAROLINE DAY, wife of H. P. GAINES, Dec. 7, 1851 - Apr.2, 1933
BYRD DAY GAINES, 1881 - 1925
LESLIE COX, wife of BYRD DAY GAINES, 1887 - 1953
H. PENDLETON GAINES, 1885 - 1942
EDMUND T. GAINES, 1887 - 1942
SIDNEY GAINES, wife of BOB CATCHINGS, 1887 - 1928
CLAIRE GAINES CATCHINGS, wife of EUGENE M. PURVIS, 1910 - 1949
~~LAWRENCE STAPLEY RICHARDSON, 1889 - 1931~~
GEORGE E. GLASS, 1859 - 1936
MARK GLASS, no dates
Wife of MARK GLASS, no dates
MISS JAMES, no dates
SALLY NORVELL WIGGINS, Feb. 1, 1895 - May 9, 1935
FRANCIS LEECH, son of PEYTON and MARY LEECH NORVELL, Mar. 20, 1894 - Feb. 1895

Oak Hill Cemetery Cont'd.

CLARA HAWES, wife of LUCIEN B. NORVELL, Jul. 9, 1837 - Jun. 5, 1901
ALICE LUCIEN, dau. of PEYTON and MARY L. NORVELL, Jan. 27, 1902 - Jun. 1903
PEYTON NORVELL, son of LUCIEN BONAPARTE NORVELL and CLARA HAWES NORVELL, b. Prince William Co. Va. Aug. 17, 1860 - d. in Jasper, Ala. Jul. 21, 1917
MARY LEECH NORVELL, wife of PEYTON NORVELL, dau. of CAPT. ELBERT LEECH, C.S.A. and FRANCES HARRIETT LEECH, b. Lowndes Co. Miss., d. Jasper, Ala. Apr. 24, 1940
CLARA LUCINE NORVELL, dau. of LUCIEN BONAPARTE NORVELL and CLARA HAWES NORVELL, b. Prince William Co. Va. Oct. 23, 1867 d. Jasper, Ala. Jul. 12, 1949
DR. W. C. ROSAMOND, Aug. 24, 1833 - May 23, 1904
MADARA, wife of DR. ROSAMOND, Nov. 15, 1842 - Oct. 24, 1881
HATTIE D., wife of DR. ROSAMOND, 1846 - 1912
MARY A. GAMBLE, wife of JUDGE F. A. GAMBLE, Jan. 16, 1846 - Feb. 24, 1920
JOHN A. GAMBLE, Jan. 1, 1861 - Feb. 18, 1946
ALEXANDER DALLAS, Mar. 8, 1864 - Nov. 11, 1900
MR. and MRS. WORTHINGTON, buried in mausoleum, no dates
SALLIE B. RICHARDSON, Apr. 4, 1878 - Mar. 19 1899
DR. and MRS. J. A. GOODWIN, no dates
JOHN L. McALONEY, Dec. 15, 1840 in Parros Barrow, Nova Scotia, died Jul. 17, 1897
ROBERT ANDREW ARGO, 1872 - 1949
ELLA DAVIS ARGO, 1884 - 1946
LETCHER C. SHERER, Jun. 29, 1871 - Jul. 19, 1951
JANIE ODOM SHERER, Mar. 23, 1876 - Apr. 15, 1950
RONIE GRACE, 1875 - 1945
W. L. HADAWAY, 1887 - 1945
JERRY M. HAYES, Dec. 30, 1867 - Dec. 5, 1949
MINNIE W. HAYES, Sep. 19, 1870 - Jun. 17, 1954

Robert Guttery Cemetery - On old home place near Townley, Alabama, Hollygrove

Sacred to the memory of: ELDER ROBERT GUTTERY, born in the State of Georgia, Feb. 25, 1801, died in Walker Co., Ala. April 6, 1877 - age 76 years, 1 mo., 10 das. He joined the Primitive Baptist Church in the year 1824 and began his Ministerial labor about the year 1826. He was a faithful Minister about 50 years.
SARAH ANN, wife of ELDER ROBERT GUTTERY, b. May 8, 1804, d. Feb. 8, 1881
B. F. GUTTERY, b. Dec. 8, 1829 - d. Dec. 22, 1830
LEVI T. GUTTERY, Mar. 27, 1839 - May 13, 1862
SARAH GUTTERY, Aug. 6, 1860 - Apr. 12, 1865

Robert Guttery Cemetery, Cont'd.

L. T. GUTTERY, Jun. 7, 1862 - Jul. 9, 1865
JOHNSON GUTTERY, Jul. 3, 1849 - Oct. 17, 1881
DAULPHIN GUTTERY, Mar. 1874 - Jul. 28, 1894
JOHNSON GUTTERY, no dates
NANCY GUTTERY, no dates
R. M. GUTTERY, Mar. 29, 1843 - Apr. 25, 1903
LUCINDA GUTTERY, Aug. 6, 1849 - Jun. 4, 1881, wife of R. M. GUTTERY
KITTY ANN, dau. of JOHN and MARY, Sep. 10, 1843 - Nov. 12, 1843
W. B., son of JOHN and MARY GUTTERY, Dec. 9, 1849 - Feb. 27, 1850
WILLIAM GUTHRIE, Dec. 29, 1828 - Apr. 23, 1868
CHARLES H. GUTHRIE, 1897 - 1930
THOMAS GUTHRIE, 1862 - 1928
EPPIE A. GUTHRIE, Dec. 12, 1866 - Jun. 13, 1910
JOHN WILLIS GUTHRIE, Feb. 24, 1838 - Jun. 20, 1926
SARAH ELIZABETH GUTHRIE, Jun. 2, 1844 - Feb. 5, 1921
Sacred to the Memory of: JOHNSON GUTTERY, born in Georgia Mar. 12, 1806, died May 26, 1876, age 70 years, 2 mos 11 das, Joined Primitive Baptist Church in the year 1826 and began his ministerial labors in the year 1839. He was a faithful minister about 37 years.
MARY, wife of JOHNSON GUTTERY, born Feb. 22, 1807 - died, Oct. 13, 1885
HETTIE GUTTERY TOWNLEY, Jun. 1812 - 1875
HENRY TOWNLEY, Jul. 15, 1808 - Sep. 4, 1842
HANNER TOWNLEY, wife of DANIEL TOWNLEY, died Dec. 1, 1855, age about 75 years. (Hanner or Hannah, was the wife of WILLIAM GUTTERY who died in Walker Co. Ala. in 1825. Daniel Townley was her second husband)
LUCINDA GUTTERY (nee TOWNLEY) died Mar. 24, 1854 - no birth date
A. S. GUTTERY, born Nov. 25, 1864 - d. Dec. 20, 1864
MARY A. GUTTERY, b. Jun. 12, 1868 - d. Dec. 28, 1868
J. R. GUTTERY, son of J. R. and BARBARA, Aug. 2, 1862 - Dec. 3, 1863
MARTHA A. GUTTERY, Jul. 20, 1873 - Aug. 29, 1876
R. R. GUTTERY, Apr. 20, 1872 - Aug. 30, 1876
G. H. GUTTERY, Sep. 22, 1870 - Mar. 2, 1877
M. V. GUTTERY, b. Sep. 6, 1842 - d. Oct.22, 1916
MARY E. GUTTERY, Feb. 8,1844 - Nov. 27, 1917
EMMER GUTTERY, Jan. 11, 1870 - Sep. 14, 1932
MARTHA CHARLOTTE (PATTON) BEASLEY, 1898 - 1950
MARGURITE BEASLEY, Jan. 7, 1871 - Jun. 30, 1930
REV. A. (JACK) BROWN, Oct. 6, 1895 - Nov. 14, 1934
MARY E.TOWNLEY, May 4, 1891 - Sep. 12, 1896
EMILY LEE McCULLAR, May 16, 1900 - Aug. 5,1912
CLARENCE MASON, Aug. 18, 1902 - Jul. 30, 1934
EDITH GWENDELINE PARVIN, Jul. 24, 1919 - Feb. 20, 1920
DONNIE MAE PARVIN, Sep. 25, 1897 - Jul. 3, 1951

Robert Guttery Cemetery, Cont'd.

WILLIAM P. TOWNLEY, 1888 - 1890
W. B. TOWNLEY, 1858 - 1891
MARY JANE ATKINS, Feb. 2, 1859 - Jun. 22, 1900
N. P. GRACE, May 2, 1897 - Oct. 3, 1911
MELISSA WESSON, Sep. 23, 1858 - Mar. 19, 1907
PERRY J. WESSON, Oct. 28, 1859 - Feb. 1, 1904
E. GUTTERY, an infant, no dates
MARY MAGDALENE (GUTTERY) HENDON, 1872 - Dec. 4, 1951
ELIZABETH GUTTERY, wife of WILLIAM GUTTERY, b. in Ala. Sep. 15, 1832, d. May 28, 1858. (She was the first wife of WILLIAM GUTTERY, son of ROBERT GUTTERY and SARAH ANN WILLIAMS. WILLIAM GUTTERY married for the second time, ELIZABETH CHRISTINE SHIRLEY and moved to Texas where both are buried.)
J. M. GUTTERY, b. Sep. 9, 1849 - d. Aug. 29, 1926
ELIZABETH MORRIS GUTTERY, no dates
HATTIE L. ALVIS, b. Apr. 10, 1881 - d. Mar. 1, 1900
BOYD N. GUTTERY, Feb. 7, 1873 - Jun. 19, 1925
NORA E. GUTTERY, Jul. 29, 1879 - Jan. 24, 1946
W. B. GUTTERY, Feb. 29, 1884 - Mar. 18, 1912
Infant dau. of J. M. & E. J. GUTTERY, no dates
BOYD NAPOLEON GUTTERY, b. May 18, 1899 - d. May, 15, 1900
WILLIE MAUD, dau. of B. N. GUTTERY, Jul. 29, 1891 - Oct. 19, 1902
ARTHUR BEASLEY, Mar. 1889 - Nov. 24, 1891
Infant son of J. M. M. and S. E. ROBINSON, b. Aug. 4, 1884 - Aug. 31, 1884
JACK GUTTERY, son of A. J. GUTTERY, Jan. 1863 - d. 1863
RACHEL GUTTERY, wife of A. J. GUTTERY, died 1863
JOHN GUTTERY, b. 1806, died Mar. 13, 1870 (son of WILLIAM and HANNAH GUTTERY)
MARY GUTTERY, wife of JOHN GUTTERY, b. 1801, d. Oct. 13, 1893
WILLIAM S. GUTTERY, Dec. 22, 1867 - no death date
JOHN R. GUTTERY, b. Jul. 9, 1869, no death date
TENNESSEE GUTTERY, b. Nov. 12, 1886, no death date
A. J. BOSHELL, b. Dec. 25, in S. C. 1815, d. Jun. 18,1901
CATHERINE (GUTTERY) BOSHELL, Mar. 22, 1824 - d. 1873
WILLIAM R. BOSHELL, Apr. 12, 1851 - Jun. 7, 1925
MARTHA KING BOSHELL, Jun. 18, 1861 - Mar. 20, 1913
J. M. BOSHELL, Aug. 25, 1856 - Jan. 9, 1931
SUSAN E. BOSHELL, Jul. 8, 1868 - Apr. 21, 1906
R. W. BOSHELL, Nov. 27, 1846 - Mar. 6, 1920
SARAH S. BOSHELL, Mar. 5, 1853 - Mar. 11, 1939
ALEMEDA BOSHELL, Oct. 14, 1907 - Apr. 11, 1908
CLYDE BOSHELL, Sep. 12, 1903 - Jan. 5, 1948
LOUIS BOSHELL, 1869 - 1948
LILLIE M. BOSHELL, Jun. 7, 1887 - Jun. 7, 1951
CHARLIE M. BOSHELL, 1882 - 1944
PORTER BOSHELL, Aug. 9, 1886 - May 25, 1933

Robert Guttery Cemetery, Cont'd.

GEORGE BOSHELL, 1890 - 1937
ALFRED BOSHELL, 1910 - 1954
JOHN W. BOSHELL, 1872 - 1944
W. J. BOSHELL, age 79 years, no further dates
DOROTHY ETHEL BOSHELL, Aug. 12, 1913 - Jun. 18, 1916
GENEVA BOSHELL, May 20, 1918 - Jun. 18, 1922
BERNICE BOSHELL, Oct. 3, 1903 - Aug. 18, 1922
Infant of P. C. and M. L. COOPER, b. Jan. 1910
HAZEL BOSHELL, Aug. 25, 1912 - Oct. 28, 1912
MAE HENDON BOSHELL, Feb. 19, 1882 - Sep. 8, 1938
ROSA BOSHELL, 1882 - 1943
JACK BOSHELL, Oct. 19, 1924 - Dec. 26, 1946
SYLVESTER BOSHELL, 1879 - 1947
ANNIE BOSHELL, 1884 - 1947
CELIA KATHERINE BOSHELL, Mar. 21, 1850 - Dec. 29, 1929
JOHN N. BOSHELL, Feb. 10, 1849 - May 13, 1919
MAGGIE BOSHELL, Jan. 23, 1884 - Jul. 28, 1918
RICHARD BOSHELL, Jul. 24, 1877 - Oct. 14, 1917
CARLOS N. BOSHELL, Apr.16, 1907 - Nov. 19, 1908
M. BOSHELL, Jan. 29, 1887 - Aug. 26, 1887
ADIE BOSHELL, Jun. 21, 1893 - Jul. 3, 1894
LUCILLE BOSHELL, Nov. 7, 1903 - Jan. 5, 1918
HARRY BOSHELL,Oct. 27, 1907 - Jun. 5, 1909
Infant son of W. R. & M. BOSHELL, Nov. 17, 1897 - d. 1897
Infant dau. of W. R. & M. BOSHELL, Aug. 16, 1911 - Aug. 22, 1911
CLAUD J. BOSHELL, Nov. 19, 1896 - Feb. 1, 1904
Infant son of D. F. & LILLIE BOSHELL, Nov. 11, 1906 - Dec. 12, 1906
J. ARDELL BOSHELL, Apr. 17, 1927 - May 27, 1932
JONAS BOSHELL, Jun. 16, 1874 - Sep. 11, 1952
BESSIE, wife of JONAS BOSHELL, May 6, 1880 - Jul. 4, 1934
MARY A. BOSHELL, Dec. 7, 1844 - Oct. 24, 1865
E. D. BOSHELL, Apr. 8, 1863 - Sep. 8, 1883
Son of COURTNEY and EARNESTINE BOSHELL, no dates
RAWLEIGH M. BURTON, 1875 - 1933
MATTIE BURTON, Dec. 8, 1878 - A g. 22, 1912
ALTHIA V. BISHOP, 1879 - 1944
MARY J. ROMINE, Jul. 22, 1839 - Sep. 26, 1903
J. B. ROMINE, Dec. 15, 1837 - Mar. 23, 1883
NANCY ROMINE, Nov. 3, 1795, Jun. 22, 1885
THOMAS C. SPEEGLE, Oct. 27, 1877 - Jan. 9, 1878
ELIZABETH J. BROWN, Oct. 21, 1836 - Dec. 1862
NANCY ANN AREY, Jul. 13, 1832 - Dec. 13, 1913
CATHERINE P. KING, Mar. 18, 1862 - Oct. 2, 1911
COLMER KING, Jan. 24, 1884 - Feb. 23, 1902
WILLIAM E. KING, Jun. 26, 1898 - Feb. 24, 1899
SAM K. PATTON, Jul. 19, 1849 - Aug. 21, 1911
W. G. TOWNLEY, Nov. 6, 1860 - Jun. 25, 1918

Robert Guttery Cemetery, Cont'd.

JAMES M. WILLIAMS, 1856 - 1929
ALABAMA WILLIAMS, 1860 - 1932
S. S. WILLIAMS, 1901 - 1921
W. A. BELL, 1888 - 1943
CLARA OLIVE BELL, 1894 - 1934
WEBSTER STEADMAN, 1883 - 1955
REBECCA S. STEADMAN, 1883 - 1921
JAMES HALL SMITH, Jul. 13, 1917 - Jul. 8, 1918
MARION C. McGILL, Apr. 30, 1861 - Nov. 28, 1915
RUTH E. McGILL, Sep. 13, 1861 - Jun. 6, 1919
ALLEN McKENDRICK, 1875 - 1952
MARGARET REINBERG VINES, b. Jun. 21,1882 -(death date not verified)
SAM C. REINBERG, b. Nov. 2, 1878 (death date not verified)
GLADYS V. SIDES, Jan. 18, 1918 - Apr. 21, 1918
MINNIE McQUEEN, Jul. 11, 1880 - Jun. 24, 1903
JOHN R. McQUEEN, Mar. 3, 1872 - Aug. 7, 1905
LEROY SMITH, 1900 - 1900
PAUL MELCHER, 1898 - 1899
C. D. SMITH, Oct. 28, 1870 - Feb. 22, 1902
MARTHA SMITH, Mar. 4, 1842 - Feb. 22, 1902
F. CLEVELAND TATE, Mar. 2, 1887 - Jul. 28, 1905
JENNINGS B. TATE, Jul. 28, 1899 - Mar. 26, 1900
WILLIAM M. TATE, Aug. 11, 1900 - 1900
J. S. TATE, Apr. 7, 1853 - Oct. 25, 1929
ELIZA JANE TATE, May 27,1862 - Dec. 11, 1937
FRANK MAYFIELD, May 16, 1916 - Jul. 8, 1917
CHESTER L. MASON, Oct. 10, 1907 - Sep.3,1953. P.F.C. World War II, Base Unit, A.A.F.
DOVIE ANDERSON, Aug. 3, 1905 - Feb. 15, 1948
SAM A. SMITH, Mar. 1, 1887 - Dec. 3, 1955
EDNA SMITH, Jun. 30, 1890 - Jun. 12, 1937
AMY C. BRAND, Jun. 30, 1870 - Feb. 14, 1955
J. A. FRANKS, Apr. 19, 1872 - Apr. 15, 1926
J. A. TIREY, Sep. 9, 1851 - Mar. 28, 1927
TISHIE TIREY, Feb. 11, 1852 - Dec. 30, 1931
W. A. TIREY, 1878 - 1935
ARTHUR AVERY, Jun. 25, 1880 - Jan. 11, 1937
EDNA AVERY, Sep. 27, 1889 - Jan. 17, 1953
JOHNNIE LEE BROWN, Jun. 13, 1918 - Apr. 5, 1937
JOHN J. FERGUSON, May 1862 - May 6, 1937
NANNIE FERGUSON, Aug. 30, 1868 - Jan. 31, 1954
HUBBARD (BERT) McLAIN, Oct. 18, 1890 - Mar. 24, 1937
MARY EVELYN McLAIN, Apr. 18, 1917 - Feb. 2, 1919
GERALDINE McLAIN McCARLEY, Feb. 23, 1915 - Jun. 30, 1948
RAYMOND ANDREWS, 1909 - 1942
THOMAS SPEEGLE, Oct. 27, 1877 - Jan. 10, 1878
B. A. SPEEGLE, Apr. 8, 1891 - Feb. 1, 1924
OZRO SPEEGLE, Aug. 28, 1888 - Dec. 5, 1907

## Robert Guttery Cemetery, Cont'd.

FRANCES SPEEGLE, 1858 - 1947
JOHN DAVID SPEEGLE, Mar. 31, 1857 - Jan. 23, 1929
WALTER A. SPEEGLE, Jun. 29, 1886 - Oct. 6, 1888
JOHN GARSON WILEY, Aug. 16, 1915 - Jul. 2, 1916
EDITH McLAIN, 1908 - 1908
Four infants by the name of ANDREWS, no dates or further data.

## Manasco Family Plot - on old home place still in the family near Townley, Alabama.

VICY (ODUM) MANASCO, born Jun. 20, 1780, d. Feb. 15, 1872
LT. JEREMIAH MANASCO, M.D., b. Jan. 16, 1832, wounded in the battle of Shiloh, April 6, died May 4, 1862.
GENERAL JOHN MANASCO, b. Mar. 28, 1800, died Nov. 23, 1895
LUCINDA, wife of GEN. JOHN MANASCO, May 2, 1809 - Dec. 11, 1892
DR. JOHN MANASCO, Feb. 9, 1852 - Apr. 16, 1923
SARAH J., wife of DR. JOHN MANASCO, Feb. 20, 1865 -Jun. 15, 1917
DR. ORIZABEE MANASCO, Jan. 28, 1882 - Apr. 9, 1919
BODINE MANASCO, 1880 - 1939
SARAH COX, dau. of GEN. JOHN MANASCO, b. Mar. 30, 1839 - d. Jun. 2, 1884
REV. DAVID MANASCO, a son of GEN. JOHN MANASCO, b. Apr. 4, 1834, d. May 17, 1884
ELIZABETH, wife of REV. DAVID MANASCO, b. Feb. 22, 1835, d. Jun. 14, 1915
F. C. MANASCO, Mar. 10, 1871 - Jan. 22, 1943
FRED MANASCO, Apr. 8,1873 - Oct. 20, 1896
ALICE MANASCO, Nov. 28, 1871 - Jul. 25, 1896
Baby ALICE, dau. of FRED and ALICE MANASCO, Jul. 14, 1896 - Jan.14, 1908
ARSINAE MANASCO STEADMAN, Oct. 25, 1862 - Mar. 17, 1939 (dau. of REV. DAVID MANASCO)
JOHN C. MANASCO, Feb. 18, 1864 - May 21, 1933
LUCILLE MANASCO, Sep. 16, 1903 - Jan. 22, 1935
J. K. P. MANASCO, son of GEN. JOHN MANASCO, Feb. 27,1845 - Jun. 7, 1923
MARTHA A., wifw of J.K.P. MANASCO, Sep. 25, 1852 - Jan. 19,1907
WILLIAM OSCAR MANASCO, 1886 - 1941
CORA V. MANASCO, dau. of J.K.P. MANASCO, Aug. 5, 1884 - Jul. 21 1895
SARAH, dau. of DR. and MRS. O. MANASCO, Apr. 26, 1918 - Jul. 1, 1921
DORTHIA, dau. of DR. JOHN and ISIE MANASCO, Jul. 5, 1920 - Jul. 4, 1921
MARTHA BOSHELL, wife of WALTER INMAN, Jan. 28, 1887 - June 26, 1916
GEORGE G.BAGWELL, Ala. Sgt. I.C.L. Med. Department,died June 8, 1939
IKE MANASCO, a slave of GEN. JOHN MANASCO
LYDIA MANASCO, a slavs of GEN. JOHN MANASCO

Guttery Gemetery - Two miles West of Townley, Alabama - Walker County

JOHN GUTTERY, b. Aug. 30, 1822, died Jan. 20, 1883
MARTHA E. GUTTERY, Jul. 24, 1866 - Aug. 14, 1876
CAROLINE GUTHRIE, Dec. 12, 1832 - May 9, 1910
W. B. GUTHRIE, 1891 - 1922
L. EARNEST GUTHRIE, Feb. 12, 1900 - Dec. 3, 1940
J. N. GUTHRIE, Feb. 12, 1884 - Jun. 29, 1948
TRACEY GUTTERY, Dec. 2, 1880 - Mar. 14, 1888
M. E. GUTHRIE, Nov. 20, 1867 - Oct. 19, 1930
ABRAHAM GUTTERY, d. Jul. 25, 1866, no other dates
H. F. GUTTERY, Dec. 16, 1894, no further date
GENE HAMILTON GUTTERY, Apr. 7, 1922, Feb. 1, 1923
ANDREW J. GUTTERY, Jul. 7, 1840 - Sep. 6, 1925
MARY J. GUTHRIE, 1862 - 1944
W, M.GUTHREY, Jun. 29, 1832 - Jun. 28, 1902- Co. L. 1st Ala. Cavalry
MAY GUTHREY, Feb. 15, 1849 - Dec. 15, 1893
J. A. GUTTERY, Nov. 8,1887 - Jul. 30, 1892
A.E. GUTHRIE, Feb. 16, 1872 - Jul. 4, 1894
BESSIE GUTHRIE, 1917 - 1953
ELZO GUTHRIE, 1921 - 1955
LOLA R. GUTHRIE, Jul. 20, 1874 - Apr. 29, 1937
JOHN W. GUTHRIE, Oct. 4, 1873 - Feb. 21, 1949
CARRIE MAE GUTHRIE, Oct. 31,1898, no further date
MALINDA E. GUTHRIE, Nov. 6, 1949, no further dats
LUE, dau. of G. W. and V. E. GUTTERY, Sep. 24, 1892 - Sep. 1894
LETTA GUTTERY, Aug. 14, 1896 - d. 1896
ROXIE GUTHRIE, 1892 - no further dates
WALTER GUTHRIE, 1882 - 1946
MARY GUTHRIE, Feb. 2, 1928- no other dates
ANNIE MAE, Jul. 24, 1916 - Feb. 1926
C. L. GUTTERY, no dates
ROBERT J. GUTTERY, 1857 - 1936
DELIA GUTHRIE, Apr. 19, 1876 - May 9, 1854
T. J. GUTHRIE, May 20, 1872 - Apr. 28, 1946
J. G. GUTTERY, May 10,1936 - Feb. 19, 1885
MARY J. GUTTERY, Feb. 7, 1848 - Oct. 8, 1895

**Note the difference in the spelling of the name GUTTERY - GUTHRIE - GUTHREY, ROBERT J. GUTTERY'S son J. N. GUTHRIE, are both listed here and spelled two ways. This has been the rule it seems, rather than the exception, for this family to use the various spellings down through the history of the family from Elbert Co. Ga. to Alabama. (Mrs. Biggerstaff)

REUBEN KEETON, Apr. 25,1832, Jan. 24, 1911
RUBY KEETON, 1914 - 1950
THOMAS KEETON, no dates

Guttery Cemetery, Cont'd.

ZOLA N. SMITH, Apr. 4, 1895 - Aug. 9, 1852
MALINDA SMITH, May 7, 1871 - Dec. 9, 1929
PLUMMER BURKETT, May 21, 1905 - Nov. 18, 1907
THOMAS NESMITH, Nov. 7, 1868 - Feb. 3, 1909
J. A. WILLIAMS, Jan. 6, 1852 - Feb. 18, 1914
MARY E. WILLIAMS, Jun. 10, 1852 - Aug. 18, 1900
CLARA ESTELL HARPER, Mar. 24, 1912 - Apr. 9, 1912
FANNIE BEVIL, Sep. 25, 1868 - Mar. 22, 1908
EARL BEVIL, 1902 - 1922
CLABORN BEVIL, 1914 - 1914
LORANGE BURKETT, Feb. 25, 1905 - Sep. 11, 1908
JESSE WILLARD BEVIL, 1916 - 1916
MARY LOU SMITH, Apr. 8, 1880 - Jun. 27, 1948
JAMES H. LAKEY, 1882 - 1940
ARTIE LAKEY, 1887 - 1926
AUSTIN WALLACE, Ala. Seaman, 2nd Class U.S.N. d. Dec. 13, 1938
THOMAS M. GRACE, 1877 - 1951
SILAS N. ROMINE, Aug. 6, 1905 - Nov. 6, 1939
HENRY ELLIS EDGIL, Mar. 30, 1929 - Apr. 8, 1930
REV. VESTER BURKETT, 1900 - 1954
STACHA CONNER, Mar. 29, 1879 - Feb. 9, 1915
MINNIE L. COONER, Oct. 29, 1899 - Aug. 8, 1901
GREENVILLE COONER, Oct. 20, 1861 - Jul. 17, 1946
JOHN W. COONER, Nov. 28, 1851 - Apr. 2, 1904
B. F. BURKETT, Feb. 11, 1842 - Oct. 18, 1914
MELROSE BURKETT, 1905 - 1926
W. H. BURKETT, Oct. 25, 1840 - Jan. 30, 1897
MARY BURKETT, Feb. 12, 1841 - Aug. 26, 1915
B. FRANK BURKETT, Apr. 15, 1876 - Jun. 29, 1948
WILLIAM G. BURKETT, Feb. 22, 1876 - Jun. 9, 1933
JOHN MATHIS, Jun. 8, 1827 - May 10, 1907
CORDELIA LOCKHART, Mar. 21, 1850 - May 29, 1929
MARY SUSAN GRIFFIN, May 14, 1880 - Feb. 17, 1911
FANNIE GRIFFIN, Feb. 16, 1883 - Mar. 1, 1899
DONNIE MESSER, Jul. 9, 1887 - Mar. 22, 1919
MELOUNIE MORRELL GRAY, b. 1928, no death date
ERNEST ATKINS, 1928 - 1950
JOHN WESLEY WAKEFIELD, Feb. 28, 1844 - Nov. 26, 1888
MALISSA WAKEFIELD, Feb. 14, 1845 - Jan. 12, 1923
FLETCHER ROSE, Sep. 25, 1897 - Dec. 3, 1932
JOHN W. WAKEFIELD, Feb. 22, 1881, Mar. 9,1900
M. C. WAKEFIELD, Jan. 19, 1849 - Dec. 18, 1904
MARY E. WAKEFIELD, Jan. 3, 1850 - Aug. 21, 1917
AMELIA ATKINS, Mar. 25, 1873 - Aug. 11, 1937
JOSEPH ATKINS, Jun. 13, 1866 - Apr. 8, 1955
DOLPHUS PHILLIPS, May 29, 1902 - no other dates
W. B. SWINDLE, 1880 - 1934
REV. T. P. SWINDLE, Oct. 1853 - Jan. 2, 1923

Guttery Cemetery, Cont'd.

G. A. SWINDLE, Nov. 12, 1852 - Feb. 25, 1917
LULA BURKETT, Dec. 30, 1880 - Mar. 19, 1920
HENRYETTA SHEDD, Dec. 28, 1856 - Nov. 21, 1916
SARAH HAZELTINE GANN, Dec. 1, 1858 - Feb. 27, 1929
M. SUSAN PIKE, 1886 - 1946
JOHN C. PIKE, 1870 - 1953
MARTHA M. PIKE, 1873 - 1904
W. A. GANN, Feb. 1, 1864 - May 19, 1908
MODENA WOODS, Jan. 12, 1885 - Jan. 1933
ARROSA BOSHELL, Mar. 29, 1876 - Dec. 23, 1914
LUCINDA KATHERINE BOSHELL, Feb. 28, 1884 - Dec. 27, 1909
MARTHA E. BOSHELL, Sep. 28, 1880 - Aug. 24, 1902
SAMANTHA BOSHELL, Dec. 30, 1890 - Jul. 4, 1891
JOHN N. BOSHELL, Jan. 6, 1855 - Feb. 4, 1891
SARAH A. BOSHELL, 1858 - 1942
J. A. WILLIAMS, Jan. 6, 1852 - Feb. 18, 1914
MARY E. WILLIAMS, Jun. 1855 - Aug. 18, 1900
MINNIE A. WILLIAMS, Feb. 7, 1884 - Sep. 1896
SARAH J. WILLIAMS, Nov. 30, 1887 - Dec. 15, 1927
SARAH G. THOMAS, Aug. 28, 1943 - Nov. 23, 1887
JAMES M. THOMAS, Jan. 16, 1845 - Dec. 1, 1925
SARAH P. KEETON, Jul. 14, 1824 - Jun. 5, 1901
HENRY N. THOMAS, Jun. 1, 1893 - Dec. 29, 1905
WILLIAM H. STACKS, Sep. 10, 1814 - Dec. 4, 1887
MARTHA STACKS, Nov. 25, 1821 - Jul. 20, 1889
L. A. GANN, 1887 - 1888
R. S. GANN, 1897 - 1898
R. B. SWINDLE, 1855 - 1888
MAUDE ELLEN TITTLE, Apr. 10, 1898 - Feb. 19, 1947
JOHN A. SWINDLE, Nov. 20, 1882 - Feb. 11, 1948
MARY BEATRICE BOSHELL, Jun. 1, 1920 - Mar. 6, 1949
FANNIE PIKE, 1885 - 1952
EMLEY PIKE, May 10, 1847 - May 4, 1912
P. C. PIKE, 1847 - 1929
IDA PIKE, 1877 - 1910
EMMA NELSON, d. 1955
SARAH NELSON, Oct. 14, 1855 - Apr. 29, 1930
HENRY H. NELSON, Pvt. 166 Ark Infantry, Jul. 13, 1933
THOMAS H. NELSON, Jun. 15, 1870 - Aug. 9, 1898
CHARLEY G. NELSON, Aug. 17, 1879 - Jan. 29, 1897
ELLIS B. SPRINGFIELD, d. Jul. 16, 1956, age 71 yrs 4mos 25das.
Infant son of J. ROE DUTTON, 1885 - no other dates
NANCY M. SWINDLE, Oct. 19, 1829 - 1905
H. W. SIDES, Nov. 4, 1820 - Aug. 6, 1892
ANNIE MAE SWINDLE, Oct. 22, 1875 - Apr. 1, 1902
THOMAS E. SWINDLE, Jun. 24, 1873 - Oct. 23, 1908
ICIE HALL, May 29, 1893 - Mar. 30, 1915

Guttery Cemetery, Cont'd.

O. R. SHEDD, 1866 - 1948
LUCINDA GRIFFIN, 1935 - 1936
ICIE GRIFFIN, 1935 - 1936
SHELTON GANN, Apr. 14, 1917 - Mar. 1, 1920

Samaria Church Cemetery - Two Miles East of Jasper - Walker County

RICHARD M. FILES, Jan. 10, 1844 - Nov. 28, 1918
MARGARET B. FILES, May 17, 1854 - Sep. 17, 1939
ABNER FILES, Jul. 12, 1842 - Jun. 6, 1904
ANGELINE STANLEY, Sep. 6, 1846 - Mar. 26, 1926
R. FILES, SR., Sep. 27, 1804 - Nov. 2, 1891
MARY FILES - Apr. 8, 1810 - Nov. 11, 1890
MARY FILES - Aug. 18, 1879 - Aug. 7, 1896
THOMAS L. FILES - May 11, 1883 - Oct. 21, 1918
S. J. BAIOCCHI, Sep. 5, 1880 - Oct. 25, 1922
I. P. BOSHELL, May 27, 1853 - Jan. 24, 1924
B. F. BOSHELL, Jan. 16, 1851 - Jul. 18, 1890
J. M. KITCHENS, May 13, 1830 - Dec. 11, 1896
MARY D. KITCHENS, May 3, 1835 - Nov. 6, 1921
JOHN M. KITCHENS, Aug. 6, 1871 - Aug. 12, 1872
MARTHA M. GARNER, Dec. 10, 1828 - Aug. 12, 1918
DAVID JOSEPH FILES, May 9, 1840 - Oct. 19, 1897
MARY BARTON, Oct. 14, 1845 - Oct. 29, 1895
T. J. SHERER, Co. K. Ala. (4th) Cavalry, C.S.A. Dec. 11, 1846
Dec. 26, 1931
NANCY ROBINSON, Nov. 28, 1813 - Mar. 31, 1889 (wife of ANDREW EGGER ROBINSON who is buried in the Old Cemetery at Jasper. She was the dau. of JAMES MEEK of York Co. S.C.)
PAMELA KIRKPATRICK, wife of W. E. KIRKPATRICK, May 3, 1828, Mar. 22, 1892.

Cemetery at Pleasant Hill Methodist Church - West of Townley, Alabama

A. J. MANASCO, 1868 - 1917
CORDELIA MANASCO, 1870 - 1942
G. H. MANASCO, 1875 - 1932
JERRY MANASCO, Sep. 6, 1846 - Jun. 30, 1917
SHERMAN CRAWFORD, Apr. 20, 1868 - Feb. 20, 1942
EDWARD THOMAS CRAWFORD, Jan. 6 1896 - Dec. 2, 1939
JOHN KING, SR., Jul. 24, 1836 Apr. 11, 1899
LUCINDA KING, Sep. 17, 1829 - Nov. 9, 1909
M. D. KING, Jan. 26, 1854 - Jan. 8, 1925
ROXINA KING, May 5, 1867 - Mar. 7, 1941
EDWARD W. KING, 1876 - 1945
SALLIE KING CUNNINGHAM, 1873 - 1947
IRA N. CUNNINGHAM, 1874 - 1941

Cemetery at Pleasant Hill Methodist Church Cont'd.

R. P. KEY, 1859 - 1949
MARY A. KEY, 1861 - 1946
J. N. NELSON, Jun. 22, 1818 - May 20, 1890 - age 77 yrs 10 mos 28 das.
CATHERINE NELSON, Dec. 24, 1827 - Nov. 11, 1891
M. J., wife of H. C. TOWNLEY, Sep. 8, 1878 - Aug. 20, 1932, age 53 yrs. 11 mos. and 11 das.
JOHN F. FIKE, Aug. 5, 1848 - Jul. 4, 1917
CAROLINE, wife of JOHN FIKE, Sep. 3, 1847 - Mar. 28, 1918
R. L. FIKE, 1874 - 1939
PALLIE, wife of R. L. FIKE, 1870 - 1946
J. L. WRIGHT, Oct. 14, 1841 - Aug. 3, 1924
MARTHA C. WRIGHT, wife of J. L. WRIGHT, Nov. 8, 1852 - Nov. 5, 1894, age 42 years, 11 mos. 27 das.
MARY J., wife of J. L. WRIGHT, b. Jan. 9, 1847 - d. Aug. 27, 1880, age 33 yrs. 7 mos. 18 das.
M. CATHERINE INMAN, Apr. 2, 1839 - Nov. 2, 1914
JOHN W. INMAN, 1891 - 1940
IDA L., dau. of W. A. & L. INMAN, Nov. 19, 1895 - Sep. 14, 1917
D. M. INMAN, Aug. 10, 1886 - Mar. 2, 1920
WILLIAM A. INMAN, 1862, no other dates
LUXORA M. INMAN, 1864 - 1941
WALTER C. INMAN, 1884 - 1945
J. B. MONFROY, 1854 - 1933
RONALD GUTHRIE, Nov. 24, 1921 - Sep. 10, 1942
ALICE C. GUTHRIE, Jun. 27, 1879 - May 19, 1946
"SUGAR DOLL" DELLA FAY HENDON, Sep. 2, 1937 - Jul. 22, 1955
JOSEPH ALLEN KNIGHT, Mar. 16, 1861 - Mar. 28, 1899, age 38 yrs. 12 das.
J. H. MEYERS, May 20, 1845 - May 9, 1921
M. C. MEYERS, Mar. 11, 1845 - Jul. 6, 1920
C. H. WOOD, Dec. 13, 1849 - Feb. 2, 1930
ZILLIE, wife of C. H. WOOD, Dec. 10, 1851 - Jun. 16, 1923
DAVID A. KEETON, Jul. 3, 1868 - Aug. 7, 1955
C. A. WOOD, Jun. 19, 1855 - Feb. 23, 1939
PHEBA CRANFORD, Sep. 18, 1861 - Aug. 5, 1934
E. T. WOOD, Jul. 20, 1817 - Aug. 29, 1884
TIM O'REAR, Sep. 2, 1876 - Sep. 18, 1892
J. W. MANN, 1855 - May 22, 1918
W. C. MANN, May 20, 1876 - May 11, 1920
BEN P. FIKE, Oct. 4, 1858 - Jul. 19, 1887
FANNIE FIKE BEVILL, Feb. 27, 1889 - Sep. 23, 1952
J. J. ODOM (ODEM) Feb. 4, 1858 - Mar. 5, 1920
ELIZABETH, wife of JAKE ODOM, Jan. 6, 1819, Nov. 22, 1905
BERTHENIE ODOM, 1857 - 1943
J. S. GURGANUS, 1848 - Apr. 1, 1913
W. R. DUTTON, May 11, 1872 - Jan. 3, 1947
TALITHA WRIGHT, wife of S. W. WRIGHT, Jun. 18, 1821 - Aug. 1903

Cemetery at Pleasant Hill Methodist Church Cont'd.

GEORGE M. WILSON, 1870 - 1940
ODESSA C. WILSON, 1875 - 1951
JOHN KEY, Mar. 13, 1836 - May 29, 1900
A, F. KEY, wife of JOHN KEY, Apr. 5, 1856 - Apr. 8, 1935
WILLIAM M. FERGUSON, Dec. 9, 1874 - Jul. 1, 1896
WALTER H. FERGUSON, 1879 - 1923
REUBEN M. SWINDLE, Jan. 12, 1849 - Feb. 15, 1900
SARAH JANE SWINDLE, Jul. 1, 1854 - Mar. 20, 1945
RUFUS D. KING, 1851 - 1891
MALINDA C., wife of RUFUS D. KING, 1853 - 1942
HORACE W. KING, Dec. 4, 1880 - May 13, 1953
MARTHA L. PRUDEN, May 18, 1878 - Oct. 25, 1910
JAMES L. KING, 1861 - 1937
MARY E. KING, 1877 - 1948
W. R. KING, Mar. 6, 1856 - Oct. 3, 1914
C. H. KING, Dec. 9, 1865 - Dec. 25, 1920
JAMES C. CUNNINGHAM, Nov. 7, 1847 - Feb. 27, 1906
NANCY KNIGHT, wife of JAMES C. CUNNINGHAM, Oct. 11, 1851 - Sep. 26, 1928
JAMES L. BEATY, Nov. 11, 1843 - Aug. 13, 1916
ELIZA A., wife of JAMES L. BEATY, Jun. 6, 1843 - May 23, 1903
ELIZABETH, wife of J. L. BEATY, Apr. 30, 1847 - Sep. 19, 1925
GEORGE O. GILL, 1881 - 1938
BETTIE CUNNINGHAM GILL, 1878 - 1943
MARGARET T. CROWNOVER, 1842 - 1921
W. GEORGE MYERS, 1864 - 1947
ELIZA L. MYERS, 1866 - 1943
JOHN SAM BOSHELL, Nov. 23,1877 - Jul. 22, 1949
FANNIE B. MELCHER, Nov. 13, 1881 - Aug. 17, 1947
JOE T. MELCHER, Sep. 6, 1872 - Aug. 18, 1949
ANDREW J. BAILEY, Dec. 16, 1872 - Jan. 7, 1949
FANNIE INMAN, wife of ANDREW J. BAILEY, Jul. 31, 1874 - Jan. 26, 1940
GEORGE C.BAKER - 1867 - no other dates
MARANDA P. BAKER, 1867 - 1934
JOHN W. REID, Feb. 11, 1871 - Jul. 27, 1940
TIMA INMAN REID, wife of JOHN W. REID, Jan. 17,1879 - Jul. 29, 1925
L. W. WRIGHT,SR., Jul. 18, 1870 - Aug. 29, 1944
ADOLPHUA WRIGHT, Sep. 7, 1873 - Jan. 13, 1951
EDWARD L. DOUGLAS, Nov. 1, 1864 - Sep. 21, 1949
JOHN B. BEATY, Mar. 11, 1880 - Nov. 15, 1950

New Hope Methodist Church Cemetery - One and a half miles East of Holly Grove

AUGUSTINE WILLIAMS, Jan. 12, 1812 - Feb. 6, 1863
MARTHA WILLIAMS, May 15, 1804 - Aug. 6, 1852
SALINA CLARK, Mar. 16, 1824 - Jun. 12, 1891

## Fike Cemetery - N.W. Pleasant Hill Church - Walker County

ISAAC NELSON, Pvt. Cowens Co. Tenn. Militia, War of 1812, died 1875
ANDREW NELSON, Aug. 8, 1829 - Apr. 6, 1915
SARAH NELSON, Feb. 1826 - May 28, 1900
CARMILIA (?) NELSON, Sep. 25, 1878 - Nov. 18, 1878
MARTHA FIKE, wife of WM. R. FIKE, dau. of RICHMOND TOWNLEY, all dates gone
WM. NESMITH, Mar. 19, 1808 - d. age 61 yrs, 28 das.

## Dutton Cemetery - Four Miles West of Jasper

L. TILLMAN DUTTON, Aug. 27, 1874 - Apr. 5, 1955
W. W. ELLIS, Oct. 14, 1861 - Aug. 12, 1932
M.F. ELLIS, 1864 - 1956
JAMES T. CARMICHAEL, Co. L. 28th Ala. Inf. C.S.A. Jan. 4, 1849 - Jan. 10, 1934
NANCY J., wife of J. T. CARMICHAEL, Mar. 15, 1848 - Apr. 15, 1916
THOMAS T. DUTTON, Feb. 14, 1849 - May 24, 1917
JACK D. BURTON, 1876 - 1952
J. SAM BURTON, May 5, 1876 - Apr. 5, 1934
THOMAS A. BURTON, 1925 - 1944
JACK S. BURTON, Jun. 29, 1925 - Nov. 10, 1945
ETTA BURTON, Jun. 1, 1870 - Dec. 31, 1932
JOHN BURTON, 1800 - Aug. 12, 1888
JANE BURTON, Sep. 8, 1800 - Mar. 4, 1904
GLENN V. BURTON, Ala. Pvt. 271 Inf. 69 Div. World War II, Feb. 24, 1926 - Feb. 19, 1945
CLEMMIE BURTON, 1897 - 1953
ROBERT S. BURTON, 1890 - 1953
GERTRUDE BURTON, May 4, 1905 - Apr. 3, 1935
JOHN W. SANDLIN, Jun. 28, 1863 - Sep. 8, 1932
LULA E. SANDLIN, Nov. 9, 1873 - May 1, 1952
NANCY CHILDERS, Jul. 1820 - Mar. 1, 1900
SAMUEL JACKSON, Jul. 25, 1831 - Sep. 18, 1879
JOHN RUSSELL, Aug. 2, 1848 - Jul. 11, 1901
MARTHA ANN RUSSELL, Apr. 20, 1857 - Jan. 31, 1930
C. C. STOCKS, Feb. 14, 1851 - Mar. 12, 1893
THOMAS ENSOR, Jul. 27, 1861 - Nov. 26, 1934
SUSAN, wife of WM. ERWIN, Nov. 8, 1823 - Mar. 31, 1894
JAS. A. LOLLAR, Sep. 27, 1840 - Oct. 3, 1914
ADELIA LOLLAR, Mar. 21, 1872 - Oct. 15, 1917
LETTICE LOLLAR, Oct. 22, 1883 - Dec. 5, 1942
ROBERT C. LOLLAR, Dec. 24, 1876 - Jul. 11, 1954
T. C. WHITWORTH, Apr. 3, 1833 - Feb. 21, 1909
BEADIE L, wife of T. C. WHITWORTH, Aug. 23, 1861 - Mar. 5, 1915

Dutton Cemetery, Cont'd.

WM. DUTTON, May 1, 1838 - May 29, 1912
MARIA DUTTON, wifw of WM. DUTTON, Nov. 23, 1839 - Nov. 14, 1900
REUBEN DUTTON, May 20, 1861 - Jul. 1, 1889
JANE ROBINSON, 1828 - 1916
MARGARETTE R. KILGORE, 1826 - 1903
ROBERT V. KILGORE, 1866- 1946
LOUANNER KILGORE, 1872 - 1906
SARAH C. HAMILTON, wife of A. J. HAMILTON, Dec. 16, 1837 - Nov. 3, 1917
A. J. HAMILTON, Feb. 24, 1839 - Jun. 15, 1902
CONN D. HARRIS, Aug. 11, 1854 - Jan. 4, 1937
CLYDE H. SHERER, Aug. 19, 1878 - Feb. 27, 1942
JAMES R. STOCKS, Nov. 29, 1889 - Jun. 26, 1953
BEN R. BEST, Nov. 20, 1868 - Mar. 6, 1947
JOHN T. CHILDERS, Sep. 1, 1854 - Mar. 15, 1900
CORA BURTON, 1902 - 1955
J. L. CARMICHAEL, Nov. 7, 1815 - Feb. 10, 1877 (son of J. A. CARMICHAEL)
BUD FLEMING, Dec. 26, 1846 - Oct. 22, 1911
LOUISA E., wife of J. T. DUTTON, Jul. 31, 1852 - Dec. 21, 1888
C. A. WHEELER, Jan. 2, 1851 - Apr. 20, 1937. Evangelist Church of Christ for 63 yrs. Baptised 6000 souls and established about 100 congregations. His influence abodes with us while his spirit is at rest.
MRS. ADELINE, wife of ELD. C. A. WHEELER, departed this life Nov.18, 1924, age 79 yrs.
J. T. BATCHELOR, Sep. 14, 1860 - Aug. 11, 1913 age 52 yrs. 10 mos. 27 das.
MINNIE, dau. of J. T. & O. L. BATCHELOR, May 10, 1891 - Mar. 11, 1913
In Memory of SAMUEL JACKSON: He was born Jul. 25, 1831 - d. Sep. 18, 1879
ELIZABETH JACKSON, May 24, 1835 - Nov. 12, 1918
SAMUEL W. JACKSON, 1861 - 1944
COLUMBUS STOCKS, Jul. 24, 1898 - 1904

Primitive Baptist Church - Mt. Zion on the Nauvoo Road:

SARAH WILSON, 1797 - Aug. 14, 1882
LEWIS WILSON, 1800 - Apr. 13, 1890
MARY A. WILSON, Mar. 18, 1800 - Jul. 15, 1890
JAMES W. WILSON, Aug. 26, 1797 - May 15, 1890
JEFFERSON DAVIS MYERS, Jul. 7, 1861 - Dec. 4, 1881
VICTOR MYERS, Dec. 23, 1868 - Oct. 25, 1888
R. J. (RUSSELL) MYERS, Sep. 15, 1834 - Apr. 27, 1899
SARAH P. MYERS, b.........d. Apr. 10, 1909

Primitive Baptist Church, Cont'd.

A. L. MYERS, Feb. 29, 1868 - Apr. 27, 1928
MART MYERS, 1871 - 1938
MARY J. MYERS, 1872 - no death date
R. V. WILLIAMS, 1862 - 1921
HENRY SIDES, Jan. 9, 1779 - Jun. 16, 1867
SUSAN SIDES, Jan. 6, 1789 - Sep. 26, 1864
SAVANNAH WILLIAMS, b........, d. Dec. 1886
ROBERT C. WILLIAMS, Apr. 11, 1877 - Jun. 8, 1887

Inactive Cemetery - West of Hillard, Ala.
One Mile back in the woods.

R. P. TOWNLEY, Sep. 18, .......... all dates gone
RUBY TOWNLEY, ...................... " " "
MARY, TOWNLEY, d. Sep, 1858
D. W. TOWNLEY, 1818 - 1856
D. TOWNLEY, 1782 - 1848 (this is DANIEL TOWNLEY who married HANNAH GUTTERY, widow of WILLIAM GUTTERY who died 1825)
ELIZABETH TOWNLEY, Dec. 9, 1793, d. 1835

Old City Cemetery (Inactive), Jasper, Ala.

AMANDA KILGORE, Jan. 1763 - Aug. 1830
WILEY KILGORE, Sep. 12, 1824 - May 12, 1864
A. E. ROBINSON, Feb. 22, 1817 - Nov, 25, 1887 (this is ANDREW EGGER ROBINSON who married NANCY MEEK in York Co. S.C.)
WM. STOVALL, b. S.C. Dec. 11,1797 - Dec. 10, 1852
WM. SHERER, b. S.C. Nov. 19, 1790 - d. Dec. 30, 1865 (father of seven sons who came to Walker Co. and all entered land here. Names of sons on his marker: JAMES G.; ELISHA; JOHN T.; ABSALOM; MADISON; JEFFERSON NEELY; WM. MINTER SHERER)
Wife of WILLIAM SHERER, died Jan. 20, 1865, age 39 yrs.
Wife of WILLIAM SHERER, Died Apr. 20, 1858, age 30 yrs.
B. F. SHERER, son of W. M. & S. E. SHERER, died Sep. 18, 1877, age 11 yrs.
W. P. O'REAR, inf. son of J.H.&M.A. O'REAR, no dates
W. L. SUTTON, inf. son of W. R. & N. J.SUTTON, no dates
THOMAS E. CAMAK, son of W. H. & F. E. CAMAK, born 1861
ELIZABETH JACKSON GILBERT, 1835 - 1862
ALEX S. GILBERT, inf.son of L. E. & E. F.GILBERT, d. Mar. 22, 1859
LILLY BROWN, Oct. 5, 1873 - Dec. 4, 1886
S. E. F.SHERER, d. Oct. 8, 1867, age 24 yrs.
W. L. SHERER, d. May 11, 1868, age 20 yrs.
A. L. B. SHERER, d. Feb. 12, 1873, age 18 yrs.
RAINEY, wife of BASALOM SHERER, May 22, 1827 - Aug. 19, 1880
LITTLE CORA, dau. of A. & S. SHERER, d. Jan. 27, 1885
MARY L., dau. of S. G. & S. C. SHERER, Mar. 10, 1881 - Jun. 11, 1883

Old City Cemetery, Cont'd.

FRANKLIN ASBURY GAMBLE, Sep. 23, 1830 - Oct.5, 1895
VIRGINIA GAMBLE, dau. of FRANKLIN ASBURY GAMBLE, Oct. 28, 1858 - May 21, 1881
IDA H. GAMBLE, Oct. 30, 1860 - Nov. 25, 1883
DOLLY W. GAMBLE, Jan. 15, 1883 - Nov. 27, 1883
JOHN FAUST GAMBLE, Nov. 6, 1884 - May 25, 1886
MARY GAMBLE, Sep. 15, 1886 - Dec. 27, 1887
MRS. JOHN B. RICHARDSON, all dates gone
LOUISA CATHERINE STEPHENSON, relict of JOHN E. STEPHENSON, Sep. 16, 1831 - Jul. 31, 1872
J. E. RICHARDSON, wife of.......(name gone) 1855 - 1877
JAMES CRANFORD, Nov. 12, 1819 - Aug. 20, 1872
RICHARD APPLING, Apr. 13, 1816 - Mar. 15, 1888
MATTIE E., dau. of E. K. DODSON, Feb. 25, 1870 - May 25, 1883
JAMES O. BURCHFIELD, son of M. D. & A. R. BURCHFIELD, Sep. 12, 1878 - Jun. 15, 1881
M. D. BURCHFIELD, Apr. 20, 1839 - Mar. 14, 1886
BENJAMIN TIERCE, Jul. 4, 1842 - Dec. 21, 1864
MERIT E. TIERCE, Jan. 15, 1860 - Apr. 30, 1861
EUGENE E. TIERCE, Nov. 29, 1839 - Dec. 19, 1861
Our Mother: PALLIE, wife of DR. WM. A. BOTELER, Nov. 23, 1875, age 34 yrs.
BENJAMIN D. BOTELER, Sep. 1847 - Oct. 19, 1860
MOSES CAMAK, Jan. 6, 1812 - Jun. 6, 1873
SAMUEL M. GUNTER, Mar. 8,1829 - Oct. 27, 1891
GRIFFIN LAMKIN, Jun. 1, 1781 - Jun. 10, 1856
GROVER LAMKIN, Nov. 13, 1884 - Aug. 28, 1885
ROBERT B. LAMKIN, Jul. 20, 1887 - Aug. 17, 1887
JAMES P. LITTLE, Jun. 20, 1844 - May 22, 1872 - age 27 yrs 11 mos 2 das.
LUCIUS G. FREEMAN, Oct. 9, 1847 - Feb. 16, 1878
FATIMA (consort) of LUCIUS G. FREEMAN, Dec. 2, 1850 - Nov. 3,1876
J. S. NEWTON CAMAK, 1852 - Aug. 13, 1884
NEWT CAMAK, Jan. 22, 1853 - Aug. 13, 1884
GEORGIA, wife of JAMES T. SHERER, Sep. 15, 1855 - death date gone
LOU N., wife of JAMES T. SHERER, Jan. 19, 1866 - Aug. 27, 1882
GENIA LEE, dau. of J. A. & S. M. JOHNSON, Mar. 9, 1888 - Apr. 16, 1888
WILLIE ANN PHIFER CRANFORD, wife of J. H. CRANFORD, all dates gone
SALLIE, wife of JAMES A. JOHNSON, b. 1862, death date gone
Another grave here, name gone, but dates are: b.1836 - d. Sep. 4, 1886
THOMAS SHERER, Nov. 20, 1808 - Sep. 15, 1888
JANE SHERER, Aug. 12, 1811 - Sep. 26, 1888

Old City Cemetery, Cont'd.

.............., wife of ........ SCOTT, Dec. 1, 1850 - Aug. 29, 1881 (names gone)
W. G. ROSAMOND, wife of W. C. ROSAMOND, Nov. 15, 1842 - Oct. 24, 1881
WM. L. STANLEY, Dec. 20, 1816 - Jun. 20, 1883
R. F. STANLEY, Jan. 15, 1831 - Sep. 30, 1851 (REBECCA F. STANLEY)
VIRGINIA STANLEY, Jan. 19, 1861 - Jul. 11, 1862
JOHN B. STANLEY, Mar. 19, 1876 - Mar. 21, 1880
MARY P. STANLEY, May 13, 1855 - Jul. 31, 1879
F. A. MUSGROVE, Jul. 22, 1865 - age 38 yrs.
JERUSHA FREEMAN, wife of F. A. GAMBLE, Nov. 29, 1835 - Mar. 14, 1875
WM. O. GAMBLE, son of F. A. & J. A. GAMBLE, Feb. 20, 1864 - Sep. 1, 1867
SALLIE M. GAMBLE, May 14, 1871 - Apr. 19, 1873
WILLIAM T. FILES, Apr. 30, 1837 - Sep. 9, 1861

Union Chapel Church Cemetery - On Hwy. 78, about six miles East of Jasper.

AMANDY GARDNER, Sep. 26, 1837 - Aug. 27, 1911
J. W. GARDNER, Jan. 4, 1837 - Jun. 11, 1920
SELY HAMBRICK, Jun. 15, 1833 - Jun. 1, 1900
ELIZABETH R., wife of B. J. WILLIAMS, Apr. 5, 1815 - Mar. 1, 1892
ELVIRA E., wife of J. P. STONE, Oct. 23, 1849 - Aug. 7, 1886
O.C. DANIEL, Jan. 2, 1856 - May 20, 1925
NANCY, wife of O. C. DANIEL, 1856 - Apr. 13, 1919
REBECCA FLOR[illegible]A BROWN, wife of E. G. BROWN, Jul. 4, 1860 - May 26, 1930
LOUIS D. SHUBERT, Mar. 10, 1870 - [illegible]. 18, 1954
MILLIE ANN SHUBERT, Jul. 15, 1870 - Mar. 16, 1944
MARY G. ELLIOTT, Oct. 17, 1835 - Jun. 7, 1904
MUTIE HUCHE, Feb. 12, 1873 - Jan. 23, 1940
ANGIE HYCHE, Mar. 27, 1875 - Jan. 13, 1953
DANIEL HICKS, Feb. 18, 1842 - Jan. 14, 1918
O. H. DUNN, Nov. 23, 1832 - Aug. 28, 1933
MRS. MARY BAGGETT GREER, Jul. 6, 1867 - Oct. 10, 1949
JAMES S. AARON, 1874 - 1951
ELIZABETH AARON, 1874 - 1948
WILEY ISAAC CARR, 1886 - 1933
ARVIL W. CARR, 1916 - 1923
W. B. STIVENER, 1876 - 1950
ELBERT S. BLACK, 1867 - 1933
J. E. BURTON, Apr. 17, 1855 - Dec. 29, 1939
LEIU, wife of J. E. BURTON, Feb. 22, 1862 - Aug. 6, 1926
NATHANIEL BARTON, Sep. 9, 1865 - Jan. 17, 1945
FRANCIS E. BARTON, May 11, 1871 - Mar. 27, 1954
MATTIE ELIZABETH, dau. of J. O. & REBECCA RIDINGS, Dec. 1, 1877 - Aug. 16, 1913

Union Chapel Cemetery, Cont'd.

SARAH AKINS, wife of J. G. AKINS, Jan. 7. 1854 - Jan. 1. 1915
J. G. AKINS, Apr. 25, 1832 - Mar. 1, 1922
W. W. HANDLEY, Jan. 15, 1853 - May 30, 1931
REV. J. M. HANDLEY, Aug. 14,1858 - Nov. 28, 1932
CATHERINE HANDLEY, May 2, 1855 - Apr. 20, 1932
JOHN W. HESTER, 1868 - 1951
ARIZONA HESTER, 1875 - 1939
JOHN W. JOHNS, 1865 - 1936
NANCY MILBERY CAMP, 1869 - 1953, wife of JOHN W. JOHNS
NATHAN B. LANGLEY, Jan. 21, 1849, Jan. 20, 1929
ELIZA E., wife of M. B. LANGLEY, Apr. 14, 1851 - Dec. 9, 1934
WILLIAM O'REAR, Jan. 2, 1858 - Dec. 12, 1935
WILLIE O'REAR, Sep. 28, 1875 - Sep. 12, 1928
NEWTON W. DAVIS, 1858 - 1923
MARY J. DAVIS, 1857 - 1923
PEARL BURTON, Jan. 24, 1893 - Jan. 26, 1935
REV. J. J. GURGANUS, Jun. 21, 1862 - Apr. 20,1933
SUSAN V. GURGANUS, Mar. 4,1859 - no death date.
DICIA BLACK, Mar. 12, 1862 - Dec.4, 1934
JAMES SULRAIN, Sep. 13, 1857 - Sep. 16, 1925
LUTHERA ANN SULRAIN, Sep. 25, 1863 - Nov.22, 1931
G. R. SHIRLEY, Aug. 3, 1838 - Jul. 27, 1931
FLORENCE, wife of G. R. SHIRLEY, May 5, 1850 - Jun. 30, 1920
NANCY S. BLACK, Apr. 3, 1856 - Jun. 4, 1904
ALEXANDER BLACK, Mar. 15, 1848 - Apr. 14,1912
TILDA J. RIVERS, wife of W. M. RIVERS, Oct. 11, 1862 - Nov. 23, 1925
WM. MOSES RIVERS, Feb. 14, 1858 - Oct. 22, 1936
J. E. HYCHE, Jun. 6, 1848 - Mar. 31, 1928
W. L. HYCHE, May 6, 1852 - Jun. 12, 1923
J. M. KIRKPATRICK, Feb. 12, 1851 - Mar. 17, 1915
JOHN MARTIN FELKINS, Dec. 24, 1832 - Jul. 21, 1888
SUSAN ANN FELKINS, Jul. 25, 1832 - Dec. 31, 1881
ALCY A. LOVEL, Sep. 23, 1858 - Sep. 9, 1889
JOHN BLACK, Jan. 12, 1818 - Feb. 10, 1896
WM. J. LOVELL, Oct. 5, 1860 - Feb. 26, 1889
ALICE S. LOVELL, Aug. 29. 1857 - Jun. 11, 1905
J. P. HEYWOOD, Mar. 8, 1871 - Mar. 9, 1938
FRANCES BLACK, Aug. 19, 1846 - Jun. 21, 1926
NAT. BLACK, Nov. 27, 1846 - Oct. 7, 1910
MARY JANE BLACK, Jan. 14, 1859 - Aug. 28, 1929

Providence Cemetery - Near Providence Baptist Church Between Parrish and Oakman, Walker County.

SUSAN LOLLAR, Sep. 1811 - Jan. 4, 1874
JOHN A. LOLLAR, Jan. 30, 1810 - May 11, 1888
ERASTUS LOLLAR, Feb. 10, 1870 - Jul. 21, 1903

Providence Cemetery Cont'd.

B. F. LOLLAR, Nov. 24, 1841 - Apr. 5, 1906
JEFFIE J. WATTS, Dec. 2, 1875 - Jul. 5, 1883
REV. J. J. WATTS, Apr. 7, 1822 - Jul. 28, 1876
ADDIE POUNDS, Dec. 29, 1859 - Jun. 13, 1894
M. C. BAKER, wife of D. P. BAKER, Sep. 5, 1848 - Oct. 27, 1887
D. P. BAKER, Feb. 13, 1853 - Sep. 18, 1879
NANCY J. LOLLAR, wife of B. F. LOLLAR, Nov. 24, 1841 - Apr. 5, 1906
DOLLIE COBB, Aug. 23, 1879 - Sep. 26, 1954
WM. COBB, Jul. 29, 1853 - June 1, 1910
GEORGE ANN AUGUST REA, Aug. 16, 1954 - Jan. 18, 1938
J. WATTS REA, Nov. 20, 1853 - Jul. 5, 1930
JACKSON N. BLANTON, Nov. 14, 1878 - Sep. 21, 1902
BEN BLANTON, 1807 - 1904
IRENE BLANTON, 1840 - 1926
ROBERT COURINGTON, Jan. 11, 1854 - Feb. 14, 1949
MONTE COURINGTON, wife of ROBERT COURINGTON, Jul. 9, 1826 - Sep. 21, 1941
DOCK CREEL, Feb. 1, 1860 - Dec. 16, 1886
JINCY, wife of J. H. STEPHENSON, Oct. 11, 1853 - Nov. 2, 1925
M. M. STEPHENSON, May 13, 1853 - Apr. 5, 1935
ADDIE STEPHENSON, Aug. 13, 1857 - Jun. 30, 1937
JESSIE LOGAN, Jul. 22, 1872 - Aug. 5, 1920
L. S. COPELAND, Dec. 22, 1858 - Sep. 19, 1924
MOSES KIRKPATRICK, May 6, 1866 - Feb. 23, 1930
MAHALA KIRKPATRICK, Dec. 17, 1871 - Nov. 28, 1938
MARY WATTS CREEL, Feb. 22, 1837 - Jun. 18, 1914
B. F. CLEMENTS, Oct. 6, 1852 - Jun. 17, 1925
MARY CLEMENTS, Feb. 16, 1857 - Dec. 17, 1943
SAMUEL H. BLANTON, 1866 - 1949
ELIZA BLANTON, 1872 - 1930
MARY E. PHIFER, Sep. 19, 1820 - Dec. 13, 1907
JOHN W. PHIFER, 1854 - 1932
MARTHA PHIFER, 1862 - 1936
JAMES J. PHIFER, Dec. 5, 1861 - Apr. 23, 1926
BATHSHEBA JONES, wife of J. R. JONES, Aug. 6, 1829 - Feb. 10, 1864
J. J. PHIFER, wife of JAMES W. PHIFER, Feb. 3, 1867 - Nov. 17, 1915
DEASON COURINGTON, died Aug. 15, 1878, aged 85 yrs (b. 1793)
JAMES M. CARMICHAEL, 1865 - 1947
RHODA M. CARMICHAEL, 1869 - 1946
SUSIE COURINGTON, Feb. 27, 1802 - Oct. 1889
MARTHA JANE COURINGTON, Feb. 11, 1840 - Dec. 3, 1917
WM. T. SARTAIN, 1801 - 1879
J. W. SARTAIN, 1865 - 1946

Providence Cemetery Cont'd.

JOHN H. ROBINSON, Oct. 28, 1849 - Jan. 19, 1923
SARAH ROBINSON, Mar. 2, 1851 - Nov. 29, 1927
ISAAC BROWN, Mar. 15, 1845 - Apr. 6, 1915
MARTHA LOLLAR BROWN, Mar. 18,1844 - Dec. 19, 1926
JOHN B. SUMNER, 1815 - 1899
EMILY SUMNER, Nov. 23, 1820 - Aug. 23, 1864
WM. R. COURINGTON, Mar. 20, 1858 - Jun. 1, 1933
J. H. THOMPSON, Aug. 8, 1843 - Feb. 4, 1924
MARY E. THOMPSON, Jul. 12, 1848 - Oct. 26, 1922
SAMUEL E. WALTON, Dec. 10, 1853 - Dec. 31, 1907
MARTHA WALTON, May 9, 1859 - May 15, 1907
W. S. WALTON, Apr. 13,1813 - Oct. 22, 1893
H. WALTON, Mar. 18, 1839 - Aug. 10, 1934
ELIZABETH BROWN, Oct. 16, 1817 - Apr. 16, 1890
SAMUEL M. STEPHENSON, Sep. 22, 1825 - Jul. 30, 1861
MARY M. STEPHENSON, Nov. 13, 1833 - Oct. 18, 1865
W. TOM WALTON, 1864 - 1939
MOLLIE WALTON, b. 1869, no death date.
J. T. POE, Jan. 12, 1858 - 1887
W. FRANK BROWN, 1867 - 1940
C. A. BROWN, wife of W. FRANK BROWN, Nov. 16, 1871 - May 20, 1921

Bethel Church Cemetery - Holly Grove, Ala.
Near Townley, Walker County

JOHN GUTHRIE, Apr. 20, 1876 - Aug. 31, 1947
DELLAH FLOYD GUTTERY, May 13, 1872 - Jul. 3, 1873
L. A. GUTHRIE, Nov.18, 1844 - Oct. 19, 1900
A. J. GUTHRIE, May 11, 1837 - Aug. 4,1889
ALICE GUTHRIE, d. Aug. 9, 1896, no birth date
LULA GUTHRIE ADAMS, d. 1948
WM. BAKER ADAMS, d. 1926
DR. VIRGIL M. MILLER, Apr. 26, 1852 - Sep. 17, 1897
LUCIUS G. MILLER, Dec. 19, 1814 - Feb. 12, 1886
MARY JANE, wife of DR. L. G. MILLER, May 1, 1823 - Oct. 2, 1903
MARTHA MILLER, was born ANNO DOMINI, 1784, departed this life, Jan. Anno Domini, 1858, age 74 yrs.
ERASTUS WASHINGTON MILLER, Mar.10, 1843 - Mar. 29, 1919
LILLIAN McKENDRICK, Feb. 15, 1854 - Oct. 28, 1924
JOHN McKENDRICK, Aug. 2, 1855 - Aug. 29, 1939
DAVID ROBY WILLIAMS, Aug. 20, 1875 - Dec. 18, 1875
FRANCIS WILLIAMS, d. Jul. 9, 1874 - age 28 yrs. 9 mos.
WM. J. WILLIAMS, Dec. 15, 1873 - Oct. 9, 1874
W. H. WILLIAMS, b. Jun. 1, 1845, departed this life the 11th day of Mar. 1863. He died a soldier at Columbus, Miss.
SIMPSON D. SMITH, Apr. 12.1845 - Nov. 23, 1870, age 25 yrs. 7 mos. 1 da.

Bethel Church Cemetery Cont'd.

JOHN P. FERGUSON, Oct. 22, 1836 - Apr. 28, 1866, age 29 yrs. 6 mos. 6 das.
JAMES T. FERGUSON, Jul. 16, 1839 - Oct. 17, 1864, age 25 yrs. 3 mos. 1 da.
EDNA TOWNLEY, Jun. 3, 1839 - Jun. 27, 1887
ELIZABETH TOWNLEY, d. May 31, 1861
MICHAEL P. BELL, May 21, 1848 - Feb. 14, 1869, age 20 yrs. 8 mos. 23 das.
LESTER G. BROWN, Aug. 7, 1910 - Oct. 1, 1915
ALBERT M. BARNNER, May 15, 1913 - Jul. 9, 1914
R. GUTTERY, Nov. 15, 1860 - Nov. 9, 1870
W. GUTTERY, Jan. 23, 1873 - Jan. 24, 1873
MARY E. TOWNLEY, dau. of W. C. & NANCY TOWNLEY, May 4, 1891 - Sep. 12, 1896
MARY A. BOSHELL, dau. of A. J. & C. B. BOSHELL, Dec. 1844, Oct. 1865, age 20 yrs. 10 mos. 17 das.
MARY S. WINGTON, 1881 - 1919
LAVINIA CATHERINE CAMAK, no dates
FRED L. CAMAK, b. Jan. 10, 1876
CHAS. MILLER CAMAK, b. Nov.5, 1881
ANNA MAE (CAMAK) FIELDS, no dates.

Pisgah Cemetery at Carbon Hill, Ala. - Walker County

W. B. SIDES, b. Aug. 29, 1832 - d. Mar. 11, 1893
SARAH SIDES, b. Dec. 16, 1835 - d. Jul. 22, 1889, age 53 yrs. 7 mos. 5 das.
FREDERICK E. SIDES, b. Mar. 17,1884 - Feb. 27, 1896
JAMES McDONALD, b. Aug. 27, 1798 -- d. Jan. 16, 1888
NAOMI McDONALD, b. May 19, 1803 - Nov. 18, age 71 yrs (d.1874)
WILLIAM FARMER McDONALD, 1866, no other dates
TIMOTHY BURTON, Aug. 6, 1847 - Nov. 23, 1919
ADALINE BURTON, Apr. 21, 1848 - Apr. 23, 1917
JAMES HOGAN, Aug. 16, 1808 - Jun. 17, 1877
ELIZABETH HOGAN, Feb. 17, 1820 - Dec. 4, 1869
THOMAS KUYKENDALL, Nov. 26, 1871 - Apr. 13, 1934
DORA SAVANNAH KUYKENDALL, Jun. 25, 1879 - Jul. 23, 1947
BEN W. LITTLE, Aug. 12, 1850 - Aug. 28, 1927
EMMA F. LITTLE, Jul. 2, 1853 - Jul. 3, 1927
DR. J. C. R. WEBB, 1836 - 1931
NANCY M. WEBB, 1839 - 1924
CHAS. H. WILLIAMS, 1853 - 1925
RHODA J. WILLIAMS, 1855 - 1918
DR. S. E. MADDOX, May 19, 1872 - Feb. 13, 1936
L. VERDREE WIGGINS, May 3, 1876 - Dec. 24, 1914
CROSBY HOWARD, 1870 - 1934
ETTA HOWARD, 1875 - 1952

Pisgah Cemetery Cont'd.

ALMA CRAWFORD HOWARD, 1826 - 1910
PEARL, wife of O. P. PEARCE, Nov. 15, 1877 - Sep. 30, 1910
MARY FLORENCE O'REAR, Feb. 18, 1877 - Dec. 12, 1939
B. M. O'REAR, May 6, 1866 - Dec. 2, 1909
JAMES THOMAS WAKEFIELD, Apr. 9, 1879 - Feb. 10, 1935
LULA STUBBLEFIELD, May 9, 1887 - Nov. 5, 1934
ALMER, wife of J. F. GUTHRIE, Nov. 12,1884 - Mar. 19, 1912
MR. A. EMBREY, Jul. 19, 1847 - Nov. 29, 1909
RUSSELL AYERS, Nov. 19, 1838 - Jun. 22, 1913
PATRICK HENRY HOUGHTON, b. Madison Co. Ala. Feb. 16, 1831 - d. Jul. 30, 1906
REBECCA, wife of S. D. MOORE, Apr. 12, 1876 - Jun. 23, 1896
J. F. BEARED or BEARD, Oct. 7, 1869 - Feb. 1, 1918
SUSAN KELLY, dau. of BARNABAS KELLY and M. KELLY, Oct. 1856 - 1862
MELVINA WEBB, Jan. 7, 1816 - May 29, 1866
JAMES MONROE WEBB, Jan. 24, 1845 - Sep. 23, 1870
GEORGE W. SHAW, 1873 - 1936
OAKLEY BYNUM FARRIS, May 12, 1845 - Oct. 1869
JANE, wife of WILLIS FARRIS, d. Sep. 10, 1887, agw 70
WILLIS FARRIS, d. Oct. 13, 1888, age 74 yrs.
THOMAS A. VINES, Aug. 28, 1830 - Mar. 4, 1880
P. A. HICKS, Mar. 22, 1849 - Jul. 9, 1933
MARTHA HICKS, Sep. 10, 1856 - Oct. 30, 1902
LOUISA P., wife of J. F.STOVALL, Dec. 19, 1825 - Aug. 23, 1898
J. F. STOVALL, Co. A. 1st Ala, Cav.
P. B. STRICKLAND, 1848 - 1920
MARY E. STRICKLAND, 1850 - 1923
G. R. PEARCE, Jan. 1, 1842 - Jul. 10, 1907
JOHN PIERCE, 1870 - 1918
ELIZABET PIERCE, 1882 - 1910
IRENE McELROY or McELVOY - all dates eroded
LUDIE BALLENGER, 1863 - 1927
J. W. BALLENGER, 1861 - 1939
MOODY FILES, 1861 - 1939
A. DOUGLAS HENDON, Oct. 5, 1903 - Jan. 24, 1954
ROZELLE MURRAY, Nov. 30, 1907 - May 18, 1949

Cemetery Near Musgrove Country Club - Jasper, Ala.

WILLIAM JONES, Feb. 12, 1802 - Jan. 17, 1856
SARAH EVANS, Mar. 15, 1823 - May 3, 1896
JOHN RYAN and wife, no dates
REV. G. W. OWEN, May 12, 1855 - Jan.21, 1927
FRED OWEN, Nov. 20, 1900 - Jul. 25, 1927
MARY C. OWEN, Sep. 14, 1817 - Dec. 25, 1890
C. P. OWEN, d. Apr. 6, 1879, age 72 yrs (A mason)

## Cemetery Near Musgrove Country Club Cont'd.

ELIZABETH, wife of W. H. CAMAK, Jan. 8, 1844 - Jan. 30, 1882
FREDONIA, wife of W. H. CAMAK, Aug. 1, 1853 - Mar. 26, 1891
ALICE CAMAK, wife of JAMES L. CRAIG, Jun. 11, 1859 - Mar. 9, 1887
B. M. SIDES, Sep. 28, 1841 - Sep. 3, 1905
MRS. B. M. SIDES, no dates
J. N. SIDES, Dec. 5, 1855 - Oct. 25, 1900
REBECCA HULSEY, wife of JOHN SNODDY, Apr. 1, 1841 - Dec. 24, 1885
BUCK LAMON, Nov. 25, 1899 - Fwb. 12, 1925
PEARL L., dau. of J. H. and M. L. ELLIOTT, Mar. 13,1881 - d. 1882
Several unmarked graves in this cemetery.

## Cemetery Near Buck Creek Bridge on Nauvoo Highway, Walker County

ELIZABETH FAUGHT, 1809 - 1866
S. W. FAUGHT, 1807 - 1841, son of JOHN and N. M. FAUGHT
MARIAH FAUGHT, Jan. 18, 1835 - Nov. 13, 1889
GEORGE W. FAUGHT, Jan. 30, 1879 - Aug. 24, 1882
JAMES I. FAUGHT, Feb. 17, 1858 - 1889
J. A. FAUGHT, Apr. 5, 1835 - Jan. 20, 1917
WILLIAM G. STAGGS, Co. G 13th Ala. Partisan Rangers, C.S.A.
SARAH, dau. of S. W. and E. FAUGHT, 1830 - 1857
This family plot is about 300 yards East of the highway

## Freewill Baptist Church Cemetery, Pocohontas, Ala.

J. H. ALVIS, 1849 - 1931
M. J. ALVIS, 1856 - 1938
R. S. EDGIL, 1860 - 1944
ALICE EDGIL, Mar. 30, 1879 - Dec. 16, 1938
I. P. GUTHRIE, Jun. 9, 1846 - Oct. 14, 1919
SAVANNAH GUTHRIE, wife of I. P. GUTHRIE, Apr. 24, 1848 - Dec. 4,
MRS. M. J. CRENSHAW, Feb. 26, 1846 - Dec. 19, 1927
L. A. ROBERTS, Jan. 29, 1854 - Dec. 31,1938
A. J. ROBERTS, Mar. 1, 1856 - Oct. 8, 1928
NANCY ANN SANDLIN, Mar. 12, 1846 - Jun. 10, 1902
V. A. DEASON, wife of W. A. DEASON, May 11, 1853 - Jan. 8, 1911
ELYSABETH ALVIS, Sep. 1, 1821 - Feb. 21, 1873
ABNER ALVIS, Dec. 12, 1812 - Feb. 19, 1871
T. C. ALVIS, Mar. 2, 1858 - Feb. 10, 1878
MARTHA L. ALVIS, dau. of F. N. & N. E. ALVIS, Jan. 20, 1866 - Sep. 8, 1874
B. E. ALVIS, Apr. 10, 1885 - Nov. 5, 1905
JAMES A. HAYNE, 1851 - Mar. 10, d. Aug. 9, 1905
MARGARET L., wife of L. GUTTERY, Jul. 30, 1855 - Apr. 11, 1898

Freewill Baptist Church Cemetery Cont'd.

BETTY M. E., wife of J. W. CLARK, Dec. 25, 1875 - Apr. 3, 1907
MRS. E. J. BELL, Dec. 22, 1853 - Aug. 31, 1917
ALONZO GUTHRIE, 1869 - 1920
LOU, wife of ALONZO GUTHRIE, 1872 - 1948
RHODA C. GUTTERY, wife of ISHAM GUTTERY, Jul. 14,1821 - Jun. 20, 1875

Faught Cemetery - Off the Nauvoo Rd. near Staggs Bridge - Farm owned at present by Mrs. Ebb O'Rear

J. H. FAUGHT, who was born Sep. 5, 1805 - d. Apr. 3, 1869, age 63 yrs. 6 mos. and 18 das.
N. A. FAUGHT, Mar. 12, 1876 - Jul. 31, 1888
JOEL R. FAUGHT, 1841 - d. 18th, other dates gone
SALLY M. CHANDLER, Aug. 17, 1840 - Sep. 20, 1914
OSA (or ASA) A. O'REAR, son of W. G. and W. D. O'REAR, b. Mar. 2, 1902 - drowned Jan. 24, 1917

Pleasant Grove Church (organized 1842) Cemetery

JOHN B. THOMAS, Mar. 5, 1855 - Aug. 29, 1915
MARY E. THOMAS, 1863 - 1929
ALABAMA SIDES, wife of ROBERT MYERS, Jan. 26, 1875 - Jun. 2, 1941
MARTHA E. SIDES, Jun. 15, 1848 - Jun. 9, 1943
JAMES H. SIDES, Jun. 7, 1852 - Feb. 22, 1933
JAMES E. THACKER, Apr. 3, 1862 - Nov. 20, 1894
BAMA, wife of R. F. JOHNSON, Oct. 23, 1875 - May 4, 1905
B. FRANK THOMAS, May 8, 1844 - Aug. 3, 1926
MARY F. THOMAS, Aug. 3, 1850 - Aug. 21, 1910
LUCIUS THOMAS, May 8, 1874 - Aug. 3, 1926
JANE CANNON, Sep. 25, 1853 - Dec. 6, 1899
MAGGIE RUTLEDGE, wife of J. M. RUTLEDGE, May 28, 1877 - Sep. 12, 1905
D. P. KILGORE, Mar. 21, 1862 - Jan. 20, 1906
MARTHA F. (RUTLEDGE) KILGORE, Oct. 1, 1864 - Sep. 21, 1947
ANDREW KILGORE, May 5, 1886 - Feb. 19, 1919
HANNAH GRACE, Nov. 15, 1835 - May 17,1887
ROSIE A. DUTTON, May 3, 1858 - Jun. 8, 1886
TAMER, wife of DR. FRANK BLANTON, Mar. 15, 1881 - Nov. 16, 1919
ISAAC BLANTON, May 1805 - Nov. 1, 1907
MARTHA, wife of ISAAC BLANTON, Oct. 13, 1835 - Oct. 17, 1920
JOHN STAGGS, Jul. 22, 1858 - Feb. 21, 1955
MARY S.STAGGS, wife of J. STAGGS, Jun. 30, 1861 -Aug. 2, 1895
LOUISE THOMAS, Jan. 10, 1872 - May 13, 1931
NANCY A. THOMAS, wife of J. J. THOMAS, May 17, 1836 - Oct. 29, 1901
JANE DAVIS, wife of ROBERT DAVIS, d. Oct. 22, 1881, age 69 yrs. 8 mos. 26 das.

## Pleasant Grove Church Cemetery Cont'd.

WILLIAM JAMES MYERS - May 2, 1844 - Oct. 6, 1900
GEORGE H. MYERS, Dec. 15, 1886 - May 9, 1955
J. A. MYERS, Jul. 15, 1851 - Sep. 7, 1922
J. B. GRACE, Jan. 8, 1860 - Mar. 16, 1943
MARTHA GRACE, Feb. 2, 1866 - Nov. 7, 1886
NICK J. JOHNSON, Mar. 12, 1851 - Dec. 20, 1906
MARTHA J. JOHNSON, Oct. 27, 1848 - Mar. 1, 1925
JACK V. JOHNSON, Dec. 4, 1877 - Feb. 14, 1931
ZILPHA JOHNSON, Jan. 14, 1854 - Mar. 6, 1917
CHARLOTTIE, wife of F. JOHNSON, Sep. 30, 1831 - Apr. 9, 1901
M. H. JOHNSON, Jun. 11, 1853 - Nov. 15, 1894
MARY S., wife of Y. J. KING, Dec. 27, 1860 - Sep. 2, 1901
ROBERT DAVIS, 1850 - 1941
SALLIE DAVIS, Nov. 24, 1855 - Jul. 26, 1930
JOHN W. DAVIS, Mar. 7, 1876 - Dec. 13, 1924
IDA DAVIS, Aug. 4, 1879 - Feb. 10, 1950
MARY GRACE, Dec. 16, 1838 - Oct. 21, 1923
JOHN N. NIX, Loundes Co. Ala. Artillery, C.S.A.
SUSAN NIX, May 2, 1841 - Jul. 27, 1931
NANNIE (MYERS) CUNNINGHAM, Jul. 30, 1890 - Mar. 21, 1956
H. N. MYERS, Dec. 24, 1846 - Aug. 3, 1919
LETHIE MYERS, Apr. 25, 1869 - Jul. 13, 1954
WAKE A. MYERS, 1852 - 1920
PATTY J. MYERS, 1852 - 1934
ED CARMICHAEL, Oct. 7, 1889 - Oct. 13, 1946
ED CARMICHAEL, JR., Apr. 30, 1930 - Nov. 4, 1934
FRANK W. CARMICHAEL, 1882 - 1934
LULA E. CARMICHAEL, 1892 - 1928
LUCY E. MYERS, wife of J. A. MYERS, Aug. 9, 1855 - Oct. 11, 1925

## Burton Cemetery - Near Sipsey, Alabama

ROBERT BURTON, (a mason), Jan. 9, 1820 - died 1871
MELISSA BURTON, Jul. 11, 1828 - May 11, 1895
S. M. BURTON, Jun. 1, 1892 - Sep. 18, 1910
D. W. BURTON, 1862 - 1934
LUCINDA BURTON, 1863 - 1917
CARIE ESTELL BURTON, Dec. 27, 1891 - May 20,1906
J. L. BURTON, Oct. 28, 1858 - Dec. 23, 1900
SUSIE BURTON, 1857 - 1929
GEORGE E. ROBERTS, Apr. 3, 1889 - Jun. 24, 1952
D. WEBSTER ROBERTS, Aug. 21, 1914 - Jul. 10, 1915
H. H. BUZBEE, Oct. 3, 1859 - Jul. 10, 1930
SARAH BUZBEE, Jun. 9, 1861 - Nov. 19, 1920
The parents of the above ROBERT BURTON were ROBERT BURTON, b. 1783, and his wife SARAH BURTON, b. 1785, taken from the 1850 census.

Brown Cemetery - (Inactive) - on West bank of Blackwater Creek - Two miles East of Nauvoo Rd.

MARTHA BROWN, dau. of HENRY and SUSAN SIDES, and wife of RUSSELL BROWN, born York Dist. S.C. Feb. 17, 1815 - d. Feb. 18, 1888
Several graves in this cemetery but no markers

Shiloh (Inactive) Cemetery - Three miles West of Thatch School on Nauvoo Road

GEN. G., son of JAMES and LAVONIA J. ELLIS, Aug. 13, 1856 - Nov. 9, 1877
SINTHIA KEY, Mar. 8, 1803 - Mar. 6, 1884
MARY C. GUTTERY, wife of W. D. GUTTERY, Dec. 24, 1854 - Oct. 4, 1889
W. S. W. KEY, Jan. 8, 1801 - Jun. 9, 1879
MARYEMERE LAMON, wife of J. W. LAMON, Oct. 3, 1876 - Oct. 10, 1893
ADONIA, wife of W. H. WILSON, Feb. 9, 1879 - Oct. 18, 1899

Burton Family Cemetery - near Macedonia Church of Christ Cemetery on road from Jasper to Townley and Hollygrove

JOHN BURTON, d. Mar. 1863
ELIZABETH BURTON, d. Feb. 5, 1886
DICY BAKER, b. Nov. 2, 1838 - d. Nov. 1, 1870
WILLIAM M. BAKER, Jan. 6, 1862 - Sep. 15, 1868
EDMOND KNIGHT, b. Jul. 15, 1826 - d. May 15, 1862

Macedonia Church of Christ Cemetery on Hollygrove Road between Jasper and Townley, Alabama

CADER BURTON, Dec. 20, 1812 - d. Sep.23, 1897
LAVINIA JOHNSON BURTON, wife of CADER BURTON, Dec. 20, 1814 - d. Aug. 12, 1900
JOHN BURTON, Co. H. 56th Ala. Partisan Rangers, C.S.A.
Wife --- no marker
P. S. BURTON, Jul. 24, 1833 - Jan. 22, 1901
MARY E. BURTON, May 12, 1835 - Jun. 5, 1904
ANNIE BURTON, 1887 - 1944
JOSHUA ATKINS, Apr. 9, 1858 - Feb. 5,1897
GEORGIA ATKINS, Oct. 16, 1859 - Jun. 1, 1911
LUCIUS B. WRIGHT, 1874 - 1944
VIRGINIA DEAN WRIGHT, wife of L. B. WRIGHT, 1867 - 1933
GILES M. BAKER, May 18, 1866 - Dec. 18, 1955
SUSIE B. BAKER, Nov. 25, 1867 - Oct. 7,1929

Macedonia Church of Christ Cemetery Cont'd.

JOHN FRANCIS BAKER, Sep. 1, 1859 - Feb. 26, 1945
SARAH WRIGHT BAKER, Mar. 11, 1867 - Feb. 19, 1946
IDA BAKER, Sep. 12, 1902 - Sep. 17, 1932
RALPH R. COOPER, 1893 - 1935
FRANCES ELIZABETH McCLESKY, Jun. 1, 1856 - Nov. 7, 1940
W. P. McCLESKY, Dec. 12, 1856 - Jan. 22, 1906
RAISH WRIGHT, 1886 - 1946
BAMA, wife of E. W. GOSS, Jun. 1, 1882 - Jul. 2, 1907
SALLIE BOSHELL, Nov. 14, 1879 - Aug. 3, 1905
JAMES B. BOSHELL, Co. H. 56th Ala. Cav, C.S.A.
SARAH, wife of J. B. BOSHELL, Feb. 23, 1843 - Nov. 21, 1913
LELAR H., dau. of J. L. & V. A. BOSHELL, 1914 - 1917
PETER N. BOSHELL, Sep. 9, 1842 - Nov. 3, 1883
LUCINDA, wife of P. N. BOSHELL, Jul. 10, 1845 - May 5, 1878
W. P. BOSHELL, Aug. 17, 1817 - Apr. 15, 1920
LURENA, wife of W. P. BOSHELL, Apr. 10, 1847 - Feb. 24, 1921
LELA BOSHELL, Apr. 25, 1885 - May 30, 1935
STACIA BOSHELL, 1881 - 1955
MALINDA ROBINSON, Nov. 10, 1872 - Mar. 31, 1947
JOHN L. BOSHELL, Jan. 10, 1869 - Jun. 12, 1932
M. M. BOSHELL, Apr. 22, 1811 - Sep. 23, 1895
M. C. BOSHELL, Oct. 16, 1814 - Oct. 8, 1894
MANICY CAROLINE BOSHELL, dau. of M. M. & M. C. BOSHELL,
May 17, 1847 - d. May 18, 1879
SELONIA BOSHELL, Jan. 6, 1851 - Nov. 25, 1871
R. O. KIMBRELL, Sep. 16, 1857 - Mar. 15, 1936
MARGARET F. BOSHELL, wife of R. O. KIMBRELL, Aug. 6, 1860 -
Oct. 27, 1941
ERIC WINSTON GUTHRIE (Minister) 1921 - 1956
ROBERT L. GUTHRIE, 1905 - 1948
MARGARET, wife of J. L. WRIGHT, Oct. 15, 1839 - Oct. 9, 1913
ELLEN I., wife of W. D. CHEATHAM, Jun. 19, 1841 - Aug. 15, 1901
W. R. FERGUSON, Jan. 18, 1858 - Mar. 17, 1933
LEONIA FERGUSON, May 12, 1859 - Jul. 20, 1941
JOHN T. McDADE, Nov. 21, 1862 - May 20, 1882
R. ROEY McDADE, Oct. 21, 1860 - Mar. 25, 1886
W. ROBERT TOWNLEY, 1871 - 1946
ALICE E. TOWNLEY, 1875 - 1948
W. J. TOWNLEY, Oct. 28, 1849 - Dec. 22, 1932
MARTHA ANN TOWNLEY, Apr. 6, 1853 - Apr. 1, 1930
PETER BURTON, Jul. 24, 1833 - Jan. 22,1902
MARY E. TOWNLEY, wife of PETER BURTON, May 12, 1835 (no death date)
JOHN H. BURTON, b. in S.C. Dec. 20, 1828, Member Co. H. 56th Ala. partisan Rangers
NANCY SIDES, wife of JOHN H. BURTON, no dates
JOHN FRANCIS BAKER, Sep. 1, 1859 - Feb. 19, 1946
GILES BAKER, May 18, 1866 - Dec. 18, 1955

## Cemetery on John Boshell Home Place Near Lost Creek

JOHN BOSHELL, d. Oct. 11, 1895 (Shown in 1870 census as age 63)
MARY BOSHELL, d. Jul. 3, 1897
A. M. WRIGHT, Jan. 30, 1857 - Jul. 11, 1915
SUSAN (BURTON), wife of A. M. WRIGHT, Mar. -- 1862 - Feb. 21, 1884
ROVIE ANN THOMAS, Dec. 22, 1861 - Mar. 1, 1887
MARTHA KNIGHT, Feb. 6, 1869 - Nov. 7, 1889

## Cemetery at Wilson Chapel - Two Miles East of Nauvoo Road, Walker Co. Near Lupton School

JOHN A. NELSON, Nov. 4, 1875 -Jun. 19, 1952
MATILDA McCULLARS, Aug. 1841 - 1876
WALTER N. MYERS, 1893 - 1931
SINTHA, wife of C.M.D. NELSON, Aug. 25, 1854 - Jul. 19, 1916
MARTHA A., wife of ALLEN SMITH, Jul. 4, 1806 - Jun. 25, 1895
ARTAMISCO, son of J. W. SMITH, May 31, 1838 - Mar. 1, 1936
REV. W. R. SMITH, 1834 - 1890
S. E., wife of REV. W. R. SMITH, May 31, 1838 - Mar. 6, 1936

## Cemetery Near Pocahontas, Alabama

OWEN HAYES SCOTT, Mar. 21, 1904 - Sep. 24, 1924
J. H. HENDON, Oct. 19, 1834 - Jul. 29, 1912
ORLENA M., wife of JAMES H. HENDON, Jan. 22, 1836 - Mar. 24, 1912
PRUDIA L., wife of LAFAYETTE TUNE, Jan. 28, 1874 - Nov. 9, 1907
MARY S. LEONARD, 1859 - 1946
WILLIAM H. LEONARD, 1858 - 1916
F. L. HALL, Sep. 2, 1860 - Feb. 28, 1907
JO ATKINS, SR., May 5, 1814 - Jul. 28, 1898
SARAH ATKINS, Sep. 30, 1831 - May 26, 1902
J. ATKINS, Sep. 2, 1877 - Mar. 12, 1897
J. M., son of J. C. & V. E. ATKINS, Aug. 19, 1874 - Jun. 30, 1921
CORTUS CRANFORD, Jan. 24, 1875 - Jan. 6, 1898
JOHN C. ATKINS, Jun. 14, 1851 - Nov. 15, 1928
VIRGINIA E., wife of J. C. ATKINS, Apr. 19, 1855 - Nov. 13, 1922
MRS. ELLA ATKINS ELLIOTT, Mar. 26, 1894 - May 14, 1947
JOHN E. CRANFORD, Co. C. 10th Ala. Inf. C.S.A. Feb. 12,1839 - Feb. 24, 1936
MARY E. COOK, 1857 - 1925
JESSIE E. COOK, 1853 - 1931
ALICE P., wife of J. W. MYERS, Mar. 20, 1831 - Jul. 3, 1915

## Cemetery Near Pocohontas, Alabama Cont'd.

REBECCA PIKE, Apr. 26, 1865 - Sep. 16, 1944
W. D. PIKE, Aug. 7, 1876 - Mar. 21, 1950
MILLIE EDGIL, Feb. 24, 1852 - Aug. 26,1937
BILL EDGIL, May 15, 1856 - Dec. 21, 1912
WILLIAM C. ATKINS, Aug. 19, 1868 - Dec. 23, 1949
HOLLIE A. ATKINS, C. 416830, Pvt. le Eng. M. Dep't. Jan. 19, 1895 - Apr. 3, 1921
ELIZABETH ATKINS, Sep. 17, 1849 - Feb. 8, 1902
J. P. COCNER, Feb. 8, 1861 - Aug. 4, 1902
D. J. SANDLIN, Nov. 23, 1836 - Mar. 2, 1928
EDDIE CANTERBERRY, Feb. 26, 1898 - age 62 yrs. - b. 1836
THOMAS B. FILES, 1st Sgt. Co. A. 1st. Ala. & Cav. - Aug. 12, 1839 - Mar. 1905
MARTHA J., wife of T. B. FILES, Mar. 16, 1834 - Jul. 26,1901
O. MATILDA COCNER, wife of DANILE COCNER, May 21, 1871 - Jun. 22, 1908
DAN G. COCNER, Feb. 27, 1871 - Sep. 28, 1954
J. FRANK HENDON, 1861 - 1940
LUCINDA COCNER, 1858 - 1920
LUNA E., wife of EDGAR FILES, Jun. 18, 1895 - May 30, 1925
J. BRACK HENDON, 1887 - 1942
ADA HENDON, Apr. 18, 1883 - Nov. 15, 1953
J. FRANK FILES, 1877 - 1944
JOHN FRAME, Dec. 30, 1859 - Nov. 12, 1944
ROBERT FRAME, Apr. 20, 1868 - Oct. 27, 1938

## New Hope Cemetery - Church of Christ - Between Oakman and Jasper, Alabama

CHESLEY CRANFORD, Feb. 5, 1833 - May 9, 1911
ELMARTHA, wife of CHESLEY CRANFORD, Mar. 15, 1835 - Jul. 22, 1910
PATSY P. CRANFORD, wife of F. M. CRANFORD, Feb. 18, 1870 - Dec. 5,1895
GEORGE SWINDLE, Dec. 20, 1858 - Jun. 4, 1951
J. W. SWINDLE, May 6, 1851 - Jan. 21, 1941
MARY JANE SWINDLE, wife of GEORGE, Aug. 18, 1859 - Sep. 9, 1952
J. H. SWINDLE, Feb. 28, 1843 - Jul. 11, 1911
L. C. SWINDLE, Dec. 7, 1848 - Oct. 14, 1928
BIRD COVIN, Jul. 13, 1898, age 62 yrs.
WILLIAM H. CAIN, Jul. 21, 1875 - Jan. 6, 1934
J. H. MORRIS, Mar. 11, 1845 - Mar. 4, 1914
S. A. MORRIS, Mar. 10, 1872 - Nov. 22, 1943
JENNETTE NOLAN DAVIS, May 30, 1846 - Apr. 18, 1922
EARLY ESTES DAVIS, May 8, 1868 - Nov. 5, 1930

New Hope Cemetery, Cont'd.

AMOS. A. MARTIN, Dec. 12,1850 - May 18, 1934
PHILLIP JEFFERSON MYERS, Jul. 11, 1848 - Jan. 23, 1929
MARY ANN, wife of PHILLIP J. MYERS, May 13, 1846 - May 24, 1925
(Mother of thirteen childred) GABRILLA, CORDELIA, TANDLY, RAEBIN L., EDDIE, DOLLY, MILIE BIRD, BODINE, JOEBIN, CLAUDE, CUMIE, MARCUS (all names appear on her stone)
MARTHA E., wife of J. H. WALKER, Aug. 22, 1858 - Jul. 22, 1916
J. B. DOBBS, Mar. 28, 1853 - Mar. 6, 1914
D. L. JONES, Jun. 16, 1859 - Jul. 29,1933
Z. C. GRAY, Jun. 22, 1860 - Jul. 9, 1945

Kitchens Family Cemetery - Three Miles West of Jasper, Alabama

JAMES MATLOCK KITCHENS, born in Tenn. Aug. 7, 1796 - d. Mar. 23, 1868
SALLY BROWN, wife of JAMES MATLOCK KITCHENS, Sep. 16, 1796, Dec. 1842
C. C. KITCHENS, Nov. 18, 1827 - Jan. 15, 1861
MARY ELIZABETH KITCHENS, Jan. 2, 1860 - Oct. 25, 1875
JESSE KITCHENS, Dec. 27, 1837 - Jun. 12, 1898
ELEANOR, wife of JESSE KITCHENS, Dec. 27, 1837 - Jun. 12, 1898
A. H. BROWN, 1844 - May 23, 1906
L. O. BROWN, wife of A. H. BROWN, dau. of T. & MARY GABBERT, Apr. 30, 1838 - d. Mar. 3, 1908
J. D. RANDOLPH, d. Feb. 28, 1870, age 72 yrs - b. 1798
COCNER .......... all that remained on the stone.

Shiloh Cemetery - Kansas, Alabama

WILLIAM ANDREW MASON, Sep. 18, 1868 - Aug. 11, 1910
ANNIE LOVE, Feb. 1, 1820 - Mar. 14, 1886
NANCY E. LOVE, Apr. 16, 1855 - Jul. 20, 1927
DEALYON LOVE, Feb. 10, 1851 - Mar. 30, 1889
JIM FIKES, 1865 - 1941
LEONA FIKES, 187[illegible] - 1943
JOHN CONN, d. Feb. 15, 1863, aged 60 yrs and 10 mos.
MARY CONN, d. 1859, age eroded on stone.
T. E. TESNEY, Oct. 2,1862 - Mar. 11, 1920
MARTHA TESNEY, wife of T. E. TESNEY, Jan. 5, 1868 - Aug. 16, [illegible]
ELIZABETH ANN, wife of E. G. TESNEY, Jun. 29, 1837 - Aug. 19, 1880
I. D. TESNEY, Aug. 14, 1867 - Mar. 13, 1898
M. J. TESNEY, Sep. 21, 1866 - Sep. 1927
E. G. TESNEY, b. S.C. Jul. 1, 1837 - d. Jul. 1895
WILLIAM ELEAM, son of D. E. & S. GALLAHER, Sep. 5, 1815 - May 1865
D. E. GALLAHER, d. Apr. 7, 1874, age 69 yrs.
EASTER, relict of JEREMIAH TESNEY, Jan. 10, 1807 - Oct. 25,1869

Shiloh Cemetery Cont'd.

R. P. McDONALD, Jan. 9, 1861- Oct. 13, 1913
MARY, wife of R. P. McDONALD, Sep. 30, 1869 - Jun. 23, 1911
WILLIAM BROWN, Dec. 4, 1872 - Nov. 13, 1899
JOHN R. BROWN, Jul. 11, 1849 - Feb. 4, 1904
ELIZABETH, wife of JOHN R. BROWN, Feb. 3, 1846 - d. age 53 yrs.
ANN TERRELL, dau. of W. S. & S. E. EPPERSON, wife of J. D. TERRELL, b. in Cherokee Co. Ga. Nov. 5, 1848 - d. Dec. 27, 1923
J. D. TERRELL, b. Cherokee Co. Ga. Sep. 25, 1840 - d. Nov. 13, 1925
JOHN M.LATHAM, Nov. 11, 1868 - Sep. 19, 1900
RICHARD L. McGOUGH, Apr. 14, 1849 - Feb. 18, 1920
MARY CATHERINE McGOUGH, Apr. 23, 1852 - Apr. 8, 1873
JOHN MASON, Aug. 23, 1821 - Apr. 8, 1879
ELIZABETH MASON, Mar. 25, 1838 - Nov. 4, 1923

Inactive Cemetery on the John Ferguson Home Place off the Nauvoo Road

MARTHA A., wife of F. R. BAKER, May 18, 1814 - Jan. 20, 1863
S. M. JONES, Dec. 23, 1840 - Feb. 20, 1869
ALBERTA, dau. of J. I. & J. F. ODOM, Jul. 27, 1888 - Mar. 13, 1889
W. H. MORRIS, Apr. 15, 1842 - Dec. 6, 1917

Mt. Vernon Baptist Church Cemetery Near Curry School

S. M. FORD, 1854 - 1936
WALTER W. MILFORD, Apr. 11,1878 - Jan. 20, 1932
.....E. HERRON, Jan. 1, 1819 - Sep. 3, 1908
JAMES H. SIDES, Oct. 12, 1867 - Mar. 10, 1950
MARY R., wife of JAMES H. SIDES, Nov. 14, 1878 - Nov. 16, 1944
SIDNEY E. HICKS, Nov. 18, 1870 - Mar. 25, 1935
LUELLER HICKS, Feb. 27, 1871 - Jul. 13, 1952
H. H. RAINES, Mar. 20, 1872 - Apr. 2, 1914
MARTIN L. SNELGROVE, Sep. 2, 1870 - Jul. 22, 1932
ANDREW McCULLAR, 1871 - 1953
JANE McCULLAR, 1873 - 1935
MARGARET HOPKINS, 1848 - 1918
G. V. MILLS, Jun. 1, 1868 - Nov. 6, 1933
NANCY BARTON, 1850 - 1942
WILLIAM E. MILLER, Jun. 5, 1875 - d. Jul. 6, 1954
J. W. MAYBERRY, Sep. 13, 1870 - Apr. 17, 1946
SAMUEL MANLEY HINTON, Sep. 23, 1867 - May 31, 1952
ALCY FRANCES HINTON, Aug. 4, 1872 - Jan. 15, 1950
JOHN I. DAVIS, 1870 - 1934
LELLA R. DAVIS, (wife), 1884 - 1952
J. W. NUNNALLEY, Dec. 11, 1872 - Jan. 4, 1927

## Mt. Vernon Baptist Church Cemetery Cont'd.

LARKIN R. HENSON, Jul. 4, 1853 - Apr. 3, 1929
SARAH M., wife of LARKIN HENSON, May 22, 1863 - Feb. 8, 1938
ELIZA BOBO, Oct. 20, 1860 - Jun. 28, 1946
J. J. STEWART, Nov. 26, 1859 - Dec. 29, 1948
MARTHA A., wife of J. J. STEWART, Dec. 13, 1863 - Jan. 25, 1948
WILLIAM J. FARLEY, Sep. 4, 1871 - Sep. 19, 1943

## Edgil Grove Church Cemetery - Off the Nauvoo Highway

JOHN W. NICKOLS, 1872 - 1945
IDA NICKOLS, 1875 - 1956
YOUNG ROWNDTREE, May 21, 1853 - Jun. 29, 1921
ANNER ROWNDTREE, Sep. 24, 1853 - Feb. 27, 1920
J. E. FERGUSON, Aug. 24, 1862 - May 29, 1934
MALINDY, wife of J. E. FERGUSON, Dec. 25, 1867 - Feb. 28, 1954
BETTY KING, wife of RANZY KING, age, all dates gone
JOSEPH EDGIL, Feb. 10, 1834 - Dec. 9, 1904
MANERVEE J., wife of JOSEPH EDGIL, Aug. 26, 1840 - Jan. 14, 1918
G. B. MADISON, Sep. 27, 1844, Feb. 28, 1918
SARAH, wife of G. B. MADISON, Feb. 27, 1846 - Feb. 8, 1925

## Cross Roads Methodist Church Cemetery

GEORGE W. BENSON, 1864 - 1947
MINNIE, wife of G. W. BENSON, 1866 - 1954
S. J. BRADFORD, Jun. 30, 1861 - Feb. 20, 1943
WILLIAM P. ELLIOTT, 1871 - 1949
JAMES MITCHELL CHISM, 1860 - 1951
MARY CHISM, 1862 - 1933
R. R. CAIN, Aug. 17, 1850 - Feb. 15, 1920
JIM S. WILSON, 1854 - 1933
M. A. (SIS) WILSON, 1855 - 1935
Wife of R. R. CAIN, name gone, Oct. 16, 1848 - Jul. 19, 1891
W. T. BUTRAM, Aug. 10, 1855 - Sep. 30, 1925
DIANA, wife of W. T. BUTRAM, Oct. 14, 1870 - Jan. 20, 1953
J. T. BRAKEFIELD, b. Chester Dist. S.C., Aug. 18, 1850 - d. Aug. 1, 1920
STEVE GILLESPIE, 1868 - 1936
SALLY GILLESPIE, 1876 - 1933
DAVIDSON DAVIS, Sep. 18, 1861 - Jan. 23, 1915
WILLIAM M. CHISM, Aug. 4, 1831 - Apr. 17, 1904
ADALINE FRANCES, wife of WM. W. CHISM, Nov. 23, 1837 - Nov. 22, 1920

Cross Roads Methodist Church Cemetery Cont'd.

LOUIS H. BARRENTINE, Jul. 18, 1861 - Nov. 16, 1943
AMANDA, wife of LOUIS BARRENTINE, Jul. 10, 1865 - Jun. 18,1941
D. T. JONES, 1869 - 1945

Patton Baptist Church Cemetery - on Patton Hill
Near Patton, Alabama

KATIE CRONNOVER, 1863 - 1949
VADIE WOODS, 1877 - 1931
JOLIE WOODS, 1871 - 1943
J. B. ROBBINS, Dec. 13, 1873 - May 6, 1933
J. W. WALLIS, 1852 - 1936
EMMA WALLIS, 1871 - 1954
WILLIAM PATTON, Nov. 18, 1846 - Oct.13, 1931
SARAH PATTON, Nov. 28, 1847 - Aug. 25, 1932
JOSEPH NEWTON PATTON, Jul. 31, 1871 - Jul. 6, 1939
EXIE LEONA PATTON, Aug. 12, 1877 - Dec. 24, 1955
J. B. MARTIN, Feb. 21, 1867 - Feb. 7, 1931
THOMAS R. KEMP, Dec. 22, 1879 - Jun. 17, 1936
JOHN D. AMERSON, Co. K. 2nd Ala. Inf. Spanish Amer. War.
b. Feb. 15,1871 - d. Aug. 21,1933
ANNA S. LAWSON, 1871 - 1951
MARION DAVIDSON, 1868 - 1950
MINNIE IDELLA SHIRLEY, Oct. 13, 1875 - Sep. 20, 1948
LOUIS L. HAGLER, Mar. 23, 1868 - Mar. 12, 1948
DELLA O. HAGLER. Oct. 12, 1871 - Oct. 17, 1942
DICIE WILCUTT, Jul. 10, 1869 - Apr. 1, 1949
MARION WILCUTT, Mar. 20, 1865 - Aug. 21, 1947
FANNIE AMERSON, Jul. 17, 1870 - Feb. 22, 1953
GEORGE PATTON, 1853 - 1931
MARY E. PATTON, 1853 - 1939
ISHAM THACKER, Jun. 6, 1877 - Jan. 3, 1950
JAMES PATTON, Jun. 15, 1848 - Mar. 4, 1929
MARY E. PATTON, Nov. 5, 1850 - Apr. 1, 1931
MARY B. PATTON, 1874 - Jan. 14 - Oct. 11, 1946
ANDY PATTON, Feb. 9, 1856 - Feb. 17, 1928
WILLIAM BROWN, 1878 - 1940
N. J. PATTON, Dec. 10, 1878 - Oct. 11, 1918
NATHAN THACKER, 1853 - 1934
MARY PATTON, wife of NATHAN PATTON, Jul. 15, 1851 - Aug. 17, 1923
W. R. THACKER, Sep. 1877 - Dec. 6, 1935
MART SMITH, Feb. 4, 1874 - Sep. 9, 1933
J. MARION EARNEST, 1864 - 1946
MARTHA EARNEST, 1861 - no death date
JOHN M. HEYGOOD, Jul. 14, 1878 - Jul. 13, 1898
PHEDIE ANN, wife of JOHN M. HEYGOOD, Oct. 17, 1857 - Aug. 9, 1910

Patton Baptist Church Cemetery Cont'd.

ROBERT CROWNOVER, son of M. E. CROWNOVER, Mar. 7, 1852 - Oct. 6, 1887
E. L. HIGGINS, Jan. 2, 1868 - Aug. 9, 1887
MARY BAKER, 1870 - 1940
DONIE C., wife of J. F. CROWNOVER, Aug. 15, 1866 - Mar. 20, 1887
J. B. CROWNOVER, May 16, 1846 - Apr. 24, 1919
S. C. CROWNOVER, wife of J. B. CROWNOVER, May 24, 1846 - Jun. 14, 1908
LEVI PATTON, Apr. 5, 1874 - Apr. 17, 1930
NANCY IDELLA, wife of L.E. PATTON, Oct. 21, 1876 - Nov. 19, 18
D. S. THOMAS, 1851 - 1918
ELIZA THOMAS, 1853 - 1931
JAMES BOWDEN, 1830 - 1941
ELIZABETH BOWDEN, Aug. 1, 1838 - May 12, 1913
JOSEPH EDGIL, 1861 - 1941
W. J. YOUNG, 1862 - 1920
DAVID E. CAIN, Apr. 3, 1879 - Feb. 24, 1934
LENA PATTON SELLERS, Sep. 1, 1875 - Nov. 27, 1955
SUSAN G., wife of G. W. WILLINGHAM, Mar. 31, 1862 - Nov. 10, 1908
BERTIE M. GUTTERY, Feb. 10, 1886, Sep. 29, 1919

Lawson Cemetery - Four Miles S.W. of Pleasant Grove Baptist Church

NANCY, wife of THOMAS DAVIS, Jan. 12, 1830 - Jan. 12, 1911
THOMAS DAVIS, May 20, 1824 - Jan. 10, 1910
SUSAN A. DAVIS, wife of W. J. DAVIS, Apr. 3, 1850 - Jun. 15, 1 4
A. J. THOMAS, Nov. 20, 1823 - Feb. 22, 1902
ELIZABETH RUTLEDGE, Feb. 1812 - Feb. 8, 1872
J. RUTLEDGE, Feb. 5, 1836 - May 26, 1860
ELIZABETH THOMAS, wife of J. J. THOMAS, Apr. 18, 1829 - Apr. 25, 1858
W. D. LOGAN, Mar. 28, 1842 - Jan. 19, 1907
M. J. LOGAN, Feb. 29, 1845 - no death date.
LAVATOR MILLER, 1860 - 1938
ELLEN MILLER, 1856 - 1948
POLLY MILLER, Sep. 12, 1832 - Dec. 2, 1916
M. J.R. TINDAL, wife of J. M. TINDAL, Feb. 22, 1859 - May 8, 1872
MINTIE J. KEY, wife of J. M. KEY, Feb. 24, 1875 - Oct. 5, 1896
CAROLINE, wife of DANIEL SWINDLE, Apr. 11, 1822 - Apr. 4, 1902
LOU IDA KEY, wife of J. M. KEY, Mar. 22, 1883 - Jul. 13, 1924
DENNIS D. SWINDLE, Oct. 17, 1848 - Mar. 29, 1921
MANDY S. SWINDLE, Apr. 16, 185 - Aug. 26, 1936
C. J. CLAUD SWINDLE, Apr. 23, 1885 - Feb. 26, 1936
HENRY ATKINS, Jul. 30, 1885 - Sep. 7, 1951

Sides Cemetery (Inactive) - Two Miles S. W. of Pleasant Grove, Alabama

HENRY SIDES, was born in the year 1734, death date gone.
WILLIAM SIDES, 1795 - Feb. 2, 1868
CEREPTA, wife of WILLIAM SIDES, Feb. 24, 1805 - Sep. 1877
MARY SIDES, dates gone
W. H. SIDES, dates gone
E. A. SIDES, dates gone
WILLIAM L. SIDES, Mar. 15, 1854 - Oct. 2, 1930
MARTHA E., wife of WILLIAM L. SIDES, Aug. 9, 1861 - Feb. 19, 1943
W. F. SIDES, 1833 - 1907
MARTHA SIDES, 1835 - 1908
HUGH R. SIDES, Jul. 22, 1819 - Dec. 30, 1855
ALVIN SIDES, 1858, all other dates gone
MANLEY SIDES, dates gone
G. F. SIDES, Co. C 13 Ala. Cav. C.S.A. Apr. 30, 1830 - Apr. 16, 1863
JAMES RUTLEDGE, Nov. 4, 1832 - May 25, 1918
E. A. RUTLEDGE, wife of JAMES, Oct. 8, 1839 - Nov. 11, 1905
GEORGE KILGORE, 1852 - 1923
MARY E. KILGORE, 1860 - 1904

Pleasant Field Baptist Church Cemetery - Seven Miles South of Parrish, Alabama

E. B. CANNON, Sep. 22, 1838 - Sep. 10, 1923
ZYLPHA CANNON, Mar. 4, 1839 - Dec. 10, 1920
B. F. SIDES, Nov. 27, 1856 - Aug. 20, 1930
JANE SIDES, 1859 - 1920
FANNIE SIDES, Oct. 20, 1858 - Mar. 31, 1905
MARY JANE, wife of F. M. SIDES, Nov. 23, 1836 - Mar. 11, 1900
C. C. DEASON, Nov. 6, 1822 - Mar. 13, 1903
J. I. ODOM, Oct. 1, 1841 - May 5, 1913
J. D. DAVIDSON, Feb. 7, 1860 - Oct. 27, 1904
M. C. DAVIDSON, Jul. 21, 1857 - Feb. 24, 1911
CAROLINE PARALEE ODOM, wife of JAMES I. ODOM, Nov. 6, 1843 - Dec. 21, 1924
JAMES T. GRACE, 1861 - 1952
PHEBA J. GRACE, 1866 - 1945
J. WASH. DEASON, 1853 - 1879
SARAH A. DEASON, 1880 - 1944
J. A. ODOM, 1868 - 1942
L. ALICE ODOM, 1875 - no further dates
JEREMIAH NEWTON ODOM, May 13, 1867 - Oct. 21, 1917
MATTELLIA LEONARD ODOM, Apr. 25, 1868 - Nov. 28, 1955
ETTA KEY, Sep. 8, 1880 - Dec. 21, 1903

Pleasant Field Baptist Church Cemetery Cont'd.

SARAH ANN HANDLEY, Nov. 14, 1860 - Dec. 5, 1940
A. H. HANDLEY, Jul. 6, 1845 - Jan. 20, 1929
MARY RICHARDSON, Feb. 14, 1848 - Aug. 9, 1911
FLORENCE DAVIDSON, 1874 - 1954
BELLE LEFAN, Apr. 19, 1867 - Feb. 5, 1954
MARION LEFAN, Nov. 10, 1854 - Dec. 9, 1935
SARAH, wife of F. M. LEFAN, May 18, 1859 - Nov. 8, 1904
JOHN RICHARDSON, Nov. 11, 1842 - Jun. 21, 1918
C. LEE KEY, 1857 - 1913
SARAH KEY, 1852 - 1936
JAMES L. LEONARD, Aug. 21, 1845 - Jul. 29, 1911
CAROLINE LEONARD, Nov. 17, 1851 - Jan. 9, 1930
C. T. KEY, 1872 - 1947
SAMUEL W. HERRON, 1872 - 1940
ALONZO J. KEY, Apr. 13, 1868 - May 9, 1947
THOMAS R. HANDLEY, May 24, 1870 - Sep. 14,1942
JAMES R. MINOR, 1847 - 1948

Gray Cemetery - Odom Memorial Church - Three Miles South of Parrish, Alabama

W. ODOM, Jul. 8, 1777 - d. Feb. 15, 1856
JAMES IVAN ODOM, May 7, 1872 - Feb. 25, 1919
SARAH JOSIE ODOM, wife of JAMES IVAN ODOM, 1877 - 1921
SAMUEL ODOM, May 15, 1846 - Oct. 11,1888
MATTIE CAROLINE, wife of L. W. ODOM, 1855 - 1918
JAMES ODOM, Sep. 9, 1811 - Apr. 1, 1906
MAHALE ODOM, Aug. 19, 1829 - Apr. 6, 1905
SUSIE ODOM, Mar. 2, 1878 - Jul. 19, 1908
ELIZABETH ODOM, Mar. 11, 1853 - Mar. 12, 1918
DALTON ODOM, Jul. 24, 1853 - May 13, 1911
BRACK C. ODOM, 1884 - 1950
MOLLIE ODOM, 1890 - 1953
J. J. KIRKPATRICK, Sep. 14, 1857 - Feb.26, 1927
ELIZA B. KIRKPATRICK, Feb. 3, 1857 - May 8,1923
DAN M. C. HERRON CORNELIUS, May 22, 1854 - Jun. 4, 1925
SARAH ELIZABETH CORNELIUS, Sep. 18, 1869 - Jan. 18, 1939
LAURA A. RUSSELL, 1866 - 1946
G. A. CARRINGTON, Jun. 17, 1879 - May 13, 1950
LORENZO DOW BAILEY, Jun. 22, 1856 - Oct. 20, 1940
SAMANTHA JANE BAILEY, Jul. 7, 1859 - Dec. 22, 1930
REV. JOSEPH WARREN, May 16, 1848 - May 14, 1922
FANNIE WEST, 1877 - 1915
MARTHA WEST, 1883 - 1955
MATTIE BROWN, Mar. 4, 1860 - Feb. 28, 1922
MARTHA E. GRAY, wife of J. P. GRAY, Jan. 25, 1853 - Apr. 21, 1921
JOHN P. GRAY, Apr. 21, 1849 - Jun. 2, 1916

Gray Cemetery Cont'd.

JOHN R. WILLIAMS, 1808 - 1886
ELIZABETH WILLIAMS, 1841 - 1913
ROBERT L. SHURLEY, Oct. 13, 1876 - Nov. 1, 1905
MILDRED E. WILSON, Apr. 29, 1859 - Sep. 11, 1913

Tubb Cemetery - Church of Christ - About Three Miles off Hwy. 69, between Jasper and Oakman, Ala.

JOHN GRACE, Feb. 14, 1798 - Nov. 16, 1888
POLLY GRACE, 1792 - 1891
N. P. GRACE, May 7, 1842 - Jan. 7, 1913
MARTHA E., wife of N. P. GRACE, Sep. 19, 1840 - Jun. 8, 1883
S. TUBB, 1823 - Sep. 27, 1902
M. E. TUBB, Mar. 15, 1825 - Jul. 2, 1887
EMILY TUBB, Oct. 7, 1827 - Sep. 20, 1918
LEE TUBB, 1858 - 1934
JULIA TUBB, 1858 - 1941
L. C. TUBB, May 30, 1856 - Oct. 28, 1904
W. H. APPLING, 1869 - 1922
MARTHA ANN, wife of J. C. APPLING, Jun. 10, 1849 - Dec. 6, 1915
JAMES C. APPLING, Co. K. 9th Ala. Cav. C.S.A.
MRS. S. S. TUBB, May 7, 1855 - Jan. 6, 1927
P. P. BLACKWELL, Nov. 9, 1846 - May 29, 1903
NANCY BROWN, Oct. 17, 1846 - Jan. 30, 1944
I. B. BROWN, Sep. 11, 1849 - Feb. 24, 1924
M. C. BROWN, Sep. 3, 1875 - Oct. 4, 1886
CELIA KATHERINE JONES, 1859 - 1861
LENA, wife of Z. H. GRAY, Jan. 19, 1870 - May 22, 1904
MARY TUBB, Jul. 22, 1866 - Oct. 24, 1894
MANCEL L. TUBB, 1860 - 1941
ALTA E. TUBB, 1872 - 1946
W. H. GRACE, May 5, 1872 - Nov. 12, 1904
J. A. GRACE, Feb. 11, 1833 - Aug. 12, 1914
EMILY GRACE, Mar. 15, 1840 - Jul. 9, 1925
GEORGE S. RANDOLPH, Feb. 6, 1866 - Mar. 27, 1915
MARTHA E. RANDOLPH, Apr. 21, 1867 - Sep. 26, 1945

Morris Cemetery - Hwy. 69 - One quarter mile south Cane Creek Bridge between Jasper and Oakman, Ala.

FRANCIS MORRIS, Jun. 15, 1849 - Feb. 28, 1872
DANIEL LEE TUBB, Aug. 7, 1827 - Nov. 5, 1857, mem. Church of Christ
MATTIE, wife of J. S. WATTS, Feb. 14, 1851 - Oct. 10, 1895
There are about 25 graves here, HUBBARD, MORRIS, CAVIN, WATTS and TUBB, no inscriptions left on them.

Cemetery Near Copeland Ferry Rd. - About One Mile from Ferry

SGT. RICHARD J. BAKER, Co. H. Partisan Rangers, C.S.A.
b. Sep. 4, 1833 - d. Apr. 17, 1888

Mt. Carmel Cemetery - Cordova, Ala.

CAPT. B. M. LONG, Nov. 5, 1827 - Jun. 17, 1903
AMANDA C. LONG, Jan. 23, 1834 - Dec. 29, 1899
POPE M. LONG, 1870 - 1956
BIRD E. LONG, 1877 - 1951
BENJAMIN NEWT. C[illegible]K, Aug. 14, 1880 - Aug. 13, 1902
DR. J. M. MILLER, Aug. 25, 1857 - Oct. 15, 1926
IDA LONG MILLER, Sep. 19, 1866 - Dec. 13, 1915
THOMAS B. COTTON, 1847 - 1951
SENA J. COTTON, 1853 - 1929
MARTHA J., wife of W. W. STAGGS, May 29, 1855 - Mar. 17, 1917
J. A. JERNIGAN, Mar. 16, 1852 - Oct. 25, 1928
MARY E. ROBERTS, wife of J. L. ROBERTS, Oct. 19, 1851 - Aug. 12, 1913
W. A. JOHNSTON, Aug. 30, 1852 - Dec. 3, 1914
M. A. JOHNSTON, Jan. 12, 1855 - May 19, 1937
SUSIE E. PRESTON, 1833 - 1927
J. N. BUTTS, Mar. 5, 1856 - Apr. 14, 1933
MRS. M. A. BUTTS, Sep. 27, 1865 - Jan. 1, 1923
DAN E. NATIONS, Dec. 13, 1857 - Nov. 25, 1928
SUSAN M. NATIONS, Sep. 19, 1867 - Jun. 8, 1913
FRANCES E., wife of JOSEPH NATIONS, Apr.27, 1828 - Feb....1902
JOSEPH NATIONS, Aug. 19, 1831 - Jun. 19, 1913
SARAH LOLLAR, Jan. 1831 - Jun. 12, 1914
FRANK WILTON WALKER, 1858 - 1930
MARGARET E. WALKER, 1851 - 1930
JOSIAH M. DUNKIN, Mar. 25, 1848 - May 13, 1903
MRS. M. J. DUNKIN, Feb. 7, 1846 - Jun. 21, 1912
REBECCA HAMRICK, 1849 - 1891
THOMAS HAMR[illegible], 1843 - 1892
HENRY ELLIS, 1840 - 1912
MARY ELLIS, 1845 - 1911
D. W. BROWN, Dec. 15, 1853 - Feb. 22, 1942
MRS. M. J., wife of E. W. COURSON, Dec. 25, 1832 - Aug. 25, 1902
JACOB A. JONES, Mar. 30, 1848 - Oct. 30, 1939
ELIZABETH JONES, Feb. 17, 1849 - Apr. 12, 1916
ALONZO CARMICHAEL, Oct. 30, 1855 - Oct. 30, 1934
TALLIE, wife of R. C. GRIZZEL, Mar. 15, 1834 - Feb. 21, 1901
C. B. NICHOLS, 1863 - 1944
ALICE NICHOLS, Dec. 11, 1863 - Feb. 13, 1907
JOHN A. DOUGLAS, 1850 - 1926
GEORGIE ANN DOUGLAS, 1855 - 1928

Mt. Carmel Cemetery Cont'd.

NANCY B. KING, 1850 - 1946
GEORGE W. STOWERS, 1849 - 1916
MARY J. STOWERS, 1858 - 1918
BETHENIA HARDIN TUBB, Oct. 15, 1855 - Oct. 6, 1939
W. G. SMITH, Sep. 5, 1856 - May 15, 1915
SARAH J., wife of W. J. FIELDS, Jan. 22, 1843 - Mar. 27, 1923
JAS. F. DUPREE, Aug. 9, 1857 - Jun. 27, 1930
MILLIE DUPREE, Mar. 16, 1862 - Dec. 6, 1930
ELIZABETH, wife of JAMES W. ELLIOTT, 1844 - 1925
JAMES H. SHEPHERD, 1856 - 1923
FRANCES E. SHEPHERD, 1858 - 1929
EDWARD WEBSTER, 1847 - 1930
LAVINA L. McCOY, Jun. 22, 185[illegible] - Dec. 26, 1928
J. T. JONES, Jan. 8, 1853 - Jan. 16,1927
MARY E. JONES, May 16, 1853 - Mar. 20, 1926
J. MARK NELSON, Sep. 22, 1847 - Aug. 20, 1904
MARTHA ANN, wife of J. B. ELLIS, Sep. 15, 1854 - Sep. 1, 1893
S. M. CLEMENTS, Apr. 15, 1847 - Apr. 19, 1909
MARY ODOM, Dec. 15, 1835 - Dec. 12, 1929
EUSTATIA GAMMON, 1849 - 1909
MARTHA GAMMON, Jul. 15, 1852 - Nov. 5, 1936

From information gathered it seems that Cordova, Ala. was settled and named for Capt. B. M. Long who came to Ala. in 1857 from Carrolton, Ga, and amassed a fortune in coal lands. The town was named for a place in Mexico.

White Church Cemetery - Near Dora, Alabama

EZEKIEL MORGAN - Aug. 21, 1797 - Nov. 26, 1881
LINNIE, wife of EZEKIEL MORGAN, Feb. 9, 1802 - Dec. 27, 1874
RICHARD HOLLY, d. Apr. 15, 1861, age 80 yrs. 1781
JAMES HENRY LOCKHART, Nov. 12, 1849 - Feb. 20, 1894
MELVIN W. MORGAN, Mar. 24, 1846- Dec. 15, 1906
SOPHRONIA MORGAN, May 27, 1847 - Mar. 13, 1932
SAMANTHA, wife of A. E. MORGAN, Feb. 20, 1855 - Dec. 25, 1892
JOHN A. MORGAN, May 30, 1871 - Jul. 31, 1953
M. C. MORGAN, Sept. 16, 1837 -- Dec. 15, 1923
G. A. MORGAN, Nov. 17, 1844 - Sep. 15, 1927
JAMES I. MORGAN, Apr. 11, 1872 -- Dec. 30, 1912
ROBERT J. MORGAN, May 6, 1834 - Aug. 6, 1916
SARAH A., wife of ROBERT J. MORGAN, Dec. 16, 1831 - Feb. 15, 1902
SARAH ANN MORGAN, Dec. 28, 1856 - Nov. 19, 1941
B. J. ALLEN, Jun. 28, 1825 - Dec. 22, 1898
MARY ALLEN, wife of B. J. ALLEN, May 16, 1833 - Nov. 8, 1897

White Church Cemetery Cont'd.

SARAH E. ADAIR, Sep. 27, 1855 - Jan. 1904
J. W. BARNES, d. Jun. 18, 1904, age 77 yrs. 1817
WM. PENN, Sargent - Feb. 19, 1844 - Nov. 8, 1908
ALLEN H. SMITH, Jun. 17, 1854 - Mar. 31, 1906
J. F. JACKSON, Apr. 22, 1877 - Sep. 3, 1910
WM. HENRY TRAVIS, Dec. 20, 1843 - Nov. 1, 1928
VIRGINIA, wife of WM. HENRY TRAVIS, Jul. 17, 1846 - Sep. 7,190[illegible]
NANCY R. CAMPBELL, Aug. 12, 1839 - Jun. 12, 1926
ELIZA WALKER, Jan. 28, 1832 - Oct. 24, 1886
T. W. DAVIS, Apr. 7, 1837 - Aug. 24, 1904
NARCISSA, wife of T. W. DAVIS, Feb. 12, 1841 - Nov. 11, 1900
MALISA SOUTHERLAND, Feb. 1, 1851 - Aug. 7, 1875
JAMES W. DAVIS, Sep. 21, 1841 - Feb. 11, 1918
SARAH E. DAVIS, wife of JAMES W. DAVIS, Mar. 1, 1846 - Apr. 16, 1906
J. M. BUTLER, Sep. 22, 1861 - Dec. 8, 1907
KERIA FRANCIS, wife of R. ESTES FRANCIS, Sep. 1, 1839 - Sep. 21, 1906
MARTHA L. POSTEN, wife of B. B. POSTEN, Jul. 24, 1855 - Feb. 2, 1892
JOHN H. DAVIS, Nov. 15, 1847 - Sep. 10, 1872
NAOMIE, wife of J. H. DAVIS, Nov. 19, 1849 - Nov. 1, 1871
DANIEL DAVIS, Jan. 12, 1816 - Aug. 7, 1874
LOUISA DAVIS, wife of DANIEL DAVIS, Sep. 2, 1819 - Feb. 21,1[illegible]
VICTORIA, wife of G. VINTSON, Nov. 29, 1850 - Nov. 28, 1887

East Dora Cemetery, Dora, Alabama

J. E. ADAIR, Apr. 23, 1849 - Nov. 5, 1929
ARENA ADAIR, wife of J. E. ADAIR, Oct. 13, 1841 - May 7, 1920
MARTHA JANE PALMER, Sep. 13, 1851 - Jan. 5, 1931
M. Y. (DOOD) CLARK, Nov. 12, 1868 - Feb. 13, 1936
FRANCIS T. LANTRIP, May 5, 1864 - No death date
MARY A. LANTRIP, Apr. 22, 1872 - Nov. 28, 1942
SARAH CATHARINE SORRELL, 1841 - 1928
ROBERT H. GLAZE, Apr. 7, 1852, Aug. 7, 1930
MARY L. GLAZE, Dec. 13, 1862 - Apr. 3, 1949
E. J. LINDLEY, Nov. 28, 1859 - Jun. 21, 1937
MARY TANNER, 1860 - 1929
JOEL D. YORK, Apr. 7, 1859 - Jun. 6, 1930
OCTIA A. YORK, Aug. 1, 1859 - Dec. 22, 1928
DOLPHUS McCARM, 1868 - 1933

Davis Cemetery - Near New Coal Valley
(Deep in the woods)

MARTHA DAVIS, d. Dec. 29, 1858, age 82 years (1776)
REV. ROBERT DAVIS, b. Jun. 12, 1806 - d. Jul. 13, 1883

Davis Cemetery Cont'd.

WM. T. DAVIS, son of JESSE T. and SARAH E. DAVIS, b. Sep. 12, 1874 - d. Dec. 25, 1889
JESSE T. DAVIS, son of J. T. and S. E. DAVIS, b. Nov. 13, 1879 d. Feb. 14, 1902
JOHN M. KEY - lies here - 1805 - 1854
CHARITY E. KEY, b. Dec. 31, 1836 - d. Mar. 9, 1890
Children of JOHN and CHARITY KEY
SARAH E. RICE, Jul. 1875 ----CAROL RICE, Nov. 3, 1877

Blanton Cemetery - Two Miles South of McColum - Hwy. 69

Three graves
SARAH MYERS, wife of WM. JAMES MYERS, b. 1817 - 1868 - Mother of - DICK, JOHN, WAKE, HOWELL, GEORGE, SARAH, SUSA, JAMES, NANCY, JEFFERSON, AMANDA, ELLEN

Copeland Cemetery - Two and one-half miles South of Jasper, Alabama

M. E. COPELAND, Feb. 2, 1875 - Jul. 16, ----
JAMES COPELAND, Sep. 22, 1849 - Jul. 27, 1922
SARAH A. COPELAND, wife of JAMES COPELAND, Apr. 21, 1856 - Dec. 15, 1919
NANCY COPELAND, Jul. 27, 1848 - Jun. 7, 1892
DELVIRA, dau. of JAMES and M. A. COPELAND, Aug. 28, 1885 - Apr. 30, 1886
SUSAN, dau. of JAMES and M. A. COPELAND, Dec. 9, 1872 - Oct. 19, 1878
ISIAH COPELAND, Jul. 12, 1847 - Mar. 29, 1876
W. J. MAIDENS, 1851 - Sep. 26, 1895
LOU MAIDENS, Nov. 13, 1870 - Feb. 24, 1891
Two graves in this cemetery, said to be WASH. COPELAND and wife.

Gaines Hill Cemetery - One Mile North of Corona, Alabama

H. P. GAINES, B. Mar. 30, 1779 - d. Jan. 1, 1865
NANCY GAINES, wife of H. P. GAINES, b. Nov. 8, 1790 - Feb. 23, 1862
GEORGE S. GAINES, b. Dec. 8, 1828 - Dec. 22, 1910
F. A. E. GAINES, wife of G. S. GAINES, Apr. 9, 1832 - Mar. 10, 1891
VINA GAINES, wife of LEWIS, Sep. 20, 1860 - Aug. 26, 1887
WILLIAM R. GAINES, 1865 - 1925
JACK GAINES, d. Aug. 4, 1892, age 64 yrs. (1828)
LAVINA J., dau. of G. S. and F. A. E. GAINES, wife of J. W. LINN, b. Feb. 12, 1854 - d. Jan. 14, 1883
EMMA L. SPEAR, wife of R. B. SPEAR, Nov. 14, 1869 - May 11, 1908

Gaines Hill Cemetery Cont'd.

PAT O'BRIEN, SR. - Mar. 3, 1822 - Dec. 25, 1905
MARY A. O'BRIEN, wife of PAT O'BRIEN, Aug. 1, 1837 - Nov. 18, 1903
MARY E., dau. of P. and M. A. O'BRIEN, wife of J. FAIRLEY, b. May 1861 - Apr. 23, 1884
ANNIE O'BRIEN, Oct. 19, 1876 - May 17, 1894
RUTHY ISBELL, Apr. 20, 1814 - Jan. 9, 1880 - age 66 yrs.
WILLIE J., son of T. J. and E. A. GRIFFITH, Jun. 15, 1868 - Oct. 18, 1887
ZEMERIAH MATHEWS, d. Oct. 23, 1898, age 35 yrs.
HENRY E., wife of J. B. ATKINS, Jan. 28, 1868 - Oct. 1, 1885
JOSEPH MILNES, d. May 26, 1901, age 60 yrs. 11 mos. 7 das.
EMMA MILNES, d. Aug. 1893, age 48 yrs.
JACK MILNES, d. Apr. 1884, age 12 yrs.
ELIJAH MILNES, d. Oct. 1886, age 2 yrs.
W. J. FIELDS, Oct. 9, 1837 - Aug. 27, 1889
J. H. FIELDS, son of W. J. and S. J. FIELDS, May 20, 1861 - Aug. 16, 1888
SARAH E., wife of B. T. WHITTEN, Oct. 14, 1858 - Dec. 1, 1895
GEORGE SHIELDS, d. Feb. 13, 1905, age 33 yrs.
SARAH ELIZABETH, wife of A. SHEPHERD, Aug. 14, 1859 - Oct. 23, 1904
SUSAN THOMAS, Mar. 25, 1828 - Dec. 1, 1888
S. J. NEAL, Dec. 26, 1854 - Aug. 8, 1892
JAMES A., son of SIMOND and MANERVY HALE, Dec. 18,1871 - Jun. 14, 1887

Cemetery Near West Corona, Alabama

MARTHA (McDOWELL) KIRK, born in Ireland, Mar. 18, 1875 - Dec. 14, 1955
HETTIAN, wife of LOUIS BAKER, Nov. 12, 1834 - Jul. 9, 1892
MATILDA S. TIPTON, mother of R. C., A. R., and S. E. HONEYCUTT, b. Mar. 1, 1847 - Aug. 19, 1916
NANCY, wife of J. W. KUKENDALL, Sep. 3, 1845 - Sep. 8, 1909
SUSIE, wife of ED. AZBILL, Apr. 8, 1879 - Dec. 6, 1906
FRANKLIN FIELDS JONES, Jul. 4, 1872 - Nov. 10, 1900
RHODA RABUT, 1872 - 1947
JANE PARRISH, Jul. 17, 1878 - Aug. 1, 1940
LEWIS D., son of G. R. and JANE FROST, Jul. 12, 1870 - Mar. 23, 1902
JENNIE C., wife of ISAAC TIPTON, Sep. 7, 1862 - Aug. 15, 1895
TOM FROST, Aug. 5, 1877 - Jan. 26, 1950
M. V., wife of E. B. FROST, Nov. 17, 1840 - Dec. 10, 1880
SEPRETA A. FROST, Apr. 11, 1880 - Jul. 27, 1951
JAMES MARION FROST, 1878 - 1948
MARY PICKETT, Jul. 4, 1833 - Sep. 14, 1910

Cemetery Near West Corona, Alabama Cont'd.

L. W. JENKINS, Jul. 21, 1835 - Sep. 3, 1895
LAROR B., wife of WALTER KINCANNON, Feb. 12, 1874 - d. 1902
ALPHA DENACE, wife of D. E. PICKETT, May 1, 1868 - Jun. 2, 1905
FATHER DAVID F. PICKETT, Jan. 9, 1860 - Aug. 29, 1917
S. H. FROST, Feb. 7, 1874 - Feb. 11, 1916
SARAH FRANCES, wife of S. H. FROST, Sep. 15, 1876 - May 18, 1940
MAX HANCOCK, 1860 - 1938
CALLINE BIRCHEAT, born about 1812 - d. Nov. 9, 1909
W. W. PICKETT, Jan. 14, 1852 - Mar. 20, 1912
W. W. SIMMONS, Sep. 24, 1862 - Apr. 25, 1903

Old Zion Cemetery - One-half Mile South of Hwy. between Jasper and Parrish, Ala. on Gorgas Road

SUDIE MUSGROVE GILES, 1867 - 1943
SARAH B. HAMBY, 1855 - 1940
J. M. MEADOWS, 1853 - 1925
SARAH MEADOWS, 1855 - 1935
CARRYE C. JONES, 1873 - 1955
WALTER H. PATTERSON, 1362 - 1937
H. D. WILLIAMS, 1865 - 1939
WILLIAM R. JONES, Sep. 20,1956 - Apr. 1, 1929
CORDELIA ANN JONES, Sep. 2, 1867 - Jun. 18, 1920
W. S. SWEENEY, Nov. 19, 1870 - Mar. 19, 1944
LULA SWEENEY, Feb. 22, 1871 - Feb. 16, 1943
ANDREW COPELAND, Jan. 13, 1850 - Jan. 18, 1915
A. B. HENDRIX, Jun. 5, 1848 - Mar. 9, 1925
WM. HENDRIX, Aug. 20, 1868 - Jun. 11, 1932
AUSBORN W. JONES, May 30, 1869 - Mar. 12, 1920
MARY L. JONES, Mar. 8, 1870 - Jul. 11, 1936
P. P. JONES, Apr. 15, 1844 - Feb. 6, 1911
PALLIE JONES, Sep. 16,1841 - Feb. 23, 1932
AUDY R. JOHNSON, 1848 - 1927
NORA JOHNSON, 1874 - 1921
EARNEST B. GODFREY, Jul. 14, 1858 - Feb. 5, 1932
J. WILSON, 1865 - 1935
M. T. HENDRIX, Dec. 25, 1842 - Jun. 24, 1913
ROBERT D. KEY, 1862 - 19 (no other date)
EDA KEY, 1871 - 1910
J. WESLEY EARNEST, Mar. 16, 1860 - Oct. 13, 1927
BIRDA EARNEST, May 6, 1873 - Jan. 21, 1929
J. M. SHERER, Dec. 20, 1841 - May 18, 1919 - age 77 yrs.
SAMARIANUS (?), wife of J. M. SHERER, Feb. 14, 1846 - Apr. 22, 1908
JAMES A. JONES, Feb. 14, 1809 - Sep. 24, 1892 - age 83 yrs. 7 mos. 10 das.

Old Zion Cemetery Cont'd.

ARTAMISSA JONES, Mar. 6, 1825 - Apr. 5, 1895 - 70 yrs. 29 das.
CAROLINE C., wife of JAMES GLAZE, Dec. 26, 1844 - Mar. 28,1902
SUSAN RICE, Apr. 13, 1865 - Dec. 31, 1917
JOHN G. JONES, 1853 - 1939
ARDEAN E. JONES, 1859 - 1933
CASSIE M., wife of A. J. JONES, Nov. 11, 1858 - May 11, 1892
J. R. JONES, Co. G 56 Ala. Partisan Rangers, C.S.A.
GERTRUDE JONES WILDER, Lan. 9, 1852 - Jul. 25, 1925
THOMAS A. CHRISTIAN, Apr. 25, 1832 - no death date
MARY E. CHRISTIAN, Feb. 23,1840 - Nov. 23, 1912
SGT. D. D. L. CARMICHAEL, Co. G 56 Rangers, C.S.A., b. Jan. 16, 1834 - Oct. 24, 1894
CELIA M. CARMICHAEL, Dec. 7,1839 - Dec. 7, 1925
ELIZA A. CARMICHAEL, Dec. 29, 1858 - Oct. 28, 1883
LAVADA A. CARMICHAEL, Apr. 27, 1877 - Dec. 24, 1895
CHARLES B. STALNAKER, 1856 - 1946
SALLIE ALICE, wife of F. E. JONES, Dec. 23, 1859 - Oct. 1, 1888
JAMES A. WILDER, Jun. 1, 1891 - age 34 yrs.
LIZZIE WILDER, 1886 - age 24 yrs.
ALICE E., wife of R. W. JONES, May 17, 1867 - Nov. 1, 1917
HAGAR, wife of J. R. JONES,Jan. 29, 1841 - Feb. 11, 1888
MARY, wife of R. W. JONES, Aug. 2, 1866 - Dec. 15, 1889
J. B. PLYLAR, Dec. 27, 1842 - Sep. 16, 1924
ELIZABETH, wife of J. B. PLYLAR, Sep. 3, 1843 - Jul. 13, 1921
MILLIE B. WEST, 1834 - 1932
HENRY H. BROOM, Mar. 6, 1851 - Mar. 14, 1949
GAYCE J. BROOM, Aug. 6,1850 - June 25, 1940
DAVID W. GARRISON, Dec. 26, 1855 - Jan. 12, 1890
MARTHA GARRISON HENDRIX, Apr. 27, 1856 - Jan. 5, 1948
SARAH J. BAILEY, 1836 - 1927
LOONEY E. BAILEY, Jan. 18, 1862 - Apr. 10, 1932
S. H. BAILEY, Jul. 27, 1875 - Nov. 14, 1921
JAMES B. KEY, 1860 - 1928
SAMANTHA J. KEY, 1864 - 1943
S. WILSON, d. Mar. 1, 1928 - age 67 yrs.
VIRGINIA DYER, wife of S. WILSON, no dates
E. Z. (ZEKE) PLYLER, Nov. 13, 1864 - Apr. 17, 1930
MARY ELLEN PLYLER, Mar. 11, 1874 - Feb. 27, 1957
NANCY PLYLER QUILLEN, 1851 - 1932
W. C. (MAC) McMILLAN, May 9, 1860 - Jan.1, 1932
MARTHA McMILLAN, Sep. 15, 1868 - Sep. 3, 1927

South Lowell Cemetery - Six Miles North of Jasper, Alabama

WINIFRED, wife of JOB RICHARDSON, dates all eroded. (first person to be buried here)
JOB RICHARDSON, Nov. 8, 1802 - Oct. 7, 1873

South Lowell Cemetery Cont'd.

RUTHA RICHARDSON, wife of JOB RICHARDSON, Jul. 16, 1831 - Jun. 12, 1894
BELZO RICHARDSON, Feb. 18, 1857 - Jun. 12, 1915
TOM RICHARDSON, Jan. 26, 1860 - May 14, 1938
JERUSHA A. RICHARDSON, wife of THOMAS BRAGDEN, May 13, 1858 - Feb. 18, 1923
L. H. COKER, May 25, 1829 - Apr. 21, 1905
ANNA COKER, Aug. 14, 1833 - Mar. 27, 1890
WM. PLIMLEY, Oct. 25, 1812 - Mar. 28, 1894
MARY ANN, wife of WM. PLIMLEY, Jan. 8, 1849 - Jan. 26, 1911
SARAH, wife of F. A. PLIMLEY, 1845 - Jan. 16, 1890
RICHARD BATES, 1868 - 1947
ETTA C. BATES, wife of RICHARD BATES, 1873 - 1949
ANDREW J. DAME, Apr. 18. 1848 - Oct. 28, 1911
MARY E., wife of T. O. PARTRIDGE, Nov. 26, 1831 - Jan. 14, 1908
UNCLE TOM PARTRIDGE, no dates
S. A. WILSON, Mar. 3, 1868 - Jan. 12, 1908
JOHN HENRY PATTON, 1862 - 1931
MARY C. (TINY), wife of JOHN HENRY PATTON, 1877 - 1906
CARRANDUS RICHARDSON, 1853 - 1921
CATHERN RICHARDSON, Sep. 23, 1858 - Dec. 14, 1893
TUTLESS, son of CARRANDUS RICHARDSON and CATHERN, 1882 - 1951
MRS. A. I. WOOD, wife of W. D. WOOD, Jul. 18, 1870 - Sep. 8, 1898
JULIA A. ROSS, wife of C. B. SPROUL, Jul. 13, 1841 - May 15, 1904
CHAS. B. SPROUL, Apr. 23, 1842 - Sep. 15, 1913
R. A. SPROUL, 1881 - 1942
W. H. SPROUL, 1877 - 1935
WM. WOOD, Jan. 3, 1835 - Jul. 28, 1908
HANNAH, wife of WM. WOOD, no dates
R. M. GOSSETT, 1846 - 1940
J. L. GOSSETT, 1860 - 1931
L. A. GOSSETT, 1882 - 1925
MAGGIE SAXTON, 1887 - 1912
BARNIE L. COKER, b. in South Lowell, Ala. Aug. 2, 1872 - Aug. 21, 1902
JOHN A. SWINDLE, Jun. 9, 1882 - Nov. 10, 1947
DELLA S. SWINDLE, Mar. 27, 1888 - Sep. 6, 1953
W. W. IRELAND, Feb. 18, 1838 - Feb. 9, 1903
ORAL RIGSBY, son of J. N. and ELVA RIGSBY, Oct. 11, 1869 - Nov. 13, 1891
S. E. McCAULLEY, wife of S. H. McCAULLEY, Nov. 16, 1841 - Sep. 15, 1905
S. H. McCAULLEY, no dates
B. F. JACOBS, Aug. 7, 1864 - Oct. 15, 1887
J. H. SMITH, Jan. 17, 1859 - Feb. 9, 1913

## South Lowell Cemetery Cont'd.

OLIVIA O'REAR, 1859 - 1923
JERRY A. O'REAR, 1855 - 1924
JOHN K. HENSON, 1873 - 1944
WM. HENSON, May 2, 1851 - Mar. 8, 1914
ALSEY HENSON, Oct. 10, 1861 - Apr. 27, 1911
W. H. HUMPHRIES, 1874 - 1931
DELLA HUMPHRIES, wife of FRED FARLEY, Mar. 28, 1902 - Oct. 30, 1932
W. J. HENSON, Aug. 2, 1876 - Feb. 9, 1949
MARGARET M. BURGETT, Jan. 13, 1849 - May 7, 1923
J. V. STOVER, May 8, 1835 - Jul. 10, 1910
L. M. WHITFIELD, Oct. 17, 1870 - May 10, 1925
R. A. KELL, Jan. 9, 1862 - Jul. 21, 1934
LUZIANNE, wife of R. A. KELL, Nov. 26, 1872 - Dec. 5, 1915
JOHN W. KING, 1876 - 1955
GEORGE W. KING, May 16, 1859 - Jan. 7, 1940
EMMA JANE KING, Dec. 1856 - Nov. 2, 1940

## Lamon Chapel Baptist Church Near Hwy. 5 N.

W. R. MARSHALL, 1845 - 1930
ALICE MARSHALL, wife of W. R. MARSHALL, 1861 - 1943
SUSAN G., wife of W. W. WILLIAMS, Dec. 17, 1842 - Feb. 27,1918
WASH. W. WILLIAMS, Feb. 14, 1848 - Aug. 20, 1916
J. W. CARTER, May 3, 1844 - Feb. 3, 1927
LAURA V. CARTER, wife of J. W. CARTER, 1854 - Dec. 11, 1927
JOE REED, Jun. 6, 1862 - Oct. 4, 1951
JANE REED, wife of JOE REED, Oct. 16, 1859 - Jan. 20, 1949
J. V. BARKER, Jul. 31, 1865 - Jun. 9, 1929
CARRIE BARKER, wife of J. V. BARKER, Sep. 27, 1859 - Nov. 26, 1923
J. F. (BUD) SIDES, Feb. 12, 1866 - Mar. 2, 1950
J. M. BSNNETT, Sep. 23, 1868 - Mar. 5, 1941
JAMES T. LEE, 1866 - 1919
TEMPA LEE, wife of JAMES T. LEE, 1871 - 1947
NANCY E. LAMON, wife of J. W. LAMON, Nov. 25, 1843 - no death date
WASH LAMON, Sep. 5, 1871 - Aug. 21, 1924
FLORENCE LAMON, wife of WASH LAMON, Dec. 16, 1879 - Jan. 29, 1855
HEWITT I. BENNETT, Oct. 3, 1882 - Dec. 14, 1940
UNCLE CHARLIE ALEXANDER, 1870 - 1945
AUNT PARALEE ALEXANDER, 1870 - 1944

## Prospect Cemetery Near Prospect Station

JAMES LESLIE SOMMERVILLE, 1855 - 1933
LILLIAN BOBO SOMMERVILLE, wife of JAMES LESLIE SOMMERVILLE, 1871 - 1935

## Prospect Cemetery Cont'd.

JAMES LESLIE SOMMERVILLE, 1907 - 1934
G. THOMAS SMITH, 1870 - 1945
NANCY LOU SMITH, wife of G. THOMAS SMITH - Jan. 2, 1874 - Jul. 15, no date
W. D. GRIFFITH
CARA GRIFFITH, wife of W. D. GRIFFITH, 1862 - 1949
JAMES STREET, 1869 - 1936
SUSIE E. STREET, wife of JAMES STREET, 1852 - 1943
W. S. JETTER, Nov. 27, 1875 - May 5, 1925
MARGARET ALICE JETTER, wife of W. S. JETTER, Nov. 15, 1875 - Aug. 8, 1940
JOHN A. HAMMETT, Mar. 10, 1856 - Feb. 25, 1934
MARGARET E. HAMMETT, Dec. 23, 1855 - Oct. 5, 1919
BRATEN M. BURT, 1855 - 1935
MATTIE J. BURT, 1862 - 1929
THOMAS BRIGDEN, Jun. 7, 1834 - Feb. 7, 1924
J. M. PRESCOTT, 1852 - 1950
C. LUSS SHERER, Mar. 15, 1875 - Nov. 15, 1948
DELIA J. SHERER, wife of C. LUSS SHERER, Dec. 28, 1872 - Oct. 2, 1946

## Boldo Methodist Church Cemetery on Hwy. 69 East

A. G. WILLIAMS, May 12, 1856 - May 11, 1929
SUSAN J. WILLIAMS, Sep. 20, 1856 - Jul. 5, 1941
REV. W. W. BARTON, Feb. 2, 1838 - Jul. 11, 1919
JACKSON W. BARTON, 1873 - 1902
FANNIE CHAPPELL, Mar. 25, 1855 - Dec. 3, 1939
ELIZABETH BANKS, Dec. 19, 1826 - Mar. 10, 1909
MARTHA A. MURRAY, Oct. 5, 1860 - Jan. 4, 1907
SCOTT MURRAY, Aug. 26, 1859 - Feb. 24, 1920
MARTHA ANN MURRAY, Oct. 15, 1831 - Jul. 25, 1905
BERRY MURRAY, Jul. 29, 1893 - Feb. 4, 1956
B. A. MURPHEE, Oct. 27, 1832 - Oct. 25, 1908
LEROY WILLIAMS, May 25, 1832 - Sep. 11, 1908
ELIZABETH WILLIAMS, wife of LEROY WILLIAMS, d. Jul. 22, 1924 age 89 yrs.
JOHN BLACK, 1865 - 1933
M. V. RICHARDSON, Oct. 3, 1864 - Sep. 18, 1936
MATILDA RICHARDSON, Feb. 23, 1871 - Feb. 9, 1911
REV. JOHN W. MURRAY, May 24, 1875 - Mar. 24, 1947
MARTHA M. MURRAY, Aug. 19, 1879, no date
NETTIE, wife of L. W. KILGO, Jan. 25, 1870 - Nov. 6, 1901
MARK LOUIS ROBINSON, Nov. 7, 1835 - Aug. 3, 1909
L. M. TUCKER, Jan. 6, 1856 - Jun. 14, 1933
SARAH E., wife of W. C. TUCKER, Oct. 12, 1834 - Sep. 3, 1918
JOSEPH MILLER, 1872 - 1928

## Boldo Methodist Church Cemetery Cont'd.

NANCY KIKER, Sep. 15, 1868 - May 5, 1936
HENRY SNOW, May 11, 1875 - May 24, 1943
HELEN SNOW, Feb. 25, 1861 - Feb. 8, 1938
S. J. ROBERTSON, Jul. 16, 1860 - Dec. 28, 1938
A. V. WOODSON, Jul. 4, 1872 - Dec. 22, 1944
MATTIE WOODSON, wife of A. V. WOODSON, Feb. 1, 1872 - Aug. 29, 1948
ELDER F. M. WOODLEY, May 26, 1867 - Dec. 11, 1946
M. WILLINGHAM, Aug. 12, 1870 - Feb. 27, 1945

## King Family Plot on Thomas J. King home place

To the memory of JOHN KING, b. in N.C., 1790, Oct. d. Mar. 10, 1828 - age 37 yrs 5 mos
To the memory of LUCY KING, b. in Va., Apr. 17, 1793 and d. May 26, 1872, age 79 yrs. 1 mo. 2 das.
THOMAS J. KING, Nov. 2, 1820 - Apr. 24, 1912, Col. 56 Cavalry, C.S.A.
MARY ELIZABETH, wife of THOMAS J. KING, b. Dec. 4, 1833 - d. Nov. 19, 1898
LUCY KING PRICE, wife of JOHN PRICE, b. Oct. 24, 1870 - Aug. 5, 1901
NANCY ELIZABETH, wife of BODINE MANASCO, Jan. 20, 1877 - Apr. 24, 1908
CHAS. M. MASON, b. in Monroe Co. Mo. Mar. 29, 1866 - married Dec. 22, 1892 - d. Jan. 26, 1846. Devoted Husband Faithful Son. At Rest.
HUSTON, son of B. D. and M. KING, b. Nov. 27, 1874 - d. Dec. 22, 1874
LENA R., dau. of R. M. and S. K.CUNNINGHAM, b. Sep. 17, 1910

## Kings Chapel Church, Hillard, Alabama

MARY S. SPARKS, May 2, 1856 - Apr. 6, 1926
ALVIN S. SPARKS, Mar. 22, 1861 - Apr. 18, 1916
ELIA SPARKS, was born the 22 day of Jan. 1835 and was married to M. C. BAKER in 1858, departed this life the 28 day of Jul , 1872, age 37 yrs, 6 mos. 6 das.
MARY C. SPARKS, wife of E. A. SPARKS, b. Sep. 3, 1840 - d. Jan. 27, 1932
J. J. STEADMAN, b. 1860 - d. 1927
CALLIE M. STEADMAN, Feb. 28, 1860 - Jun. 11, 1940
JAS. S. STEADMAN, Jul. 30, 1854 - Oct. 6, 1885
SARAH L., wife of JAMES S. STEADMAN, Jan. 14, 1857 - Jul.23,1876
JOHN HOCKER, Apr. 12, 1862 - Mar. 19, 1936
MARY JANE HOCKER, Sep. 17, 1869 - Apr. 22, 1951
WILLIE HOCKER, son of J. E. and M. J. HOCKER, Dec. 17, 1886 - Jan. 15, 1909
LOUISA CAROLINE WILLIAMS, b. the 6th of Oct. 1838, d. 15th of Oct. 1895

Kings Chapel Church Cont'd.

JOHN TOWNLEY, b. Apr. 3, 1835 - d. Nov. 3, 1868
A. F. TOWNLEY, b. May 31, 1859 - d. Oct. 20, 1888
IRENE, dau. of O. E. S. and M. F. BURTON, b. Feb. 24, 1918 - d. Oct. 27,1918

Palmer Cemetery - Four Miles S.W. of Townley, Alabama

RARDERN BEVILLE, Feb. 26, 1793 - Mar. 12, 1877
HENRY PROCTOR, Apr. 15,1815 - Mar. 18, 1865
J. W. NELSON, Sep. 22, 1873 - Aug. 16, 1894
W. A. NELSON, Oct. 11, 1868 - Feb. 23, 1893
NANCY A. BEVILL, wife of F. K. BEVILL, Feb. 25, 1860 - Jul. 22, 1887
G. W. ARY, 1854 - 1936
M. A. ARY, 1855 - 1936
THOMAS A. ROGERS, Jan. 15, 1849 - Aug. 23, 1878
DAVIS KNIGHT, b. in Ga. Mar. 12, 1815 - Aug. 2, 1875
SARAH KNIGHT, Nov. 17, 1820 - Oct. 11, 1880
WILLIE ARY, son of G. W. and M. A. ARY, Feb. 16, 1880 - Oct. 15, 1908
LOU T. ARY, dau. of G. W. and M. A. ARY, Dec. 16, 1887 - Dec. 9, 1908
JOHN A. BAKER, Feb. 15, 1851 - Dec. 3, 1918
MARY E. BAKER, wife of JOHN A. BAKER, b. Feb. 25, 1847 - Aug. 13, 1927
ELIZABETH A., wife of R. T. PALMER, Dec. 27, 1821 - Aug. 31, 1880
DORA K. PALMER, wife of R. H. PALMER, Mar. 27, 1863 - Oct. 3, 1885
MOLVIN AMERSON, 1883 -1944
MALISSA C. AMERSON, wife of JOHN A. AMERSON, d. May 19, 1886, age 45 yrs.
MARSHAL M. AMERSON, May 6, 1860 - Mar. 9, 1932
MARTHA JANE AMERSON, Feb. 6, 1865 - Dec. 24, 1945
WM. ERASTUS AMERSON, Jan. 10, 1869 - Mar. 30, 1932

Old Canean Cemetery - Sellers Family Plot - Near Summiton, Alabama

LUTHER SELLERS, Sep. 29, 1813 - Jan. 21, 1897
MARGARET SELLERS, wife of LUTHER SELLERS, Apr. 4, 1824 - Feb. 16, 1889
MILLIE, wife of MILTON SELLERS, Apr. 15, 1844 - Nov. 14, 1919
SAM SELLERS, Oct. 26, 1865 - Mar. 19, 1930
DOLLIE SELLERS, Mar. 9, 1867 - no death date
LUCY M., wife of J. P. WILLIAMS, Jan. 1830 - Apr. 2, 1903
LIZZIE, dau. of J. P. WILLIAMS, Sep. 4, 1872 - Mar. 25, 1903
W. A. PARTAIN, SR., Dec. 26, 1868 - Jul. 2, 1919
MARY M. PARTAIN, Jun. 13, 1866 - Apr. 17, 1910
RANDOLPH SELLERS, Mar. 4, 1883 - Sep. 25, 1948
DELLIE SELLERS, Dec. 31, 1887 - Jan. 25, 1945

Phillips Cemetery - Delworth Mines, Walker Co.

G. WASH. PHILLIPS, Feb. 7, 1846 - Jan. 9, 1874
JEFF D. PHILLIPS, Sep. 15, 1861 - Oct. 6, 1946
LOUELLA PHILLIPS, May 17, 1868 - Oct. 16, 1946
MARTHA E. PHILLIPS, Jan. 7, 1878 - Apr. 20, 1905
SAMUEL MARTIN, Feb. 2, 1882 - Aug. 30, 1884
S. BYRD PHILLIPS, Sep. 1, 1842 - Jul. 31, 1902
MARY A. PHILLIPS, Nov. 25, 1849 - Aug. 13, 1895
ROBERT L. PHILLIPS, Apr. 3, 1884 - May 31, 1924
DOVER P. PHILLIPS, Oct. 5, 1889 - Jul. 28, 1929
OATHER PHILLIPS, (M.D.), Oct. 30, 1890 - Dec. 30, 1933
PHELAN PHILLIPS, (M.D.), Nov. 30, 1888 - Sep. 16, 1938
J. M. PHILLIPS, May 7, 1871 - May 11, 1945
S. B. (DOCK) PHILLIPS, May 1, 1876 - Oct. 21, 1948
JOHN W. PHILLIPS, Feb. 18, 1880 - Jan. 26, 1950
J. W. HANDLEY, Jul. 27, 1866 - Jul. 26, 1909
KEDRICK B. HANDLEY, Feb. 4, 1901 - Jul. 22, 1947
BOB HANDLEY, Dec. 9, 1907 - Mar. 1, 1955
CONROE E. HANDLEY, Dec. 17, 1903 - May 29, 1918
DORA PHILLIPS HANDLEY, no dates
MR. GUTHRIE, Mar. 17, 1881 - Oct. 17, 1938
THOMAS M. GUTHRIE, Dec. 28, 1876, no further dates
MARY ALLEN GUTHRIE, Jan. 11, 1875 - Nov. 14, 1945
LILLY GUTHRIE, Aug. 17, 1899 - Jul. 12, 1914
G. H. GUTHRIE, 1873 - Mar. 11, 1951
NANCY GUTHRIE, Dec. 8, 1847 - Apr. 12, 1939
B. M. GUTHRIE, Feb. 1841 - Oct. 11, 1912
MRS. S. J. KNOTT, Jan. 7, 1828 - Jun. 10, 1912
H. H. RICE, 1861 - Jun. 11, 1901
MARTHA, wife of J. H. CLARK, May 6, 1816 - Mar. 23, 1897
TINE AARON, wife of J. W. AARON, Apr. 15, 1876 - Oct. 27, 1918
JOHN W. AARON, Oct. 30, 1872 - Jul. 9, 1946
ELI DAVIS, 1846 - 1934
J. H. HOLLY, May 1848 - Aug. 26, 1912
J. H. CLARK, Aug. 8, 1808, Dec. 23, 1888
W. R. CLARK, Dec.15,1841 - Apr. 7, 1921
ELIZABETH M. CLARK, Oct. 11, 1851 - Apr. 20, 1919
WARREN IVY, Oct. 14, 1843 - Jan. 7, 1914
CHAS. L. PHILLIPS, Mar. 31, 1872 - Feb. 15, 1929
ETTA PHILLIP, Jan. 11, 1872 - May 24, 1913
E. J. PHILLIP, (JACK), 1843 - May 6, 1933
MARK PHILLIP, May 12, 1874 - Jan. 1, 1914
OLA M. PHILLIP, Jan. 15, 1887 - Sep. 14, 1942

Easley Cemetery - One Mile South of Dr. A. L. Hendon Home, Townley, Ala.

JOSIAH EASLEY, 1780 - 1850
ELIZABETH EASLEY, wife of JOSIAH EASLEY, May 26, 1783 - Feb. 4, 1852
DR. A. L. HENDON, Oct. 15, 1849 - Apr. 29, 1924

Easley Cemetery Cont'd.

SARAH A., wife of DR. A. L. HENDON, Jun. 1, 1859 - Apr. 7, 1932
BURWELL L., son of DR. A. L. HENDON and S.A. HENDON, Mar. 4, 1878, Dec. 27, 1905
KATIE K., dau. of DR. A. L. and S. A. HENDON, Feb. 4, 1893 - Dec. 16, 1905
FERNANDO G. HENDON, Jun. 21, 1880 - Jul. 4, 1918
THOMAS STAPLES HENDON, 1853 - 1935
ARMINTA ANN, wife of T. S. HENDON, Feb. 4, 1863 - Nov. 29, 1891
BESSIE, dau. of T. S. and A. A. HENDON, Nov. 5, 1883 - Oct. 24, 1905
JOHNSON HENDON, Feb. 11, 1834 - Oct. 12, 1862
MARGARET, wifw of JOHNSON HENDON, Nov. 22, 1831 - Dec. 6, 1891
J. A. HENDON, Aug. 5, 1812 - Mar. 15, 1890
ELIZABETH W., wife of J. A. HENDON, Jan. 8, 1814 - Apr. 17,1890
E. T. HENDON, Jul. 28, 1860 - Dec. 25, 1941
NANNIE, wife of E. T. HENDON, Jan. 7, 1873 - Dec. 6, 1909
NAN HENDON KOZAK, Dec. 5, 1909 - Mar. 12, 1941
JONATHAN SIDES, Nov. 1, 1817 - Jan. 25, 1898
FRANCIS, wife of JONATHAN SIDES, Jul. 31, 1826 - Feb. 26, 1906

Liberty Grove, Primitive Baptist Church Cemetery
One Mile South of Nauvoo

Sacred to the Memory of: WILEY S. ALLISON, who was born in Green Co. Ga. Feb. 10, 1797, was married Nov. 20, 1824, was a member of the Primitive Baptist Church departed this life in triumph of that faith Feb. 21, 1873, age 76 yrs and 17 das.
Sacred to the Memory of: SUSAN B., wife of WILEY ALLISON, who was born in Warren Co. Ga. Feb. 15, 1807, died a member of the Primitive Baptist Church, age 68 yrs. 7 mos.
FRED C. McKEEVER, 1886 - 1955
GUSS McKEEVER, 1884 - 1951
THOMAS P. McGOUGH, Jan. 28, 1885 - Jul. 5, 1940
M. A. McGOUGH, Mar. 10, 1862 - May 20, 1940
PAT McGOUGH, Jan. 14, 1851 - Jan. 25, 1919
SARAH, wife of M. A. McGOUGH, Dec. 30, 1862 - Nov. 25, 1939
CLEO McGOUGH, Jan. 14, 1883 - Aug. 7, 1909
S. J. DAVIS, Dec. 8, 1875 - Nov. 8, 1893
ARMANDA K., wife of G. C. DAVIS, May 28, 1840 - Jun. 2, 1913
GEO. J. DAVIS, Co. H 43 Ala. Inf. C.S.A. b. Sep. 8, 1838 - d. Feb. 17, 1923, age 85 yrs, 7 mos and 19 das.
ELIZABETH DAVIS, Aug. 11, 1850 - Dec. 5, 1929
WILLIAM T. DAVIS, 1856 - 1952
LUCINDA E. DAVIS, 1853 - 1918
L. RANSOM DAVIS, Sep. 1, 1850 - Aug. 25, 1927
IDA MAY DAVIS, dau. of L. R. and ELIZABETH C. DAVIS, Fsb. 24, 1890 - Feb. 6, 1907
In Memory of: MILEY DAVIS, May 27, 1883 - Jul. 4, 1887

## Liberty Grove Cemetery Cont'd.

DAVID M. DAVIS, Dec. 20, 1813 - Apr. 26, 1903, age 89 yrs 4 mos. 5 das.
SARAH A., wife of D. M. DAVIS, dau. of JACKSON HARWELL, Apr. 16, 1818 - Feb. 19, 1891
A. J. McGOUGH, Apr. 4, 1853 - Jan. 29, 1924
MARY ANN McGOUGH, Mar. 29, 1856 - Feb. 3, 1956
MILLIE E., wife of Z. D. ALLISON, Apr. 22, 1850 - Sep. 23, 1918
R. S. LOVELADY, May 1, 1847 - Mar. 3, 1915
ALITHA, wife of R. S. LOVELADY, Apr. 21, 1839 - Feb. 26, 1924
E. W. WINDHAM, Oct. 13, 1818 - Oct. 10, 1900
CORNELIA JACKSON, Feb. 15, 1795 - Jan. 23, 1851, age 72 yrs. 4 mos. 1 da.
MARY A. JACKSON, Mar. 11, 1859 - age 39 yrs. 11 mos.
J. C. ROBERTS, Nov. 20, 1815 - Nov. 1, 1862
ELIZABETH M., wife of J. C. ROBERTS, d. Nov. 1, 1880, age 65 yrs
LECLA, wife of J. A. MILLER, Aug. 1, 1832 - Jul. 7, 1902
W. E. WILLIAMS, Sep. 23, 1863, Sep. 4, 1914
MINNIE L., dau. of L. C. and B. F. KELLEY, wife of W. L. WILLIAMS, Feb. 15, 1867 - Oct. 1, 1903
MARY L. STOCKMAN, wife of G. E. STOCKMAN, Mar. 19, 1866, Feb. 6, 1914
In Memory of: GEO. J. DAVIS, May 3, 1862 - Oct. 28, 1889, age 27 yrs. 5 mos. and 5 das.
In Memory of: SUSAN GILL, Nov. 27, 1803, Apr. 22, 1891
LEWIS WILLIAMS, Apr. 9, 1862 - Nov. 19, 1887

## Good Hope Cemetery - Coleman, Alabama

DANIEL TUBBS, Feb. 17, 1794 - Mar. 25, 1882
MATILDA TUBBS, Dec. 29, 1861 - Jul. 8, 1886

## Lindsey Cemetery - South of Hwy. 69 West of Warrior River

NANCY, relict of JOHN MYERS, b. 1790, d. 1870
Several graves are here but dates are gone.

## Richardson Cemetery - In fork of Riley Creek - Near Warrior River

HIRAM RICHARDSON, 1799 - Jan. 21, 1859
EUGHAMA RICHARDSON, Oct. 2, 1806 - Jul. 12, 1887
JOSIAH RICHARDSON, 1846 - only date on stone
JAMES RICHARDSON, 1840 - (No further dates, not stated if birth or death)
SINA RICHARDSON, 1840 - (No further dates, not stated if birth or death)
GEORGE RICHARDSON, Sep. 10, 1875 - Nov. 7, 1876
SALINA THOMPSON, May 11, 1826 - Nov. 1, 1879

Romine Cemetery - West of Macedonia Church on Hollygrove Rd. - Near Lost Creek

NICHOLAS BOSHELL, Oct. 27, 1786 - Dec. 22, 1862
SARAH, wife of NICHOLAS BOSHELL, Jan. 6, 1788 - Sep. 23, 1858
W. R. BOSHELL, Dec. 2, 1823, Dec. 29, 1860
MACK ROMINE, Jan. 16, 1846 - Jul. 3, 1870
WILEY BROGDEN, Co. K, 5 Tenn. Inf.
......BROGDEN, Mar. 22, 1870 - Dec. 6, 1887

Gibson Hill Cemetery - Corona, Alabama

W. R. THACKER, May 20, 1859 - Jun. 14, 1947
ANNIE THACKER, Feb. 1, 1863 - May 14, 1943
EDDIE T. JONES, Feb. 26, 1868 - Aug. 19, 1949
JOSEPH J. FILES, Mar. 7, 1865 - Feb. 22, 1947
SUSIE E. FILES, Mar. 9, 1875 - no death date
JERRY F. FILES, Nov. 10, 1876 - Jun. 20, 1947
GEORGE W. THACKER, 1846 - 1938
HULDA THACKER, 1851 - 1938
JOHN KIMBRELL, Dec. 13, 1877 - Sep. 27, 1921
MAGGIE KIMBRELL, Sep. 13, 1877 - Aug. 20, 1920
MARY WILCUTT, 1872 - 1950
R. J. AMERSON, Jun. 30, 1841 - May 5, 1917
MARTHA A. UPTON, Feb. 8, 1872 - Mar. 7, 1934
W. J. EARNEST, 1869 = 1925
NANCY EARNEST, 1871 - 1933
HENRY EARNEST, 1858 - Aug. 25, 1931
GEORGE B. KILGORE, Jan. 28, 1878 - Apr. 3, 1943
FRANK SUTER, 1879 - 1942
JAMES TAYLOR, Aug. 31, 1863 - Aug. 27, 1942
SUSAN TAYLOR, Nov. 16, 1861 - Jan. 14, 1936
CORDELIA HARRIS, wife of D. N. HARRIS, Dec. 10, 1879 - Dec. 7, 1948
S. H. CUNNINGHAM, Mar. 12, 1851 - May 14, 1913
CATHERINE, wife of JAKE TAYLOR, Mar. 10, 1831 - Oct. 15, 1917
SUVILLER, wife of R. B. KILGORE, Jun. 12, 1874 - Jul. 29, 1931
ELBERT POE, May 4, 1862 - Jul. 20, 1934
BELLE POE, Jul. 13, 1867 - Oct. 22, 1931
MARY SUSA, wife of JOHN WALLACE, Dec. 10, 1875 - Mar. 12, 1926
E. W. WILCUTT, May 9, 1843 - May 2, 1917
MANDY, wife of E. W. WILCUTT, Sep. 25, 1849 - Dec. 8, 1915
REV. J. T. JONES, 1850 - 1910
MALISSA JONES, 1840 - 1925
J. EDWARD FROST, Jan. 7, 1878 - Feb. 9, 1939
JOHN T. PITTS, Apr. 12, 1856 - Oct. 9, 1918
MRS. SAVILLA F. PITTS, Jan. 19, 1859 - Aug. 17, 1922
OSCAR GIBSON, Sep. 22, 1880 - Mar. 12, 1946

## New Canena Church Cemetery - Six Miles North of Sipsey, Alabama

IRA ROBBINS, 1874 - 1939
NIMY ROBBINS, Apr. 10, 1826 - Nov. 20, 1928
NANCY ROBBINS, Jan. 21, 1857 - Feb. 25, 1918
WILLIAM L. CHAMNESS, Oct. 10, 1867 - Jan. 4, 1935
NARCISSIS, wife of J. W. ROBBINS, Aug. 20, 1859 - Oct. 9, 1938
JAMES A. HIGHT, 1869 - 1932
SUDIE HIGHT, 1875 - 1952
LUTHER OWENS, Jul. 3, 1871 - Feb. 17, 1939
CAROLINE MILLER, Mar. 11, 1872 - Mar. 23, 1951
BASCOM MORROW, Aug. 17, 1860 - Jul. 10, 1947
BEN OWENS, 1844 - Apr. 3, 1903
S. G. OWENS, wife of BEN OWENS, Jul. 8, 1851 - Nov. 12, 1896
J. C. PELT, May 5, 1864 - Nov. 18, 1943
THOMAS BAILEY, Mar. 24, 1853 - Feb. 15, 1940
BETTY BAILEY, Jan. 9, 1847 - Jul. 12, 1928
MARY OWENS, Sep. 9, 1862 - Sep. 24, 1938
A. W. OWENS, Jan. 4, 1861 - Apr. 10, 1938
GEORGE CHILDERS, Mar. 30, 1869, Apr. 12, 1942
M. J. GIPSON, Oct. 15, 1869 - May 28, 1946
JESSE H. JAGOOD, Jan. 26, 1868 - Oct. 30, 1930
ROBERT CAPPS, Jun. 6, 1864 - Apr. 9, 1939
EVA CAPPS, Dec. 5, 1866 - Feb. 26, 1940
SAM ROBERTS, Oct. 8, 1878 - Jan. 17, 1939
P. H. WAIT, Aug. 31, 1870 - Apr. 11, 1944
IDA WAIT JUSTIS, Jun. 22, 1870 - Feb. 17, 1948

## Lollar Family Plot - On Holly Grove Road - Three Miles West of Jasper

WILLIAM LOLLAR, d. Aug. 21, 1875 - age 65 yrs.
MARY, wife of WILLIAM LOLLAR, May 25, 1892 - age 78 yrs.
ETTA CHRISTIAN, dau. of JAMES A. and MARTHA J. LOLLAR, b. Jan. 15, 1882 - d. Sep. 20, 1882
VANDORN, son of W. H. & A. A. LOLLAR, Oct. 25,1874 - Nov. 12, 1877
NEILY, son of W. H. & A. A.LOLLAR, Feb. 6, 1876 - Nov. 5, 1877

## Cemetery - Eldridge, Alabama

JAMES HERRON, Nov. 4, 1849 - Oct. 21, 1935
BRYANT T. ASHMORE, M.D., Mar. 17, 1862 - May 9, 1931
ALICE EUGENIA CHENAULT, wife of BRYANT T. ASHMORE, M.D., Aug. 21, 1876 - d. Feb. 28, 1941
J. W. ROGERS, Jan. 13, 1840 - Feb. 8, 1916
ELLA, wife of J. W. ROGERS, May 13, 1853 - May 12, 1919
B. D. KELLY, Dec. 16, 1843 - Sep. 12, 1926

Cemetery - Eldridge, Alabama Cont'd.

ROXANNA KELLY, Jan. 8, 1854 - Apr. 4, 1940
PERRY W. KENDRICK, Sep. 22, 1857 - Sep. 18, 1951
W. A. ALDRIDGE, Mar. 10, 1862 - 19.....(not legible)
DORA ALDRIDGE, Aug. 27, 1876 - Oct. 21, 1937
JAMES L. LATHAM, Mar. 3, 1843 - Aug. 24, 1925
SARAH LATHAM, May 31, 1860 - Apr. 14, 1940

Oakman Cemetery - Oakman, Alabama

W. B. DAY, Mar. 8, 1817 - Jul. 16, 1901
NANCY DAY, wife of W. B. DAY, b. Tenn. Oct. 22,1817 - d. Jan. 15, 1883
MARGARET C. DAY, wife of W. B. DAY, Feb. 5, 1831 - Mar. 8, 1900
M. M. DODSON, Sep. 4, 1844 - Apr. 15, 1918
ALBERT G. WHITSON, Jul. 6, 1816 - Apr. 22, 1890
MRS. E. J. WHITSON, Mar. 17, 1831 - Sep. 22,1893
JAMES NEWTON MASTERSON, b. Tenn. Oct. 15, 1814 - Jul. 3, 1899
MAHALA, wife of J. H. MASTERSON, Aug. 20, 1855 - Jan. 3, 1897
SALLIE STEPHENSON, Aug. 23, 1863 - Nov. 18, 1948
H. W. STEPHENSON, M.D., 1854 - 1942
W. T. MASTERSON, M.D., Feb. 5, 1855 - Mar. 17, 1911
SARAH ELIZABETH, wife of W. T. MASTERSON, M.D., Apr. 5, 1857 - Sep. 25, 1921
ANNIE POUNDS, Nov. 10, 1856 - Jan. 1, 1895
JOSEPH M. HUBBERT, Apr. 8, 1829 - Apr. 2, 1903
D. GAINES HUBBERT, Dec. 27, 1853 - Sep. 25, 1899
SID MOORE, 1865 - 1933
LOU MOORE, 1866 - 1947
JOEL ELMORE, 1858 - Aug. 7, 1887
NANCY, wife of JOHN ELMORE, d. Dec. 26, 1884, age 68 yrs.
MARY E. WILLIAMS, wife of L. W. WILLIAMS, Jan. 17, 1859 - Jun. 24, 1888
G. H. DAY, May 14, 1848 - Mar. 4, 1921
LAURA E. DAY, Jan. 15,1854 - May 31, 1932
SAM B. DAY, May 3, 1867 - Apr. 27, 1935
MRS. M. E. DAY, wife of S. B. DAY, 1874 - 1931
DAVID MARION DAY, Nov. 30, 1842 - Apr. 27, 1903
SARAH ANN, wife of D. M. DAY, Oct. 18, 1842 - Apr. 8, 1918
WM. H. DAY, Sep. 17, 1878 - Jan. 29, 1927
LELIA C. DAY, Mar. 17, 1879 - Jan. 31, 1935
NANCY D. WILCOX, 1874 - 1935
T. L. DICKINSON, Jun. 22, 1857 - Aug. 4, 1904
ELIZABETH E., wife of T. L. DICKINSON, Jan. 6, 1862 - Jul. 31, 1898
ARCHEVIE JOHNSTON CARDEN, wife of E. S. CARDEN, May 1, 1872 - Oct. 10, 1904
JAMES R. MOORE, Mar. 24, 1860 - Dec. 12, 1926
ELIZA ANN, wife of J. R. MOORE, Feb. 28, 1873 - Nov. 9,1916

Oakman Cemetery Cont'd.

H. L. MONTGOMERY, Nov. 23, 1861 - Feb. 2, 1911
JAMES S. WATTS, Sep. 28, 1850 - May 12, 1933
JOSIE REID WATTS, Apr. 5, 1866 - Dec. 10, 1946
W. A. REID, Sep. 4, 1833 - Mar. 23, 1907
ALLEN H. JOHNSTON, Feb. 1, 1830 - Nov. 3, 1906
MARIA LOUISA JOHNSTON, wife of ALLEN H. JOHNSTON, Nov. 23, 1836
Oct. 28, 1924
FLEMING JOHNSTON, D.D.S., Jan. 13, 1871 - Jul.18, 1935
MOLLY K. PARKER, May 20, 1850 - May 18, 1935
F. M. LEITH, Feb. 8, 1838 - Mar. 24, 1915
SARAH F. LEITH, Sep. 22, 1852 - Aug. 29, 1923
JACOB HOLBROOK, Apr. 5, 1818 - Mar. 17, 1904
FATIMA E., wife of JACOB HOLBROOK, Oct. 7, 1833 - Jun. 14, 1912
MARION P. HOLBROOK, Mar. 24, 1853 - Oct. 21, 1897
P. E. HOLBROOK, 1856 - 1916
CHARLEY CROWNOVSR, Oct. 30, 1896 -- Apr. 27, 1901
URSULA CROWNOVSR, Jan. 18, 1862 - Jan. 9, 1933
WM.FRANKLIN CROWNOVER, SR., Feb. 22, 1855 - Dec. 6, 1933
B.F. CROWNOVER, Jun. 18, 1858 - Apr. 8, 1932
CELIA COX CROWNOVER, Oct. 19, 1862 - Nov. 15, 1949
MOLLIE KITCHENS HOCUTT, Jun. 12, 1869 - May 18, 1915
M. C. HOCUTT, no dates, eroded
MILLIE BLANTON HUTTO, 1858 - 1950
WM. TINSON, 1854 - 1916
ADA HUTTO MOSELY, 1877 - 1896
THOMAS N. BARNETT, Jan. 16, 1853 - Dec. 12, 1931
SARAH A. BARNETT, May 12, 1852 - Feb. 21, 1922
ANGELINE, wife of REV.ROBERT WILSON, Dec. 22, 1851 - Oct. 27, 1905
GRANDPA MARTIN, 1819 - 1907
MARTHA E. POSEY, 1849 - 1920
LEWIS H. POSEY, Jan. 10, 1843 - Jun. 16, 1926
WM. T. SAVAGE, 1860 - 1932
ADALINE M. SAVAGE, 1860 - 1940
M. L. SMITH, Sep. 14, 1859 - Feb. 7, 1928
CARRIE DOLBY BOYKIN, Dec. 11, 1874 - Apr. 4, 1950
REV. JOHN H. POOL, Jun. 8, 1853 - Oct. 13, 1926
SUSAN EMILY POOL, Fsb. 1, 1861 - Jan. 24, 1929
P. M. STEWART, Mar. 11,1857 - Jan. 22, 1908
E. H. SUBER, May 8, 1854 - Oct. 2, 1902
MARY M., wife of W. N. ALDRIDGE, Mar. 30, 1852 - May 14, 1914
SEBASTIAN MORRIS, 1860 - Jul. 10, 1945
SAMUEL W. INMAN, Feb. 9, 1863 - Mar. 11, 1948
PAUL P. DELENNE, 1855 - 1913
ANNIE DELENNE, 1858 - 1956
ALBERT PIERRE, SR., 1861 - 1947
BERTHA JOSEPHINE PIERRE, 1864 - 1945

Oakman Cemetery Cont'd.

MRS. S. D. KARRH, Mar. 26, 1851 - Feb. 3, 1926
S. L. KARRH, Sep. 11, 1875 - Jul. 30, 1930
JOHN ROSE, Jul. 16, 1852 - Jun. 10, 1938
EMILY BYRD ROSE, Apr. 11, 1852 - Feb. 18, 1927
SUSAN A. LOLLAR, 1857 - 1940
CHARLES HENRY CAIN, b. Warrick Co., Ind. Apr. 22, 1861 - d. Aug. 24, 1929
EFFIE GARRISON CAIN, Sep. 3, 1868 - May 3, 1950
WILEY W. HUTTO, Dec. 25, 1857 - Dec. 22, 1931
MILDRED DAY HUTTO, 1874 - 1934
LOUISE CHAMBOREDOM, 1850 - 1937
EDWARD C. CHAMBOREDOM, b. St. Paul France, Nov. 1, 1844 - d. Jan. 4, 1918
MARIE R. DELEUNE, b. France, Feb. 18, 1827 - Oct. 26, 1890
FRANK M. McMILLAN, 1836 - 1931
SARAH A. WHITSON McMILLAN, 1846 - 1930

Kelly Csmetery - Two Miles West of Eldredge, Ala. On Byler Road

JOHN KELLY, Mar. 29, 1805 - Sep. 12, 1883
MARTHA ANN, wife of JOHN KELLY, dau. of EASON FRANKLIN, 1815-1887
1ST. LT. JAMES M. KELLY, Co. B. 10th Ala. Cav. C.S.A.
C. C. KELLY, 1849 - 1911
M. E. KELLY, 1855 - 1937
CAPT. ED KELLY, May 27, 1836 - May 22, 1900
MRS. S. S. KELLY, Sep. 1, 1858 - May 6, 1906, wife of F. M. KELLY
MRS. LYDA ROBUCK, 1860 - 1929
ALICE McCLUSKEY, May 11, 1886 - Apr. 4, 1927
F. M. COLBURN, Mar. 15, 1855 - Jan. 18, 1929
W. T. COLBURN, Sep. 18, 1861 - Jul. 27, 1941
P. M. CLAYTON, Feb. 13, 1844 - Nov. 29, ....
F. M. CLAYTON, Jun. 22, 1833 - Sep. 22, 1903
CHARLEY B., son of H. B. & R. K. BAGWELL, Apr. 4, 1883 - Jul. 28, 1904
DREW McCLESKEY, 1872 - 1940
SARAH McCLESKEY, 1872 - 1940
JOHN LARKIN, M.D., 1866 - 1928
MARTHA LOUELLA LARKIN, 1872 - 1920
MARTHA W. KELLY, wife of CAPT. E. D. KELLY, May 22, 1845 - Dec. 2, 1912
NANCY A. BUTLER, wife of JOHN BUTLER, Mar. 22, 1859 - Feb. 5, 1896
DREW M. McCLUSKEY, 1857 - 1929

Kelly Cemetery Cont'd.

G. W. CASTLEBERRY, Nov. 21, 1856 - Aug. 13, 1937
AMANDA CASTLEBERRY, Feb. 24, 1856 - Nov. 1, 1923
MIRIAM CASTLEBERRY, Jul. 1833 - Apr. 9, 1900
S. L. CASTLEBERRY, Sep. 24, 1831 - Dec. 16, 1899
MARTHA ABLES, Apr. 11, 1875 - Mar. 22, 1896
WM. M., son of J. H. & NANCY M. SHAW, Jul. 16, 1849 - Oct. 1, 1866
WILMER, wife of S. B. WEST, May 27,1859 - Jul. 10,1903
SARAH M. TUCKER, Dec. 1, 1850 - Dec. 24, 1932
WM. M. TUCKER, Apr. 25, 1836 - Feb. 2, 1892
L. J. WILLIAMS, wife of J. H. WILLIAMS, Dec. 16, 1822 - Jun. 23, 1912
SGT. SAMUEL A. REED, Co. K 26th Ala. Inf. C.S.A.
REBECCA REED, Jul. 5, 1835 - Sep. 11, 1907
MATTIE REED ATKINS, 1854 - 1913
VETURIA, wife of J. T. STUBBLEFIELD, Jul. 28, 1861 - Aug. 19, 1891
NANCY GRAHAM STUBBLEFIELD, b. at Travelers Rest in Coosa Co. Ala. May 10, 1852 - Sep. 29, 1904
CHARLEY KNIGHT, Oct. 7, 1886 - May 30, 1908
L. D. KNIGHT, Dec. 16, 1850 - Dec. 6, 1895
JULIA JEDEMIA KNIGHT, wife of L. D. KNIGHT, Jan. 16, 1859 - Aug. 29, 1915
E. R. GUESS, wife of S. B. GUESS, May 1, 1831 - Sep. 4, 1894
S. B. WEST, Nov. 20, 1845 - Aug. 20, 1900
NANCY, wife of S. B. WEST, Jul. 12, 1846 - Aug. 21, 1885
H. L. TUCKER, Dec. 28, 1835 - Oct. 27, 1913
L. C., wife of H. L. TUCKER, Mar. 19, 1843 - Nov. 21, 1904
V. E., son of H. L. & L. C. TUCKER, Jul. 12, 1868 - Dec. 3, 1897
THOMAS EASON BAGWELL, son of J. T. & T. L. BAGWELL, Dec. 28, 1853, age 29 yrs.
LOUISA BAGWELL, wife of JOHN T. BAGWELL, Mar. 12, 1830 - Nov. 16, 1889

Sardis Nazarene Church -Cemetery - About Five Miles South of Jasper, Alabama

SAMUEL JACKSON, b. 1799 - d. Apr. 21, 1895
N. B. POSEY, Jun.11, 1824 - Aug. 26, 1904
EFFIE, wife of N. B. POSEY, May 21, 1826 - May 21, 1906
H. C. CRUMP, Jan. 7, 1845 - Mar. 10, 1928
MRS. M. E. CRUMP, wife of H. C. CRUMP, Jan. 25, 1848 - Aug. 14, 1950
JAMES B. COURINGTON, Co. I, 67th Ala. Inf. C.S.A.
IRENE COURINGTON, wife of JAMES B. COURINGTON, Jul. 12, 1854 - Mar. 3, 1933
N. CAL POSEY, 1855 - 1930
SUSAN F. POSEY, 1858 - 1934

Sardis Nazarene Church Cemetery Cont'd.

G. W. POSEY, Jul. 24, 1874 - Oct. 5, 1951
LAURA E. POSEY, Mar. 7, 1876 - Oct. 22, 1952
EMILY L. POSEY, 1832 - 1884
JAMES DAVIS CHILDERS, 1878 - 1957
M. A. POSEY, May 27, 1859 - Dec. 24, 1925
MRS. E. A. POSEY, Apr. 27, 1858 - Apr. 13, 1951
JOHN REECE DOUGLAS, Aug. 2, 1879 - Feb. 2, 1950
ALEX DOUGLAS, 1843 - 1915
H. J. CRUMP, Feb. 4, 1871 - Feb. 23, 1925
G. C. DOUGLAS, Nov. 1, 1873 - Oct. 15, 1913
ELISHA CLEMENTS, Nov. 8, 1858 - Oct. 31, 1867
M. M. CLEMENTS, Dec. 2, 1860 - Jan. 2, 1898
JOSEPH E. CLEMENTS, Mar. 4, 1829 - Jun. 27, 1902
LOUISE CAROLINE CLEMENTS, Apr. 2, 1834 - Apr. 24, 19...
WARREN COOPER, May 5, 1862 - Sep. 15, 1940
MINTY COOPER, Mar. 2, 1863 - Dec. 14, 1953
EMMA DOUGLAS, 1850 - 1926
MRS. L. A. FULLER, 1862 - 1918
T. B. ODOM, Feb. 13, 1862 - no further date
MARY A. T. ODOM, Sep. 11, 1864 - Dec. 2, 1941
J. H. LAWRIMORE, Feb. 11, 1859 - Jan. 8, 1944
JOHN COPELAND, Oct. 5, 1874 - Feb. 16, 1948
J. C. KITCHENS, Jul. 29, 1877 - Apr. 22, 1953
J. E. LIDDELL, Dec. 13, 1869 - Sep. 13, 1943

Cemetery on Key Hill - Antioch, Ala. - Northwest of Oakman, Alabama

TOM WOOD, Apr. 9, 1867 - Apr. 7, 1956
ELVIRA WOOD, Jul. 18, 1862 - Jan. 16, 1946
MANURVA, wife of THOMAS REED, b. S.C., Feb. 14, 1810 - d. Feb. 9, 1895
SUSANAH, wife of DR. R. P. GRIFFIN, Jul. 22,1856 - Apr. 10,1881
HENRY BARENTINE, Jun. 9, 1853 - Dec. 21, 1900
JOSEPH G. SHANNON, Feb. 8, 1857 - Apr. 27, 1932
MARTHA ANN GUTTERY, (2nd wife of JOSEPH M. CORRY) Dec. 24, 1834 - d. Apr. 18, 1872
DANIEL W. CORRY, 1860 - 1938
WALTER G. CORRY, 1870 - 1942
BENJAMIN FRANKLIN CORRY, 1868 - 1940
ALLIE MONROE CORRY, 1870 - 1948
ELIZABETH MANERVY (McCARNS), wife of JOSEPH M. CORRY, b. May 16, 1828 - d. Apr. 18, 1867
ABRAHAM MYERS ROBBERTS, (stepfather of JOSEPH M. CORRY), Jul. 18, 1814 - d. Jan. 2, 1855
THOMAS KEY, Furrier, 13 BN, Ala. Partisan Rangers, C.S.A. b. Sep. 8, 1833 - d. Aug. 20, 1910

Cemetery on Key Hill Cont'd.

EDITHA ESABELLA CORRY, GAINES, DAVIS, dau. of JOSEPH M. CORRY, b. Nov. 30, 1855 - d. Aug. 1888
ELIZABETH DAVIS, wife of WILEY DAVIS, Oct. 25,1882 - age 46 yrs.
WILEY DAVIS, Mar. 22, 1842 - Jun. 15, 1905
ELIZA J., wife of ANDREW PATTON, Aug. 13, 1865 - Sep. 21, 1884
MORGANA, wife of R. S. BALGH (?), Aug. 5, 1849 - Oct. 12, 1878
EVELINE SANDERS, Oct. 31, 1859 - Feb. 22, 1928
JOHN WOOD, 1859 - 1889
G. T. SANDERS, Mar. 20, 1863 - Jun. 17, 1917
SUSAN M. LAWSON, Nov. 12, 1873 - Mar. 13, 1937
J. W. BLANTON, Nov. 28, 1843 - Oct. 12, 1880
CURTIS M. WOOD, 1873 - 1950
VIRGIA ETHEL MYERS, WOODS, Mar. 4, 1895 - Jun. 18, 1920

Patton Family Plot - Deep in the woods near Patton, Ala.

ANDREW PATTON, b. Jul. 6, 1772 - d. Oct. 12, 1846
Other graves here but stones eroded and not readible.

Swindle Cemetery, near Oakman, Alabama

WILLIAM SWINDLE, Sep. 16, 1811 - Mar. 13, 1893
LUCIUS C. SWINDLE, 1852 - 1928
M. H. W. SWINDLE, wife of LUCIUS SWINDLE, Nov. 24, 1854 - Mar. 3, 1893
W. LAFAYETTE CRANFORD, b. Feb. 7, 1860, married ETTA SWINDLE, Oct. 23, 1881, d. may 27, 1896
GEORGE T. DAVIDSON, Sep. 25, 1842 - Jun. 31, 1900
MATHEW L. JAMES, 1854 - 1931
MARGARET E. JAMES, 1858 - no death date
SUE, wife of JOHN RUTLEDGE, Jun. 8, 1847 - Dec. 1928
JEAN LOUIS FONTANE, b. France, Dec. 13, 1852, Jun. 6, 1913
W. D. WREN, Jan. 13, 1849 - May 10, 1911
ELLEN J. KIRKWOOD, Dec. 4, 1849 - Aug. 30, 1894
FRANCOIS LEFEVER, b. France, 1841 - d. 1895
MARGARET M. WOLF, Mar. 1, 1851 - Jun. 2, 1914 -
ZELLON E., wife of J. R. PURDEN, Aug. 8, 1870 - Dec. 7, 1905
LORENA, wife of J. R. PURDEN, d. May 18, 1888, age 30 yrs.
GEORGE BURT, d. Aug. 12, 1894, age 43 yrs.
JEPTHA C. JONES, Co. A. 24 Ala. Inf. C.S.A.
W. L. GROOM, Jun. 27, 1866 - Apr. 2, 1920
LUCINDA GROOM, wife of W. L. GROOM, Dec. 22, 1870 - Mar. 29, 1927

Files Cemetery - About One Mile West Beech Grove Freewill Baptist Church

JACOB FELTMAN, Aug. 27, 1799 - Feb. 5, 1879
JESSE TYREE, b. Va. Mar. 29, 1767 - d. Aug. 8, 1870, age 103 yrs 4 mos. and 12 das.

Files Cemetery Cont'd.

MARTHA TYREE, wife of JESSE TYREE, b. Tenn. May 21, 1782, d. Oct. 15, 1873, age 91 yrs. 4 mos. and 28 das.
JOHN NORRIS, d. 1864, age 70 yrs. (b. 1794)
JOHN LAWSON, d. Nov. 3, 1883, age 103 yrs. (b. 1780)
SARAH, wife of JOHN LAWSON, d. Jun. 14, 1885, age 92 yrs. 9 mos. 22 das. (b. 1792-3)
W. M.RUTLEDGE, 1809-1866
E. P. ALEXANDER, Mar. 21, 1860 - Feb. 8, 1934
MARTHA JANE ALEXANDER, Oct. 29, 1867 - Jan. 15, 1912
ANNA FILES, 1879 - 1940
MARY, wife of J. W. RUTLEDGE, Feb. 26, 1846 - Nov. 10, 1916
A. J. (ABB) FILES, Oct. 7, 1861 - May 1,1940
M. H. MARY FILES, Aug. 13, 1864 - Jun. 16, 1948
MARY C. FILES, Oct. 26, 1860 - Sep. 11, 1935
M. Q. FILES, wife of J. J. FILES, Jan. 20, 1866 - Oct. 7, 1890
A. J. FILES, Nov. 14, 1822 - Dec. 12, 1888
E. A. FILES, 1831 - 1922
B. F. FILES, Co. A. 1st Ala. Cav.
J. M. FILES, Jan. 30, 1868 - Jan. 24, 1930
W. A. FILES, Dec. 5, 1876 - Sep. 20, 1902
TALATHA J. FILES, wife of W. F. FILES, May 16, 1878, Sep. 5, 1901
E. J. FILES, dau. of J. M. & RHODA FILES, Apr. 9, 1841 - May 27, 1892
RHODA E. FILES, wife of JERRE F. FILES, Apr. 22, 1837 - Dec. 29, 1892
GEORGE M. EDGIL, Ala. Pvt. 318 - 80 Div. d. Mar. 16, 1937
D. L. MITCHELL, 1873 - 1953
JESSE V. TITTLE, Feb. 17, 1862 - Apr. 6, 1950
MINTY TITTLE, Aug. 23, 1869 - Jan. 6, 1950
ROBERT A. HARBIN, Jan. 24,1861 - May 3, 1935
WM. O. TIREY, Sep. 2, 1863 - Mar. 2, 1921
GEORGAN TIREY, May 31, 1865 - Nov. 8, 1935
EXEY V. TIREY, Aug. 22, 1879 - Nov. 23, 1883
D. P. (DOSH) BROWN, 1861 - May 1, 1940
M. B. (LOU) BROWN, 1867 - 1930
MONROE COONER, Nov. 26, 1868 - Nov. 24, 1930
JAS. C. CARP COONER, Co. G 1st Ala. Cav.
MAHALA, wife of J. C. COONER, Apr. 24, 1833, Dec. 23, 1927
J. B. ALEXANDER, Dec. 8, 1803 - Nov. 18, 1915
MRS. I. E. ALEXANDER, 1855 - 1941
J. HENRY THORNTON, Oct. 16,1863 - Jan. 29, 1925
ELIZA A.THORNTON, Feb. 10, 1870 - Feb. 2, 1917
MARY A. RUTLEDGE, wife of J. W. RUTLEDGE, Feb. 26, 1846 - Nov. 10, 1910

Cemetery - Beech Grove Baptist Church

JOHN E. L. ALEXANDER, Oct. 2, 1823 - Dec. 20, 1872
MALINDA ALEXANDER, Dec. 19, 1822 - Nov. 20, 1900

Cemetery - Cedar Creek Church of Christ
Beat 10 - Walker Co.

WM. M. JACKSON BUSH, Nov. 22, 1876 - Mar. 12, 1948
MARGARET E. BUSH, Apr. 29, 1950 - May 14, 1899
EDWARD SANFORD, Sep. 17, 1867 - Jan. 28, 1957
IZUMA, wife of EDWARD B. SANFORD, Feb. 19, 1872 - Jul. 5, 1916
B. F. GANUS, Jan. 30, 1858 - Dec. 4, 1894
R. C. COURINGTON, Apr. 25, 1862 - Dec. 4, 1894
MRS. FANNIE COURINGTON, Apr. 1, 1867 - Jan. 17, 1935
K. P. GANT, 1872 - 1931
T. P. THOMPSON, Dec. 2, 1860 - Aug. 4, 1922
M. B. THOMPSON, Sep. 1, 1863 - Aug. 3, 1920
SUSAN, wife of K. P. GANT, May 6, 1871 - Mar. 24, 1915
VAN H. HOLLAND, Jul. 27, 1875 - Jan. 3, 1940

Central Church of Christ - Beat 23

AMANDA GURGANUS, Feb. 1, 1855 - Dec. 3, 1935
WILLIAM H. GURGANUS, 1872 - 1940
JOHN GURGANUS, Apr. 11, 1852 - Dec. 21, 1932
SALLIE EVANS, 1872 - 1946
MARGARET EVANS, 1874 - 1940
CHARLES S. POWELL, May 1, 1867 - Mar. 14, 1948
L. O. EVANS, Feb. 23, 1866 - Jan. 30, 1950

Family Cemetery - One Mile West of Tutwiler
School - Beat 10 - Walker Co.

WILLIAM ODOM, 1801 - Jan. 21, 1876

Cemetery Near Cannon Bridge, Beat 10 - Walker County

HIRAM CARADINE, Sep. 1793 - d. Dec. 1877
M. A. THOMPSON, Apr. 9, 1859 (not identified as birth or death date)

Cemetery - Beat 10 - Walker Co.

L. A. THOMPSON, Jul. 25, 1865 - Sep. 30, 1926
J. W. THOMPSON, Nov. 15, 1852 - Dec. 9, 1928
JAMES B. ROWE, Aug. 14, 1860 - Apr. 12, 1923
JANE P. ROWE, Feb. 9, 1864 - Nov. 12, 1925

Inactive Cemetery - Fork of Lost Creek - One Mile South Pleasant Grove Church

JAMES PATMAN COONER, Apr. 10, 1787 - 1855
MARTHA LOLLAR COONER, Dec. 3, 1794 - 1856

Gilchrist Cemetery - Beat 23 - Walker County

MARY GILCHRIST, Feb. 14, 1832 - Feb. 2, 1909
EDMON GILCHRIST, Feb. 19, 1791 - Jul. 9, 1875
ROBERT GILCHRIST, Jan. 7, 1867 - Jan. 22, 1939
THULA GILCHRIST, May 7, 1867 - Feb. 26, 1945
PIE McDUFF, Feb. 27, 1873 - no other dates
J. A. ROBBINS, May 24, 1833 - Jun. 26, 1901
JOSEPHINE ROBBINS, Dec. 12, 1860 - May 6, 1935
WALTER R. MARTIN, 1854 - 1924
W. T. MARTIN, Dec. 29, 1839 - May 18, 1902

Bible Church of God Cemetery - One Mile West of Wyatt Station

GEO. W. MAULDIN, Aug. 5, 1839 - Nov. 23, 1910
J. W. THOMPSON, Jan. 10, 1840 - Oct. 24, 1895
MARY ANN THOMAS, 1839 - 1923
JAMES LESTER THOMAS, Jan. 15, 1861 - Nov. 26, 1926
W. H. BRASFIELD, Jan. 8, 1845 - Mar. 26, 1926
NANCY E. BRASFIELD, Dec. 10, 1849 - no other dates
MATILDA QUINN, Mar. 27, 1873 - Jan. 30, 1919
CORNELIA G., dau. of W. H. & N. E. BRASFIELD, Jan. 24, 1872 - May 7, 1893

Cemetery - Near Cordova, Ala. on Shell Cotton's Farm, Inactive

HAWKINS BORDON, d. 1842 (First sheriff of Walker Co.)
This is the only grave here with an inscription or stone, although there are many graves in the plot.

Cemetery Near Warrior River - Black Family

SAMUEL BLACK, b. 28, Oct. 1801 - d. Dec. 11, 1873
ELIZABETH BLACK, wife of SAMUEL BLACK, dates eroded. (Elizabeth BLACK was ELIZABETH BURTON before her marriage in S.C.)

Cemetery at Wilson Chapel - Near Lupton School off Nauvoo Road

MARTHA A., wife of ALLEN SMITH, b. Jul. 4, 1806 - Jan. 25, 1895
REV. W. P. SMITH, Mar. 7, 1834 - Jan. 3, 1900

Cemetery at Wilson Chapel Cont'd.

S. E. SMITH, wife of REV. W. P. SMITH, May 31, 1838 - Mar. 6, 1936
ARTIMISSA SMITH, Feb. 15, 1859 - 1884
C. M. D. WILSON, Jan. 20, 1850 - Feb. 7, 1915
SINTHIA WILSON, wife of C. M. D. WILSON, Aug. 25, 1854 - d. Jul. 9, 1910
HIRAM W. LOVELADY, b. Ga. Oct. 10, 1835 - Mar. 15, 1870
MATILDA R. N. McCULLARS, Aug. 1, 1841 - Oct. 19, 1876

Cemetery at Mt. Hope Church on Hwy. Jasper to Parrish, Alabama - Old Road

DAVIS D. MANUEL, 1860 - 1945
MARY E. MANUEL, 1862 - 1946
LT. JONES, Jun. 22, 1857 - Jan. 7, 1931

Antioch Cemetery on old Hwy. from Jasper to Parrish, Alabama

W. J. JONES, Mar. 13, 1836 - Jan. 12, 1907
EDA JONES, Mar. 6, 1836 - Sep. 22, 1893
CHARLES L. ROBINSON, Jan. 5, 1824 - Mar. 28, 1889 - joined Baptist Church 1871
MARGARET ROBINSON, Oct. 12, 1824 - Dec. 3, 1899
MISSIE BLACKWELL, Oct. 29, 1871 - Aug. 31, 1907
THOMAS B. HYCHE, Co. G. 13th Ala. Partisan Rangers, C.S.A.
DELILA FILES, d. Oct. 18, 1872, stone broken, birth date gone

Goodsprings Cemetery - Goodsprings, Ala.

AMEY CHRISTIAN, 1802 - 1880
JULIA ANN SANFORD, Jan. 18, 1848 - Jul. 20, 1934
THOMAS JEFFERSON SANFORD, Oct. 22, 1844 - Apr. 7, 1919
JOHN W. WINN, 1854 - 1933
ANNIE E. WINN, 1865 - ....
JAMES S. JENT, Nov. 8, 1855 - Apr. 4, 1911
A. W. GROVE, Dec. 1, 1853 - Mar. 3, 1917
GEORGE W. JONES, 1857 - 1939
LUSINA JONES, 1853 - 1944
MRS. M. E. SNOW, wife of JOHN SNOW, SR., May 20, 1858 - Jun. 13, 1923
JOHN W. SNOW, SR., Aug. 9, 1853 - Sep. 9, 1936
JOHN BORDEN, d. Apr. 9, 1891, age 69 yrs.
JAMES M. BORDEN, Apr. 7, 1852 - Dec. 1, 1933
JAMIMA ADALINE BORDEN, Dec. 21, 1856 - Jan. 24, 1914
GEORGE P. BORDEN, 1868 - 1937
BETTIE MAE BORDEN, 1877 - 1943

Goodsprings Cemetery Cont'd.

J. H. WEEMS, Co. B. 62nd Ala. Inf. C.S.A. Nov. 27, 1847 - Jun. 11, 1916
POLKEY KEY, May 31, 1858 - Mar. 25, 1924
JOHN C. KEY, 1846 - 1887
JULIA A. KEY, 1847 - 1928
C. J. GARNER, 1857 - 1920
NANCY E. GARNER, Dec. 24, 1859 - Jun. 29, 1941
ROBERT SPRINGFIELD, Feb. 1, 1832 - Oct. 12, 1910
D. J. DAVIS, Mar. 5, 1832 - Sep. 26, 1871
G. R. SANFORD, 1861 - 1927
SARA A. SANFORD, May 7, 1862 - Sep. 10, 1941
WILLIAM P. SANFORD, Aug. 7, 1846 - Feb. 21, 1908
ISIAH SANFORD, 1818 - Dec. 5, 1867
JOHN W. SANFORD, 1821 - 1866
ELIZA ADALINE SANFORD, 1840 - 1878

Cemetery at Kansas, Alabama

SUSAN SMITH, Mar. 4, 1854 - Jul. 28, 1868 - age 15, dau. of A. A. SMITH
ELIZABETH JENKINS, Dec. 1, 1852 - Nov. 11, 1872, married to L. W. JENKINS, Oct. 11, 1871
MANISA E., wife of A. A. SMITH, Jun. 9, 1831 - Jun. 5, 1888
A. A. SMITH, Apr. 9, 1832 - Apr. 22, 1908
SAMUEL CLARK, May 22, 1786 - Apr. 15, 1863, age 66 yrs. 11 mos. 23 das.
MARY ANN, wife of SAMUEL CLARK, May 22, 1817 - Jan. 16, 1898
MARTHA J., wife of WM. P. HAYNEY, Dec. 16, 1833 - Jul. 20, 1889
JOHN W. STRONG, Mar. 12, 1849 - Apr. 22, 1901
REBECCA McCOLLOUGH, wife of W. McCOLLOUGH, Nov. 13, 1806 - age 35 yrs.
LIENELLA (or LIWELLA), wife of J. I. PRINCE, Oct. 19, 1859 - Nov. 12, 1892
CATHERINE, wife of WM. R. McDONALD, Feb. 3, 1831 - Mar. 22, 1910
WM. R. McDONALD, Jan. 31, 1828 - Aug. 3, 1890
WM. G. JOHNSON, Mar. 4, 1851 - Feb. 24, 1914
F. M. TREADWAY, Mar. 18, 187.. - Feb. 22, 1897
SARAH M., wife of F. M. TREADWAY, Dec. 1, 1849 - Jul. 22, 1893
A. K. RUTLEDGE, Aug. 4, 1840 - Feb. 4, 1901
ELIZA J. RUTLEDGE, Nov. 25, 1847 - Jul. 8, 1932
SAVANNAH E. RUTLEDGE, Aug. 4, 1865 - Oct. 15, 1931
JAMES L. RUTLEDGE, May 27, 1887 - Jan. 1, 1908
ALICE RUTLEDGE, Mar. 1, 1884 - Dec. 31, 1918

## Cemetery - Wyatt Station Baptist Church

JEREMIAH SHEPHERD, d. Jan. 26, 1869, age 70 yrs (b. 1799)
KISIAH SHEPHERD, May 4, 1799 - Dec. 28, 1874
ISAAC H. SHEPHERD, Nov. 23, 1845 - Jun. 17, 1903
HATTIE SHEPHERD SYKES, 1878 - 1909
ELIZABETH SHEPHERD, Nov. 14, 1832 - Sep. 19, 1846
REV. W. H. PETERSON, Apr. 3, 1860 - May 5, 1905
NANCY, wife of REV. W. H. PETERSON, Jun. 30, 1861 - Dec. 22, 1944
W. F. PETERSON, Nov. 1830 - Dec. 1916
SARAH M. PETERSON, wife of W. F. PETERSON, Jan. 28, 1829 - Mar. 28, 1895
HIRAM F. PETERSON, Jan. 13, 1856 - Dec. 14, 1893
EMMA J. PETTERSON, Aug. 13, 1877 - Mar. 1, 1896
EDNA PETERSON, b. S. C. Jun. 16, 1804, d. May 24, 1891
NANCY LANTRIP PETERSON, wife of WM. F. PETERSON, Mar. 17, 1858 - Jul. 21, 1882
SARAH G. HAYES, dau. of WM. & SARAH M. PETERSON, Nov. 29, 1865 Dec. 8, 1883
SARAH ANN LANTRIP, Nov. 15, 1825 - Jan. 28, 1891
SARAH ANN, wife of C. T. LANTRIP, Sep. 30, 1825 - Dec. 23, 1877
MALINDA, wife of L. M. SUMMERS, Aug. 19, 1872 - Sep. 30, 1902
R. F. WYATT, Mar. 11, 1869 - Nov. 23, 1943
EUDORA WYATT, Feb. 24, 1873 - Feb. 24, 1949
ROSEANA HAYES, Aug. 10, 1839 - Dec. 1, 1896
JOHN S. HAYES, Feb. 9, 1819 - Aug. 14, 1895
MARY HOOD, Aug. 16, 1800 - Apr. 14, 1887
CATHERINE, wife of JOS. WILLIAMS, Jun. 28, 1807 - May 31, 1854
ANGELINE PRESCOST, Sep. 6, 1840 - May 6, 1877
NANCY JANE, dau. of ANGELINE PRESCOST, Dec. 12, 1860 - Feb. 18, 1922
MARY SHERER, May 3, 1842 - Aug. 1, 1891

## Cemetery - Shanghi Baptist Church - Near Quinton, Alabama

LUCINDA, wife of S. G. BRASFIELD, May 3, 1855 - May 14, 1908
W. R. ANDREWS, Jun. 10, 1842 - Mar. 6, 1912
S. M. ANDREWS, Apr. 24, 1850 - Aug. 24, 1926
R. H. ANDREWS, Aug. 17, 1844 - Jul. 31, 1927
MARY ANN, wife of G. T. LANTRIP, Nov. 15, 1869 - Jan. 9, 1915
JOHN ODEN, 1863 - 1922
CLARA ODEN, 1860 - 1946
J. L. KILGORE, Jul. 25, 1859 - Feb. 28, 1920
ELLEN KILGORE, Oct. 17, 1869 - Aug. 12, 1923
J. H. PARKER, Mar. 18, 1863 - Aug. 19, 1905
JALEY FRANCES, wife of J. H. PARKER, 1863 - Sep. 14,1928
G. H. PARKER, Co. G. 28th Ala. Inf. C.S.A.

Cemetery - Shanghi Baptist Church Cont'd.

SAMUEL J. SELLERS, Feb. 9, 1809 - Apr. 21, 1887
REBECCA, wife of SAMUEL J. SELLERS, Oct. 9, 1820 - Oct. 23,1899
SAMUEL T. SELLERS, Mar. 1, 1859 - Apr. 12, 1935
DANIEL JENKINS, Aug. 17, 1838 - Jun. 24, 1899
DOROTHY R. JENKINS, Mar. 18, 1839 - Mar. 27, 1913
MARY ALICE LOVELADY, Apr. 12, 1869 - Mar. 18, 1956
G. W. THAXTON, Apr. 21, 1845 - Feb. 1, 1899
DAVID M. MORGAN, Nov. 19, 1858 - Jan. 26, 1939
ADDIE W. MORGAN, Mar. 3, 1862 - other date gone
JOHN L. GLOVER, Apr. 23, 1827 - Dec. 15, 1893
L. SAMUEL GLOVER, Apr. 4, 1854 - Nov. 19, 1882
MARTHA JANE LAWSON, Jul. 29, 1857 - Oct. 30, 1881
MARY K. LAWSON, Nov. 14, 1859 - Sep. 29, 1939
JOHN R. LAWSON, Oct. 17, 1851 - Aug. 24, 1927
REV. T. P. VANDIVER, Nov. 28, 1852 - Dec. 25, 1916
FRANCES VANDIVER, Nov. 14, 1852 - Nov. 26, 1940
HARL. NICHOLS, Dec. 7, 1867 - 1897
MARTHA LAWSON, Jan. 2, 1827 - Feb. 19, 1911
MARY N. BLACK, Feb. 18, 1858 - Dec. 18, 1895
JAMES L.BLACK, Jul. 2, 1862 - May 7, 1954
FANNIE BRASFIELD, 1841 - Jul. 16, 1913
A. J. SUMNER, 1857 - 1919
ISABEL, wife of A. J. SUMNER, Apr. 3, 1862 - Mar. 8, 1902
JACOB CROCKER, May 11, 1848 - Nov. 7, 1911
JOHN ANDREWS, Mar. 17, 1869 - Feb. 23, 1931

Cemetery - Sardis Primitive Baptist Church
South of Warrior River Bridge, Hwy. 78 East
On the River Road

HENRY FERGUSON, Oct, 16, 1783 - Feb. 24, 1874
MARY S., wife of HENRY FERGUSON, Nov. 24, 1811 - Jan. 12, 1866
HIRAM BARTON, Apr. 10, 1801 - m. SARAH WILLIS, 1821, d. Mar. 25, 1876, age 74 yrs. 11 mos. 15 das.
SARAH BARTON, Aug. 15, 1803 - Apr. 15, 1877
MOSES BARTON, Feb. 18, 1818 - m. Feb. 2, 1840 - d. Apr. 14,1890
MARGARET A. BARTON, wife of MOSES BARTON, b. Lawrence Co. Ala. Jan. 19, 1819 - d. Oct. 5, 1893
HIRAM BARTON, May 18, 1821 - Jul. 1, 1893
RACHEL BARTON, Jul. 4, 1836 - Feb.16, 1906
JAMES H. BARTON, Dec. 17, 1864 - Sep. 26, 1947
MARTHA JANE BARTON, Jan. 15, 1869 - Feb. 8, 1948
VESTER BARTON, 1874 - 1906
WASH BARTON, Feb. 20, 1862 - Sep. 4, 1937
MOLLIE BARTON, Oct. 27, 1869 - Jan. 27, 1951
JOHN M. BARTON, 1852 - 1930
MARY E. BARTON, 1859 - 1950

Cemetery - Sardis Primitive Baptist Church Cont'd.

G. W. BARTON, JR., Nov. 21, 1876 - Mar. 9, 1939
MOLLIE F. BARTON, Nov. 22, 1873 - Oct. 13, 1931
HIRAM S. BARTON, Mar. 7, 1875 - Feb. 19, 1940
VONA, wife of H. A. BARTON, Jan. 16, 1872 - Feb. 8, 1899
M. W. BARTON, May 9, 1827 - Sep. 11, 1902
MARTHA H. BARTON, Sep. 25, 1829 - Dec. 5, 1915
J. T. McADAMS, Jan. 9, 1850 - Sep. 14, 1921
J. H. McADAMS, dates gone
C. A. McADAMS, dates gone
MITTIA RAINS, 1822 - 1843
J. H. MYERS, 1839 - 1897
DANIEL W. DRUMMOND, Dec. 29, 1862 - no death date
ADALINE, wife of SANIEL DRUMMOND, Feb. 2, 1866 - Jun. 9, 1930
J. M. JOHNSON, Dec. 11, 1859 - no death date
MANDY, wife of J. M. JOHNSON, Jun. 5, 1860 - Mar. 18, 1932
BOB JOHNSON, 1862 - 1937
LETY JOHNSON, 1867 - no other date
H. A. WILLINGHAM, Mar. 10, 1855 - Jan. 2, 1940
A. H. HAMPTON, 1868 - 1927
MOLLIE HAMPTON, 1866 - 1925
VICIE YARBOROUGH, Jun. 24, 1861 - Sep. 24, 1918
B. F. IVY, Apr. 17, 1843 - Jan. 11, 1902
MARGARET, wife of B. F. IVY, Dec. 12, 1848 - May 27, 1922
REV. SANFORD V. ARGO, Aug. 10, 1834 - Sep. 26, 1894
JOHN W. ARGO, Aug. 25, 1856 - Sep. 20, 1900
JAMES E. STREET, Nov. 8, 1856 - Jul. 30, 1931
SARAH E. STREET, Jul. 26, 1867 - Sep. 28, 1917
F. M. SIMS, Jan. 28, 1835 - May 29, 1897
JAMES R. COLE, Jan. 14, 1843 - Jun. 22, 1920
MARRISSA COLE, wife of JAMES R. COLE, Nov. 9, 1847 - Sep. 8, 1927
WILLIAM BUTT, Feb. 24, 1834 - Oct. 1913
MARY A., wife of ENOCH MINOR, Nov. 22, 1825 - Jul. 22, 1894
WILLIAM BANKS, Aug. 23, 1832 - Nov. 31, 1900
ELIZABETH BANKS, Jul. 18, 1830 - Jun. 20, 1901
EVALINE, wife of J. N. BANKS, Sep. 28, 1857 - Jun. 25, 1909
J. N. ROBERTS, Jun. 24, 1854 - Jan. 1, 1916
IRENA ROBERTS, Jun. 4, 1860 - Jan. 26, 1941
JAMES ALEX HUNTER, 1877 - 1949
W. P. STOVALL, Jul. 29, 1856 - Aug. 28, 1930
At lease 100 unmarked graves in this cemetery, many built up like a bed with rocks.
HUGH BARTON, Jan. 1, 1846 - Feb. 12, 1919
IRENA BARTON, 1854 - 1928
JAMES H., son of J. A. & M. BARTON, Dec. 9, 1870 - Dec. 16, 1878

Cemetery - Sardis Primitive Baptist Church Cont'd.

MARTHA McADAMS, Jul. 10, 1803 - Dec. 18, 1883
MERICA F., dau. of W. A. & M. A. FIELDS, Mar. 28, 1876 - Feb. 6, 1891
WILLIAM A. FIELDS, Apr. 27, 1852 - Feb. 25, 1929
MARTHA A., wife of WILLIAM A. FIELDS, Sep. 24, 1851 - Jan. 31, 1928
JOHN C. MORROW, Jul. 23, 1824 - Mar. 4, 1918
MARGARET MORROW, d. Jan. 19, 1901, age 60 yrs.
SAMUEL MORROW, Sep. 27, 1871 - Aug. 6,1947
IDA, wife of SAMUEL MORROW, Jun. 20, 1870 - Mar. 9, 1944
HIRAM MORROW, Apr. 2, 1857 - Nov. 19, 1929
SARAH ELIZABETH, wife of HIRAM MORROW, Sep. 22, 1855 - Jun. 25, 1938
THOMAS B. MORROW, Jul. 30, 1849 - Jun. 15, 1930
MARTHA, wife of THOMAS B. MORROW, Jan. 17, 1851 - Jan. 10, 1917
REV. MODE B. MORROW, Jan. 2, 1848 - 1938
MRS. CYNTHIA MORROW, wife of REV. MODE B. MORROW, May 26, 1847 - Jan. 2, 1933
ADAM MORROW, Feb. 25, 1821 - Nov.1, 1863
TALITHA MORROW, wife of ADAM MORROW, Nov. 6, 1825 - Jul. 10, 1902
J. WASH GARNER, Jun. 14, 1856 - Nov. 13, 1939
M. J., wife of J. WASH GARNER, Sep. 29, 1857 - Apr. 8, 1905
MOSES SANDERS, 1829 - Sep. 1, 1897
CAROLINE SANDERS, wife of MOSES SANDERS, 1836 - Jan. 5, 1910

Cemetery - Liberty Grove Baptist Church
Above Buck's Creek, North on Nauvoo Road

ANDY SIDES, Jul. 17, 1827 - Aug. 31, 1912
MARY M. SIDES, Nov. 15, 1829 - Feb. 8, 1918
W. O. WILSON, Jul. 3, 1850 - Jan. 29, 1923
TIMA WILSON, Mar. 30,1851 - Jul. 18, 1941
CATHERINE, wife of JOHN KEETON, Apr. 6, 1838 - Jun. 30, 1899
W. C. ATKINS, Jul. 3, 1846 - Apr. 13, 1925
MINERVY M. ATKINS, Feb. 20, 1858 - Jan. 7, 1904
MARTHA JANE, wifs of ARCHABEL KEETON, Jul. 31, 1832 - Apr. 16, 1912
MARTHA J. SMITH, wife of J. W. SMITH, Mar. 3,1866 - Dec. 8, 1890
N. L. HARKNESS, wife of E. O. HARKNESS, Oct. 18, 1842 - Apr. 18, 1895
J. H. ALLIS, (ELLIS); Oct. 2, 1863 - Sep. 20, 1900
GEORGE, son of W. H. & M. S. BENSON, May 1, 1875 - Jul. 8, 1906
T. J. MOTE, 1847 - Aug. 1, 1900
MRS. M. C. MOTE, Apr. 15, 1860 - Sep. 21, 1941

## Cemetery - Liberty Grove Baptist Church Cont'd.

OLLIE G. SIDES, 1879 - 1945
W. M. KEETON, 1864 - 1941
JANE KEETON, 1869 - no date
FRANK FERGUSON, 1864 - 1949
BESSIE FERGUSON, 1868 - 1951
WILLIAM H. PIKE, 1869 - 1950
LOU A., wife of W. H. PIKE, Jan. 28, 1873 - May 25, 1920
J. C. PIKE, Dec. 8, 1833 - Jun. 16, 1916
MARTHA M. PIKE, no dates
ORA LOVE FAUGHT, 1909 - 1930
TINY GRACE FAUGHT, 1889 - 1934
G. W. ROBBINS, Feb. 11, 1855 - Nov. 23, 1928
M. C. ROBBINS, Oct. 12, 1857 - Feb. 3, 1834
MARY V., dau. of J. R. & O. E. DUTTON, May 16, 1834 - Mar. 15, 1901
CHARLES FISHER, Co. D. 4th Ky. Inf., Dec. 7, 1841 - Nov. 18, 1937
W. F. McCULLAR, Aug. 4, 1849 - Nov. 16, 1933
MARY E. McCULLAR, Apr. 9, 1854 - Mar. 26, 1905
JULIA ODOM, Jan. 1, 1866 - Nov. 6, 1932
JAMES IRA ODOM, May 6,1859 - Dec. 6, 1941
JOHN R. FERGUSON, Jun. 14, 1872 - Dec. 14, 1946
EFFIE FERGUSON, 1887 - 1933
L. T. SMITH, 1875 - 1937
MARGARET L. SMITH, 1879 - 1953
NANCY J. MORRIS, Aug. 1, 1846 - Feb. 7, 1937

## Fairview Cemetery - Near Reynolds School

RICHARD N. BELL, Apr. 3, 1875 - Mar. 26, 1943
IDA BELL, Sep. 17, 1873 - Nov. 6, 1951
K. S. HERRON, Jan. 28, 1862 - Aug. 1888
MALISSA, wife of J. W. GURGANUS, Apr. 11, 1833 - Nov. 13, 1894
MARTHA F. GURGANUS, Dec. 24, 1864 - Jun. 12, 1938
MARAND J.GURGANUS, Feb. 27, 1856 - Feb. 7, 1926
GEORGE W. GURGANUS, Oct. 30, 1858 - Oct. 18, 1876
THOMAS P. DAVIS, Apr. 12, 1843 - Oct. 25, 1916
NANCY M. DAVIS, May 28, 1866 - Apr. 24, 1945
JAMES M. BROWN, Nov. 27, 1860 - no other dates
M. C. BROWN, wife of JAMES BROWN, Jun. 14, 1865 - May 9, 1926
DICY ALLICE EARNEST, Dec. 25, 1853 - Nov. 8, 1902
J. B. THOMPSON, Co. G. 56th Ala. Partisan Rangers, C. S. A. Mar. 20, 1833 - Apr. 28, 1910
ARMINDA MILLER THOMPSON, Jan. 8,1872 - Feb. 21, 1951
FELMAN A. THOMPSON, 1869 - 1915
M. I. DOROUGH, Jul. 10,1835 - Aug. 24, 1891
ARMINTA, wife of JOHN COURINGTON, Feb. 5, 1858 - Jan. 2, 1923

Fairview Cemetery Cont'd.

JAMES F. GANT, Co. K. 50th Ala. Inf. C.S.A. Nov. 11, 1842 - Aug. 28, 1901
JOSEPHINE GANT, Mar. 16, 1862 - Dec. 2, 1935
B. J. HERRON, Jul. 27, 1864 - Dec. 27, 1917
MISSOURI HERRON, Jan. 1, 1862 - Oct. 26, 1955
EBENEZER BROWN, d. Feb. 25, 1914, age 78 yrs.
GEORGE ANN BROWN, Aug. 20, 1847 - Jun. 19,1917
JOSEPH H. HERRON, Co. K. 50th Ala. Inf. C.S.A.
SAMPSON BROWN, Co. K. 50th Ala. Inf. C.S.A.
LUIZER WETHERED, d. Feb. 11, 1877 - age 75 yrs.
ZACHARY GURGANUS, 1854 - 1937
BELLE GIRGANUS, 1860 - 1899
CALTON D. FIKE, Nov. 25, 1863 - Apr. 1, 1923
MARTHA FIKE, Feb. 17, 1864 - Jun. 13, 1926
S. E. GANT, Mar. 9, 1876 - Oct. 26, 1896
JOHN UPTAIN, Fowler's Ala. Artillery, C.S.A.
NATHANIEL O. DUNN, Fowler's Ala. Artillery, C.S.A.
SARAH DUNN, Dec. 15, 1852 - Apr. 14, 1938
BENJAMIN OZE GURGANUS, Sep. 30, 1861 - Aug. 11, 1952
ROSIE E. GURGANUS, Mar. 27, 1884 - Oct. 15, 1955
DR. S. W. GURGANUS, Mar. 12, 1884 - May 18, 1936
JACK BLACKSTON, 1867 - 1931
SAVILLA BLACKSTON, 1874 - 1929
JOHN W. WHITEHEAD, Dec. 31, 1871 - Apr. 4, 1953
MARGARET WHITEHEAD, Apr. 11, 1879 - Dec. 15, 1935
S. J. GARRETT, 1861 - 1935
LUCY A. GARRETT, 1866 - 1953
ALEX T. HUTTO, 1876 - 1950
ROBERT LEE SELBY, 1871 - 1936
R. WILLIE WAID, Feb. 18, 1867 - Mar. 12, 1922
MRS. M. E. WAID, Jan. 16, 1860 - Sep. 29, 1937
RUFUS F. DAVIS, 1871 - 1953
MARY R. DAVIS, 1875 - 1943

Liberty Hill Cemetery - S. W. Walker Co.

JAMES CAIN, d. Jan. 14, 1883, age 89 yrs. (b. 1794)
ELIZABETH, wife of JAMES CAIN, Oct. 30, 1803 - Nov. 16, 1870
RICHARD W. CAIN, Aug. 31, 1847 - Jun. 23, 1898
G. A. CAIN, Jul. 15, 1847 - Aug. 7, 1927
JAMES W. CAIN, Jul. 28, 1869 - Jul. 19, 1902
SAMUEL W. CAIN, Aug. 10, 1871 - Nov. 4, 1947
EDD M. EVANS, Dec. 5, 1862 - Aug. 22, 1955
ROXIE A. EVANS,Nov. 13, 1873 - Mar. 18, 1923
T. S. CALDONIA ROSE, Jan. 8, 1875 - 1908
B. P. (DOC) GURGANUS, 1877 - 1934
J. M. MELLOWN, Nov. 26, 1856 - Nov. 3, 1925
MRS. J. M. MELLOWN, Mar. 17, 1856 - Nov. 29, 1929

Liberty Hill Cemetery Cont'd.

POWELL JOHNSON, Dec. 10, 1869 - Aug. 6, 1942
A. PICKNEY WALDROP, Feb. 10, 1856 - Dec. 26, 1934
MAKINNEY M. WALDROP, Mar. 20, 1857 - Oct. 30, 1936
NELLIE GANT, Apr. 1, 1859 - Apr. 26, 1934
ALLEN GANT, Aug. 22, 1855 - Aug. 23, 1924
SAMUEL A. MULLINAX, Oct. 14, 1856 - Feb. 4, 1934
ORPHA C. MULLINAX, Mar. 12, 1859 - Mar. 28, 1943
ABNER KNIGHT, Co. K. 43rd Ala. Inf. C.S.A. Dec. 21, 1830 - Oct. 23, 1902
NANCY C. KNIGHT, Sep. 25, 1832 - Jun. 2, 1916
MATHEW MELLOWN, Dec. 26, 1812 - Feb. 28, 1900
DAVID A. MORRIS, Co. E. 28th Ala. Inf. C.S.A. Aug. 14, 1846 - Feb. 2, 1917
JESSE P. DAVIS, Steeles Co. Miss. Cav. C.S.A. Jun. 6, 1844 - Dec. 11, 1931
SARAH DAVIS, wife of JESSE P. DAVIS, May 12, 1843 - Dec. 11, 1931
MARY JANE, wife of D. A. MORRIS, 1849 - 1939
G. B. WALDROP, Mar. 6, 1831 - Jul. 21, 1889
EDWARD M. EVANS, Co. I 32nd Ala. Inf. C.S.A., Oct. 22, 1841 - Jul. 13, 1905
B. H. HUTTO, SR., Aug. 4, 1874 - Apr. 26, 1948
J. E. HANDLEY, 1861 - 1899
J. T., wife of W. W. HUTTO, Oct. 6, 1864 - Jan. 8, 1897
ELIZABETH CORLEY, Sep. 27, 1821 - Sep. 3, 1877
ASA TILMAN POE, Aug. 9, 1850 - Sep. 6, 1927
DORINDA RABURN POE, Mar. 26, 1854 - May 28, 1895
W. W. (WID) WETHINGTON, 1842 - Jun. 10, - Jun. 7, 1916
ELIZABETH, wife of W. W. WETHINGTON, Aug. 1, 1847 - Dec. 15,1895
THOMAS V. WETHINGTON, Jul. 3, 1872 - Sep. 16, 1894
MARTHA S. (SISTER), Oct. 11, 1875 - Sep. 25, 1883
R. E., wife of A. T. HANDLEY, Mar. 11, 1862 - Jul. 3, 1888
M. A., wife of A. T. HANDLEY, Mar. 4, 1843 - Dec. 14, 1881
JOICY B. CHILTON, Jan. 27, 1841 - Dec. 28, 1880
S. J. CHILTON, Apr. 8, 1837 - Nov. 4, 1899
SUSAN SWINDLE, Oct. 16, 1838 - Feb. 6, 1905
J. M. SWINDLE, Dec. 7, 1873 - Jun. 9, 1900
MARTHA JANE, wife of J. M. GARRETT, Jul. 26, 1868 - Oct. 19,1888
MARGARET L., wife of J. R. DAVIDSON, Oct. 5, 1857 - May 29, 1893
MARY EVANS, Sep. 22, 1860 - 1878
EMILY GANT, May 28, 1834 - Nov. 1, 1890
TINSON SHEPHERD, 1808 - 1879
MANERVA SHEPHERD, 1814 - 1845
CLEMENT CORLEY, All dates gone
I. M. MINOR, Aug. 5, 1851 - Mar. 7, 1882

Liberty Hill Cemetery Cont'd.

MARTHA MELLOWN, 1813 - 1878
MALIBA KILGORE, Feb. 2, 1849 - Mar. 12, 1894
ISAAC KILGORE, Co. K. 50th Ala. Inf. C.S.A. Aug. 13, 1840 -
ELIZA GARRETT, Jul. 3, 1834 - Jan. 11, 1926
SARAH EARNEST, 1827 - May 9, 1852
ANNIE YOUNG, Dec. 25, 1827 - May 8, 1910
S. GRANT, 1817 - 1877
WM. A. THOMPSON, Nov. 10, 1831 - Feb. 8, 1918
ELIZABETH THOMPSON, Mar. 14, 1838 - Jun. 10, 1906
SUSAN B., wife of W. W. HUTTO, May 12, 1859 - Jul. 22, 1888
ELIZABETH HUTTO, Sep. 2, 1837 - Feb. 10, 1903
JOHN C. HUTTO, b. Abbeville Dist. S.C. Aug. 25, 1830 - May 15, 1887
M. BELLE COBB, 1867 - 1943
J. R. KILGORE, Dec. 7, 1858 - Aug. 11, 1888
MARY E. KILGORE, Oct. 25, 1828 - Feb. 12, 1904
THOMAS W. PRICE, Aug. 24, 1817 - Apr. 6, 1860
MARTHA, wife of W. S. SMALLWOOD, 1808 - Aug. 10, 1893
MARTHA J. SAVAGE, 1845 - 1915
JAMES V. SAVAGE, Phelan's Co. L. Ala. Artillery, C.S.A. - 1844 - 1912
REV. MACK F. CORNELIUS, all dates gone
NANCY PALANTINE, wife of I. W. GURGANUS, Mar. 24, 1858 - Jun. 10, 1886
W. F. MINOR, Sep. 18, 1874 - Feb. 26, year not indicated
MARY EVALINE EVANS, Mar. 17, 1837 - Aug. 25, 1902 (wife of J. D. EVANS)
J. D. EVANS, Dec. 14,1831 - Mar. 2, 1880

Cemetery - Old Union Primitive Baptist Church -
About Four Miles From Eldredge, Ala. on Nauvoo Road

GEORGE M. BONNER, Co. K Ala. Cav. C.S.A. married Dec. 19, 1867 - b. Mar. 30, 1845 - d. Jan. 12, 1939, a Primitive Baptist for 57 yrs.
FRANCES ADALINE CONN BONNER, Jul. 8, 1838 - Oct. 12, 1921, a Primitive Baptist for 39 yrs. (wife of GEORGE M. BONNER)
JOHN McGOUGH, Feb. 9, 1834 - Alg. 1, 1919, Co. K. 4 Ala. Cav. C. S. A.
ROBERT DOWNEY, Mar. 25, 1844 - Aug. 14, 1919 - in the Cav.
MARY E. DOWNEY, Sep. 17, 1835 - Apr. 3, 1903
MARTHA J. JACKSON, Feb. 14, 1871 - Nov.22, 1908
ROBERT M. INGLE, Co. A. 1st Miss. Mounted Rifles, Mar. 27, 1840 Oct. 2, 1912
SIMEON TUCKER, Co. K. 1st Ala. Cav. Aug. 28, 1850 - Oct. 11, 1911
J. M.CLOWERS, Co. K. 4th Ala. Cav. C.S.A.
ANDREW J. HOLT, Co. M. 1st Ala. Cav. Dec. 8, 1844 -Sep. 9, 1927
JULIA ANN HOLT, Aug. 20, 1846 - Jan.15, 1922

## Spring Hill Church Cemetery - Between Eldredge and Nauvoo, Alabama

BARNABUS KELLY, Oct. 1810 - Jun. 26, 1887
J. F. KELLY, Mar. 9, 1850 - Jun. 5, 1898
THANIEL M. SMITH, Co. F. 20th Ala. Inf. C.S.A. 1830 - 1913
NANCY SMITH, 1837 - 1913
MARTHA M. PERRY, May 20, 1852 - Mar. 18, 1931
FRANK M. YATES, Feb. 10, 1654 - Apr. 8, 1928
MARY M. HENSON, Mar. 8, 1848 - Aug. 2, 1900
ARTHUR LAWSON, Pvt. 327th Inf. 32nd Div. Dec. 9, 1825 - Apr. 27, 1888
H. B. FOWLER, 1846 - Feb. 8, 1911

## Scott Cemetery - Ebenezer Church - Between Saragassa, Ala. and Holly Grove

HENRY FERGUSON, Sep. 9, 1832 - Jun. 5, 1911
CYNTHIA FERGUSON, Jan. 19, 1832 - Nov. 8, 1908 (wife of HENRY FERGUSON)
JOSEPH FERGUSON, b. Chester Dist. S.C. Dec. 25, 1794 - d. Sep. 21, 1886
LURANIA FERGUSON, b. York Dist. S.C. Dec. 23, 1809 - d. Sep. 12, 1888
MILLIE FERGUSON, b. Chester Dist. S.C. May 6, 1826 - d. Jul. 19, 1882
JOHN N.FERGUSON, Sep. 9, 1855 - Dec. 1, 1881
ROXANNA FERGUSON, Dec. 2, 1862 - Apr. 5, 1882
J. W. FERGUSON, Jun. 4, 1834 - Aug. 24, 1911
ELIZABETH, wife of J. W. FERGUSON, Oct. 10, 1838 - Jun. 9,1917
WM. H. FERGUSON, Feb. 22, 1867 - May 11, 1954
C. S. FERGUSON, Jan. 2, 1858 - Sep. 7,1917
SUSAN, wife of C. S. FERGUSON, Apr. 3, 1859 - Jun. 8,1920
RICH TOWNLEY, Dec. 5, 1833 - Mar. 11, 1905
MARY, wife of RICH TOWNLEY, Feb. 4, 1841 - Aug. 9, 1901
D. J. TOWNLEY, Oct. 28, 1838 - Mar. 23, 1894
ELIZABETH, wife of D. J. TOWNLEY, Nov. 17, 1843 - Nov. 17, 1891
S. D. TOWNLEY, Feb. 23, 1861 - Aug. 13, 1927
ALMA TOWNLEY, wife of GEORGE TOWNLEY, Mar. 10, 1866 - Mar. 4, 1948
M. J. STEADMAN, Mar. 8, 1842 - Oct. 14, 1923
JAMES J. STEEDMAN (?), b. Aug. 31, 1799, Chester Dist. S.C., - d. Apr. 8,1874
MARY A. STEEDMAN, b. York Dist. S.C. Jun. 27, 1804 - d. Jan. 4, 1890
J. B. STEEDMAN, Jan. 2, 1835 - Nov. 14, 1911
MARTHA J. STEEDMAN, Feb. 24, 1833 - Apr. 25, 1896
MARY JANE BOSHELL, Feb. 18, 1859 - Jan. 1, 1881

Scott Cemetery - Cont'd.

JOHN F. LATHAM, Sep. 25, 1862 - Dec. 12, 1881
ELIZUAR LATHAM, Jan. 1, 1865 - Oct. 13, 1881
R. T. LATHAM, Jan. 9, 1825 - Sep. 16, 1887
HIRAM HERRON, Jul. 25, 1850 - Sep. 15, 1909
MARTHA, wife of HIRAM HERRON, Feb. 18, 1850 - Jan. 15, 1927
JOHN W. KING, Aug. 6, 1855 - Dec. 28, 1893
W. R. KING, SR., Aug. 9, 1817 - Apr. 6, 1903
MARY L. KING, wife of W. R. KING, SR., b. Madison Co. Ga. - Oct.14, 1827 - d. Mar. 17, 1888
GEORGE W. KING, Jan. 9, 1851 - Dec. 16, 1881
JANE D. KING, Oct. 6, 1863 - Apr. 1, 1889
JOHN F. TUNE, Dec. 12, 1825 - Apr. 19, 1907
J. F. TUNE, Oct. 22, 1861 - Jan. 15, 1920
J. W. CHEATHAM, Nov. 3, 1837 - Jul. 28, 1909
WYATT CHEATHAM, b. Iredell Co. N.C. Mar. 5, 1807 - joined the Baptist Church of Christ, Jun. 1844 - d. Feb. 19, 1884
M. L. KING, dau. of J.W. & L. A. CHEATHAM, wife of WM. R. KING, JR., b. Jan. 29, 1869 - d. Aug. 15, 1888
L. W. CHEATHAM, Mar. 28, 1845 - Aug. 8, 1894
MISSOURI T.CHEATHSM, wife of R.T. CHEATHAM, May 3, 1850 - Mar. 4, 1892
ELIZABETH, wife of W. L. DAVIS, Feb. 16, 1838 - Feb. 13, 1914
WM. L. DAVIS, Nov. 18, 1835 - Feb. 6, 1919
MARY A. DAVIS, wife of WM. L. DAVIS, Mar. 22,1841 - Jun. 24, 1882
JOHN P. BLACKWELL, Mar. 2,1837 - Aug. 11, 1875
SOPHIA BLACKWELL, 1807 - Mar. 21, 1880
DAVIDSON BLACKWELL, Oct. 7, 1809 - Jun.22, 1887
W. R. BLACKWELL, Dec. 20, 1845 - Aug. 4, 1916
MARY ANN F. BLACKWELL, Dec. 29, 1852 - May 25, 1928
EMILE E. RADEN, Apr. 26, 1859 - Aug. 18, 1893
ELIZABETH, wife of REV. WM. PERRY, Oct. 9, 1797 - Apr. 15, 1886
J. A. WILSON, Jan. 15, 1825 - Sep. 25, 1901
MARY A., wife of J. A. WILSON, Jun. 9, 1829 - Jan. 24, 1901
R. P. CHANDLER, Mar. 23, 1850 - May 27, 1920
JOSEPH WALTER SCOTT, Sep. 5, 1856 - Sep. 21, 1877
H. W. SCOTT, Aug. 18, 1877 - Aug. 13, 1896
CARTER SCOTT, Feb. 16, 1821 - Mar. 21, 1897
MALINDA JANE, wife of CARTER SCOTT, Oct. 8, 1841 - Sep. 6, 1915
SARAH SCOTT, Jan. 5, 1818 - Jan. 18, 1863
DR. JOHN M.SCOTT, Jul. 25, 1848 - Oct. 12,1876
ABSALOM SHURLEY, Nov. 26, 1818 - Oct. 6, 1898
NANCY SHURLEY, Aug. 20, 1830 - Apr. 4, 1915

## Dorsey Creek Primitive Church Cemetery - 23 Miles East of Jasper - Culman County

W. J. MORGAN, May 8, 1841 - Jun. 9, 1944 (at rest, age 103 yrs)
BRACKIE MORGAN, Dec. 24, 1853 - Feb. 24, 1918
MARTHA GARRISON, Mar. 10, 1851 - Nov. 16, 1951
RICHARD S. GUNTER, Apr. 15, 1859 - Mar. 29,1937
SYLVIA GUNTER, Apr. 18, 1856 - Jul. 25, 1929
D. D. GRAVES, Mar. 11, 1875 - Mar. 31, 1943
M. J. ALLRED, 1857 - 1939
G. W. FINE, 1850 - 1905
ISABELLE FINE, 1865 - Mar. 5, 1912
B. J. GRAVES, Jan. 30, 1846 - Sep. 11, 1918
W. M. D. PHILLIPS, 1858 - 1934
MARY L. PHILLIPS, Mar. 4, 1828 - Apr. 11, 1894
MARY ELEN FIELDS, 1865 - 1936
MATILDA ROBBINS WALLS, Jun. 20, 1850 - Apr. 4, 1914
WASHINGTON LUTHER BRIDGES, Feb. 23, 1836 - Sep. 7, 1885
IDA CALLANS, Jul. 20, 1875 - Jun. 1, 1912
FRANCIS JOHNSON, Feb. 1846 - Feb. 15, 1901
EZEKIEL CHILDERS, May 31, 1808 - Jun. 5, 1870
NELLY, wife of EZEKIEL CHILDERS, Sep. 18, 1812 - May 5, 1884
J. C. CHILDERS, Feb.12,1859 - Apr. 5, 1934
THOMAS CHILDERS, Apr. 2, 1851 - May 7, 1916
MARTHA CHILDERS, Mar. 27, 1867 - Jul. 16, 1898
LUCY CHILDERS, wife of THOMAS CHILDERS, Dec. 23, 1858 - Jul. 14, 1897
JONATHAN CHILDERS, Oct. 9, 1842 - Nov. 23, 1915
MARGARET CHILDERS, 1838 - Feb. 28, 1922
JOHNNIE CHILDERS, May 1, 1871 - Nov. 3, 1945
MONROE CHILDERS, May 29, 1877 - Mar. 12, 1889
J. A. CHILDERS, Co. D 1 Ala. Inf. C.S.A.
MARY ANN, wife of J. A. CHILDERS, Dec. 23, 1845 - Jun. 8, 1888
MARY JANE CHILDERS, wife of J. A. CHILDERS, Feb. 23, 1845 - Nov. 23, 1903
NICHOLAS CHILDERS, Dec. 16, 1847 - Feb. 2, 1937
SARAH J. (AUNT SALLY CHILDERS), May 10, 1868 - Mar. 24, 1949
MARSHALL DANIELS, May 28, 1878 - Dec. 31, 1942
MARTHA DANILES, Feb. 9, 1848 - Jul. 22, 1916
DAVID DANILES, May 13, 1852 - Sep. 5, 1901
GEORGE W. DANILES, 1840 - 1921
B. W. BRAZIL, Aug. 26,1859 - May 25, 1932
NANCY E. BRAZIL, Sep. 6, 1856 - Dec. 23, 1943
EDMOND T. MINOR, Apr. 22, 1849 - Dec. 16,1883
WILLIAM B. CHANEY, Jan. 25, 1861 - May 5, 1882
JOHN COLWELL, Sep. 8, 1900 - age 55 yrs.
CHARLEY MOTES, Jun. 27,1871 - Jan. 22, 1912
W. J. NICHOLAS, Oct. 22, 1865 - Jan. 22, 1927

Cemetery Shady Grove Primitive Baptist Church - Near Arkadelphia, Cullman County

J. RUSSELL GUTTERY, no dates
BARBARA GUTTERY, no dates
WM. M. PARKER, b. Oct.11, no other dates
NICIE E. PARKER, May 20, 1848 - Nov. 19, 1913
SURRENIA DILL, Feb. 7, 1842 - Apr. 30, 1915
J. P. DILL, Dec. 30, 1831 - Aug. 7, 1919, Co. B 1st Ala. Cav. C.S.A.

Arkadelphia Cemetery - Cullman County

DR. CHARLES DRENNEN, Sep. 6, 1842 - death date gone - (a son of R. W. WALTER B. DRENNEN & MATILDA H. CROMWELL DRENNEN) no date

Harmony Baptist Church Cemetery - South of Arkadelphia, Alabama - Cullman County

R. W. WALTER B. DRENNEN, May 29, 1817 - Jun. 9, 1871
IRA ROBBINS (second wife)
A son GORDON ROBBINS, dates lost

Valley Springs Church Cemetery - South of Arkadelphia, Cullman County Alabama

JOHN L. GUTHRIE, Nov.17, 1867 - Aug. 7, 1943
REBECCA GUTHRIE, May 10, 1872 - no death date

Lebanon Cemetery - 2.3 Miles North of Blue Water Trace - Corona, Ala. Fayette Co.

JESSIE JOHNSTON, 1784 - Mar. 1861
Children named on his stone were: LEVI, ALFRED, CALVIN, LARKIN, ELIZA, POLLY ANN, ALLEN H., FRANKLIN JOHNSTON
ALONZO, son of A. & M. A. KILGORE, Jul. 20, 1875 - Mar. 23, 1890
MARY A., wife of A. KILGORE, Dau. of B. & M. EARNEST, May 20, 1843 - Jun. 22,1887
GEORGE W., son of A. & M. A. KILGORE, Apr. 1, 1866 - Feb. 27, 1886
JOHN W. THACKER, Co. I 32nd Ala. Inf. C.S.A. 1825 - 1909
OWEN G. KILGORE, Dec. 16, 1840 - Dec. 7, 1903
THOMAS PATTON, Jan. 18,1853 - Feb. 19, 1884
JANE HANDLEY, mother of A. T. HANDLEY, Nov. 1, 1805 - Nov. 30, 1859
TOM HANDLEY, 1827 - 1887
SARAH HANDLEY, 1863 - 1889

Lebanon Cemetery Cont'd.

WILLIAM PRESTON, Nov. 27, 1864 - Oct. 22, 1893
R. L. BURNER, Mar. 8, 1866 - Jul. 5, 1884, age 18 yrs. 3 mos. 7 das.
HETTY STRICKLAND, Dec. 15, 1871 - Mar. 2, 1894
M. A. KIMBRELL, dau. of H. & O. E. KILGORE, Jan. 29, 1848, married to A. J. KIMBRELL, Sep. 11, 1867, d. Jun. 10, 1916, baptized into the Missionary Baptist Church at the age of 17, Deaconness for 40 yrs. (What more could a person want in any record)
JOHN W., son of W. P. & N. A. EARNEST, Nov. 16, 1853 - Apr. 11, 1878
W.M. KILGORE, 1833 - Jan. 10, 1909
JOHN HANDLEY, Apr. 1, 1837 - Oct. 20, 1883
JOSEPH, son of W. M. & M. A. KILGORE, Jun. 17,1874 - Nov. 16, 1895
MARY A., wife of W. M. KILGORE, Jan. 13, 1838 - May 16, 1891
ROBERT, son of W. M. & M. A. KILGORE, Aug. 7, 1868 - Sep. 12, 1884
NANCY, wife of JOHN HANDLEY, Oct. 18, 1837 - Oct. 15, year gone
ABERHAM KIMBRELL, Nov. 19,1873 - Jun. 15, 1927
ELIZABETH O., wife of JOHN TURNER, Mar. 8, 1824 - Mar. 30,1890
GEORGE KILGORE, Dec. 25, 1805 - Feb. 4, 1892
HETY KILGORE, Jun. 12, 1808 - Jul. 24, 1890
GEORGE, son of G. & H. KILGORE, Dec. 10, 1836, killed in battle at New Hope Church Ga. Jul. 4, 1864 (In Grateful Remembrance of our Confederate Dead)
MARY, dau. of G. & H. KILGORE, Mar. 24, 1828 - Apr. 30, 1883
MARGARET, dau. of G. & H. KILGORE, May 20, 1840 - May 5, 1860
ROBERT, son of G. & H. KILGORE, Apr. 5, 1850 - Sep. 25, 1878

Boley Springs Cemetery - Seven Miles South of Corona, Ala. on road from Corona to Wiley- Fayette County

CELIA JONES, Feb. 5, 1800 - Sep. 7, 1839
J. J. WILLIAMS, Mar. 10, 1850 - May 30, 1912
LIHUE (?P DAVIS, 1878 - 1935
R. B. GANT, 1874 - 1949
LEE NORA GANT, 1879 - 19 --
A. BASTUN TIERCE, Jan. 4, 1858 -- Dec. 13, 1939
L. ALICE TIERCE, Jan. 1, 1866 - Aug. 8, 1954
W. J. POE, Feb. 4, 1856 - Nov. 8, 1927
LACNILLY (?) E. POE, Oct. 15, 1826 - Nov. 17, 1908
MARTHA A. POE, Dec. 6, 1860 - Jun. 21, 1883
REUBIN PENDLY, May 20, 1807 - d. 1885
J. L. PENDLY, Feb. 11, 1864 - Jul. 4, 1938
MARTHA E. PENDLY, Feb. 23, 1873 - Apr. 18, 1947

Boley Springs Cemetery Cont'd.

LELA A., wife of R. C. HONEYCUTT, Jan. 16, 1877 - Mar. 4, 1897
ELLA M. RAYNES, Jun. 7, 1880 - Jan. 22, 1922
HANSFORDT WESTBROOK, 1850 - 1937
MARGARET A. WESTBROOK, 1860 - 1934
LULA, wife of J. W. RAYNES, 1879 - 1914
DELILIAM SMITH, Feb. 14, 1873 - Jul. 9, 1927
REBECCA ANN CUNNINGHAM, Jun. 16, 1839 - Aug. 18, 1925
J. WILEY BAKER, 1879 - 1947
CLEO A. GOODE, 1839 - 1918
HENRY H. GOODE, Mar. 25, 1837 - Jan. 22, 1922
FRANCES HELEN, wife of J. L. MILLER, Mar. 30,1874 - Sep. 16, 1903
LUTHER BAKER, 1878 - 1945
JAMES-FULTON PHELANS, So. L. Ala. Artillery, C.S.A. Mar. 22, 1845 - Sep. 15, 1932
G. M. BAKER, Dec. 21, 1856 - Sep. 9, 1914
ELIZABETH FULTON, Apr. 15, 1852 - Mar. 21, 1935
NANCY FULTON, Jun. 13, 1841 - Dec. 5, 1923
WILLIAM FULTON, 1843 - 1889
L. B. BIRCHEAT, Jun. 20, 1878 - Jun. 20, 1878 - May 30, 1948
CYNTHA A. BIRCHEAT, Mar. 20, 1850 - Mar. 17, 1920
JOHN M. COURINGTON, Jan. 16, 1855 - Jun. 8, 1937
J. R. MULLINAX, 1870 - Sep. 21, 1935
MARTHA JANE MULLINAX, 1869 - May 2, 1949
J. A. BIRCHEAT, May 20, 1853 - Feb. 12, 1930
SARAH BIRCHEAT, Nov. 14, 1859 - Apr. 24, 1923
MARY ANN PRUETT, Jun. 23, 1837 - Aug. 20, 1916
ALMEDA WILLIAMS, Jan. 31, 1858 - Apr. 20, 1912
JANNIE S., wife of L. A. SMITH, Mar. 5, 1874 - Mar. 5, 1904

Grave in Ed. Stricklan's Yard - Near So. Ry. between Alta & Berry Ala. - Fayette County - Listed by Mrs. Herman Poe

A. B. PERKINS, b. 1760 - d. 1838

Salem Cemetery - Four Miles South of Corona, Ala. Fayette County

N. J. FROST, Feb. 4, 1842 -- Mar. 29, 1888
A. J. POE, Aug. 20, 1850 - Apr. 23, 1911
NANCY GIBSON, Aug. 8, 1815 - Dec. 4, 1891
WILLIAM NELSON GIBSON, Oct. 9, 1815 - Dec. 20, 1891 (made a Mason, 1853)
ASA R. POE, Jul. 19, 1864 - Jan. 5, 1935
REV. LEE A. WEATHERS, 1871 - 1946
SMITH W.WESLEY, 1864 - 1898

## Salem Cemetery Cont'd

RELITHA WESLEY, 1869 - 1950
JAMES MONROE DAVIS, Jan. 2, 1857 - Dec. 13, 1915
JUDA C., wife of G. W. POE, Sep. 4, 1853 - Oct. 16, 1891
GEO. W. POE, SR., Dec. 6, 1848 - Feb. 17, 1934
A. J. ROBISON, Aug. 22, 1875 - Feb. 25, 1910
FRANK ROBINSON, Jun. 14, 1873 - Oct. 13, 1919
L. M. J. POE, Sep. 18, 1874 - Dec. 7, 1917
GEO. T. DAVIS, 1873 - 1920

## Union Grove Cemetery - Fayette County - Ten Miles South of Corona, on old Tuscaloosa Rd.

MATILDA N. CANNON, Jul. 25, 1867 - Apr. 3, 1934
JOHN N. CANNON, Oct. 3, 1862 - Jul. 28, 1933
F. W. LOLLAR, Aug. 18, 1870 - no death date
WILLIAM D. DAVIS, Dec. 3, 1874 - Apr. 16, 1929
MARY BAKER GURGANUS, 1876 - 1938
W. W. GARRISON, May 1, 1860 - Feb. 3, 1921
WILEY GARRISON, Mar. 17, 1867 - May 6, 1939
ELIZABETH, wife of WILEY DAVIS, Aug. 8, 1853 - Feb. 10, 1925
LITHA WALLIS, Oct. 29, 1854 - Dec. 28, 1913
LUCINDA WALLIS, Sep. 20, 1835 - Jun. 29, 1911
NANCY C. ALDRIDGE, Dec. 20, 1847 - Nov. 16, 1918

## Zion Cemetery - Three Miles N. of Bankston, Ala. on the Byler Road - Fayette County

ELIZABETH, wife of SAMUEL DYER, b. Greenville Dist. S.C. 1789 d. 1859
SARAH POWELL, b. Laurens, S.C. Jan. 1, 1791 - d. Aug. 22, 1869
J. W. R. BAILEY, Mar. 12, 1830 - Oct. 25, 1893, age 63 yrs. 2 mos. 13 das.
MRS. J. W. R. BAILEY, Nov. 3, 1828 - Dec. 4, 1902
W. A. ELLIS, Mar. 24, 1835 - Mar. 20, 1918
L. H. ELLIS, Nov. 6, 1841 - Jan. 10, 1924
H. T. FORTENBERRY, Aug. 13, 1835 - Apr. 10, 1880
W. N. J. FORTENBERRY, Jun. 30, 1834 - Oct. 24, 1923
DANIEL ARY, Oct. 17, 1851 - Jan. 28, 1929
M. I. ARY, Aug. 27, 1849 - Sep. 25, 1917
ISERAL E. FOWLER, Nov. 15, 1821 - Nov. 14, 1892
J. E. FOWLER, Apr. 16, 1857 - Dec. 13, 1886
F. E. FOWLER, Nov. 17, 1835 - Jun. 29, 1910
ROSEA C. FOWLER, Apr. 10, 1876 - Jul. 8, 1910
SIDNEY P. JENKINS, Mar. 19, 1856 - Jul. 22, 1920
MARY C. JENKINS, Dec. 8, 1858 - Jan. 22, 1939
H. W. CHANEY, b. Williamson Co. Tenn. Jan. 27, 1827 - Dec. 23, 1957

## Zion Cemetery - Cont'd.

ARMINDA H. OAKLEY, Jan. 7, 1860 - Mar. 8, 1895
REV. JESSE FREEMAN, Aug. 14, 1804 - 1885
REBECCA, wife of REV. JESSE FREEMAN, Mar. 22, 1799 - Apr. 26, 1882
JOHN KELLER, Co. C. Ill. Inf. no further date
F. A., wife of S. P. TRAWEEK, Oct. 18, 1837 - Aug. 8, 1905
JACOB G. MILLER, Mar. 5, 1826 - Feb. 8, 1901
RHODIA M. MILLER, Mar. 5, 1825 - Mar. 8, 1895
HARRISON MILLER, Nov. 15, 1836 - Dec. 27, 1900
McAJAHH MILLER, May 17, 1850 - Sep. 13, 1922
ELIZABETH J., wife of McAJAHH MILLER, Jan. 9, 1852 - Sep. 8, 1919
J. R. WEBB, Apr. 1, 1851 - Sep. 9, 1914
CYNTHIA COTTON, Dec. 25, 1812 - Jul. 26, 1916
J. W. HAMMACK, Co. D. 22nd Ga. Inf. C.S.A.
RUDOLPHUS COTTON, Jun. 6, 1877 - Jan. 29, 1904
E. J. COTTON, 1848 - 1932
G. H. COTTON, 1839 - Oct. 13, 1899

## Cemetery on Byler Road - North of New River Baptist Church - Fayette County

J. R. PHILLIPS, Nov. 27, 1845 - Apr. 14, 1911
NANCY E. PHILLIPS, Aug. 25, 1862 - Oct. 1, 1942
JOHN and NANCY PHILLIPS, all dates gone
MARY McCOLLUM, Jul. 22, 1852 - Jan. 16, 1906
G. W. WAKEFIELD, Dec. 14, 1804 - Jul. 11, 1882
NANCY MAHALA WAKEFIELD, Nov. 2, 1814 - Jan. 5, 18[illegible]
MOSES EASON, 1832 - 1912
BETTIE EASON, 1836 - 1912
[illegible]. F. DOSIER, 1875 - 19.. no other dates legible
C. H. DOSIER, 1872 - 1943
S. W. HALLMARK, Jul. 10, 1858 - Apr. 15, 1923
M. R. HALLMARK, May 15, 1866 - Oct. 14, 1938
F. L. PHILLIPS, Dec. 14, 1847 - Aug. 30, 1922
DONIA PHILLIPS, Sep. 14, 1853 - Jan. 28, 1943

## New River Baptist Church Cemetery - On the Byler Road - Fayette County

JAS KILLINGSWORTH, d. Oct. 21, 1883, age 81 yrs
MARTHA M. KILLINGSWORTH, Dec. 11, 1813 - Jul. 22, 1892
FREEMAN KILLINGSWORTH, Aug. 6, 1832 - Aug. 14, 1893
CHARLES L. KILLINGSWORTH, Mar. 15, 1872 - Aug. 15, 1956
MOLLIE KILLINGSWORTH, Dec. 5, 1869 - Jan. 9, 1936
W. J. KILLINGSWORTH, 1840 - 1918
HENRY A. KILLINGSWORTH, 1876 - 1956
ALBERT DOBBS, Oct. 15, 1835 - Mar. 16, 1912

## New River Baptist Church Cemetery Cont'd.

J. H. DOBBS, Apr. 5, 1822 - Jul. 2, 1899
ELIZABETH E. DOBBS, Aug. 30, 1827 - Feb. 22, 1889
J. N. M. PARKER, May 22, 1811 - Aug. 31, 1893
JAMES C. HOKET, Sep. 17, 1860 - Jan. 20, 1941
JOHNATHAN D. SHERER, Sep. 6, 1842 - Jun. 21, 1911
MARY B. SHERER, Apr. 10, 1846 - Apr. 1911
J. M. SHERER, Jun. 5, 1874 - Aug. 24, 1907
IRA E. SHERER, 1876 - 1952
J. E. EASON, Mar. 28, 1859 - Oct. 4, 1888
W. D. DOSIER, Aug. 19, 1871 - Sep. 7, 1909
E. H. TIDWELL, wife of J. C. TIDWELL, Oct. 31, 1846 - Aug. 28, 1873
MARY KILLINGSWORTH, Sep. 8, 1858 - Nov. 18, 1883
SUSAN DEPOISTER, Nov. 18, 1842 - Oct. 21, 1897
J. M. HALLMARK, Jan. 18, 1855 - Jun. 6, 1916
J. R. FOWLER, 1871 - 1943
S. J. FOWLER, 1879 - 19.. date illegible
MRS. S. J. WEDGWORTH, Oct. 4, 1814 - Feb. 14, 1837
JULIA C, WOODWARD, Apr. 12, 1867 - Jun. 10, 1922
J. M. WAKEFIELD, Co. K. 4th Ala. Cav. C.S.A. Apr. 12, 1846 Aug. 8, 1920
A. J. PICKLE, Aug. 8, 1867 - Sep. 16, 1942
W. H. HALLMAKR, Apr. 1, 1856 - Nov. 1, 1942
C. T. HALLMARK, Feb. 22, 1866 - Jan. 6, 1948
WM. MILTON WOODWARD, Mar. 27, 1866 - Apr. 21, 1939
MARTHA J. WOODWARD, Jun. 8, 1865 - Jun. 6, 1941
J. T. WOODWARD, Jul. 29, 1870 - Mar. 11, 1934
JULIA WOODWARD, Mar. 20, 1875 - Apr. 28, 1940
STEPHEN WOODWARD, May 21, 1835 - Feb. 5, 1908
MRS. E. J. WOODWARD, wife of STEPHEN WOODWARD, Mar. 16, 1835- Dec. 31, 1921

## Cemetery at Berry, Ala. - Fayette County

CHARLIE E. BOWEN, 1878 - 1935
F. A. NELSON, Feb. 19, 1849 - Nov. 17, 1910
WM. N. GIBSON, Oct. 30, 1858 - Jun. 25, 1935
ALICE R., wifw of W. M. GIBSON, Dec. 10, 1860 - Mar. 8, 1922
J. R. STEPHENS, Jun. 8, 1845 - Oct. 26, 1928
DELLA MOORE, wife of JOHN E. MOORE, Dec. 25, 1868 - May 28, 1872
WM. FRANK TRAWEEK, Jan. 25, 1878 - Aug. 28, 1932
E. F. FALLS, 1871 - 1938
M. S. FALLS, 1870 - 1934
WM. P. GEER, Oct. 11, 1866 - Jan. 14, 1930

Cemetery at Berry, Ala. Cont'd.

KATE DAVIS, 1847 - 1938
WM. T. OSBORN, Feb. 24, 1852 - Feb. 16,1921
SUSAN FRANCES OSBORN, Jun. 9, 1855 - Oct. 23, 1927
HOPE WELL DOSS, Jul. 1, 1829 - Feb. 9, 1910
FRANK BAKER, 1868 - 1928
B. J. BAKER, Jun. 30, 1880 - Jan. 27, 1931
M. A. LAWSON, Sep. 20, 1860 - Jan. 17, 1919
J. D. LAWSON, Sep. 16, 1861 - Apr. 4, 1920
JOHN B. GARRARD, Oct. 19,1870 - Mar. 10, 1914
ADA F. GARRARD, Mar. 12, 1876 - Aug. 17, 1954
FRED W. JOHNSON, Sep. 30, 1880 - May 9, 1955
ALICE, wife of FRED W. JOHNSON, Dec. 22, 1880 - Apr. 15, 1919
VELMA JOHNSON, Aug. 29, 1889 - Nov. 30, 1943
MOLLIE NORRIS, Jul. 23, 1850 - Jan. 3, 1928
WILLIE UTLEY, 1862 - 1956
BAMA UTLEY, 1869 - 1955
C. J. BAKER, Aug. 1842 - Nov. 25, 1923
ANNIE C. BAKER, wife of C. J. BAKER, Oct. 26, 1846 - Nov. 17, 1929
G. W. JOHNS, Feb. 17, 1861 - Jan. 23, 1924
MARTHA C. JOHNS, Oct. 10, 1865 - Aug. 14, 1935
C. A., wife ofM. L. CLINE, Dec. 7, 1876 - Oct. 4, 1915
OLIVER C. DOBBS, 1847 - 1907
SARAH A. DOBBS, 1850 - 1943
J. P. TRAWEEK, Nov. 29, 1844 - Feb. 20, 1922
L. C. TRAWEEK, May 1, 1839 - Dec. 22, 1917
NANCY A. EARNEST, wife of W. T. EARNEST, Feb. 18, 1830 - Jul. 9, 1906
VIRGINIA V., wife of THOMAS L. JEFFERIES, Nov. 8, 1851 - Jun. 12, 1919
WILLIAM THOMAS JEFFERIES, Jan. 16, 1878 - Feb. 1, 1924
W. R. ADAMS, Oct. 19, 1832 - Sep. 22, 1924
MAHALE ADAMS, Sep. 16, 1835 - Oct. 21, 1927
JAMES W. SHEPHERD, Nov. 25, 1881 - Jan. 13, 1941
JOHN COGER SHEPHERD, Oct. 30, 1875 - Apr. 7, 1949
ESTELLE ETHEL SHEPHERD, Sep. 16, 1855 - Oct. 21, 1927
AUGAMIRAH, wife of JOHN N. BERRY, Feb. 22, 1845 - Jan. 24, 1921
WM.T. STUDDARD, Sep. 28, 1878 - Jun. 11, 1927
J. J. BAKER, Sep. 11, 1848 - Apr. 5, 1920
CHARLES MALCOLM HANKINS, Jun. 4, 1855 - Jan. 12, 1915
LAFAYETTE DAVIS, Feb. 10, 1871 - Oct. 5, 1915
JAMES B. SOUTH, 1855 - 1910
CLOVE D. SOUTH, 1874 - 1951
MARY BROCK, Sep. 9, 1871 - Jun. 15, 1947
E. A. WILLINGHAM, Apr. 1, 1847 - Feb. 28, 1928
D. F. FREEMAN, 1831 - Jul. 7, 1900
L. M. FREEMAN, Jun. 6, 1834 - Jul. 14, 1900

Cemetery at Berry, Ala. Cont'd.

J. A. BROWN, Jun. 18, 1852 - Oct. 1, 1936
ROBERT G. JONES, Mar. 27, 1834 - Mar. 14,1922
MARY C. JONES, Feb. 9, 1833 - Oct. 27, 1914
MOLLIE THOMPSON JONES, 1860 - 1923
BENJAMIN ELLIOTT JONES, Aug. 31, 1860 - Oct. 20, 1939
WYATT P. BOONE, 1861 - 1925
MARTHA W. BOONE, 1865 - 1919
FELIX AUSTIN GRAY, Apr. 14, 1877 - Jun. 16, 1943
MARTELIA SHEPHERD, Apr. 15, 1848 - Apr. 20, 1924
C. C. SMITH, Mar. 11, 1856 - Mar. 1, 1931
ELLA SMITH, wife of C. C. SMITH, Jan. 1, 1858 - Feb. 8, 1906
G. W. L. STOKES, Nov. 7, 1835 - Feb. 15, 1903
MRS. MARY F. STOKES, Jan. 3, 1843 - Nov. 6, 1921
HENRIETTA STOKES, Oct. 16, 1874 - Sep. 14, 1956
PALATINE HAYSELLETTE, wife of N. H. KIMBRELL, Nov. 10, 1872 - Dec. 5, 1935
MALISSA J. HAYSELLETTE, Oct. 25, 1845 - Jan. 14, 1905
CARRIE JULIAN, wife of C. C. SMITH, Feb. 22, 1869 - Feb. 1,1948
DR. J. N. PATTERSON, Jul. 29, 1847 - Apr. 29, 1916
NANCY ANN PATTERSON, wife of DR. J. N. PATTERSON, Jul. 8, 1845- Jun. 26, 1924
LONIA PATTERSON, Oct. 22, 1871 - Feb. 24, 1910
LIZZIE PATTERSON, Jan. 26, 1869 - Mar. 12, 1909
NANNIE, wife of J. L. LINDSEY, Sep. 21, 1878 - Mar. 19, 1909
JAKEL LINDSEY, Jul. 19, 1875 - Oct. 14, 1910
WM. P. JENKINS, Jun. 9, 1863 - Jan. 25, 1925
FRANCES E. JENKINS, Aug. 16, 1868 - Dec. 1, 1941
SARAH FRANCES HIDE, 1874 - 1949
DR. JAMES WILLIAMS COLLINS, Dec. 17, 1850 - Dec. 26, 1913
DR. GEORGE W. OLIVE, Jul. 12, 1862 - Sep. 23, 1940
MARTHA ROSETTA OLIVE, wife of DR. GEO. W. OLIVE, Jun. 27, 1866- Mar. 21, 1912
FRANCIS MARION DOBSON, Feb. 8, 1852 - Mar. 7, 1926
MRS. ZORA E. DOBSON, Mar. 7, 1880 - Nov. 7, 1907, wife of FRANCIS MARION DOBSON
D. W. JOHNSON, Nov. 7, 1857 - Apr. 9, 1932
JOE BUCK JOHNSON, Aug. 23, 1867 - Oct. 27, 1940
ELLEN ODOM JOHNSON, Jan. 1, 1868 - Aug. 30, 1955
SNOW CANNON, Nov. 3, 1876 - Jul. 8, 1927
MARY E. DAVIS CANNON, Jul. 27, 1885 - Nov. 30,1936
C. M. STRICKLIN, Nov. 6, 1874 - May.18, 1922
JAMES B. GRIFFIN, Jul. 26, 1870 - Mar. 25, 1939
JAMES T. MOORE, 1861 - 1932
MARY MOORE, 1860 - 1934
WM. W. WORTHINGTON, Jul. 26, 1853 - Nov. 23, 1922
CANDY WORTHINGTON, Feb. 1,1857 - Nov. 8, 1936
JOEL H. SUGGS, Apr. 1, 1852 - Dec. 17, 1925

Cemetery at Berry, Ala. Cont'd.

LETHIA A. SUGGS, Dec. 15, 1859 - Nov. 14, 1901
JOHN N. FREEMAN, Dec. 28, 1868 - Sep. 26, 1940
MILTON E. CAMPANY, Feb. 12, 1856 - Jan. 21, 1935
IDA M. CAMPANY, Oct. 6, 1870 - Aug. 20, 1934
MACK B. BERRY, 1878 - 1949
LAURA FOWLER, May 15, 1873 - May 12, 1923
JAMES R. BRASHER, 1869 - 1942
G. A.HOCUTT, 1868 - 1941
W. RANZO STRICKLAND, Mar. 17, 1872 - Dec. 27, 1948
MARY ANN STRICKLAND, Dec. 5, 1875 - Oct. 10, 1946
MRS. SUSAN SIMPSON, Aug. 16, 1853 - Jul. 7, 1928
WM. T. SIMPSON, Jan. 10, 1849 - Mar. 10, 1917
DANIEL STRICKLAND, Sep. 18, 1877 - Feb. 13, 1942
R. T. STRICKLAND, Feb. 2, 1856 - Jan. 8, 1914
MARY E. STRICKLAND, Nov. 20, 1875 - Apr. 22, 1954
LEE STEWART, 1868 - 1913
CORDELIA STEWART, 1875 - 1947
GEORGE A. THOMPSON, Mar. 11, 1868 - Apr. 12, 1939
JESSIE APPLING JOHNSON, 1863 - 1945
WILLIAM ALFRED JOHNSON, 1862 - 1947
JAMES MOORE, Feb. 28,1873 - Feb. 17, 1953

Sands Springs Church Cemetery - Better Known as Friendship Church located three miles East of Hwy. 171 & 43, near Glen Allen, Ala. - Fayette County (Copied by Mrs. Lucas)

JAMES G. LAWRENCE, Mar. 14, 1837 - Feb. 5,1907
SARAH LAWRENCE, Oct. 30, 1807 - Apr. 8, 1886
GEORGE LAWRENCE, Jul. 2,1807 - Dec. 20, 1884
WILLIE B. LAWRENCE, 1878 - Dec. 10, 1898
SIDNEY LAWRENCE,Jan. 17, 1871 - Jan. 11, 1898
ARCHIEN KIMBRELL, Nov. 19, 1874 - Feb. 15, 1897
W. J. STANLEY, Dec. 21, 1813 - Jun. 7, 1888
M. J. STANLEY, Oct. 1840 - Apr. 14, 1911
JEFFERSON, Harbin, Feb. 20, 1830 - Dec. 1915
JAMES W. WHITE, Apr. 23, 1826 - Feb. 12, 1891
C. W. S. THOMPSON, Jul. 17, 1822 - Sep. 4, 1884
N. J. REEVES, Nov. 19, 1860 - Sep. 10, 1896
ARON JONES' wife, May 4, 1862 - Apr. 27, 1895

Bethaberry Church Cemetery - Near Berry, Ala. on Hwy. to Oakman in Fayette County

M. A.STEWART, Apr. 22, 1817 - Nov. 5, 1891
J. A. STEWART, 1847 - 1924
EXIE NELSON, 1882 - 1936
MARY HARBIN, wife of L. B. HARBIN, Jul. 10, 1813 - Dec. 18, 1885

## Bethaberry Church Cemetery Cont'd.

REV. L. B. HARBIN, Jan. 31, 1811 - Nov. 21, 1897
SARAH E. HARBIN, wife of T. J. HARBIN, Mar. 10, 1853 - Oct. 2, 1905
JAMES L. HARBIN, Mar. 13, 1836 - May 16, 1914
N. H. HARBIN, Jun. 16, 1851 - Nov. 16, 1925
MARY E. HARBIN, wife of N. H. HARBIN, Feb. 14, 1848 - Dec. 8, 1924
I. N. AWTRY, Apr. 29, 1834 - Nov. 29, 1904
ELIZABETH AWTRY, Feb. 20, 1835 - May 2, 1913
HENRY NELSON, Mar. 6, 1906 - Aug. 6, 1951
W. H. KIMBRELL, Sep. 26, 1842 - Dec. 2, 1914
ELIZABETH, wife of WM. KIMBRELL, Mar. 22, 1845 - Nov. 22, 1930

## Cemetery on the Byler Road Between New River Baptist Church and Walker County Line - Fayette County

A. J. TIDWELL, Dec. 15, 1820 - Oct. 26, 1920
MARGARET, wife of A. J. TIDWELL, Jul. 22, 1823 - Jul. 20, 1887
S. J. TIDWELL, Jan. 20, 1844 - Jan. 4, 1928
GRACY J. TIDWELL, wife of S. J. TIDWELL, Oct. 22, 1854 - Aug. 16, 1924
MARY J. WHITEHEAD, wife of G. W. WHITEHEAD, Feb. 25, 1846 - Aug. 20, 1878
MARTHA ALICE SHAW, Jan. 28, 1869 - Jun. 10, 1909
MARGARET E. LAWRENCE, Dec. 20, 1870 - Feb. 17, 1941
MARTHA A. BUICE, Mar. 12, 1848 - Apr. 29, 1927
AARON HERREN, May 15, 1835 - Jul. 13, 1915
MARY A. HERREN, Mar. 29, 1841 - Apr. 25, 1932
WILLIAM SPARKS, Mar. 31, 1821 - Jul. 25, 1893
ELVIRA SPARKS, 1825 - Alg. 13, 1897
R. T. SPARKS, Jul. 25, 1847 - Dec. 25, 1913
SUSAN S. SPARKS, 1841 - 1888
MARGARET KELLY, Jul. 15, 1877 - 1908
G. W. TUCKER, Jul. 8, 1848 - Jan. 31, 1934
IRENA TUCKER, Jul. 25, 1855 - Oct. 30, 1928
W. T. TUCKER, 1880 - Nov. 29, 1925

## Cleveland Church of Christ Cemetery - Near Bankston, Ala. on Byler Road North Fayette County

J. N. SMITH, b. Elbert Co. Ga. Nov. 9, 1826, d. Dec. 3, 1901
DAVID W. GURLEY, 1861 - 1947
MARY M. GURLEY, 1861 - 1916
F. M. HYDE, Feb. 14, 1867 - May 31, 1901
N. H. HYDE, Mar. 2, 1849 - Mar. 6, 1888
W. A. HYDE, Sep. 15, 1833 - May 22, 1907

## Cleveland Church of Christ Cemetery Cont'd.

CAROLINE, wife of W. A. HYDE, b. near Newnan, Ga. Dec. 10, 1834, d. Mar. 1, 1909
JAMES HARMON HYDE, Jan. 31, 1859 - Nov. 28, 1887
J. T. HYDE, Oct. 28, 1846 - May 6, 1936
MRS. N. T. HYDE, Mar. 20, 1853 - Nov. 25, 1883
JERRY C. HYDE, Sep. 22, 1871 - Sep. 24, 1934
EMILY FLORENCE, wife of D. W. JOHNSON, Jan. 29, 1856 - Aug. 31, 1894
JIM BOWLES, 1862 - 1936
MIRAM BOWLES, 1863 - 1928
MARTIN L. SMITH, Feb. 26, 1854 - Jul. 12, 1880
J. M.ALLRED, Sep. 10, 1853 - Nov. 16, 1928
RACHEL ALLRED, Apr. 11, 1857 - Jan. 10, 1938
MOSES P. BAILEY, Apr. 23, 1857 - Apr. 15, 1929
FANNIE, wife of MOSES P. BAILEY, Jun. 30, 1855 - Oct. 12, 1908
MRS. A. M. MARTIN, 1844 - 1915
W. D. PERRY, Apr. 2, 1859 - Sep. 5, 1883
A. L. SMITH, Dec. 28, 1811 - Oct. 8, 1885
TABITHA, wife of A. L. SMITH, 1813 - Jan. 28, 1912
JOSEPH ELLIS, 1863 - 1901
ALICE ELLIS,1865 - 1945
ALEX BRANDENBURG, Feb. 8, 1851 - Jan. 22,1927
SARAH BRANDENBURG, Jun. 13, 1851 - Aug. 19, 1910
EMILY C., wife of W. E. JULIAN, Feb. 21, 1857 - Sep. 14, 1883
J. D. HYDE, 1811 - Oct. 19, 1876

## Pleasant Hill Church Cemetery - About Two Miles N. W. of Berry, Ala. - Fayette County

T. J. JEFFERIES, Aug. 12, 1842 - Feb. 25, 1930
THOMAS JEFFERIES, Dec. 22, 1842 - Sep. 29, 1886
W. B. JEFFERIES, Dec. 7, 1815 - Oct. 17, 1886
ADALINE JEFFERIES, Feb. 22, 1816 - Jun. 28, 1889
ARMINTA JEFFERIES, Mar. 6, 1854 - Mar. 9, 1868
KATHERINE E. JEFFERIES, Nov. 12, 1849 - Nov. 24,1861
JOSIAH P. JEFFERIES, Sep. 28, 1837 - Apr. 2, 1863
WM. R.WILLINGHAM, May 30, 1835 - Feb. 16, 1886
THOMAS L. WILLINGHAM, Apr. 23, 1807 - Nov. 8, 1888
SUSAN A., wife of THOMAS L. WILLINGHAM, Jul. 3, 1817 - Aug. 20, 1900
EULAH E. WILLINGHAM, Aug. 14. 1861 - Nov. 17, 1897
W. L. WILLINGHAM, Aug. 9, 1871 - Apr. 29, 1911
ANGELINE WILLINGHAM, 1852 - 1932
A. O. JACKSON, 187[illegible] - 1946
WM. H. JACKSON, Feb. 10, 1855 - Jul. 19, 1935
ELIZABETH JANE, wife of JESSE F. JACKSON, Oct. 23, 1833 - Sep. 29, 1905

Pleasant Hill Church Cemetery Cont'd.

JESSIE F. JACKSON, Jan. 18, 1825 - Dec. 30, 1904
SAMUEL G. COLE, Apr. 8, 1844 - Aug. 10, 1955
JOHN E. COLE, Oct. 2, 1802 - Aug. 30, 1849
LITTLETON COLE, Sep. 3, 1810 - Aug. 7, 1871
NARCISSA COLE, Apr. 4, 1814 - Sep. 20, 1847
WM. M. COLE, Feb. 10, 1841 - Jul. 16, 1864 - was drowned in the Ala. River
MANLEY COLE, Aug. 25, 1815 - Jul. 20, 1848
SUSAN COLE, Nov. 4, 1813 - Sep. 22, 1844
LESTER COLE, Oct. 6, 1888 - Jan. 24, 1953
MARY ANN COLE, dau. of J. B. & TERRISA COLE, Jun. 8, 1839 - Feb. 5, 1905
MATTIE PINION SOUTH, Nov. 27, 1870 - Jan. 9, 1947
SAMUEL LAFAYETTE SOUTH, Oct. 30, 1867 - Oct. 15, 1945
ETTA, wife of A. W. PINION, Dec. 18, 1848 - Sep. 29, 1903
WM. T. BERRY, Jun. 15, 1883 - Sep. 22, 1912
MALLISA J., wife of H. B. BERRY, Nov. 6, 1851 - Oct. 6, 1921
HENRY B. BERRY, Dec. 6, 1829 - Apr. 22, 1895
ALLEN M. OAKLEY, Jan. 3, 1857 - Aug. 22, 1896
ELIZA HARDY, Feb. 10, 1834 - Mar. 3, 1902
SUSAN JOHNSON, Mar. 10, 1823 - Apr. 17, 1896
SUE JOHNSON, wife of FRED JOHNSON, Sep. 13, 1855 - married Sep. 16, 1888 - d. Dec. 18, 1914
LUCY JOHNSTON, Jun. 26, 1813 - Aug. 27, 1838
G. W. JOHNSTON, d. Mar. 28, 1865, aged 68 yrs, b. 1797
FRED JOHNSON, Aug. 10, 1836 - Sep. 8, 1915
VIRGIL HALL, Apr. 17, 1885 - Sep. 17, 1948
MARY JOHNS HALL, wife of VIRGIL HALL, Sep. 15, 1886 - Apr. 21, 1945
J. LUTHER STANLEY, Aug. 1, 1880 - Dec. 13, 1951
MATTIE STANLEY, Jul. 2, 1881 - Jan. 29, 1910
LEWIS T. STANLEY, Jun. 20, 1815 - Nov. 17, 1896
SUSANNAH STANLEY, May 14, 1842 - Dec. 1, 1896 - (Susannah F. Stanley is also called SUANNAH in family records.) She is the wife of LEWIS STANLEY.
LUCY FREEMAN, Oct. 21, 1818, married JAMES CHAPPELL, Jan. 15, 1838, d. Aug. 18, 1895
JAMES M., son of J & L CHAPPELL, May 10, 1851 - Jan. 2, 1874
DAVID H. STANLEY, Co. F. 38th Ala. Inf. C.S.A.
D. M. F. WYNNE, d. Feb. 6, 1863 - age 36 yrs.
ELIZABETH (BETTIE), wife of D. M. T. WYNNE, Sep. 22, 1837 - Sep. 6, 1910 -(dau. of MILES and PRISCILLA PARKER CHAPPELL - note by Mrs. Guttery)
MARY J., wife of WM. KIRKLAND, May 18, 1844 - d. age 38 yrs. 9 mos. 16 das.
THOMPSON BERRY, b. Orange Co. N.C. Dec. 18, 1801 - d. Jan. 8, 1870
JOHN N. BERRY, Feb. 14, 1825- Oct. 3, 1885

Pleasant Hill Church Cemetery Cont'd.

WM. P. BERRY, Co. F. 38th Ala. Inf. C.S.A.
VINEY JONES, d. Aug. 29, 1840, aged 48 yrs. 3 mos. 9 das. b. 1792
GATTIE ANN WILLIAMSON, Mar. 6, 1849 - Aug. 27,1916
J. M. WILLIAMSON, husband of GATTIE WILLIAMSON, May 9, 1850 - Mar. 5, 1908
PEARL PENINA SCOTT, Sep. 4, 1859 - Aug. 10,1928
JUDITHA POE, May 19,1822 - May 9, 1894
W. F. KIRKLAND, Apr. 3, 1839 - Nov. 4, 1907
MARY J., wife of W. F. KIRKLAND, May 18, 1844 - May 4, 1883
R. G. WILLINGHSM, Sep. 8, 1815 - Oct. 21, 1872
ELIZABETH, wife of R. G. WILLINGHAM, Jun. 30, 1800 - Oct. 15, 1884
WM. R. WILLINGHAM, Mar. 25, 1833 - Mar. 2, 1864
F. S. GRIGG, Jan. 6, 1835 - Aug. 6, 1874
MARY G. GRIGG, Dec. 30, 1836 - Sep. 25, 1910
E. T. PERKINSON, Sep. 16, 1815 - Oct. 26, 1869
JOHN MOORE, 1816 - 1896
HANNAH MOORE, 1832 - 1889
S. G. BAGWELL, May 21, 1832 - Feb. 24, 1896
ELIZABETH YORK, 1800 - May 15, 1893, age 93 yrs.
Y. M. YERBY, 1876 - no other dates
VERRILA YERBY, 1881 - 1942
TALLERT YERBY, 1847 - 1926
LUCY P. YERBY, 1853 - 1931
L. W. WHITSON, son of J & M. B. WHITSON, Jul. 7, 1851 - Mar. 4, 1868
REBUEN DAVIS, Co. I. 26th Ala. Inf. C.S.A.
VALUTIA A. V. DAVIS, wife of REUBEN DAVIS, Nov. 12, 1848 - Apr. 14, 1917
RICHARD DAVIS, Oct. 4, 1812 - Jun. 19, 1874
NANCY F. DAVIS, Apr. 7, 1820 - May 16, 1900
JAMES COLE, Nov. 18, 1896 - Nov. 7, 1941
W. D. COLE, Nov. 20, 1864 - Apr. 23, 1940
ELIZABETH, wife of W. D. COLE, Sep. 21, 1867 - Apr. 1, 1944
FRANCES T. DARDEN, Mar. 9, 1823 - Nov. 10, 1884
SAMPSON H. DARDEN, Dec. 23, 1810 - Mar. 6, 1885
MARTHA McCLAIN, Sep. 5, 1799 - Nov. 8, 1853

Oak Grove Methodist Church Cemetery - On Hwy. to Fayette, Ala. - Fayette County

M. A. TAYLOR, Apr. 23, 1830 - Jul. 13, 1914
S. P. TAYLOR, Feb. 22, 1827 - Sep. 2, 1900
DICY E. TAYLOR, Feb. 6, 1848 - Apr. 18, 1927
JOHN Y. TAYLOR, Jul. 1854 - Mar. 1923
L. E. TAYLOR, wife of JOHN Y. TAYLOR, 1856 - Nov. 5, 1912
Y. O. SEXTON, Jul. 24, 1867 - May 23, 1910

## Oak Grove Methodist Church Cemetery

J. H. SEXTON, Dec. 23, 1866 - Jan. 18, 1940
JOSEPH A. LANE, Co. A. 26th Ala. Inf. C.S.A.
SARAH J. LANE, May 1, 1855 - Dec. 10, 1920
J. M. DOBBS, 1867 - 1930
M. J. DOBBS, 1870 - 1925
W. A. VICK, Jan. 12, 1859 - Dec. 22, 1925
S. A. VICK, Jan. 24, 1857 - Jun. 13, 1931
PERRY GARDNER, 1863 - 1947
JAMES AMOS SPILLER, Busket's Ala. Guards, C.S.A.
MARGARET E. SPILLERS, Apr. 12, 1848 - Dec. 30, 1913
T. J. HOBBS, Jul. 11, 1847 - Jul. 18, 1914
SARAH E. HOBBS, Apr. 8, 1859 - Apr. 28, 1951
BELLE GUESS, 1861 - 1950
WM. D. STOUGH, 1853 - 1928
MARY F. STOUGH, 1858 - 1928
ENOCH KIZZIRE, Co. H. 41st Ala. Inf. C.S.A.
MARY J. KIZZIRE, May 28, 1840 - Nov. 25, 1905
W. M. GRAY, Aug. 14, 1851 - Dec. 26, 1914
WILLIAM E. ROBERTS, Aug. 5, 1852 - Apr. 1, 1947
RHODIA LAWSON, 1869 - 1955

## Pleasant Grove Baptist Church Cemetery - Five Miles South of Carbon Hill, Ala. - Fayette Co.

MARY ANN JOHNSON, Jul. 29, 1844 - Mar. 2, 1910
M. L. JOHNSON, Co. L. Ala. Cav.
C. C. JOHNSON, Co. A. 1st Btn. Miss. M.F.D. Rifles
SARAH F. JOHNSON, Sep. 9, 1839 - Mar. 24, 1929
MARTHA E. JOHNSON, Aug. 10, 1862 - Apr. 1, 1912
J. T. JOHNSON, Oct. 3, 1853 - Jun. 2, 1902
H. F. JOHNSON, 1861 - 1941
LUCY A. KITCHENS, dau. of S. H. & LUCY WOOD, Feb. 23, 1827 - Jul. 30, 1903
MRS. A. M. KITCHENS, Apr. 4, 1858 - Jul. 12,1924
JAMES KITCHENS, Sep. 21, 1885 - Dec. 26, 1929
L. J. KITCHENS, Sep. 12, 1851 - Nov. 17, 1935
J. H. KITCHENS, Nov. 14, 1852 - Mar. 18, 1935
GEO. H. KITCHENS, 1874 - 1948
SABRINA KITCHENS, 1880 - 1951
W. C. C. BROWN, Jan. 27, 1856 - Dec. 14, 1934
N. C. BROWN, Jan. 6, 1858 - Dec. 28, 1952
SUSAN, wife of J. M. BARTON, Nov. 11, 1842 - Apr. 8, 1889
CHARLEY TIDWELL, Sep. 12, 1860 - Sep. 12, 1945
MARY TIDWELL, Nov. 9, 1867 - Jan. 22, 1947
ELIZABETH M. TIDWELL, Jul. 7, 1854 - Mar. 20, 1894
SARAH ANN TIDWELL, Jun. 3, 1867 - Mar. 26, 1940
NANCY TIDWELL, Apr. 11, 1834 - Jul. 10, 1922

Pleasant Grove Baptist Church Cemetery Cont'd.

JAMES K. DOBBINS, Jun. 17, 1840 - Oct. 19, 1910
MARY DOBBINS, Dec. 4, 1840 - Jun. 30, 1921
M. E. McDADE, Sep. 14, 1866 - May 6, 1931
JOHN F. MYERS, Sep. 16, 1840 - Jul. 20, 1924
MARY S. MYERS, Mar. 4, 1843 - Apr. 3, 1926
MARY D. MYERS, 1879 - 1947
MARY E. MYERS, 1878 - 1900
MARCU O. MYERS, 1871 - 1949
BEADIE RODEN, Apr. 15, 1820 - Feb. 3, 1893
L. E. DOBBINS,Jan. 21, 1865 - Fsb. 8, 1888
G. B. McGOWEN, Sep. 13, 1858 - Oct. 17, 1932
R. A. KITCHENS, Nov. 13, 1834 - Nov. 27,1909
SAMUEL H. KEY, Dec. 11, 1842 - Aug. 18, 1906
ZIPPORAH KEY, Sep. 25, 1851 - Jul. 16, 1926
N. C. PHILLIPS, Aug. 8, 1853 - Jul. 17, 1885
MILLIE CAMPBELL BROWN, 1831 - 1891
S. H. CAMPBELL, Nov. 22, 1854 - Feb. 8, 1928
M. E., wife of S. H. CAMPBELL, Oct. 24, 1852 - May 23, 1921
ROBERT FORD, Apr. 20, 1846 - Aug. 27,1923
DILLIE FORD, Sep. 12, 1871 - Oct. 16, 1947
FANNIE ALDRIDGE, Jul. 12, 1854 - Oct. 22, 1936
J. W. ALDRIDGE, Sep. 3, 1852 - Nov. 10, 1917
JOHN T. STOVALL, Jul. 10, 1856 - Mar. 29, 1939
F. S. STOVALL, Nov. 19, 1867 - Jan. 8, 1913
RUTITIA BEVILL, wife of R. BEVILL, Aug. 12, 1828 - Dec. 13, 1911 (she was the wife of RARDON BEVILL, see 1812 War Pension application earlier in this book .....Mrs. M. B. B.)
DAVID RUTLEDGE, Jul. 14, 1833 - Dec. 9, 1915
ELIZABETH SLLEN RUTLEDGE, 1849 - 1920
LOUIS A. RUTLEDGE, Aug. 14, 1864 - Jan. 29, 1888
HUGH R. SIDES, Mar. 4, 1856 - Jan. 3, 1927
SUSAN K. SIDES, Nov. 3, 1862 - Apr. 28, 1888
S. E. BROWN, Jun. 15, 1865 - Aug.12, 1906
L. C. WOODWARD, Sep. 19, 1858 - May 15, 1892
M. L. JOHNSON, Jun. 7, 1857 - Dec. 18, 1905
J. W. JOHNSON, Feb. 4, 1855 - Apr. 30, 1930
MIRA STRICKLING, 1831 - Jan. 27, 1907
W. J. F. STRICKLAND, Aug. 26, 1851 - Sep. 27, 1915
M. A. STRICKLAND, Sep. 5, 1853 - Sep. 9, 1935

Mt. Vernon Methodist Church Cemetery - On Hwy. 18 Between Fayette and Vernon, Ala. - Fayette Co.

WILLIAM S. HARKINS, Mar. 23, 1799 - Dec. 4, 1858
W. B. HARKINS, Sep. 19, 1840 - Apr. 14, 1921
MARY CAROLINE, wife of W. B. HARKINS, Sep. 6, 1848 - Nov. 3, 1921

Mt. Vernon Methodist Church Cemetery Cont'd.

HUGH SMITH HARKINS, Feb. 3, 1878 - Apr. 25, 1950
R. W. WILEY MILES, May 1, 1811 - Dec. 6, 1879
ELIZABETH MILES, Apr. 9, 1831 - 1891
JOSEPHINE MILES McCLURE, Jun. 1839 - married Mar. 5, 1861 - d. Jul. 26,1863
MARY FOSTER, 1831 - 1872
A. E. FOSTER, Nov. 18, 1814 - Oct. 7, 1885
W. L. MILES, Jan. 29, 1836 - Jul. 15, 1900
MARY M. MILES, wife of W. L. MILES, Oct. 1, 1843 - Jul. 6, 1856
VALENTINE PRATER, Co. L., 41st Ala. Inf. C.S.A.
MRS. FANNIE ROBERTSON, wife of R. J. ROBERTSON, Jun. 29, 1862- Sep. 16, 1923
HIRAM COCHRAN, Sep. 23, 1845 - Nov. 17, 1927
J. W. ABBOTT, 1866 - 1932
CALLIE L. ABBOTT, 1868 - 1932
JOHN T. RENFRO, Jan. 4, 1866 - Mar. 2, 1956
H. L. SMITH, Dec. 8, 1863 - Dec. 4, 1884
J. A. SMITH, Nov. 3, 1846 - Jan. 12, 1884
B. G. DUDLEY, Jul. 11, 1843 - Sep. 13, 1913
SALLIE DUDLEY, Oct. 26, 1862 - Sep. 14, 1933
G. W. EDWARDS, 1836 - 1909
DR. JONATHAN SHELTON HOLLIS, May 4, 1856 - Jul. 28, 1928
MARY ANN BROCK HOLLIS, Fsb. 16, 1863 - Mar. 6, 1926
BENJAMIN F. McCLURE, 1839 - 1911
ELLEN FOSTER McCLURE, Feb. 28, 1842 - Feb.20, 1933
WALTER B. HUTTO, Co. K. 1st Ala. Inf. Spanish Amer. War
REV. M. M. BROCK, Aug. 31, 1859 - Dec. 25, 1929
HARRIETT BROCK, Feb. 18, 1859 - Aug. 8, 1900
J. R. NICHOLS, Feb. 21, 1860 - Nov. 4, 1925
ROSANAH C. NICHOLS, wife of J. R. NICHOLS, Dec. 10, 1861 - Sep. 9, 1918
GEORGE CARGILE, 1850 - 1921
JULIA ANN CARGILE, 1852 - 1897
JESSE T. APPLING, 1858 - 1939
MELISSA M. APPLING, 1861 - 1943
A. NE MAN, Jul. 25, 1839 - Jun. 27, 1909
ANGELINE BUCKNER NEWMAN, Jun. 3, 1840 - May 18, 1922
H. S. SMITH, Sep. 25, 1857 - Dec. 24, 1930
SAMANTHA C. SMITH, Sep. 8, 1858 - Mar. 24, 1927
T. R. EDWARDS, Mar. 12, 1837 - Jun. 6, 1915
E. J. EDWARDS, 1842 - 1927
F. A. MILES, Feb. 18, 1847 - Jun. 18, 1917
R. E. MILES, wife of F. A. MILES, May 24, 1846 - Jan. 11, 1923
COL. AUSTIN PRICHETT, 1882 - 1953
JESSE C. CRUMLEY, Nov. 24, 1861 - Jan. 28, 1914
J. B. PRICE, 1864 - 1931
ADDIE PRICE, 1868 - 1942

Mt. Vernon Methodist Church Cemetery Cont'd.

WM. J. SMITH, 1851 - 1909
NANCY SMITH, 1866 - 1948
F. W. McCLURE, Jun. 5, 1847 - Dec. 4, 1908
FRANCES N. McCLURE, Dec. 28, 1852 - May 30,1928
DAVID HOLLIS, Mar. 28,1861 - Jul. 1, 1938
AURA HOLLIS, Oct. 10, 1859 - Oct. 29, 1928
JOEL W. RASPBERRY, Apr. 12, 1859 - Oct. 10, 1935
BIDDIA A. RASPBERRY, Apr. 25, 1860 - May 25, 1938
W. L. BOBO, Jun. 28, 1825 - Jan. 4, 1902
MARY BOBO, Jun. 4, 1838 - Sep. 25, 1903
WILLIS ABBETT, Feb. 18, 1823 - Feb. 18, 1907
S. F. RIELLY, Dec. 21, 1850 - Aug. 5, 1913
JAMES W. PINCKERTON, 1855 - 1930
NARCISSA PINCKERTON, 1852 - 1924

Hopewell Primitive Baptist Church Csmetery - Six Miles North of Fayette, Ala. on Hwy. 171 - Fayette County

J. H. BRYAN, Jan. 11, 1798 - Jun. 23, 1871
S. W. BRYAN, Sep. 16, 1808 - Jul. 23, 1866
I. W. PAYNE, Jan. 29, 1834 - Dec. 9, 1927
E. A. PAYNE, Feb. 20, 1844 - Jul. 11, 1937
W. M. RILEY, Oct. 21, 1817 - Jul. 26, 1890
MRS. ANN RILEY, May 11, 1838 - May 31, 1913
L. C. GUTTERY, Aug. 11, 1856 - Dec. 11, 1888
WILLIAM M. RILEY, Pvt. Co. E. 9th Reg. Ala. Inf. C.S.A. - Oct. 21, 1817 - May 29, 1863
DAVID N. MOORE, Oct. 20, 1845 - Jul. 18, 1891
SALLIE L. MOORE, Apr. 23, 1846 - Jun. 20, 1916
MARY A. LAWRENCE, wife of J. G. LAWRENCE, 1840 - 1876
GLENN A. THORNTON, 1850 - 1914
MINNIE THORNTON, 1863 - 1933
M. E. THORNTON, Apr. 6, 1822 - Mar. 30, 1882
WILLIAM THORNTON, Jan. 17, 1811 - Nov. 2, 1895
CHRISTIAN HARKINS, Jan. 20, 1807 - Jul. 29, 1849
ANDREW HARKINS, Oct. 16, 1802 - Apr. 6, 1871
T. S. HARKINS, Dec. 13, 1834 - Nov. 26, 1859
JAMES N. HARKINS, May 18, 1848 - Sep. 26, 1880
NANNIE IRVING, 1833 - 1913
CALEB EHL, Aug. 14, 1840 - Oct. 15, 1900
SARAH J. EHL, wife of CALEB EHL, Apr. 23, 1850 - Oct. 31, 1910
JAMES FORD, Mar. 22, 1821 - Jul. 26, 1892
ELIZABETH M. FORD, Feb. 17, 1841 - Jun. 24, 1882
RICHARD T. HAMNER, 1861 - 1945
JESSIE R. HAMNER, 1875 - 1948
J. Q. BRADLEY,Jun. 12, 1852 - Apr. 9, 1933
MANDY BRADLEY, May 22, 1851 - Mar. 4, 1905

Hopewell Primitive Baptist Church Cemetery Cont'd.

JAMES W. HENDRIX, 1850 - 1914
NANCY E. HENDRIX, 1853 - 1946
DAVID R. WATSON, Co. B 4th Ala. Cav. C.S.A.
S. B. KILLINGSWORTH, Mar. 29, 1859 - Jan. 29, 1929
CORP. M. D. KILLINGSWORTH, Co. I, Ala. Inf. C.S.A.
M. A. KILLINGSWORTH, Feb. 18, 1839 - Dec. 17, 1888
S. P. KILLINGSWORTH, Feb. 12, 1840 - Aug. 25, 1871
REV. C. L. JONES, Mar. 16, 1851 - Apr. 14, 1925
JOHN M. MOORE, Aug. 14, 1861 - Nov. 22, 1940
FANNIE J. MOORE, Sep. 30, 1858 - Apr. 21, 1941
GEORGE H. MOORE, Jun. 4. 1829 - Apr. 4, 1908
M. E. WEST MOORE, Jan. 12, 1829 - Aug. 5, 1898
ALLIS S. MOORE, May 5, 1856 - Jan. 3, 1930
E. S. JONES, Jun. 17,1846 - Aug. 11, 1927
FLORAH JONES, wife of E. S. JONES, Mar. 4, 1850 - May 10, 1923
JAMES H. RUSSELL, May 2, 1832 - Jul. 12, 1891
M. J. RUSSELL, Nov. 9, 1837 - Oct. 16, 1908
D. R. WATSON, 1830 -1905
CAROLINE WATSON, 1832 - 1886
J. W. SHEPHERD, Dec. 22, 1833 - Oct. 10, 1880
MARY FRANCIS JONES, Oct. 16, 1837 - Mar. 17, 1930
CHARLES A. STEWART, Nov. 15, 1811 - Sep. 5, 1871
J. F. DICKSON, Mar. 2, 1855 - Sep. 22, 1939
M. E. DICKSON, Mar. 11, 1855 - Jul. 3, 1934
ROBERT CORKREN, 1864 - 1947
BETTY CORKREN, 1853 - 1933
S. L. WHITE, Jun. 21, 1852 - Apr. 19, 1939
VIRGINIA JONES WHITE, wife of S. L. WHITE, Feb.7, 1857 - Sep. 28, 1953
GEORGE W. GRIFFIN, Jul. 17, 1833 - Jul. 7, 1903
S. E. GRIFFIN, Jul. 10, 1837 - Nov. 14, 1910
IRA POPE, Nov. 1812 - Nov. 1893
ELIZABETH POPE, Sep. 1812 - Sep. 1902
ELIZABETH HULSEY, Apr. 1805 -Dec. 1886
OLIVIA E.WHITE, wife of T. G. WHITE, Nov. 15, 1856 - Mar. 12, 1925
MARTHY G. WHITE, wife of T. G. WHITE, Jun. 24, 1826 - Sep. 6, 1884
G. B. BRAZIL, Jun. 20, 1815 - Aug. 18, 1899
NANCEY BRAZIL, May 15, 1825 - Nov. 26, 1906
HANNAH G. BAILEY, Mar. 1849 - Jul. 10, 1908
ROBERT PICKLE, Mar. 21, 1838 - Mar. 12, 1915
SARAH E. PICKLE, Sep. 3, 1848 - Jan. 9, 1929
REBECCA, wife of J. D. GILLILAND, Apr. 17, 1846 - Dec. 8, 1896
SARAH E. SMITH, Nov. 11, 1850 - Aug. 23, 1933
JOHN STAMP, Mar. 17, 1831 - Apr. 29, 1887
SARAH J. STAMP, Nov. 20, 1844 - Apr. 6, 1931

Hopewell Primitive Baptist Church Cemetery Cont'd.

JOHN N. BERRY, Sep. 26, 1823 - Aug. 12, 1877
ELIZA BERRY, wife of JOHN N. BERRY, 1826 - Apr. 26, 1908
MARTHA, wife of J. T. DAVIS, Dec. 16, 1855 - Jan. 21, 1937
LUCINDA REEVES, Apr. 11, 1823 - Aug. 17, 1905
HENRY N. REEVES, Co. K 7th Ga. Inf. C.S.A. Feb. 20, 1823 - Jul. 27, 1897
H. D. ROYCROFT, Palmer's Co. Ala. Res. C.S.A.
W. L. JONES, Aug. 16, 1819 - Dec. 29, 1887
ELIZABETH JONES, wife of W. L. JONES, Sep. 7, 1831 - Dec. 2, 1925
CHARLES H. REEVES, Co. D 2nd Ga. Cav. C.S.A.
MARY E. WHITE, Sep. 30, 1855 - Jan. 4, 1923
M.L. THORNTON WHITE, Nov. 2, 1855 - Oct. 30, 1940
JOHN W. JONES, Dec. 25, 1841 - Jul. 11, 1897
C. J. PARKER, 1861 - 1922
M. L. PARKER, 1857 - 1928

Cedar Creek Cemetery - On paved road between Berry and Alta Station - near Southern Railroad - Listed by Mrs. Herman Poe, Corona, Ala.

THOMAS W. ANDERSON, Dec. 14, 1859 - Apr. 3, 1916
FRANCES ANDERSON, May 1, 1857 - Nov. 21, 1898
H. G. AMERSON, Oct. 22, 1837 - Apr. 15, 1918
TELITHA, wife of H. G. AMERSON, Nov. 19, 1833 - Nov. 27, 1909
JOHN S. GOODE, Mar. 9, 1872 - Oct. 19, 1876
JENCIE A. KIMBRELL, Nov. 30, 1873 - Aug. 13, 1949
MISSOURI A. GAMMON, May 17, 1853 - Oct. 4, 1956
L. FIDELUS GAMMON, Jul. 31, 1855 - May 9, 1906
ZILPHA MOORE, May 1, 1843 - Sep. 12, 1908
CLEMME POE, Sep. 5, 1866 - Jun. 9, 1935
JOHN SEABORN MOORE, Jun. 24, 1875 - Mar. 15, 1940
TOLLIE R. MOORE, 1877 - 1948
EDWARD DURRELL DICKERSON, Dec. 25, 1873 - Feb. 11, 1915
RICHARD A. BAKER, 1854 - 1929
JIM M. AMERSON, Mar. 1, 1849 - Jan. 13, 1897
Y. R. AMERSON, Dec. 3, 1813 - Jun. 7, 1895
LOUISA P., wife of R. A. BAKER, Mar. 31, 1855 - May 17, 1884
MARY W., wife of REV. R. BAKER, Feb. 4, 1858 - May 10, 1909
RICHARD H. BAKER, Apr. 10, 1879 - Dec. 12, 1903
ANN M. C. POE, Nov. 3, 1820 - Dec. 23, 1839
NANCY KIMBRELL, b. 1735 - d. 1876 -(death date could not be verified)
M. (MUGGIE) KIMBRELL, 1862 - 1944
B. M. KIMBRELL, 1857 - 1917
MRS. D. A. KIMBRELL, Apr. 1, 1854 - Sep. 18, 1935
REV. J. M. KIMBRELL, Sep. 10, 1852 --- no other date
DAVID H.STRICKLAND, Apr. 13, 1865 - Mar. 20, 1939

## Cedar Creek Cemetery Cont'd.

MAGGIE D. STRICKLAND, Jul. 4, 1873 - Jan. 9, 1946
RHODA ROGERS, wife of W. S. POE, Nov. 18, 1837 - Dec. 4, 1916
WILLIAM S. POE, Apr. 26, 1837 - Jan. 24, 1917
NUGGIE A., wife of G. T. GOBLE, Oct. 19, 1874 - May 20, 1903
MATILDA P. KIMBRELL, 1843 - 1920
ELIZABETH KIMBRELL, May 1, 1829 - Jan. 30, 1877
B. M. KIMBRELL, May 4, 1827 - Mar. 4, 1889
BUCKNER KIMBRELL, b. in 1782 - d. Sep. 1858
A. J. KIMBRELL, 1822 - 1874
ELIZABETH KIMBRELL, 1815 - 1887

## Good Hope Baptist Church Cemetery on Hwy. 78 About Six Miles from Walker Co. line on road to Birmingham - Jefferson County

CATHERINE, wife of JOHN H. McBEEM, Mar. 16, 1856 - Sep. 12,1908
ALEX GOGGANS, Jan. 24, 1861 - Sep. 20, 1879
FRANCES GOGGANS, wife of WM. D. GOGGANS, Jan. 20, 1828 - Dec. 7, 1896
T. H. ROBBINS, May 5, 1848 - May 17, 1904
JOHN T. PAYNE, Apr. 9, 1828 - Jan. 12, 1903
J. R. (BOB) PAYNE, Feb. 14, 1869 - Mar. 6, 1951
MOLLY, wife of J. R. PAYNE, Oct. 9, 1864 - Dec. 4, 1936
NANCY E. DAVIS, Jan. 6. 1860 - Jul. 18, 1894
REV. A. F. ALLUMS, 1866 - 1937
N. J. ALLUMS, 1869 - 1937
ROBERT MAXWELL ROBBINS, Sep. 28, 1860 - Feb. 17, 1934
LOUISE FRANCES ROBBINS, Sep. 16, 1861 - Jan. 6, 1943
MAGGIE BLACKBURN, Mar. 28, 1865 - Oct. 8, 1932
DANIEL W. ROBBINS, 1860 - 1932
JOEL W. MANNING, 1850 - 1913
LOUISA J. MANNING, 1854 - 1940
D. J. GLOVER, May 10, 1864 - Aug. 11, 1913
JOHN T. MYRICK, Nov. 11, 1857 - Aug. 23, 1909
J. T. MYRICK, Apr. 10, 1858 - Apr. 30, 1887
SARAH MYRICK, 1843 - 1923
E. A. ROBBINS, Jan. 16, 1865 - Mar. 5, 1897
EMLA FRANCES, wife of E. N. ROBBINS, Jan. 13, 1833 - Oct. 20, 1919
E. N. ROBBINS, Aug. 1, 1869 - Dec. 28,1902
HARVEY N. ROBBINS, 1861 - Sep. 16, 1894
MARGARET ROBBINS, 1864 - 1952
JOHN W. MYRICK, Jan. 20, 1856 - Oct. 23, 1902
WM. H. GOGGANS, Oct. 3, 1847 - Dec. 13, 1920
ROSE A. GOGGANS, Jul. 18, 1843 - Jan. 12, 1917
SARAH MISSOURI GOGGANS, Apr. 12, 1868 - Sep. 12, 1889
W. P. HULSEY, Nov. 26, 1826 - Nov.6, 1867

## Good Hope Baptist Church Cemetery Cont'd.

ELIAS WOOD, Jun. 6, 1830 - May 5, 1915
MALINDA, wife of ELIAS WOOD, Feb. 5, 1841 - Oct. 8, 1901
MINNIE J. NORRIS, Jan. 1, 1863 - Jun. 17, 1938
J. R. NORRIS, May 3, 1851 - Jun. 13, 1950
K. A. WEBSTER GRAY, Mar. 30, 1859 - Jul. 2, 1935
JAMES W. WHITE, Dec. 8, 1857 - Spe. 13, 1947
FRANCES CONNELL, 1864 - 1909
FRANCIS TANNER, 1851 - 1941
JIM R. ROBBINS, 1856 - 1908
MARY E. ROBBINS, 1859 - 1911
JAMES D. WHITE, Co. M. 10th Tenn. Cav.
GRANNY: JANE CURRIER, Aug. 1, 1800 - Apr. 15, 1890
AMANDA C, CURRIER, Aug. 10, 1846 - Nov. 21, 1889
MARGARET PAYNE, Mar. 6, 1845 - Feb. 11, 1917
TERRELL JACKSON BOYD, 1859 - 1900
WILLIE SUMNER BOYD, 1856 - 1941
LARRELL, wife of J. C. JONES, Aug. 9, 1842 - Mar. 2, 1906
GEORGE W. JONES, Co. A. 2nd Ala. Inf. Spanish Amer. War
JOHN HENRY CRAVEN, Dec. 13, 1849 - Apr. 12, 1924
MARY JANE CRAVEN, Jan. 7, 1847 - Jun. 21, 1923

## McCormack Church Cemetery - Near Summiton, Ala. Jefferson Co.

J. M. LAWLER, Aug. 15, 1877 - Apr. 7, 1948
GEO. W. PHILLIP, Dec. 23, 1872 - Mar. 31, 1934
OCTAVIA PHILLIP, May 2, 1867 - Aug. 6, 1950
CHARLIE M. ALLRED, 1876 - 1952
N. C. CLIFTON, 1869 - 1940
LEWIS WADE [illegible], Aug. 25, 1868 - Feb. 21, 1944
BYRD A. MILLER, May 22, 1878 - Feb. 23, 1952
J. T. ALLUMS, Feb. 27, 1871 - Dec. 13, 1951
MARY ALLUMS, Jan. 11, 1872 - Jan. 13, 1942
C. J. SCOTT, Feb. 27, 1860 - Jun. 26, 1942
MILLIE SCOTT, May 9, 1865 - Jul. 6, 1940
MARGARET HINTON, 18[illegible]4 - 1930
NANCY ODEN, Jul. 12, 1870 - Nov. 9, 1940
A. J. ODEN, Nov. 16, 1862 - Apr. 4, 1945
A. W. McCORMACK, Mar. 8, 1870 - Mar. 4, 1956
JANOLA McCORMACK, Apr. 10, 1871 - Apr. 15, 1931
W. J. McCORMACK, Dec. 23, 1847 - Apr. 23, 1930
SUSAN M. McCORMACK, Sep. 27, 1846 - Sep. 30, 1919
L. M. DOBBS, Mar. 6, 1847 - Jan. 31, 1928
C. A. ROBBINS, Aug. 9, 1853 - Oct. 2, 1925
THENIA J. ROBBINS, Apr. 13, 1850 - May 23, 1918
MRS. M. A. DODD TERRELL, May 4, 1851 - Jul. 16, 1941
NOAH S. DANIEL, 1858 - 1923
EFFIE DANIEL, 1870 - 1942

McCormack Church Cemetery Cont'd.

LINSEY LONG, 1831 - 1904
DELONIA WALKER LONG, 1837 - 1920
CAROLINE HOLLIS, Apr. 11, 1830 - Jul. 18, 1899
MARTHA L, wife of E. M. HOLLIS, Jul. 27, 1848 - May 10, 1911
FRANCIS HOLLIS, 1857 - 1935
MARY HOLLIS, 1862 - 1941
JOHN HOLLIS, May 1, 1833 - Aug. 23, 1911
RACHEL ANN, wife of JOHN HOLLIS, May 30, 1833 - 1907
HIRAM PUTNAM, Jan. 3, 1852 - Oct. 13, 1936
MARY E. PUTNAM, Apr. 27, 1862 - no death date
JOHN SPEARS, Feb. 1, 1865 - Mar. 14, 1940
ANGELINE SPEARS, 1863 - 1920
JOSEPH WILEY PITTMAN, 1868 - 1926
MAGGIE EVELYN PITTMAN, 1871 - 1930
MARTHA E. REYNOLDS, 1846 - 1932
DREW TANNER, 1853 - 1944
LOU TANNER, 1852 - 1930
HENRY JAMES, 1866 - 1942
ROSA JAMES, 1868 - 1938
PINKNEY GOODWIN, Jul. 12, 1852 - Jan. 9, 1928
MARTHA A. GOODWIN, Oct. 18, 1846 - Sep. 17, 1944
JOHN GLOVER, Oct. 11, 1857 - Sep. 21, 1950
MATILDA ANN GLOVER, Aug. 18, 1855 - Jun. 28, 1929
SERENIA CAROLINE BAGLEY, Apr. 18, 1862 - Sep. 3, 1927
W. E.HAWKINS, Jan. 1, 1854 - May 25, 1925
J. B. BLAND, Jan. 30,1871 - Mar. 9, 1942
N. A. YARBROUGH, Aug. 28, 1860 - Jul. 23, 1928

Lawler or Lollar Cemetery - About one mile from the Walker Co. Line on Hwy. 78 - Jefferson Co.

ELIJAH H. VINSON HOLLIS, d. May 23, 1865, age 78 yrs (b.1788)
SUSANNAH LISBORN, Jun. 11, 1787 - Apr. 20, 1871
JOAB LOLLAR, 1804 - Aug. 19, 1868
JENNETTE LOLLAR, wife of JOAB LOLLAR, 1819 - Mar. 18, 1896
ELIZA LOLLAR, Jul. 20, 1844 - Jul. 23, 1881
J. A. LOLLAR, Sep. 30, 1879 - Feb. 1,1953
W. H. LOLLAR, Jun. 19, 1856 - Sep. 3, 1929
NANCY E. LOLLAR, wife of W. H.LOLLAR, Mar. 21, 1855 - Aug. 27, 1890
I. M. LAWLER, Oct. 29, 1852 - Jan. 23, 1924
MARY ELIZABETH LAWLER, Oct. 23, 1852 - Jun. 18, 1940
J. A. BLACK, Sep. 20, 1814 - 1885
JOHN W. BAGLEY, 1859 - 1953
NANCY E. BAGLEY, 1868 - 1955
NANCY WILLIAMS, Apr. 8, 1842 - Feb. 5, 1917
ETHEL WILLIAMS, Jan. 31, 1842 - May 18, 1877
SUANER C. WILLIAMS, Nov. 20, 1866 - May 1879
ED WILLIAMS, 1816 - Feb. 10, 1865

Lawler or Lollar Cemetery Contd.

RICHARD BERRY TURNER, Jun. 1, 1873 - Jul. 22, 1956

Old Union Baptist Church Cemetery - Two Miles East of Bear Creek - Marion Co.

SUSAN DOWNEY, dau. of JOHN and CATHERINE DOWNEY, Jan. 27, 1849- Jan. 9, 1882
JOHN DOWNEY, Sep. 25, 1788 - Jul. 25, 1890 (102 yrs. of age)
M. J. DOWNEY, Feb. 27, 1853 - Dec. 5, 1883
M. J. DIKES, wife of R. P. DIKES, Sep. 6, 1858 - Sep. 8, 1905
THOMAS WALKER, Jan. 29,1790 - Dec. 13, 1875
NANCY, wife of THOMAS WALKER, Jan. 14, 1793 - Jun. 1, 1868
FERNANDOS WALKER, Mar. 3, 1833 - Feb. 24,1874
THOMAS WALKER, Craven Co. N. C. Militia, War of 1812
WM. N. RODEN, M.D., Mar. 12, 1803 - Nov. 7, 1886
LETHA, wife of WM. N. RODEN, M.D., Mar. 30, 1815 - Mar. 1, 1878
MARTIN STRANGS, 1812 - Jul. 22, 1878
ANNIE STRANGE, Jul. 29, 1833 - Aug. 9, 1910
NATHANIEL COX, Jan. 3, 1810 - Feb. 16, 1895
MAHALEY COX, Dec. 18, 1809 - May 30, 1865
E. M. DEGRAFFENREID, Jul. 4, 1841 - May 25, 1926
Other graves in this cemetery not copied by Mrs. Guttery.

Zion Cemetery - On Legion Rd. Two Miles N.E. Winfield, Ala. - Marion Co.

ROBERT BOWLAN, Sep. 30, 1782 - Jul. 8, 1851
MARY, wife of ROBERT BOWLAN,Jul. 1788 - Oct. 19, 1848
JAMES CAROL BOWLAN, Feb. 7,1848 - May6, 1898
MARGARET ELLEN BOWLAN, Jan.26, 1850 - Jun. 3, 1938
HENRY N. BOWLAN, May 3, 1825 - married MARTHA C. BYERS, Jan. 1, 1845 - d. Dec. 29, 1898
W. T. HULSEY, 1847 - 1923
NANCY HULSEY, Mar. 24, 1844 - Jul. 8, 1919
GEORGE W.BENTON, Sep. 18, 1826 - Aug. 10, 1882
NANCY EMILY BENTON, Sep. 1, 1835 - Sep. 17, 1914
DAVID S. HARRIS, Jan. 24, 1826 - m. to MALINDA BOWLAN, Jan. 24, 1844 - d. Sep. 26, 1884
MALINDA HARRIS, Nov. 26, 1823 - Sep. 12, 1901
ELD. A. W. GREEN, Nov. 26, 1848 - Jan. 10, 1938
ORPHA R. GREEN, Nov. 13, 1852 - Sep. 4, 1907
JOSEPH F. SHIRLEY, May 13, 1853 - Nov. 6, 1926
MANERVEA G. SHIRLEY, Nov. 30,1852 - Jul. 21, 1909
DAVID H. SHIRLEY, Aug. 1, 1849 - Sep. 25, 1904
MELVINA, wife of DAVID H. SHIRLEY, Oct. 25, 1848 - Jan. 15,1929
SEMMEL J. STANLEY, 1857 - 1928
MARTHA A. STANLEY, 1851 - 1926

Zion Cemetery Cont'd.

JOHN W. KIRK, Jan. 19, 1849 - Sep. 8, 1915
DICY A. KIRK, Feb. 6, 1841 - Mar. 20, 1915
ABRAM SHIRLEY, Aug. 5, 1834 - Apr. 8, 1914
SUSAN A. SHIRLEY, Jul. 19, 1854 - Feb. 11, 1937
MARGARET SAPHRONIA SHIRLEY, Jan. 31, 1834 - Dec. 7, 1889
H. L. ADKINS, May 19, 1866 - May 26, 1906
DANIEL SIZEMORE, Jan. 2, 1852 - Oct. 18, 1921
REBECCA SIZEMORE, 1852 - 1937
T. W. BERRYHILL, 1860 - 1913
OPHELIA BERRYHILL, 1865 - 1953
W. H. MARKHAM, Mar. 1, 1848 - Jan. 19, 1917
H. J. MARKHAM, Jan. 12, 1846 - Mar. 25, 1915
L. N. MARKHAM, Oct. 4, 1843 - Sep. 13, 1917
LUCY JANE MARKHAM, Aug. 29, 1851 - Jun. 1, 1942
REV. ANDERSON MARKHAM, Apr. 4, 1816 - ordanied May 1852 - d. Jul. 3, 1889
MARY MARKHAM, Mar. 8, 1813 - Jun. 24, 1882
MARTIN SHIRLEY, Sep. 27, 1816 - May 30,1889
ELIZABETH SHIRLEY, wife of MARTIN SHIRLEY, May 30, 1811 - Jun. 1, 1889
REUBEN SHIRLEY, Jun. 14, 1838 - Mar. 23, 1910
CHARITY EMALINE SHIRLEY, Dec. 9, 1840 - death date gone
SARAH, wife of R. SHIRLEY, Dec. 25, 1833 - Sep. 19, 1921
M. E. BSNTON, Sep. 3, 1869 - Nov. 27, 1928
THOMAS R. BENTON, Oct. 24, 1860 - Nov. 11, 1898
CARROLL REED, 1852 - 1941
MARGARET REED, 1856 - 1935
JULIAN DOSS, 1850 - 1927
POLLY DOSS, 1859 - 1951
SIMEON ESTES, Oct.20, 1821 - Dec. 23, 1876
ELIZABETH ESTES, Dec. 12, 1826 - May 4, 1868
MARY E. ESTES, May 16, 1856 - Apr. 22, 1878
JULIA ANNIE, wife of N. M. CHAMBLESS, Jan. 25, 1844 - m. Jan. 15, 1865, d. Dec. 24, 1867
J. H. MAY, May 1, 1860 - Oct. 26, 1938
L. L. MAY, Jul. 23, 1828 - Sep. 13, 1883
M. L. MAY, Jul. 27, 1828 - Apr. 22, 1898
MARY S. TAYLOR, Nov. 9, 1859 - Oct. 10, 1897
S. M. MADDOX, wife of B. J. MADDOX, Feb. 11, 1836 - Sep. 10, 1887
E. J. SPANN, May 17, 1828 - Jan. 21, 1871
WILLIAM SPANN, Jul. 13, 1803 - Jun. 24,1862
MATILDA A. SPANN, May 16, 1807 - Jul. 5, 1877
MARTHA G. BYARS, Jan. 9, 1824 - married H. M. BOWLAN, Jan. 1, 1845, d. May 11, 1898
E. L. ADKINS, Feb. 4, 1840 - Nov. 4, 1896
THOMAS N. ADKINS, May 11, 1859 - Jul. 28, 1884
WILLIAM F. JONES, Jul. 21, 1854 - Jan. 13, 1936

Zion Cemetery Cont'd.

ESSIE J. JONES, Nov. 26, 1855 - Feb. 27, 1939
J. T. GREEN, May 10, 1857 - Nov. 2, 1929
MARTHA A. GREEN, Nov. 15, 1857 - May 6, 1933
A. J. LANGLEY, Aug. 29, 1849 - Dec. 13, 1915
SUSIE L., wife of T. J. SPRINGFIELD, Sep. 24, 1850
M. A. FIELDS, 1864 - 1935
L. P. FIELDS, 1868 - 1942
JOHN T. HOWELL, Mar. 7, 1866 - Jun. 19, 1949
LOUISA A. HOWELL, Oct. 9, 1868 - Feb. 17, 1934
DANIE HAWKINS, 1859 - no death date
MINTA A. HAWKINS, 1862 - 1934
JOHN J. DAVIS, Sep. 20, 1867 - Feb. 27, 1940
CATHERINE DAVIS, Feb. 27, 1867 - Nov. 12, 1949

Siloam Missionary Baptist Church Cemetery - Organized 1884 - Three Miles from Winfield, Ala. On Hwy. to Fayette - Marion Co.

J. C. KIRKLAND, Apr. 4, 1812 - Nov. 12, 1889
PERMELIA, wife of HON. J. C. KIRKLAND, Feb. 6, 1817 - Oct. 26, 1900 (note: she was a dau. of MILES and PRISCILLA CHAPPELL)
JAMES W. WARD, 1858 - 1946
JULIA M. WARD, d. Feb. 1, 1958 - aged 87 yrs.
JOHN ALBERT WARD, d. Feb. 7, 1959 - age 87 yrs. 7 mos. 21 das.
CLARA DOT WARD, d. Jul. 26, 1958 - age 45 yrs 8 mos 13 das
ETTA WARD, Sep. 10, 1869 - Mar. 1939
B. L. WARD, Jun. 8, 1860 - May 13, 1923
A. WARD, Apr. 18, 1857 - Oct. 25, 1873
B. F. WARD, Nov. 30, 1835 - Nov. 19, 1906
MARY M. WARD, Jun. 2, 1838 - Sep. 1, 1926
C. E. WARD, 1861 - 1894
JOHN W. MELTON, May 6, 1833 - Apr. 25, 1909
ELIZABETH MELTON, May 20, 1833 - Jan. 15, 1915
E. ERWIN, 1824 - Aug. 14, 1908
ROBERT Z. ERWIN, 1859 - 1937
MARGARET M. ERWIN, 1869 - 1938
SUSAN LANGLEY, 1854 - 1947
W. N. BURLESON, Aug. 30, 1851 - May 29, 1913
NANCY BURLESON, 1866 - 1953
MANNING VANDIVER OWING, 1859 - 1941
SUANNAH OWING, 1869 - 1905
R. MARC OWING, Sep. 15, 1810 - Dec. 10, 1895
F. E. MILLS, Jul. 14, 1847 - Jul. 10, 1929
J. E. MILLS, Sep. 24, 1847 - Jun. 17, 1929

Old Cemetery - Seven Miles South of Talladega, Ala. On Jackson Tracc - Talledega County

ABNER LAWLER, Sep. 1, 1798 - Feb. 1846
LYDIA LAWLER, Sep. 24, 1794 - Aug. 25, 1858
MRS. MARY SMOOT, Feb. 4, 1764 - Mar. 28, 1848
CALEDONIA MILL, dau. of B. A. & E. A. SMOOT, Jun. 8, 1835 - Oct. 27, 1856
SARAH ELIZA, dau. of B. A. & E. A. SMOOT, May 1845 - Mar. 14, 1953
THOMAS J. FARISS, b. Lincoln Co. Neb. Oct. 24, 1796 - Oct. 27, 1875
LAFAYETTE FARISS, Dec. 9, 1825 - Jul. 8, 1835
ANNIS CAMERON, consort of WM. CAMERON, d. Aug. 14, 1841 - age 63 yrs. (b. 1778)
JAMES G. HANCOCK, Nov. 15, 1795 - Sep. 7, 1842
HENRY SIMS, d. Jun. 21, 1890, age 86 yrs.
AMANDA, wife of JAMES G. HANCOCK, Oct. 2, 1807 - May 25, 1880
ADELAIDE, dau. of J. G. & A. H. HANCOCK, Dec. 27, 1832 - Mar. 1860
ELIZABETH JANE, dau. of J. G. & A. H. HANCOCK, May 14, 1828 - May 12, 1845
WM. H. HANCOCK, son of J. G. & A. H. HANCOCK, Mar. 17, 1840 - Apr. 6, 1881
ISAAC KILLOUGH, 1808 - Jun. 5, 1834
MARY GALLEY, b. 1775 - Nov. 26, 1843
SARAH GALLEY, b. 1807 - d. Jun. 2, 1835
SARAH FRANCES GALLEY, Dec. 2, 1838 - 1838
SURGN. SAMUEL M. HOGAN, Conf. Army, C.S.A.
WILBER FISK HOGAN, Co. A. Conf. Cav. C.S.A.
AUNT: ELIZA JANE HOGAN, Mar. 11, 1840 - May 29, 1914
JAMES M. KENDALL, Aug. 29, 1839 - d. age 29 yrs (b.1810)
M. P. GADIE, b. 1802 - Dec. 18, 1899
SARAH A. GADIE, 1812 - Jun. 1, 1879
MARY A. BEAVERTON, Jun. 24, 1849 - age 30 yrs (b. 1819)
RICHMOND ROBB, Feb. 14, 1859 - Mar. 23, 1906
LEWIS W. ROBB, Dec. 5, 1862 - 1884
MARY H. WOODRUFF, wife of M. WOODRUFF, Jan. 1, 1837 - Jan. 9, 1863
ALWILDA TRUEHART, dau. of EDWIN & LOUISE GIBBS, Mar. 27, 1850 - no other date
THOMAS W. FARRIES, Aug. 18, 1831 - Mar. 7, 1847
EMILY FARRIES, Aug. 1, 1811 - Aug. 5, 1834
THOMAS CALLEY (or Galley), 1761 - 1861
MRS. M. E. SLAUGHTER, consort of COL. M. H. SLAUGHTER, Sep. 21, 1830 - Nov. 21, 1861 -
JOHN BYARS, Sep. 14, 1802 - Aug. 12, 1889
JESS C. TERRY, Feb. 21, 1837 - Jul. 5, 1921
MARY L. MABERLY (MOBERLY), wife of J. C. TERRY, Apr. 27, 1842 - Apr. 4, 1887

Old Cemetery Cont'd.

EULA TERRY, Dec. 15, 1872 - 1937
THOMAS W. TERRY, Aug. 9, 1847 - Nov. 28, 1904

Cemetery on Stanley Old Home Place - Tuscaloosa Co. One Mi. South of Sterling Ch. Cemetery - Land Now Owned by Nina Searcy of Tuscaloosa

BENJAMIN STANLEY, Feb. 7, 1791 - Apr. 23, 1867
NANCY THOMAS STANLEY, all dates eroded

Sterling Church Cemetery - Tuscaloosa Co.

MILES CHAPPELL, Jun. 15,1790 - Mar. 24, 1887
PRISCILLA PARKER CHAPPELL, Apr. 10, 1797 - Aug. 27, 1889
DR. F. B. APPLING, Dec. 23, 1829- Jul. 26, 1900
ELVIRA APPLING, Jun. 17, 1828 - Feb. 13, 1904
JESSE M. STANLEY, May 15, 1829 - Dec. 27, 1896
MARTHA (CHAPPELL) STANLEY, May 29, 1831 - Sep. 20, 1909

Inactive Cemetery - Deep in the woods, five miles N. E. of Sterling Church, Tuscaloosa Co.

C. R. BAKER, Aug. 8,1807 - Oct. 25, 1869
WM. APPLING, son of F. B. & ELVIRA APPLING, Jan. 27,1861 - Aug. 12, 1863
FRANK APPLING, Nov. 23, 1865 - Jan. 7, 1866
E. J. BAKER, 1871 - 1871

Whitson Cemetery - on Hwy. 69 near Jesse Dunn Home Tuscaloosa Co. (By Mrs. Herman Poe of Corona)

W. T.WHITSON, Jul. 28, 1848 = May 15, 1882
SUSAN HAMNER, Jul. 23, 1853 - Jun. 20, 1878
MATTIE L. LOLLAR, wife of J. W. LOLLAR, Jan. 10, 1861 - Dec. 24, 1901
A.W. LOLLAR, Oct. 18, 1837 - Jan. 7, 1896
RANDY LOLLAR, wife of F. W. LOLLAR, Dec. 5, 1871 - Aug. 7, 1899
WILLIAM DUNN, Jun. 22, 1824 - Mar. 9, 1902
SAMUEL DUNN, 1857 - 1927

Evergreen Cemetery - Tuscaloosa, Alabama - Tuscaloosa Co.

JOHN S. FITCH, b. in Norwich, Oct. 15, 1792 - d. Sep. 20, 1870
CAROLINE UNICE FITCH, Sep. 15, 1816 - Jun. 21, 1892
ELIZA JENNETT, wife of JOHN ABSOLOM PARK, Dec. 7, 1836 - May 8, 19...

Evergreen Cemetery Cont'd.

MARTHA ESTHER, wife of ROBERT I. MERIWETHER, d. Jul. 22, 1911, aged 69 yrs.
HARRIETT, COLVIN, wife of JAS. S. COLVIN, Mar. 6, 1839 - Jun. 24, 1915
JOHN S. HANLY, Aug. 29, 1844 - Jan. 6, 1905
MARTHA ANN HANLY, Jan. 29, 1853 - Aug. 30,1914
SAMUEL BARTLETT JONES, 1846 - 1899
LULA ALDREDGE JONES, 1855 - 1880
MARY SOMERVILLE JONES, 1824 - 1952
RICHARD COLVIN McCALLA, SR., Mar. 15, 1826 - Feb. 18, 1899
MARGARET ELIZA LEWIS, Jan. 21, 1830 - Jul. 4, 1914
BENJAMIN HARRISON, Sep. 17, 1813 - Jul. 7, 1872
ADALINE HARRISON, Feb. 5, 1825 - Dec. 7, 1908
J. LUTHER FOSTER, May 31, 1837 - Dec. 9, 1905
JAMES M. McGOWEN, Apr. 23, 1813 - Feb. 18, 1895
JULIA LOUISE McGOWEN, Mar. 5, 1828 - Apr. 25, 1911
REV. J. T. YERBY, Feb. 2, 1826 - Sep. 3, 1895
PERMELIA ANN MILLER YERBY, Mar. 24, 1824 - Jun. 6, 1905 (wife of REV. YERBY)
THOMAS NEWTON HAYS, Oct. 1836 - Mar. 5, 1894
MILTON A. STRICKLAND, Apr. 7, 1825 - Mar. 15, 1902
MARGARET COLLIER, Apr. 22, 1833 - Nov.17, 1911
C. C. KILGORE, Sep. 26, 1848 - Jan. 12, 1938
ELIZABETH FORTNER KILGORE, wife of C. C. KILGORE, Aug. 24, 1855-Jun. 24, 1946
J. L. CLEMENTS, Nov.6, 1844 - Dec. 16, 1915
BANNIE CLEMENTS, May 12, 1849 - Oct. 19, 1902
MARGARET T. LOVE, Sep. 8, 1833 - Nov. 7, 1905
LUTHER MORGAN CLEMENTS, M.D., Capt. Co. F. 41st Ala. Vol. C.S.A. Nov. 15, 1825 - Nov. 1, 1903
CHRISTOPHER J. HAUSMAN, Aug. 26, 1839 - Jul. 9, 1913
ADELIA HAGLER HAUSMAN, Jan. 16, 1850 - Jan. 12, 1939
MARIA L. ALLEN, Mar. 23, 1830 - Nov. 8, 1902
M. E. J. MARR, Sep. 9, 1828 - Feb. 2, 1885
NANCY GREEN, relict of WM. M. MARR, Sep. 19, 1789, m. Dec. 20, 1807, d. Mar. 11, 1856
THOMAS LUNCH CARSON, Sep. 13, 1816 - Apr. 17, 1867
CHAS. JEROME FIQUET, Sep. 14, 1811 - Oct. 6, 1869
STERLING ALEXANDWR MARTIN WOOD, Mar. 17, 1823 - Jul. 26, 1891
LELIA ELIZABETH WOOD, Sep. 19, 1825 - Jan. 14, 1891
MARGARET NABORS MALONE, Nov. 11, 1843 - Sep. 10, 1914
CHARLES P. MALONE, Aug. 26, 1842 - Jan. 18, 1912
JOHN ABSALOM PARKER, Dec. 7, 1836 - May 8, 1911
JOSEPH THOMAS GARNER, b. Claborn Co. Sep. 14, 1844 - d. Tuscaloosa Dec. 25, 1908
SUE JOHNSON, wife of J. T. GARNER, dau. of WILLIAM JOHNSON and HANNAH BYLER, Aug. 19, 1844 - Sep. 24, 1918
JOHN TOWNSEND, Dec. 16, 1848 - Jan. 8, 1924

Evergreen Cemetery Cont'd.

NANCY M. BISHOP, Jun. 14, 1842 - Jan. 19, 1912
M. E. TOWNSEND, May17, 1834 - Sep. 30, 1910
WALTER C. HARRIS, 1848 - 1934
JAMES LINDSEY BARR, son of JAMES & MARY ELIZABETH BARR, b. Charleston, S.C. May 14, 1840 - d. Tuscaloosa Co. Nov. 4, 1908, aged 68 yrs.
BETHENIA HARDEN PHIFER, Feb. 26, 1834 - May 5, 1908
SUSAN W. BOSWELL, Aug. 4, 1842 - May 22, 1926
ROBERT WILSON, 1840 - 1911
ISABELLE HENRY WILSON, 1850 - 1916
W. Z. JONES, SR., May 3, 1836 - Jul. 10, 1912
ALGE LESUEUR, wife of W. Z. JONES, SR., Apr. 6, 1852 - Aug. 26, 1927
SARAH JANE WEATHERFORD, dau. of WILLIAM & MARY A. WEATHERFORD, wife of D. D. DURRETT, Oct. 1, 1847 - Oct. 6, 1919
D. D. DURRETT, Dec. 4, 1843 - Jul. 21, 1923
JOHN DERSHIDE, Nov. 10, 1843 - Aug. 27, 1929
ANNIE DERSHIDE, May 26, 1845 - Sep. 5, 1931
DR. G. W. BORCUGHS, Sep. 2, 1841 - Jul. 14, 1921
ELENA JOSEPHINE, wife of J. H. PRATT, Jun. 14, 1848 - Sep. 30, 1929
MONTGOMERY INGE, Mar. 31, 1849 - Sep. 26, 1925
MARTHA ELEN, wife of WM. B. TAYLOR, Dec. 24, 1847 - Sep. 29, 1914
S. E. JONES, Jun. 30, 1849 - Jul. 23, 1919
DR. GEORGE LITTLE, Feb. 11, 1838 - May 15, 1924
CAROLINE PATILLO DOAK, wife of DR. GEORGE LITTLE, b. Jun. 12, 1842, Clarksville, Va. d. Tuscaloosa, Oct. 12, 1914
ROSA BRITTEN TURNER, b. Madison, N.J. May 15, 1843 - d. Jun. 15, 1922
THOMAS S. JOHNSON, Jul. 28, 1807 - Nov. 17, 1873
JOSEPHINE S. JOHNSON, Aug. 1, 1812 - Jan. 2, 1882
H. HESTER JOHNSON, Jun. 29, 1845 - Dec. 2, 1939
W. H. JOHNSON, Mar. 3, 1846 - Sep. 24, 1916
MARGARET KING JONES, Jul. 22, 1830 - Apr. 20, 1904
LUCRETIA ELIZA OWEN, wife of WM. W. PRUDE, dau. of THOMAS OWEN, 1789 - 1849
WILLIAM WELLINGTON PRUDE, Jan. 31, 1824 - Oct. 14, 1895 - son of WILLIAM PRUDE, 1774 - 1883.
MARY E. KENNEDY, Jun. 8, 1824 - Sep. 26, 1883
JOHN S. KENNEDY, Oct. 1, 1818, May 2, 1899
JAMES SPENCE, b. near Edenboro, Scotland, Jan. 20, 1838 - d. Aug. 18, 1916
ANNA COWLES PRICE, wife of JAMES SPENCE, dau. of LOUISA SHEARER and JAMES L. PRICE, b. Apr. 24, 1848 - d. in her 80th year

Evergreen Cemetery Cont'd.

EUGENE ALLEN SMITH, Oct. 27, 1841 - Sep. 7, 1927
JENNIE GARLAND, wife of EUGENE ALLEN SMITH, Apr. 26, 1847 - Dec. 15, 1930
ROBERT JEMISON STONE, 1832 - 1915
SARAH STAPPE JONES, 1842 - 1920
REV. ROBERT BROWN McALPINE, Jan. 25, 1848 - Jul. 5,1920
W. T. DAVIS, Oct. 7, 1835 - Sep. 19, 1907
MARY ANN CROSSLAND, wife of W. T. DAVIS, Sep. 7, 1837 - Nov. 23, 1914
LUCINDA FRANCES RABUN, wife of ADKIN RABUN, 1848 - 1926

Williamson Cemetery - Northport, Ala.
Tuscaloosa County

MARYLAND FREEMAN, Jan. 12, 1839 - Sep. 19, 1907
AMANDA E. SMITH, Aug. 19, 1848 - Mar. 27, 1904
ROBERT H. WILLIAMSON, Aug. 11, 1859 - Dec. 16, 1921
ADDIE W. WILLIAMSON, Aug. 18, 1859 - Aug. 1, 1897
ZIMRI SHIRLEY, Jun. 10, 1843 - Oct. 5, 1923
CHERIE WILLIAMSON, wife of Z. SHIRLEY, Jul. 29, 1849 - Jan. 13, 1912
REV. E. A. POWELL, May 17, 1817 - Sep. 1, 1892
AMANDA MELVINA POWELL, May 27, 1824 - Mar. 9, 1872
JAMES H. RICE, Feb. 26, 1833 - May 15, 1896
CATHERINE RICE, wife of W. W. STRONG, Jul. 10, 1831 - Jan. 12, 1913
W. W. STRONG, Dec. 12, 1823 - Oct. 11, 1893
THOMAS F. RICE, Jul. 17, 1835 - Sep. 16, 1897
MARYETTA P. RICE, Aug. 19, 1839 - Mar. 16, 1885
SUSAN DURRETT STRONG, wife of W. L. CHRISTIAN, Mar. 11, 1831 - Oct. 21, 1912
WM. LOUIS CHRISTIAN, Oct. 14, 1824 - Nov. 20, 1898
W. R. DODSON, Nov. 16, 1829 -Oct. 21, 1921
ANNIE PALMER DODSON, wife of W. R. DODSON, Nov. 6, 1830 - Sep. 20, 1904
W. H. BAKER, Apr. 4, 1841 - Sep. 25, 1925
MARY PALMER, wife of W. H. BAKER, Mar. 7, 1854 - Jun. 2, 1909
CHARLOTTE CAIN, wife of THOMAS PRICE, Oct. 10, 1828 - Jun. 2, 1913
D. W. WYLIE, Mar. 7, 1832 - Sep. 14, 1912
MISS S. D. HARDIN, Jan. 29, 1821 - May 20, 1913
JOHN C. ANDERS, Jul. 10, 1848 - Apr. 3,1914
TOLBERT C. RICE, Aug. 10, 1846 - May 11, 1930
SARAH ELIZABETH RICE, Mar. 10, 1848 - Aug. 5, 1917
C. A. THOMAS, May 27, 1848 - Apr. 1, 1926
LOIS ELLEN THOMAS, Jul. 28, 1854 - Oct. 10, 1935

Williamson Cemetery Cont'd.

JAMES C. McGEHEE, May 6, 1832 - Dec. 27, 1884
MARY L. McGEHEE, Jul. 24, 1849 - Dec. 8, 1925
P. K. THOMSON, Nov. 18, 1844 - May 17, 1888
CYNTHIA THOMSON, Jul. 1, 1846 - Oct. 9, 1899
FRANCES J. GOODMAN, Feb. 6, 1839 - May 23, 1902
ALLEN LINDSEY, Mar. 30, 1846 - Aug. 27, 1917
SARAH LINDSEY, Sep. 2, 1843 - Aug. 26, 1912
JENNIE LINDSEY, Nov. 28, 1858 - Jan. 17, 1928
J. C. BOWERS, Sep. 23, 1833 - Aug. 1, 1916
MRS. MALINDA ANTHONY McGEE, Dec. 23, 1829 - Jan. 27, 1901
REV. GEORGE TIERCE, Aug. 21, 1818 - Dec. 11, 1901
SARAH E. TIERCE, Oct. 20, 1819 - Apr. 13, 1891
JOSIAH H. FREEMAN, Oct. 17, 1821 - Jan. 31, 1895
LUCY M., wife of JOSIAH H. FREEMAN, Feb. 26, 1839 - Aug. 23, 1890
LEON P. FREEMAN, Nov. 5, 1851 - Mar. 26, 1904
SARAH E., wife of R. F. PALMER, Feb. 23, 1836 - Oct. 12, 1892
RICHARD F. PALMER, Jan. 30, 1822 - Aug. 8, 1885
REUBEN D. PALMER, Aug. 6, 1876 - Oct. 18, 1899
SPENCER WASHINGTON, d. Mar. 23, 1897 - aged 56 yrs.
ADKIN CAIN, Aug. 23, 1832 - May 29, 1899
BETTY HAGLER CAIN, Mar. 30, 1846 - Jan. 28, 1943
S. M. HAMNER, May 8, 1827 - Jan. 19, 1914
DEMPSEY WILLIAMSON, Nov. 15, 1812 - May 25, 1869
REBECCA E. WILLIAMSON, Dec. 25, 1822 - Jul. 16, 1896
JOHN B. WILLIAMSON, 1855 - 1939
ADDIE, wife of J. B. WILLIAMSON, Mar. 16, 1856 - Dec. 23, 1880
JAMES LEWIS WILLIAMSON, 1853 - 1916
J. H. SMITH, Oct. 6, 1841 - Feb. 14, 1909
MRS. SARAH P. JOHNSON, wife of SAMUEL M. HAMNER, May 14, 1829 - Jul. 25, 1912
MILLIE F. WILLIAMSON, 1855 - 1929
JAMES S. SMITH, Dec. 28, 1819 - May 4, 1890, aged 70 yrs, 4 mos. 6 das.
THOMAS W. SMITH, Aug. 10, 1822 - Mar. 24, 1900
SARAH J. SMITH, Jul. 17, 1826 - Apr. 2, 1878
J. G. BELL, May 16, 1840 - Oct. 20, 1889
RABAGA A. BELL, Oct. 8, 1846 - Feb. 14, 1923
MOSES SHIRLEY, Dec. 18, 1811 - married Feb. 11, 1839 - d. Jun. 5, 1878
MARGARET LOUISE, wife of THOMAS W. SMITH, Apr. 15, 1852 - Jan. 1, 1929
JAMES D. BELL, Jan. 8, 1823 - May 17, 1887
LOUISE C. RICE, wife of J. D. BELL, Jul. 18, 1838 - Jul. 26, 1907
ROBERT S. COX, Oct. 19, 1837 - Jun. 14, 1901

Williamson Cemetery Cont'd.

MARY A. COX, Mar. 8, 1816 - Jun. 19, 1890
CHAS. J. SPENCER, Oct. 19, 1838 - death date not verified
MARTHA HELEN SPENCER, Jan. 1, 1843 - death date not verified
SAM M. FREEMAN, Jul. 29, 1852 - Jul. 19, 1925

Macedonia Methodist Church - Hwy 69 North of Tuscaloosa, Alabama

BENJAMIN TIERCE, 1785 - Feb. 18, 1869
SUSANNAH TIERCE, Jun. 13, 1787 - Apr. 29, 1862
JULIA FRANCES TIERCE, Jan. 28, 1868 - Apr. 7, 1901
E. G. TIERCE, Dec. 17, 1827 - Mar. 21, 1906
FRANCES C. TIERCE, Dec. 3, 1831 - Mar. 13, 1900
EUGENE B. TIERCE, May 15, 1865 - Aug. 30, 1918
MRS. VETURIA TIERCE, Nov. 22, 1869 - Jun. 21, 1907
E. ANDER, JR., May 26, 1807 - Aug. 19, 1881
MARY E. SAVAGE, Mar. 8, 1839 - Jul. 5, 1871
JOHN P. HAMNER, Oct. 4, 1845 - Dec. 18, 1905
ANNIE M. HAMNER, wife of JOHN P. HAMNER, Jan. 10, 1846 - Jan. 2, 1931
G. H. HAMNER, Mar. 12, 1837 - Feb. 13, 1909
SALLY HAMNER, wife of G. H. HAMNER, Oct. 1848 - Jul. 28, 1931
THOMAS CLEMENTS, 1828 - 1900
FRANCES CLEMENTS, 1846 - 1927
MANEN CLEMENTS, Jan. 17, 1833 - May 8, 1907
SUSIE LANGLEY, 1841 - 1913

Inactive Salem Baptist Church Cemetery - Near Hwy. 43 North of Tuscaloosa, Ala.-Tuscaloosa Co.

JAMES RICE, Sep. 20,1799 - Jan. 8, 1881
MARIA RICE, wife of JAMES RICE, Oct. 29, 1805 - Sep. 5, 1869
DR. WILLIAM BAKER, Apr. 23, 1831 - Dec. 1868
NIMROD FREEMAN, Nov. 14, 1804 - Jan. 23, 1878
RHODA FREEMAN, Jan. 9, 1803 - Oct. 29, 1882
A. N. FREEMAN, May 17, 1847 - Dec. 30, 1879
MALINDA G., wife of S. T. TINION, Aug. 26, 1841 - Nov. 30, 1887
J. W. TOWNS, d. Dec. 29, 1870, age 49 yrs.
T. C. DAVIS, Jan. 23, 1840 - May 3, 1927
ELI M. DAVIS, Jun. 13,1837 - Oct. 20,1908
CALDONIA, wife of Z. T. SAVAGE, d. A g. 20, 1887, age 27 yrs.
(see Boone Cem. for another wife of Z. T. SAVAGE.)

Boone Cemetery - New Lexington - Tuscaloosa Co. Hwy. 43, N.

ISAAC CANNON, Apr. 19, 1792 - Feb. 12, 1885
SARAH CANNON, Oct. 14, 1799 - Feb. 5, 1860

Boone Cemetery Cont'd.

WILLIAM FOWLER, Mar. 4, 1814 - Jul. 17, 1890
INDIA EITSON FOWLER, wife of WILLIAM FOWLER, Dec. 6, 1845 - Apr. 26, 1908
J. S. CANNON, Apr. 4, 1842 - Feb. 27, 1921
ELIZA A.CANNON, wife of J. S. CANNON, Jan. 13, 1844 - Dec. 6, 1899
JOHN W. OLIVE, May 16, 1850 - Nov. 19,1898
A. J. OLIVE, Sep. 30, 1822 - Jul. 24, 1880
NANCY OLIVE, wife of A. J. OLIVE, Dec. 19, 1826 - Mar. 6, 1879
MATILDA P. MOORE, 1818 - 1848
L. M. RICE, Nov. 7, 1831 - Oct. 8, 1893
CATHERINE RICE, Jun. 12, 1840 - Apr. 1, 1925
JAMES L. FOWLER, Nov. 15, 1862 - Feb. 19, 1927
HELEN BELLE FOWLER, Dec.14, 1876 - Mar. 22, 1920
S. P. TAYLOR, Jun. 27, 1853 - Mar. 9, 1924
HELEN MENERVA CLEMENTINE TAYLOR, Jun. 26,1857 - May 26,1925
ISAAC ALLEN BROM, Apr. 5, 1830 - Jun. 15, 1918
MARY ELIZABETH BROM, Aug. 10, 1840 - Mar. 12, 1922
SALLIE SAVAGE, Dec.18, 1859 - Apr. 6, 1929
Z. T. SAVAGE, Nov. 18, 1859 - May 11, 1926
A. L. JOHNS, Mar. 16, 1871 - Jul. 8, 1941
REPPIE D. JOHNS, Feb. 27, 1870 - Sep. 26, 1952
ROBERT JOHN MOORE, Sep. 26, 1958 - Dec. 10, 1939
JENNIE VIRGINIA MOORE, Oct.-27, 1867 - Apr. 5, 1947
S. A. JOHNS, Apr. 10, 1834 - Jan. 28, 1929
LUCY JOHNS, wife of S. A. JOHNS, Aug. 15, 1837 - Aug. 5, 1911
REV. I. L. COLLINS, Sep. 11, 1856 - Feb. 20, 1907
ANGELINE COLLINS, Sep. 11, 1833 - May 14, 1896
M. R. I. COLLINS, Jul. 25, 1878 - Jul. 14, 1916
MELISSA FRANCES DOUGHTY, Aug. 24, 1851 - no death date
MONROE DAVIS, Jul. 23, 1867 - Apr. 26, 1912
MARTHA EVELINE DAVIS, wife of MONROE DAVIS, May 11, 1874 - Nov. 14, 1897
F. C. DAVIS, Mar. 1, 1871 - Mar. 23, 1897
THINY DAVIS, wife of T. L. DAVIS, Aug. 29, 1876 - Jan. 2, 1947
VIRELLA DAVIS, wife of T. L. DAVIS, Aug. 25, 1869 - May 25,1913
J. D. WATKINS, Dec. 1, 1846 - Mar. 3, 1942
ANNIE B. WATKINS, Jun. 6, 1868 - Apr. 3, 1897
LOVELLA WATKINS, May 2, 1874 - Apr. 5, 1898
M. D. WATKINS, Mar. 8, 1873 - May 2, 1908
L. H. WATKINS, Oct. 1, 1850 - Feb. 24, 1926
C. C. WATKINS, wife of L. H. WATKINS, May 25, 1851 - Nov. 7, 1924
W. B. DAVIS, May 29, 1861 - Nov. 1, 1915
JOHN M. DAVIS, Aug. 18, 1824 - May 14, 1905
L. E. DAVIS, May 4,1852 - May 5, 1932
HELEN DAVIS, Dec. 4, 1859- Jan. 9, 1903

Boone Cemetery Cont'd.

G. N. DAVIS, Nov. 17, 1848 - Feb. 28, 1915
MATILDA DAVIS, wife of G. N. DAVIS, Nov. 24, 1849 - Aug. 17, 1900
J. M. DAVIS, Mar. 4, 1814 - Sep. 30, 1891
W. J. DAVIS, Mar. 11, 1861 - Oct. 25, 1938
JANE G. TAYLOR, wife of W. J. TAYLOR, Aug. 15, 1854 - Mar. 8, 1914
SARAH J. TAYLOR, Nov. 18, 1835 - Sep. 9, 1880
SARAH A. E. SCUTH, Jan. 18, 1850 - Oct. 4, 1890

Piney Woods Baptist Church Cemetery - on Hwy. 69 N. of Tuscaloosa, Ala. - Tuscaloosa Co.

JIM CHRIS, Jun. 10, 1800 - Dec. 12, 1841
MARY CHRIS, Mar. 1800 - Oct. 21, 1871
T. W. CHRIS, Aug. 7, 1830 - Sep. 9, 1847
WM. MOORE, Mar. 4, 1840 - May 6, 1860
MAHALEY MOORE, Sep. 12, 1835 - Apr. 3, 1855
WILLIAM MORRISON, Jan. 1, 1802 - Oct. 8, 1865
JENER LOGAN, Oct. 10, 1800 - Apr. 9, 1910
JESSE BARGER, Aug. 14, 1844 - Feb. 20, 1917
M. P. BARGER, wife of JESSE BARGER, Oct. 14, 1839 - Jan. 16, 1910
JOHN HOWELL, Dec. 9, 1864 - Apr. 4, 1936
J. NATHANIEL BANKS, Oct. 24, 1846 - Sep. 7, 1928
ELIZABETH SWINDLE BANKS, Feb. 14, 1852 - Feb. 2, 1937
TRILLY SWINDLE, Jul. 7, 1838 - Apr. 6, 1887
SERENE C. SWINDLE, May 29, 1830 - May 11, 1883
WILEY A. SWINDLE, May 27, 1800 - Oct. 6, 1870
AMANDA REID, Nov. 25, 1843 - Feb. 3, 1875
REBECCA SWINDLE, Aug. 8, 1803 - Sep. 14, 1857
B. A. MADDOX, Apr. 11, 1814 - May 17, 1885
WILLIAM C. MADDOX, Jul. 12, 1871 - Jun. 24, 1893
JAMES W. CHRISTIAN, Dec. 29, 1879 - Feb. 18, 1900
LEVI W. CHRISTIAN, 1854 - 1932
ANN V. CHRISTIAN, 1853 - 1930
J. H. CHRISTIAN, Nov. 27, 1856 - Aug. 28, 1896
J. M. CHRISTIAN, Apr. 22, 1822 - Feb. 13, 1887
UPHEMY CHRISTIAN, Nov. 8, 1817 - May 20, 1910
JESSIE FRANCIS CHRISTIAN, Oct. 12, 1861 - May 7, 1930
M. R. CHRISTIAN, Dec. 21, 1873 - Apr. 8, ..... date gone
RACHEL WILCUTT, wife of H. B. JONES, d. Nov. 5, 1916, age 53 yrs
MARGRET WILCUTT, Jul. 4, 1837 - Jul. 29, 1874
BRAZZELL MANUEL McPHERSON, Jul. 3, 1844 - Apr. 29, 1927
MATILDA McPHERSON; wife of BRAZZELL McPHERSON, Dec. 14, 1854 - Jul. 7, 1892
A. W. MILES, May 27, 1870 - Jun. 10, 1930

Piney Woods Baptist Church Cemetery Cont'd.

LEVI WILSON EARNEST, 1850 - 1930
MANDY FRANCES ROBERTSON, Jan. 2, 1853 - Feb. 2, 1925
ELLEN CHRISTIAN, 1861 ...... no other date
MANDA HAMNER, wife of J. M. HAMNER, age 46 yrs. no other date
J. W. FIELDS, Dec. 14, 1857 - Mar. 3, 1931
JOHN A. BINGHAM, Sep. 11, 1866 - Jan. 9, 1939
HENRY LUTZENHISER, 1837 - 1924
JOHN WILSON EDWARDS, Apr. 2, 1862 - May 4, 1947
SARAH ANN EDWARDS, 1861 ....Apr. 4, 1929
ZANCE (or YANCE) COLLINS, 1843 - 1929
IDA J. COLLINS, 1853 - 1930
JOHN A. CALHOUN, Oct. 3, 1853 - Feb. 7, 1926
HARRIETT CALHOUN, Sep. 18, 1853 - Sep. 1, 1939

Old Liberty Primitive Baptist Church Cemetery
Evanstown Settlement - S.E. of Sterling Ch.
Tuscaloosa Co.

SARAH CLIFTON, Mar. 29, 1796 - Nov. 12, 1863
LUISA EVANS, Apr. 8, 1822 - Nov. 20, 1886
J. EVANS, Dec. 23, 1833 - Sep. 7, 1869
J. W. EVANS, Mar. 2, 1852 - Aug. 5, 1880
T. J. EVANS, Sep. 20, 1847 - Jun. 23, 1891
ELIZABETH EVANS,Nov. 15, 1849 = Sep. 30, 1945
SYLVANUS EVANS, Sep. 13, 1847 - Aug. 23, 1884
MARTHA EVANS, wife of SYLVANUS EVANS, Jan. 27, 1853 - Jan. 23, 1891
MANDY EVANS, wife of D. L. EVANS, Mar. 17, 1858 - Mar. 12,1880
D. L. EVANS, Jun. 22, 1851 - Jun. 2, 1911
JOSIAH EVANS, Jun. 23, 1825 - Oct. 30, 1896
CAROLINE EVANS, Nov. 12, 1827 - Aug. 13, 1896
W. R. EVANS, Sep. 8, 1875 - May 25, 1910
A. EVANS, wife of D. L. EVANS, May 11, 1854 - Jun. 1, 1917
M. A. JOHNSON, Jan. 27, 1853 - Jan. 23, 1891
S. L. DUREN, Aug. 2, 1867 - Feb. 2, 1944
MRS. S. M. C. JONES, wife of S. M. JONES, May 22, 1858 - Nov. 5, 1914
G. W. HOCUTT, d. Mar. 26, 1884, age 52 yrs.
MARTHA A.HOCUTT, d. Jun. 27, 1904, age 44 yrs (wife of G. W. HOCUTT)
JAMES T. MARKEY, Feb. 4, 1871 - Oct. 25, 1904
MARY IDA MARKEY, wife of JAMES T. MARKEY, Aug. 31, 1874 - Jun. 23, 1898
HENRY PINKIE McMILLIAN, Feb. 1, 1868 - Dec. 8, 1941
JOHN THOMAS McMILLIAN, Feb. 5, 1870 - Feb. 10, 1923
JONATHAN ESARY and wife MARGARET, no dates
J. M. UTLEY, Dec. 7, 1860 - Nov. 9, 1941
ELIZA ANN UTLEY, wife of J. M. UTLEY, Jun. 28, 1855 - Mar. 22, 1919
REBECCA ANN, wife of S. R. UTLEY, Oct. 10, 1859 - Aug. 27, 1922

Cemetery One Mile W. of Sipsey River Bridge, Winston County, Ala.

ZEPTCHNIAH ESTES, Co. B. 2nd Ga. reserves, C.S.A.

Hatters Cemetery - Five Miles N.E. of Arley, Ala. - Winston County

SOLOMON B. BUMBLORD, Dec. 8, 1804 - Jun. 3, 1883
WM. WILLIAM, d. Mar. 10, 1900 - age 84 yrs.
ARRY B. FINCHER, Mar. 30, 1859 - Apr. 16, 1888
MOSES B. FINCHER, Mar. 10, 1826 - Jan. 1, 1886
HARVEY SMITH, Nov. 15, 1860 - Dec. 20, 1941
MARY M. SMITH, wife of H. E. SMITH, Feb. 24, 1862 - Aug. 2, 1923
CATHERINE, wife of J. N. WOODLEY, Dec. 1, 1838 - Dec. 23, 1883
URIAH WOODLEY, Dec. 27, 1829 - Dec. 19, 1909
ELIZABETH, wife of W. C. WILLIAMS, Dec. 1, 1849 - Nov. 1, 1880

Cemetery on Hwy. - Five Mi. N. and Two Mi. over Walker Co. Line in Winston Co. Ala.

S. D. SPAIN, Oct. 14, 1858 - Feb. 7,1947
NANCY G., wife of S. D. SPAIN, May 30, 1860 - 1922
JOHN SIHEINICK, Jun. 11, 1870 - Oct. 15, 1945
JOHN ABBOTT, Jan. 13, 1874 - Nov. 15, 1955
REV. ROBERT MONCRIEF, May 6, 1873 - Oct. 31, 1951

Inactive Cemetery - One Mile N. of Sipsey River Bridge, Winston Co. Ala.

ANDREW NELSON, Pvt. Tate's Va. Troops, Revolutionary Soldier, b. York Co., Pa. 1762. A friend to his country. D. Nov.1850, his memory an inspiration.
JOHN HILL, b. May 13, 1795, married to CATHERINE BARNWELL, Feb. 20, 1823, d. Feb. 21, 1870

Fairview Cemetery - Near Double Springs, Winston Co., Ala.

THOMAS JEFFERSON MILLICAN, Jun. 26, 1826 - Jan. 11, 1912
JULIA A. MILLICAN, May 20, 1831 - Jun. 26, 1904
GEORGE M. MILLICAN, 1852 - 1904
MARY F. MILLICAN, 1852 - 1934
F. L. HADDER, Mar. 29, 1852 - Sep. 17, 1889
THOMAS J. COWERT, Nov. 20, 1830 - May 31, 1911
LYDIA A. COWERT, Aug. 18, 1834 - Nov. 11, 1911
DAVID S. McVAY, Co. I. 5th Ala. Cav. C.S.A.
OCTAVIA NEWMAN, wife of P. H. NEWMAN, Apr. 16, 1843 - Oct. 20, 1923
MANDY BONDS, wife of A. J. BOND, Jul. 19, 1859 - May 10, 1928

Fairview Cemetery Cont'd.

CATHARINE BONDS, Apr. 29, 1806 - Jul. 24, 1894
MARTHA JANE, wife of T. M. BONDS, Mar. 13, 1860 - Jun. 12, 1942
ALBERT J. BONDS, SR., Jan. 3, 1855 - Nov. 5, 1887
W. R. BONDS, SR., Nov. 3, 1829 - Feb. 9, 1918
SARAH S. BONDS, Mar. 8, 1835 - Jun. 14, 1919
THOMAS M. BONDS, Dec. 14, 1858 - Jun. 4, 1955
JAMES M. OVERTON, Dec. 29, 1854 - Mar. 18, 1908
MARTHA O. OVERTON, May 28, 1860 - Mar. 8, 1950
A. J. INGLE, 1820 - 1896
REBECCA INGLE, 1828 - 1894
REV.S. N. WILSON, May 4, 1857 - Nov. 7,1936
MARGARET F. WILSON, Jul. 30, 1856 - Jan. 5, 1929
MARGARET OVERTON, d. Oct. 11, 1906 - age 73 yrs.
W. R. ADKINS, Feb. 12, 1839 - Sep. 17, 1903
CREOLA YEATES EZELL, Feb. 28, 1858 - Sep. 30, 1930
DR. FRANKLIN P. EZELL, Mar. 11, 1853 - Apr. 19, 1910
ETTA LOONEY, 1860 - 1944
THOMAS J. DENSON, Jan. 20, 1863 - Sep. 14, 1935
AMANDA DENSON, wife of THOMAS J. DENSON, Jan. 7, 1861 - Sep. 19, 1910
SARAH E. GIBSON, Mar. 27, 1855 - May 6, 1924
ISHAM PRINCE, Jun. 22, 1854 - Jun. 2, 1895
JANE BAIRD, d. Dec. 1894 - age 46 yrs.
MOLLIE E. CURTIS, Jan. 9, 1867 - Sep. 21, 1898
GEORGE W. BLAKE, 1848 - 1922
RACHEL A. BLAKE, 1848 - 1938
J. A. ROBINSON, Dec. 6, 1859 - Feb. 20, 1908
M. C. ROBINSON, wife of J. A. ROBINSON, Jun. 21, 1859 - Mar. 9, 1904
MELVINA E. BUTTRAM, Aug. 29, 1869 - Mar. 18, 1906
MELVINA GLENN, Apr. 11, 1861 - Apr. 14, 1900
S. C. E. HARRIS, Nov. 22, 1850 - May 11, 1933
WM. C. CHAMBERS, Sep. 21, 1851 - Jan. 15, 1929
L. ADELINE CHAMBERS, Sep. 26, 1856 - Nov. 10, 1926
J. T. FERRELL, May 22, 1848 - Jul. 7, 1912
MARY ANN FERRELL, May 22, 1848 - Jul. 7, 1912
JAMES M. TINGLE, Apr. 26, 1865 - Aug. 24, 1929
SARAH HASFORD, Jun. 5, 1860 - Mar. 1, 1927
REV. JOHN H. CORBIN, Mar. 2, 1857 - Jul. 26, 1940
MARY CORBIN, Jan. 12, 1859 - May 5, 1945
W. G. BAILEY, Nov. 25, 1845 - Apr. 3, 1920
MEDORIA ANN SNODDY, Jul. 24, 1866 - May 13, 1949
JAMES S. SNODDY, SR., Dec. 6, 1861 - Sep. 17, 1942
CREASY PRUITT, Jan. 22, 1851 - Apr. 19, 1948
G. A. PRUITT, May 18, 1833 - Jul. 28,1908
PERMELIA HOWELL, Feb. 2,1842 - Oct. 22, 1908
JOHN A. HOWELL, May 25, 1841 - Sep. 6, 1878

Fairview Cemetery Cont'd.

J. H. McCOLLUM, Sep. 28, 1867 - Aug. 29,1919
S. McCOLLUM, Oct. 23, 1843 - Dec. 10, 1915
AMANDA McCOLLUM, wife of S. McCOLLUM,Oct. 13, 1848 - Jun. 17, 1941
FRANCES INDIANA McCOLLUM, Jun. 8, 1860 - Feb. 11, 1935, wife of J. H. McCOLLUM
S. J. CURTIS, Mar. 12, 1859 - Jan. 30, 1923
TEMPIE MINA CURTIS, wife of S. J. CURTIS, Sep. 7, 1865 - Feb. 12, 1949
J. H. HEFNER, Co. K., 1st Ala. Cav.
J. M.BONDS, Jun. 19, 1835 - Aug. 30, 1921
SARAH BONDS, wife of J. M. BONDS, Oct. 17, 1834 - Jun. 8, 1918
GEORGE SHIPMAN, b. N. C. d. Apr. 17, 1881, age 68 yrs. 8 mos. 20 das.
MARGARET SHIPMAN, wife of GEORGE SHIPMAN, b. N.C. Apr. 17, 1814 d. Apr. 13, 1891
E. T. CHAMBERS,Apr. 7, 1852 - Mar. 6, 1919
W. I. PAINTER, 1845 - 1900
JOHN R. SIDES, Jun. 12, 1850 - Oct. 13, 1923
A. J. McCULLAR, Dec. 6, 1860 - Jun. 3, 1928
SARAH A.McCULLAR, Jan. 11, 1866 - Oct. 11, 1927
FANNIE BAILEY, Mar. 11, 1862 - Nov. 15, 1942
MARY E. BAIRD, Dec. 4, 1855 - Nov. 28, 1932
THOMAS GUTHRIE, May 1, 1856 - May 14, 1926
JESSIE G. WILLIAMS, Feb. 14, 1850 - Feb. 14, 1929
RHODA E., wife of J. G. WILLIAMS, Jan. 18, 1853 - Sep. 18, 1918

Corinth Church Cemetery - Seven Miles S.E. of Double Springs out in the woods - Winston County

MOTHER: HULSEY MOTE, Jun. 1, 1832 - Jan. 17, 1916
WM. H. MOTE, Feb. 19, 1860 - Jan. 10, 1894
UNCLE: JOE HILTON, Jan. 28, 1861 - Sep. 27, 1922
S. C. COOPER, Aug. 30, 1851 - May 20, 1900
ROBERT A. HILL, Jul. 8, 1838 - Jun. 17, 1923
S. MARGARET HILL, Mar. 10, 1843 - Dec. 20, 1895
JOE TAYLOR PUTNAM, Dec. 19, 1844 - Apr. 10, 1917
MARGARET PRUETT, wife of J. T. PUTNAM, Aug. 27, 1844 - Jun. 1, 1930
G. W. HILTON, Jan. 12, 1839 - Mar. 22, 1910
G. C. HILTON, wife of G. W. HILTON, Sep. 11, 1844 - Feb. 4, 1926
RHODA, wife of BASIL FALLS, Oct. 10, 1861 - Apr. 5, 1912

Old Cemetery - On Hwy. 195 S. of Delmer, Ala.
Winston County

JOROYAL BARNETT, Co. G. 7th Ill. Cav.
LEWIS BARNETT, Co. B. 12th Ala. Inf. C.S.A.
M. C. DODD, b. Jan. 1, 1851 - d. Nov. 1, 1875
C. W. DODD, d. Dec., age 24 yrs. no further info. on him
ELIZABETH DODD, Jul. 22, 1823 - Jul. 29, 1896
LOUISA, wife of G. HYDE, May 9, 1840 - Dec. 28,1909
CALIP HYDE, husband of L. HYDE, d. Aug. 28, 1912, no other date.

Rock Creek Church Cemetery - About Six Miles East
of Double Springs, Winston Co., Ala.

ISAAC MARTIN, Co. G. 1st Ala. and Tenn. Vidette Cav.
ELIZA A. MARTIN, Dec. 8, 1838 - Mar. 1, 1911
ELENDER CAGLE, Sep. 1, 1845 --No other dates
JOSEPH SHIPMAN, Jul. 3, 1821 - Nov. 20, 1900
WM. P. SHIPMAN, 1838 - Dec. 22, 1886
D. E. SHIPMAN, Feb. 9, 1845 - Nov. 27, 1911
JOSEPH N. CURTIS, May 15, 1846 - Oct. 3, 1910
E. R., wife of J. N. CURTIS, Aug. 29, 1839 - Sep. 3, 1906
JOE J. CURTIS, Oct. 23, 1864 - Oct. 25, 1918
G. W. TAYLOR, Mar. 24, 1858 - Mar. 24, 1926
J. P. HARPER, Sep. 8,1856 - Nov. 4, 1926

Arley Cemetery - Arley, Ala. - Winston County

JAMES H. HORSLEY, Jul. 7, 1864 - Mar. 13, 1948
MARY ANN LINDLEY, Jan. 9, 1849 - Feb. 18, 1935
WILBURN ABBOTT, Mar. 12, 1855 - Dec. 2, 1919
WILLIAM T. LINDLEY, Jul. 29, 1846 - May 2, 1918
J. H. LINDLEY, Jan. 23, 1868 - Feb. 5, 1916
THOMAS M. WODSWORTH, 1841 - 1897
TALLY WODSWORTH, 1859 - 1935
JAMINA, wife of JOHN FOSTER, Apr. 4, 1832 - Nov. 27, 1909
NOAMA INGLE, 1859 - 1931
G. W. INGLE, May 3, 1852 - Jan. 25, 1914
W. A. SMITH, Feb. 14, 1859 - Feb. 26, 1927
SOPHA JANE SMITH, Oct. 8, 1860 - Sep. 14, 1938
JOHN T. COOK, Mar. 6, 1849 - Mar. 14, 1923
ALICE UDORA COOK, Dec. 15, 1859 - Mar. 28, 1922
MARY I. DOVER, Apr. 19, 1862 - Mar. 22, 1930
ANNA E. BATTLE, Dec. 10, 1827 - Jul. 30, 1905
N. DOVER, Sep. 7, 1868 - Dec. 10, 1936
S. E.TAYLOR, Nov. 12, 1861 - Sep. 13, 1924
J. I. TAYLOR,Oct. 20, 1854 - Oct. 23, 1915
M. A., wife of W. T. THOMPSON, Aug. 18, 1848 - Apr. 16, 1909

Arley Cemetery Cont'd.

J. W. AARON, Feb. 9, 1861 - May 6, 1919
M. B. H. WALKER, Aug. 23, 1832 - Mar. 3, 1913
JAMES LANE, Sep. 28, 1829 - Aug. 16, 1906
S. J. WOLF, Sep. 7, 1852 - May 11, 1928
W. S. E. WOLF, Jun. 5, 1854 - Jul. 24, 1911
MELVINA, wife of H. J. WILSON, Aug. 24, 1850 - Jan. 28, 1909
S. R. CRUMPTON, Dec. 15, 1855 - Oct. 25, 1911
MARTHA CRUMPTON, 1858 - 1939
ANNIE HANDLEY, Feb. 4, 1837 - Feb. 5, 1893
JAMES O. FARLEY, Co. D, 12 Tenn. Cav.
ELIZABETH FARLEY, Apr. 19, 1841 - Jan. 1, 1921
G. B. BALDWIN, Co. D. 12th Tenn. Cav.
SAMUEL J. HILLER, Aug. 11, 1841 - Jan. 22, 1897
SARAH REBECCA HILLER, Feb. 3, 1849 - Feb. 29, 1916
ALFRED J. FINE, 1837 - 1900
JULIA C. FINE, 1851 - 1909
LEVI WILSON, 1837 - 1893
JOHN W. PHILLIPS, Nov. 14, 1848 - Dec. 20, 1912
P. C. W. PHILLIPS, Aug. 1, 1841 - Feb. 22, 1909
ANNIE A. HARRIS, Sep. 22, 1828 - Jan. 27, 1908
J. P. GILLILAND, Aug. 29, 1862 - Oct. 16, 1897
MARY F. HORSLEY, Apr. 16, 1866 - May 1, 1906
SARAH BENSON, Dec. 22, 1859 - Dec. 13, 1908
REV. GEO. W. GIBSON, Mar. 24, 1861 - Dec. 5, 1941
JOSEPHINE AMELIA GIBSON, Sep. 29, 1861 - Sep. 27, 1937
CLAUDIUS CLIFTON HILLER, Dec. 9, 1877 - Feb. 21, 1941
FAYETTE KNIGHT, Aug. 18, 1865 - May 9, 1940

Wakefield Cemetery - 3½ Miles S. of Lynn, Ala. on old Hwy. - Winston County

PETER INGLE, d. Dec. 1849 - Age 88 yrs. (b. 1761)
CATHERINE INGLE, d. Nov. 9, 1868, age 66 yrs.
S. E. INGLE, Sep. 5, 1867 - Oct. 24, 1898
SUSAN E. INGLE, wife of PAUL INGLE, Jun. 20, 1839 - Dec. 30, 1928
PAUL INGLE, Feb. 28, 1827 - Mar. 4, 1891
KISIAH L. INGLE, May 18, 1863 - death date - age 36 yrs.
NANCY C. MERPHEW, dau. of P. & K. INGLE, Aug.21, 1850 - Oct. 20, 1887
JOHN INGLE, Mar. 23, 1826 - Jul. 10, 1866
SARAH E. HENSON, dau. of PAUL INGLE, Feb. 23, 1852 - Mar. 18, 1880
J. N. BAUGHN, Co. L. 1st Ala. Cav. Sep. 9, 1833 - Apr. 26, 1891
.. A. BAUGHN, Jan. 23, 1837 - Aug. 12, date gone

Wakefield Cemetery Cont'd.

MARGARET, wife of R. G. VINES, Jan. 25, 1876 - Nov. 26, 1893
NANCY THREADGIL, dau. of J. N. & B. A. BAUGHN, Jul. 26, 1864 - Aug. 4, 1886
NANCY BAUGHN, 1819 - death date gone
PEYTON BAUGHN, 1869 - death date gone
JOHN A. SMITH, Sep. 23, 1853 - Aug. 11, 1864
SARAH ELIZABETH, wife of A. J. NORRIS, dau. of W. W. & A. J. JOHNSON, b. Jul. 14, 1876 - d. Jul. 4, 1894
KIZZIE JANE, wife of L. J. HAYNES, Nov. 6, 1870 - Sep. 18, 1905
SARAH F. GAN, dau. of J. N. & B. A. BAUGHN, Mar. 17, 1861 - Aug. 9, 1897
MARY E. LAMBERT, dau. of J. N. & B. A. BAUGHN, Aug. 26, 1862- Nov. 1, 1887
HUBBARD BAUGHN, Dec. 11, 1857 - Jan. 3, 1938
NANCY, wife of HUBBARD BAUGHN, May 2, 1863 - Sep. 17, 1920
ALZANY, wife of T. F. BRIM, Jul. 27, 1876 - Aug. 12, 1899
JASPER HOLT, Mar. 20, 1841 = Jul. 25, 1868
YOUNG NORRIS, May 12, 1831 - Oct. 31, 1867, age 37 yrs.
MARGARET, wife of Y. P. INGLE, Jul. 23, 1860 - Jul. 1, 1923
Y. P. INGLE, Oct. 29, 1852 - Feb. 23, 1917
ELLEN, wife of G. F. LAWSON, May 17, 1844 - Mar. 13, 1887
JAMES BRANNAN, Sep. 28, 1796, Mar. 2, 1882
T. M. WAKEFIWLD, Feb. 26, 1835 - Jan. 2, 1880, age 44 yrs. 10 mos.
ELIZABETH, wife of T. M. WAKEFIELD, Jul. 15, 1838 - Mar. 18, 1886
MARY ANN EDORA, wife of J. P. WILLIAMS, Feb. 5, 1867 - Dec. 16, 1890
MARY E. (nee WAKEFIELD) wife of J. B. WEAVER, Feb. 16, 1883 - Feb. 19, 1904
L. T. HOPSON, Aug. 12, 1859 - Jul. 11, 1940
AMANDA F. HOPSON, Nov. 15, 1859 - no death date
DEE C. WAKEFIELD, 1858 - 1937
ELIZA WAKEFIELD, 1865 - 1936
ISIAH HOPSON, May 2, 1833 - Jul. 5, 1904
KISIE HOPSON, Oct. 20, 1833 - Mar. 15, 1920
ALICE B., wife of W. C. HOPSON, Feb. 15, 1861 - Jul. 6, 1916

ADDENDA

Tombstone Inscriptions taken from a later list of: Mt. Zion Primitive Baptist Church, on the Nauvoo Road, Walker County
Refer to page 76

W. W. WILSON, Sep. 8, 1825 - Dec. 13, 1908
JOHN P. WILSON, Nov. 4, 1847 - Sep. 24, 1869
LOUISA CAROLINE WILSON, Feb. 12, 1858 - Oct. 29, 1870

## Mt. Zion Primitive Baptist Church Cont'd.

W. S. WILSON,May 1, 1864 - Mar. 19, 1907
B. A. SIDES, Oct. 26, 1854 - Jun. 21, 1917
MAHALEY SIDES, Jun. 12, 1826 - Oct. 26,1878
ELIJAH SIDES, Jan. 4, 1825 - Mar. 28, 1900
J. I. MORRIS, son of J. & M. E. MORRIS, Nov. 6, 1869 - Jan. 9, 1895
MILLEY MORRIS, Jun. 19, 1881 - (death date) age 18 yrs 5 mos 24 das
SARAH MORRIS, d. Sep. 17, 1888, age 20 yrs.
SARAH MORRIS, Mar. 28, 1868 - Nov. 5, 1894
ELIZABETH MORRIS, Feb. 26, 1845 - Jun. 25, 1918
JAS. LARRY MORRIS, Jan. 22, 1839 - May 1, 1916
J. L. FAUGHT, 1836 - 1929
NANCY SIDES, Feb. 20, 1820 - Apr. 12, 1886
ALETHA ADKINS, b. Chambers Co. Ala. Apr. 22, 1832 - d. Apr. 14, 1882
HENRY W. WILLIAMS, son of R. V. & N. E. WILLIAMS, Sep. 30, 1896 1899
DANIEL H. HARRIS, Feb. 16, 1828 - Jan. 2, 1890

..........................................................

Additions to: Sardis Primitive Church, South of Warrior River, Walker County - Refer to page 131

ANNIE J. BARTON, Aug. 24, 1874 - Oct. 19, 1948
W. H. BARTON, 1877 - 1891
HUGH S. MORROW, 1861 -1927
MARY A. MORROW, 1862 - 1945
WILLIS M. GUNTER, 1866-- no death date
NANCY J. GUNTER, 1865 - 1941
NANCY J. NATIONS, no dates, seven other graves on this lot.
ADA IVEY, Dec. 3, 1880 - Oct. 25, 1908
THOMAS B. MORROW, Jul. 30, 1849 - Jun. 15, 1930
MARY E., wife of BRADFORD BARNETT, Mar. 1, 1833 - Mar. 12, 1917
ED. DAVIS, Jun. 9, 1867 - Nov. 27, 1945
S. C., wife of ED DAVIS, Nov. 20, 1868 - Jun. 25, 1916

..........................................................

Additions to the Kelly Cemetery - Eldridge, Ala. See page 119

JOHN T. BAGWELL, d. Feb. 10, 1830, age 62 yrs. (b. 1768)
JESSE W.LANE, 1856 - 1915
MARY A.LANE, 1861 - 1885
GEORGE THOROGOOD, Aug. 5, 1840 - Aug. 13,1912
WM. THOROGOOD, d. May 4, 1852, age 48 yrs. 9 mos. 14 das.
HENRY THOROGOOD, 1853 - 1928
L. R. CANEY, Aug. 26, 1837 - Feb. 16, 1925

..........................................................

Addition to the Cedar Creek Church of Christ - see page 124

MILLISSIA GANUS, Jun. 3, 1867 - Jun. 8, 1937

INDEX

AARON, 8,16,79,112,178
ABBETT,155
ABBOTT,154,174,177
ABLES, 120
ADAIR, 102
ADAMS, 82,145
ADCOCK,5
ADKINS,13,41
AKINS, 80,162,175,180
ALDREDGE, 5,15,17
ALDRIDGE, 117,118,142,153
ALEXANDER,4,8,14,108,123,
124
ALFORD, 11
ALLEN, 2,4,5,11,22,101,166
ALLIS, 131
ALLISON, 113,114
ALLRED, 35,149,159
ALLUMS, 158,159
ALVIS, 9,12,19,65,85
AMERSON, 18,95,111,115,157
AMISS, 59
ANDER, 170
ANDERSON, 67,157
APPLING, 20,62,78,99,154,
165
ANDREWS, 13,15,16,17,67,68,
128,129
ARCHER, 54
AREY, 66
ARGO, 57,63,130
ARY, 111,142
ASHLEY, 11
ASHMORE, 116
ATKINS, 26,65,70.88,90,91,
96,104,120,131
ATWOOD, 12
AVERY, 67
AWTRY, 148
AYERS, 84
AZBILL, 104
BACHELOR, 6
BAGLEY, 4, 160
BAGWELL, 14,68,119,120,151,
180
BAILEY, 13,74,98,106,116,
142,149,156,175,176
BAIOCCHI, 72
BAIRD, 175,176
BAKER, 3,4,9,11,18,43,45,
74,81,88,89,93,96,
100,104,110,111,141,
145,157,165,170
BALDWIN, 178
BALEY, 5
BALGH, 122
BALLARD, 15
BALLENGER, 7, 84
BANKHEAD, 58,59
BANKS, 13,10,19,109,130,172
BARGER, 172
BARKER, 51,108
BARNES,102
BARNETT, 118,177,180
BARNWELL, 174
BARR, 27,167
BARRENTINE, 95,121
BARRETT, 13
BARRNER, 83
BARTON, 4,7,8,12,14,18,32,
48,49,72,79,93,109,
129,130,152,180
BATCHELOR, 76
BATES, 8,59,107
BATTLE, 177
BAUGHN, 178,179
BEACH GROVE, 37
BEASLEY, 5,6,18,19,64,65
BEATTY, 35,36
BEARD, 12,84
BEATY, 74
BEAVERTPN, 164
BELL, 6,17,67,82,86,132,169
BELLAH, 5
BELLAMY, 7
BENNETT, 9,108 (see errata)
BENNS, 11
BENSON, 94,131,178
BENTON, 161,162
BERRY, 41,145,147,150,151,
157
BERRYHILL, 162
BESS, 8
BEST, 15,76
BEVILL, 28,21,29,30,70,73,
111,153
BEVILLE, 111

BILLINGLY, 4
BINGHAM, 173
BIRCHEAT, 105,141
BIRD, 19
BIRDWELL, 9,30,31
BISHOP, 66,167
BLACK, 8,12,14,15,18,51,
55,79,80,109,125,
129,160
BLACKBURN, 10
BLACKSHEAR, 34
BLACKSTON (BLACKSTONE),
13,16,133
BLACKWELL, 3,4,12,16,99,
126,137
BLACKWOOD, 16
BLAKE, 175
BLAND, 160
BLANKENSHIP, 9
BLANKS, 42
BLANTON, 2,10,13,81,86,122
BLEVIN, 6,9,17
BOATRIGHT, 11
BOBO, 94,155
BOND(S), 174,175,176
BONNER, 135
BOON(E), 20,146
BOOTH, 38
BORDEN, 9, 126
BORDON, 125
BOROUGHS, 167
BOSHELL, 3,14,16,17,18,19,
20,43,55,65,66,68,71,
72,74,83,89,90,115,
136
BOSWELL, 167
BOTELER, 78
BOUCHELLE, 55
BOWDEN, 96
BOWEN, 144
BOWERS, 169
BOWLAN, 161,162
BOWLES, 149
BOX, 5,13
BOYD, 15,7,159
BOYKIN, 118
BOYLE (OR BOYLES), 42,57
BRADDEY, 42
BRADFORD, 6, 94
BRADLEY, 4, 155
BRAKE, 7
BRAKEFIELD, 15,94
BRANCH, 6
BRAND, 67
BRANDENBURG, 149
BRANNAN, 179
BRASFIELD, 125,128,129
BRASHER, 147
BRAZEAL, 5,11,15
BRAZIL, 138,156
BREAKFIELD, 15,56
BRETT, 11
BRIGDEN, 107,109
BRIDGES, 138
BRIGGS, 61
BRIM, 179
BROCK, 11,145,154
BROCKMAN, 58
BROCKWAY, 60
BROGDEN, 115
BROM, 171
BROOM, 106
BROWN, 2,4,5,6,9,10,18,20,
25,28,30,33,39,64,66,
67,77,79,82,83,88,92,
93,95,98,99,100,123,
132,133,146,152,153
BRYAN, 17,155
BRYANT, 13
BRYSON, 7
BUICE, 148
BUMBLORD, 174
BURCHFIELD, 60,78
BURDEN, 8
BURGETT, 108
BURKE, 15,24,35
BURKETT, 16,17,19,70,71
BURLESON, 163
BURLISON, 12
BURNER, 140
BURNS, 7,8,50
BURNUM, 4
BURT, 109,122
BURTON, 3,4,8,14,17,19,20,
46,47,49,55,66,75,76,
79,80,83,87,88,89,90,
111,125
BUSBEE, 14,15
BUSBY, 10,12,14,15,16
BUSH, 124

BUTCHER, 7
BUTLER, 16,28,30,61,102,119
BUTRAM, 94
BUTT, 7,8,48,130
BUTTRAM, 175
BUTTS, 100
BUZBEE, 87
BYARS, 162,164
BYERS, 161
BYLER, 166
CAGLE, 3,4,11,177
CAIN, 6,10,46,51,58,91,94,
96,119,133,169
CALHOUN, 173
CALLAHAN, 8
CALLAN, 138
CALLEY, 164
CALVERT, 6,11
CAMAK, 2,5,12,17,77,78,83,
85,100
CAMBELL, 8
CAMERON, 164
CAMP, 80
CAMPANY, 147
CAMPBELL, 17,60,102,153
CANEY, 180
CANNON, 7,11,17,86,97,142,
146,170,171
CANTABERRY, 31,91
CAPPS, 116
CARADINE, 18,124
CARDEN, 117
CARGILE, 154
CARMICHAEL, 14,19,43,75,76,
81,87,100,106
CARR, 79
CARRINGTON, 98
CARROLL, 38
CARROWAY, 9
CARSON, 166
CARTER, 17,108
CASE, 7
CASTLEBERRY, 9,18,120
CATCHINGS, 46,62
CATHY, 11
CAVIN, 99
CHAEAK, 6
CHAMBERS, 175,176
CHAMBLESS, 162
CHAMBOREDOM, 119
CHAMNESS, 116
CHANCE, 7
CHANDLER, 49,86
CHANEY, 138,142
CHAPPEL, 19,20,38,39,41,42,
44,52,54,55,109,150,
163,165
CHEATHAM, 89,5,137
CHENAULT, 116
CHILDERS, 4,11,16,59,75,
76,116,121,138
CHILDRES, 12
CHILTON, 8,12,57,134
CHISM, 94
CJRIS, 172
CHRISTIAN, 106,116,126,172
173
CLAGHORN, 8
CLANCEY, 5
CLARK, 6,9,14,16,74.86,102,
112,127
CLAY, 54
CLAYTON, 7,119
CLEERE, 4
CLEMENTS, 4,10,11,13,24,35,
81,101,121,166,170
CLEMMONS, 9,15
CLIFTON, 159,173
CLINE, 145
CLOWERS, 135
COBB, 10,17,27,61,81,135
COCHRAN, 9,154
COCKRAN, 13
COFFEE'S BRIGADE, 39
COKER, 20,107
COLBERT, 42
COLBURN, 119
COLE, 8,9,15,57,130,150,151
COLEMAN, 58
COLLIER, 166
COLLINS, 12,14,16,17,146,
171,173
COLVIN, 2,166
COLWELL, 138
COMER, 9
CONLEY, 5
CONN, 56,92,135
CONNELL, 159
CONNER, 15,70
CONWAY, 6,8,9,13
COOK, 90,177
COONER, 10,14,70,91,92,123,125

COOPER, 89,121,176
COPELAN (COPELAND), 5,6, 13,17,25,27,81,103, 105,121
CORBIN, 175
CORKREN, 156
CORLEY, 6,10,13,134
CORNELIUS, 98,135
CORY (CORRY), 36,43,49,50, 121,122
COTTON, 100,125,143
COURINGTON, 10,14,81,82, 120,124,132,141
COURSON, 100
COVIN, 10,12,15,91
COWERT, 174
COX, 13,14,15,17,18,62,68, 161,169,170
CRAIG, 19,85
CRAMEEN, 4
CRANFORD, 10,12,18,60,59,73, 78,90,91,122
CRAVEN, 159
CRAWFORD, 3,9,10,72
CREEL, 15,81
CREIGHTON, 54
CRENSHAW, 85
CROCKER, 56, 129
CROFT, 8
CROMEENS, 11
CROMWELL, 139
CRONEY, 9
CROSSWHITE, 12
CROW, 59
CROWNOVER, 74,96,95,118, (see errata)
CRUMLEY, 154
CRUMP, 120
CRUMPTON, 178
CULLMAN CO., 40
CULWELL, 11
CUMMINGS, 20
CUNNINGHAM, 3,15,72,74,87, 110,115,141
CURRIER, 159
CURTIS, 58,175,176,177
DALLAS, 63
DAME, 107
DANIEL (DANIELS), 4,14,17, 79,138,159
DARDEN, 151
DARIEN, (GA.), 24
DAVIDSON, 95,97,98,122,134
DAVIS, 4,5,6,7,8,10,12,13, 14,15,16,17,18,19,41, 80,86,87,91,93,94,96, 102,103,112,113,114,122, 127,132,133,134,137,140, 142,145,151,157,158,162, 170,171,172,180
DAY, 6,11,16,62,117
DEAN, 11
DEASON, 85,97
DEGRAFFENREID, 161
DELENNE (see DELEUNE), 118
DELEUNE (see DELENNE), 119
DENSON, 175
DENT, 15
DEPOISTER, 144
DERSHIDE, 167
DESKIN, 6, 9
DEWEESE, 20,49,62
DICKENSON, 8, 117
DICKERSON, 157
DICKSON, 156
DIKES, 161
DILL, 4,12,17,139
DILWORTH, 58
DISON, 15
DISSFAIN, 43
DOAK, 167
DOBBINS, 153
DOBBS, 143,92,144,145,152, 159
DOBSON, 146
DODD, 11,59,159,177
DODSON, 117,78
DOROUGH, 132
DOSIER, 143,144
DOSS, 145,162
DOUGHTY, 171
DOUGLAS, 74,100,121
DOVER, 177
DOWDY, 10
DOWNEY, 135, 161
DOYLE, 7
DRENNEN, 7,139
DRAYTON, 28,29
DRUMMON, 8,15,130

DUDLEY, 154
DUFFEE, 59
DUNKIN, 17
DUNKLIN, 100
DUNN, 7,10,79,133,165
DUNSTON, 57
DUPEY, 4
DUPREE, 101
DUREN, 173
DURRETT, 167
DUTTON, 4,71,73,75,76,86, 132
DYER, 106,142
EARNEST, 5,9,95,105,115, 132,135,139,140,145, 173
EASLEY, 3,12,112
EASON, 143,144
EAST, 28
EDGIL, 10,32,85,91,94,95, 123
EDWARD(S), 10,11,16,61,154, 173
EHL, 155
ELBERT CO. GA., 52
ELEAM, 92
ELKINS, 9
ELLIOTT, 79,11,85,90,94, 101
ELLIS, 9,14,17,19,75,88,100, 101,131,142,149
ELLISON, 9
ELMORE, 17,117
EMBRY, 9, 84
ENIS, 9
ENSOR, 75
EPPERSON, 93
EPPES, 19
ERWIN, 2,75,163
ESARY, 173
ESTES, 162,174
EVANS, 9,84,124,133,134,135, 173
EZELL, 175
FAIRLEY, 104
FALLS, 144,176
FARLEY, 94,108,178
FARRIES, 164
FARRIS, 12,84,164
FAUGHT, 10,85,86,132,180
FAYETTEVILLE (TENN), 25,27
FEARS, 14
FELKINS, 80
FELTMAN, 14,122
FELTON, 11
FERGUSON, 10,11,13,17,67, 74,82,93,94,129,132, 136
FERRELL, 175
FIELDS, 8,83,101,104,131, 138,163,173
FIKE, 18,73,75,92,133
FILES, 9,12,14,16,17,18, 20,72,79,84,91,115, 123,126
FINCHER, 174
FINE, 138,178
FINLEY, 11
FIQUET, 166
FISHER, 132
FITCH, 165
FLEMING, 2,76
FLOIA, 31
FLOWERS, 9
FONTANE, 122
FORD, 4,16,93,153,155
FORTENBERRY, 142
FOSTER, 18,154,166
FOWLER, 135,142,144,147,171
FRAME, 91
FRANCIS, 102
FRANKLIN, 6,8,119
FRANKS, 67
FRASER, 12
FREEMAN, 13,20,36,41,78, 79,143,145,147,150, 169,170
FRETWELL, 11
FROST, 9,104,105,115,141
FULLER, 8
FULLERTON, 26,30,32
FULTON, 141
GABBERT, 2,15,16,92
GADDY, 14
GADIE, 164
GAINES, 8,9,14,15,44,45, 57,62,103,122
GALLAHER, 23,33,92
GALLEY, 164

GAMBLE, 2,12,13,14,15,16,
17,18,21,23,37,63,78,
79
GAMMON, 101,157
GAN, 179
GANN, 71,72
GANNERT, 15
GANT, 13,124,133,134,140
GANUS, 124,180
GARDNER, 79,152
GARNER, 42,48,49,127,131,
166
GARRARD, 145
GARRETT, 10,133,134,135
GARRISON, 9,2,106,138,142
GEER, 144
GESIRE, 3
GIBBS, 164
GIBSON, 7,8,10,115,141,
144,175,178
GILBERT, 10,13,77
GILCHRIST, 10,125
GILES, 105
GILL, 74,114
GILLESPIE, 94
GILLILAND, 156,178
GILMORE, 16
GIPSON, 116
GLASS, 62
GLAZE, 4,102,106
GLENN, 175
GLOVER, 12,15,129,158,160
GOBLE, 158
GODFREY, 7,105
GOGGANS, 158
GOODE, 141,157
GOODMAN, 169
GOODWIN, 12,63,160
GOOKEY, 23
GORDON, 44,57,61
GOSS, 89
GOSSETT, 107
GRACE, 19,63,65,70,86,87,
97,99
GRANT, 135
GRAVES, 138
GRAVLEE, 7,9,15,26,58
GRAY, 2,6,13,16,57,61,70,
92,98,99,146,152,159
GREEN, 6,161,163,166
GREER, 79
GRIFFIN, 18,23,24,70,72,
121,146,156
GRIFFITH, 104,109
GRIGG, 151
GRIZZEL, 100
GROOM, 122
GROVE, 126
GROVELAND, 61
GUESS, 14,120,152
GUINN, 10
GUNTER, 2,59,78,138,180
GURGANUS, 5,13,18,73,80,
124,132,133,135,142
GURLEY, 148
GUTHREY, 69
GUTHRIE, 64,69,73,82,84,
85,86,89,112,139,176
GUTTERY, 3,6,9,12,15,16,
17,18,19,20,23,28,
33,40,42,43,44,45,
50,51,52,53,56,57,
58,61,63,64,65,69,
77,82,83,85,86,88,
96,121,139,155
GUY, 60
HADAWAY, 63
HADDER, 174
HADDRILLS POINT (S.C.),35
[illegible], 95
HAGOOD (see errata), 116
HALE, 104
HALEY, 62
HALL, 71,90,150
HALLMARK, 143,144
HAMBRICK, 79
HAMBY, 105
HAMILTON, 4,5,6,13,14,15,
16,17,18,42,60,76
HAMMACK, 143
HAMMETT, 109
HAMNER, 9,42,155,165,169,
170,173
HAMPTON, 130
HAMRICK, 100
HANCOCK, 7,14,15,16,105,
164
HAND, 14
HANDLEY, 80,98,112,134,
10,139,140,178
HANKINS, 145
HANLEY, 166

HARBIN, 123,147,148
HARBISON, 6, 10
HARDCASTLE, 3
HARDEN, 12
HARDY, 150
HARKINS, 153,154,155
HARKNESS, 131
HARPER, 70, 177
HARPOOL, 50
HARRIS, 4,6,16,17,18,19,76, 115,161,167,175,178, 180
HARRISON, 4,166
HARVEY, 4
HARVILLE, 9
HARWELL, 114
HASFORD, 175
HASSELL, 19
HAUGHTON, 57
HAUSMAN, 166
HAWES, 63
HAWKINS, 160,163
HAY(S), 57,166
HAYES, 60,63,128
HAYNE, 85,179
HAYNEY, 127
HAYSELLETTE, 146
HAYWOOD, 13
HAZELTON, 62
HEADRICK, 4
HEARD, 4,5
HEFNER, 176
HENDON, 22,23,73,3,5,16,22, 31,32,33,66,84,90,91, 112,113
HENDRIX, 105,106,156
HENRIX, 12
HENSON, 9,16,94,108,136,178
HERREN, 148
HERRON, 17,93,98,116,133, 132,137
HESTER, 7,12,80
HEWITT, 19
HEWLETT, 2,7
HEYGOOD, 95
HEYWOOD, 80
HICKS, 8,11,79,84,93
HIDE, 146
HIGGINBOTHAM, 12
HIGGINS, 96
HIGHT, 116
HILL, 3,12,174,176
HILLER, 178
HILTON, 176
HINTON, 93, 159
HOBBS, 152
HOCUTT, 12,118,147,173
HOGAN, 83,164
HOKET, 144
HOLBROOK, 118
HOLCOMBE, 42
HOLLAND, 9,124
HOLLIS, 16,18,154,155,160
HOLLOWAY, 11
HOLLY, 10,14,32,101,112
HOLSHOUSER, 25,26,27
HOLT, 135,179
HONEYCUTT, 104,141
HOOD, 128
HOOKER, 4,110
HOOPER, 53
HOPSON, 179
HOPKINS, 93
HOPPER, 20
HORSLEY, 177,178
HOUGHTON, 84
HOUSEWORTH, 14
HOWARD, 11,83,84
HOWEL (L), 9,162,172,175
HUBBARD, 15,99
HUBBERT, 117
HUDSON, 14,19,49,54,55
HUGGINS, 61,60
HUGHES, 10,34
HULSEY, 4,56,85,156,158,161
HUMPHRIES, 14,108
HUNTER, 13,18,130
HUTTO, 5,12,18,118,119,133, 134,135,154
HYAM, 40
HYCHE, 79,80,126
HYDE, 41,148,149,177
HYRA, 9
INGE, 167
INGLE, 5,11,13,135,175,177, 178,179
INMAN, 6,68,9,73,74,118
IRELAND, 107
IRVIN, 49
IRVING, 155
IRWIN, 3,4,49
ISBELL, 15,104
IVEY, 180
IVY, 112,130

JACKSON, 4,5,11,13,17,18, 34,38,39,49,57,75, 76,102,114,120,135, 149,150
JACOBS, 107
JAMES, 6,9,62,122,160
JEFFCOAT, 51
JEFFERIES, 145,149
JEFFERS, 4
JENKINS, 13,17,18,105,127, 129,142,146
JENT, 32,126
JERNIGAN, 100
JETT, 12
JETTER, 109
JETTON, 7
JOHNS, 80,145,150,171
JOHNSON, 2,7,9,14,15,16,17, 43,48,52,78,86,87,105, 127,130,134,138,145, 146,147,149,150,152, 153,166,167,169,173, 179
JOHNSTON, 11,15,100,118,139, 150
JONES, 2,6,8,9,10,12,13,14, 15,16,17,18,20,23,81, 84,92,93,94,99,100, 101,104,105,106,115, 122,126,140,146,147, 151,156,159,162,163, 166,167,172,173
JULIAN, 146,149
JUSTICE, 17
JUSTIS, 116
KARRH, 119
KEATON, 3
KEETON, 16,69,71,73,131,132
KELL, 108
KELLER, 143
KELLEY, 114
KELLY, 14,84,116,117,119, 136,148
KEMP, 7,8,14,95
KENDALL, 164
KENDRICK, 117
KENNEDY, 167,7
KEY, 6,10,12,13,14,15,17,18, 26,73,74,88,96,97,98, 103,105,106,121,127,153
KIDD, 21,35,36
KIKER, 12,56,110
KILGO, 109
KILGORE, 5,10,12,15,56,60, 76,77,86,97,115,128, 135,139,140,166
KILLINGSWORTH, 143,144,156
KILLOUGH, 164
KIMBRELL, 12,18,89,115,140, 148,157,158
KINCANNON, 105
KING, 3,4,6,10,11,13,14,16. 17,18,19,27,43,60,66, 72,74,87,94,101,108, 110,137
KINNEY, 11
KIRK, 104,162
KIRKLAND, 19,150,151,163
KIRKPATRICK, 51,56,57,72, 80,81.98
KIRKWOOD, 122
KITCHENS, 12,4,14,43,46, 60,72,92,121,152,153
KIZZIRE, 152
KNIGHT, 9,13,10,14,19,55, 57,61,73,74,88,90, 111,120,134,178
KNOTT, 112
KOZAK, 113
KUDER, 61
KUKENDALL, 104
KUYKENDALL, 83
LACEY, 58,60,61
LACKEY, 12
LAKEY, 70
LAMBERT, 179
LAMERT, 61
LAMKIN, 58,5,78
LAMON, 85,88,108
LAND, 2
LANE, 5,152,178,180
LANG, 29
LANGLEY, 80,162,163,170
LANGYARD, 10
LANKFORD, 5,19
LANTRIP, 13,58,102,128
LARKIN, 119
LATHAM, 17,93,117,137
LAWLER, 159,160,164
LAWRENCE, 6,147,148,155
LAWRIMORE (LOWRIMORE), 4, 9,121
LAWSON, 3,10,16,95,122, 123,129,136,145,152, 179

LAY, 6
LEE, 42,108
LEECH, 62,63
LEETH (LEITH), 12,15,19,30, 57,118
LEFAN, 98
LEFEVER, 122
LEGG, 62
LEONARD, 3,9,90,98
LESTER, 16
LESUEUR, 167
LETSON, 35
LEWIS, 166
LIDDELL, 121
LINDLEY, 102,177
LINDSEY, 8,114,146,169
LINN, 103
LISBORN, 160
LITTLE, 4,12,58,78,83,167
LIVINGSTON, 6,11
LOCHART, 101
LOCKEY, 12
LOCKHART, 15,17,19,70
LOGAN, 81,96,172
LOGGINS, 11
LOGIN, 17
LOLLAR, 4,10,49,50,56,62,75,77 80,81,82,100,116,119, 142,160,165
LONG, 2,13,17,57,58,60,61, 62,100,101,160
LOONEY, 57,175
LOSS CREEK, 41
LOVE, 50,92,166
LOVELADY, 114,126,129
LOVELL (or LOVEL), 80
LOVETT, 9
LOVING, 12
LOYD, 3
LUMPKIN, 9
LUND, 59
LUSTER, 19
LUTZENHISER, 173
LYNN, 62
LYON, 59
McADAMS, 8,48,130,131
McALLESTER, 18
McALONEY, 63
McANNALY, 59
McAULEY, 59
McBEEM, 158
McCALLA, 166
McCARLEY, 67
McCARM, 102
McCARN, 7,121
McCAULLEY, 107
McCLAIN, 3,68,151
McCLELLAND, 3
McClENDON, 8
McCLESKEY, 14,89,119
McCLUNG, 3,20,26
McCLURE, 154,155
McCLUSKEY, 119
McCOLLOUGH, 61,127
McCOLLUM, 17,143,176
McCORMACK, 159
McCOY, 101
McCRACKEN, 13
McCRORY, 15
McCULLAR, 64,90,93,126,132, 176
McDADE, 5,89,153
McDANIEL, 15
McDONALD, 5,83,93,127
McDOWELL, 104
McDUFF, 10,13,125
McELROY, 5,84
McFEARSON, 13
McFERIN, 7,8
McGEE, 169
McGEHEE, 169
McGILL, 67
McGOUGH, 13,15,16,17,93,113, 114,135
McGOWEN, 16,153,166
McGREGOR, 61
McGUIRE, 5,35
McKEEVER, 113
McKENDRICK, 67,82
McKINLEY, 4
McLAIN, 67
McMAHAN, 42
McMILLAN, 106,119
McMILLIAN, 173
McMINN, 41
McNUTT, 3,4,5
McPHERSON, 172
McQUEEN, 67
McVAY, 174
MABERLY, 164
MACON, 13
MADDOX, 83,162,172
MADISON, 21,36,37,38,94
MAGBY, 9
MAIDENS, 103
MALLARD, 5

MALLARD, 5
MALONE, 15,166
MANASCO, 3,5,11,12,14,15,
17,19,20,55,68,72,110
MANLY, 6
MANN, 73
MANNING, 158
MANUEL, 17,126
MARAWHEATHER, 22
MARKEY, 173
MARKHAM, 162
MARKS, 6
MARR, 166
MARSHALL, 42,108
MARTIN, 6,9,17,21,33,34,35,
60,91,95,112,118,125,
149,177
MASON, 5,13,64,67,92,93,110
MASTERSON, 117
MATHEWS, 21,104
MATTHEWS, 21,22,23,24
MATHIS, 70
MATON, 17
MAULDIN, 125
MAY, 162
MAYBERRY, 93
MAYFIELD, 67
MAYHALL, 2
MEADOWS, 105
MEANS, 35
MEDLIN, 5
MEEK, 50,51,72,77
MELCHER, 67,74
MELLOWN, 133,135
MELTON, 163
MERIWETHER, 22,23,166
MERPHEW, 178
MESSER, 70
METCALF, 38
MEYERS, 73
MIGHT, 61
MILES, 154,172
MILFORD, 93
MILL, 164
MILLER, 3,5,14,17,24,30,43,
49,58,82,93,96,100,109,
114,116,141,143,166
MILLICAN, 174
MILLIGAN, 6
MILLS, 7,93,163
MILNES, 104
MINOR, 5,6,13,16,130,134,
135,138
MITCHAEL, 12
MITCHELL, 15,123
MOBERLY, 164
MONCRIEF, 174
MONFROY, 73
MONTGOMERY, 9,4,118
MONTEITH, 17
MOONEY, 56,11
MOORE, 4,5,18,55,84,117,
144,146,147,151,155,
156,157,171,172
MORGAN, 15,16,101,129,138
MORRIS, 10,15,16,17,21,31,
32,33,91,93,99,118,
132,134,180
MORRISON, 12,172
MORROW, 8,48,49,116,131,180
MOSELY, 118
MOTE(S), 131,138,176
MUGFORD, 12
MULLENS, 14,16
MULLINAX, 134,141
MURPHEE, 109
MURPHEW, 11
MURPHY, 2
MURRAY, 109,84
MUSGROVS, 2,5,13,35,58,79
MYERS, 7,8,18,39,74,76,78,
87,90,92,103,114,122,
153
MYRICK, 158
NABOURS, 29
NATIONS, 8,17,100,180
NEAL, 104
NELSON, 18,19,28,71,73,75,
90,101,111,144,147,
148,174
NESMITH, 15,19,70,75
NEWMAN, 154,174
NEWTON, 5
NICHOLAS, 138
NICHOLS, 100,154
NICKOLS, 94
NICKOLSON, 15
NIX, 87
NORRIS, 11,16,123,145,159,
179
NORVELL, 62,63
NUNNALLEY, 93
OAKLEY, 143,150
OATES, 57
O'BRIEN, 104
ODEN, 128,159

ODOM, 15,17,19,73,93,97,98,
101,121,124,132
ODUM, 10
OLIVE, 146,171
O'REAR, 4,6,9,16,18,30,35,
46,56,61,62,59,73,77,
80,83,86,108
ORR, 6
OSBORN, 145
OVERTON, 175
OWEN, 13,16,84,116,167
OWING, 163
PACE, 4
PAINTER, 176
PALANTINE, 135
PALMER, 13,57,58,102,111,
169
PARK, 165
PARKER, 6,11,16,19,118,128,
139,144,150,157,165,
166
PARRISH, 104
PARTAIN, 111
PARTRIDGE, 107
PATTERSON, 105,146
PARVIN, 64
PATE, 11.5,10
PATTON, 8,10,64,66,95,96,
107,122,139
PAYNE, 6,9,10,60,155,158,
159
PEAK, 7
PENDLY, 140
PENN, 3
PEARCE, 84
PELT, 116
PENN, 102
PERKINS, 141
PERKINSON, 151
PERRY, 59,136,137
PERSON, 42
PETERS, 11
PETERSON, 13,17,128
PHELANS, 141
PHELTMAN, 16
PHIFER, 12,13,53,81,167
PHILLIP(S), 5,8,9,15,17,57,
70,112,138,143,153,159,
178
PICKETT, 104,105
PICKLE, 144,156
PIERCE, 84
PIERRE, 118
PIKE, 3,9,10,71,91,132
PINCKERTON, 155
PINION, 150
PINKNEY, 38
PITTMAN, 160
PITTS, 115
PLIMLEY, 107
PLYLAR, 106
PLYLER, 106
POE, 82,115,140,134,141,142,
151,157,158
POOL, 4,19,118
POPE, 156
PORTER, 39
POSEY, 118,120,121
POSTEN, 102
POUNDS, 81,117
POWELL, 61,124,142
PRATER, 154
PRATT, 167
PRESCOAT, 128 (see errata)
PRESCOTT, 15,109
PRESTON, 61,100,140
PREWETT, 4,9
PRICE, 7,13,110,135,154,167
PRICHETT, 154
PRINCE, 11,127,175
PROCTOR, 111
PRUDE, 167
PRUETT, 141,176
PRUITT, 175
PURDEN, 122
PURDY, 5
PUTNAM, 160,176
PYLER, 4
QUILLEN, 106
QUINN, 13,125
RABEN, 10
RABUN, 10
RABUT, 104
RADEN, 4,137
RAINES, 93
RAINS, 4,8,9,20,130
RAMEY, 17
RANDOLPH, 4.12,13,15,16,17,
24,92,99
RANEY, 17
RASPBERRY, 155
RAYNES, 141
REA, 81
READ, 38
REED, 2,5,6,10,15,108,120,
121,162

REEVES, 147,157
REID, 7,30,31,74,118
REINBERG, 67
RENFRO, 154
RENOW, 9
REYNOLDS, 37,38,160
RHEA, 6,14,18
RHODES, 7,11
RICE, 7,8,13,15,103,106, 112,169,170,171
RICHARDS, 9
RICHARDSON, 4,5,12,16,18, 57,62,63,78,98,106, 107,109,114
RIDINGS, 79
RIELLY, 155
RIGGS, 4
RIGSBY, 107
RILEY, 155
RIVERS, 80
ROBB, 164
ROBBERTS, 121
ROBBINS, 116,125,132,139, 158,159
ROBERTS, 8,10,14,49,85,87, 100,114,116,130,152
ROBERTSON, 4,9,35,110,154, 173
ROBESON, 33
ROBINS (ROBBINS), 3,4,7,8, 9,13,15,18,61,95
ROBINSON, 12,50,51,65,72, 76,77,82,89,109,126, 142,175
ROBUCK, 119
RODEN, 11,153,161
ROE, 4
ROGERS, 7,111,116,158
ROLLINS, 18
ROMINE, 15,3,18,21,30,31, 66,70,115
ROQUEMORE, 60
ROSAMOND, 14,63,79
ROSE, 15,70,119,133
ROSS, 9,107
ROSSER, 46,60
ROWE, 14,16,17,61,124
ROWNDTREE, 94
ROYCROFT, 157
RUSSEL, 8
RUSSELL, 15,75,98,156
RUTHERFORD, 7,30,35,39
RUTLEDGE,10,14,39,40,86,96, 97,122,123.127,153
RYAN, 84
SAMPLE, 11
SANDERS, 8,17,18,40,43,46, 60,61,62,122,131
SANDLIN, 6,11,17,75,85,91
SANFORD, 14,16,124,126,127
SAPP, 6
SAPPINGTON, 9
SARTAIN, 2,14,15,58,81
SAVAGE, 15,118,135,170,171
SAXON, 56
SAXTON, 107
SCOGGINS, 3
SEARCY, 165
SCOTT, 4,17,79,90,137,151, 159
SEETON, 15
SELBY, 133
SELF, 11, 17
SELLERS, 96,111,129
SESSION, 12
SEXTON, 151,152
SHANNON, 121
SHAVERS, 6
SHAW, 16,60,84,120,148
SHEATS, 6
SHEED, 71,72
SHEPHERD, 2,7,10,12,13,14, 16,18,57,58,101,104, 128,134,145,146,156
SHEARER, 167
SHERER, 18,19,48,56,57,61, 63,72,76,77,78,105, 109,128,144
SHIELDS, 2,13,58,60,62,104
SHIPMAN, 176,177
SHIRLEY, 43,65,80,95,161, 162,169
SHORT, 5,6,17,60
SHUBERT, 79
SHUCK, 49
SHURLEY, 99
SIDES, 3,4,10,11,14,17,19, 30,35,40,67,71,77,83, 85,86,88,89,93,97,108, 113,131,132,153,176,180
SIHELNICK, 174 (see errata)
SIMMONS, 3,105
SIMPSON, 16,147
SIMS, 130,164
SIZEMORE, 162
SLAUGHTER, 164
SMALLWOOD, 135
SITTON, 7,8

SKELTON, 17
SKINNER, 27
SMALLWOOD, 10
SMITH, 3,5,6,8,9,12,13,14, 15,16,17,18,46,56,58, 61,67,59,70,82,90,95, 101,102,107,109,118, 125,126,127,131,132, 136,141,146,148,149, 154,155,156,169,174, 177,179
SMOOT, 47,164
SNELGROVE, 93
SNODDY, 85,175
SNOW, 3,5,9,110,126
SOMMERVILLE, 108,109
SORRELL, 102
SOUTH, 12,14,145,150,172
SOWELL, 58
SPAIN, 174
SPANN, 162
SPARKS, 4,15,16,18,19,46, 49,110,148
SPAULDING, 7
SPEAR(S), 103,160
SPEEGLE, 6,66,67,68
SPENCE, 1[illegible]7
SPENCER, 170
SPILLER(S), 152
SPRINGFIELD, 71,127,163
SPROUL, 107
STACKS, 23,24,71
STAGGS, 85,86,100
STALNAKER, 106
STAMP, 156
STANLEY, 17,20,24,36,40,41, 42,43,44,48,52,53,54, 57,72,79,147,150,161, 165
STEADMAN, 18,67,68,110,136
STEED, 30
STEEDMAN, 18,136
STEEL, 7
STEPHENS, 17,144
STEPHENSON, 6,78,81,82,117
STEWARD, 7,8,11
STEWART, 3,11,94,118,147, 156
STIVENER, 79
STOCKMAN, 114
STOCKS, 75,76
STOKES, 3,4,146
STONE, 79
STOUGH, 152
STOVALL, 7,5,31,32,59,77, 84,130,153
STOVER, 3,57,108
STOWERS, 101
STRANGE, 161
STREET, 109,130
STRICKLAND, 84,140,141,147, 153,157,158,166
STRICKLIN, 146
STRICKLING, 153
STRONG, 34,127
STUBBLEFIELD, 14,57,84,120
STUDDARD, 16,145
STURGIS, 46,47
SUBER, 115,118
SUGGS, 146,147
SULLIVAN, 7
SULRAIN, 80
SUMMERS, 128
SUMNER, 14,15,18,82,129
SUSA, 115
SUTHERLAN, 8
SUTTON, 8,77
SWEENEY, 105
SWINDLE, 10,16,21,24,25, 26,27,45,61,70,71, 74,91,96,107,122,134, 172
SYKES, 128
TANNER, 102,159,160
TARRANT, 57
TATE, 67
TAYLOR, 2,7,10,11,16,42,115, 151,167,171,172,177
TEAGLE, 10,12
TEAGUE, 8
TEARCE, 37
TERRELL, 93,159
TERRY, 164,165
TESNEY, 92
TETSON, (see Letson), 35
THACKER, 9,10,86,95,115,139
THAXTON, 129
THOMAS, 3,11,17,20,22,33,41, 53,54,71,86,90,95,96, 104,125
THOMPSON, 5,6,13,14,15,16, 18,33,82,114,124,125, 132,135,147,177
THOMSON, 169
THORNTON, 33,34,123,155
THOROGOOD, 180

THREADGIL, 179
THURMAN, 15
TIDWELL, 144,148,152
TIERCE, 78,140,169,170
TINDALL, 96
TINGLE, 175
TINION, 170
TINSON, 118
TIPTON, 104
TIREY, 67,123
TITTLE, 11,71,123
TOLLEVER, 9
TOWNLEY, 3,12,13,18,19,46, 53,64,65,66,73,75,77, 83,89,111,136
TOWNS, 170
TOWNSEND, 166,167
TRAVIS, 102
TRAWEEK, 143,144,145
TREADWAY, 127
TRICE, 21
TRUEHEART, 164
TRUSSEL, 6
TUCKER, 5,11,109
TUBB(S), 4,13,39,40,41,99, 101,114
TUCKER, 120,135,148
TUNE, 16,90,137
TURNER, 5,6,13,15,16,167, 161
TUTTLE, 8
TWEEDY, 61
TYRA, 9
TYREE, 122,123
UNDERWOOD, 13,18
UPTAIN, 133
UPTON, 10,17,115
USSELTON, 7
UTLEY, 145,173
VANDIVER, 14,15,18,129
VEST, 6,12,17
VICK, 152
VINES, 67,84,179
VINTSON, 102
WADE, 26
WADKINS, 9
WAID, 14,133
WAIT, 116
WAKEFIELD, 70,83,143,144, 179
WALDEN, 5
WALDROP, 18,134
WALKER, 13,92,100,102,161, 178
WALLACE, 70,115
WALLIS, 5,95,142
WALLS, 42,138
WALTON, 18,82
WALTY, 18
WARD,7, 163
WARREN, 98
WASHINGTON, 25,26,169
WATKINS, 171
WATSON, 156
WATTS, 81,99,118
WEATHERFORD, 167
WEATHERS, 141
WEATHINGTON, 10,54
WEAVER, 179
WEBB, 6,83,84,143
WEBSTER, 101
WEDGEWORTH, 11,144
WEEMS, 127
WELBORN, 57
WELCH, 15
WELLS, 14,5
WESLEY, 141,142
WESSON, 65
WEST, 11,98,106,120
WESTBROOK, 141
WESTON, 6
WETHERED, 133
WETHINGTON, 134
WHEELER, 53,76
WHITE, 3,4,12,13,35,147,156, 157,159
WHITEHEAD, 133,148
WHITFIELD, 18,108
WHITLEY, 15,16
WHITSON, 9,41,117,151,165
WHITTEN, 104
WHITWORTH, 75
WIGGINS, 62,10,83
WILCOX, 117
WILCUTT, 12,95,115,172
WILDER, 106
WILEY, 6,68
WILHITE, 9,49
WILLIAM, 13,174
WILLIAMS, 3,6,7,9,10,11,12, 13,14,15,16.17,18,19, 20,43,47,48,49,52,61, 65,67,70,71,74,77,79, 82,83,99,105,108,109, 110,111,114,117,120, 128,140,141,160,174, 176,179,180
WILLIAMSON, 10,39,151,169

WILLINGHAM, 96,110,130,145, 149,151
WILLIS, 12,129
WILLSON, 24
WILSON, 5,8,14,15,17,62,74, 76,88,94,99,105,106, 107,118,126,131,137, 167,175,178,179,180
WIMBERLEY, 24
WINDERS, 59
WINGTON, 83
WINDHAM, 114
WINN, 126
WINSLETT, 62
WINTERS, 4
WODSWORTH, 177
WOLF, 122,178
WOOD, 9,10.13,73,107,121, 122,152,159,166
WOODALL, 6
WOODLEY, 110,174
WOODRUFF, 164
WOODS, 19,60,61,71,95
WOODSON, 110
WOODWARD, 144,153
WORTH, 34
WORTHINGTON, 63,146
WORTHY, 33
WREN, 122
WRIGHT, 14,15,17,19,20,33, 45,55,73,74,88,89,90
WYATT, 128
WYNNE, 41,150
YARBOROUGH, 130
YARBROUGH, 160
YATES, 135
YERBY, 151,166
YORK, 102,151
YOUNG, 3,6,18,96